RESTLESS AS MERCURY

Also by Gopalkrishna Gandhi

Fiction
Refuge

Non-fiction
Of a Certain Age: Twenty Life Sketches
Abolishing the Death Penalty: Why India Should Say No To Capital Punishment

Plays
Dara Shukoh: A Play

Translations
The Tirukkural
Koi Achha Sa Ladka (Translation of *A Suitable Boy*
by Vikram Seth into Hindustani)

Books edited by Gopalkrishna Gandhi
Gandhi and South Africa (with E. S. Reddy)
Gandhi and Sri Lanka
Nehru and Sri Lanka
India House, Colombo: Portrait of a Residence
Gandhi is Gone: Who Will Guide Us Now?
A Frank Friendship: Gandhi and Bengal: A Descriptive Chronology
The Oxford India Gandhi: Essential Writings
My Dear Bapu: Letters from C. Rajagopalachari to Mohandas Karamchand Gandhi

MOHANDAS KARAMCHAND
GANDHI

RESTLESS AS MERCURY

MY LIFE AS A YOUNG MAN

Edited by
GOPALKRISHNA GANDHI

ALEPH

ALEPH BOOK COMPANY
An independent publishing firm
promoted by Rupa Publications India

First published in India in 2021
by Aleph Book Company
7/16 Ansari Road, Daryaganj
New Delhi 110 002

Copyright © Gopalkrishna Gandhi 2021

All rights reserved.

The author has asserted his moral rights.

The views and opinions expressed in this book are those of the author and the facts are as reported by him, which have been verified to the extent possible, and the publishers are not in any way liable for the same.

The publisher has used its best endeavours to ensure that URLs for external websites referred to in this book are correct and active at the time of going to press. However, the publisher has no responsibility for the websites and can make no guarantee that a site will remain live or that the content is or will remain appropriate.

No part of this publication may be reproduced, transmitted, or stored in a retrieval system, in any form or by any means, without permission in writing from Aleph Book Company.

ISBN: 978-81-948741-4-0

3 5 7 9 10 8 6 4 2

Printed at Thomson Press India Ltd., Faridabad

This book is sold subject to the condition that it shall not, by way of trade or otherwise, be lent, resold, hired out, or otherwise circulated without the publisher's prior consent in any form of binding or cover other than that in which it is published.

This work is dedicated to
Mahadev Desai
*Gandhi's secretary and translator of his autobiography
remembering, with gratitude,
six path-finders to all his biographers*

Joseph J. Doke
Millie Graham Polak
Prabhudas Chhaganlal Gandhi
James D. Hunt
Pyarelal
Enuga S. Reddy

CONTENTS

Preface   xi

BOOK I
1869 to 1888

One	The Gandhis	3
Two	My Father	7
Three	My Mother	11
Four	Childhood	14
Five	Marriage	19
Six	A Confession	23
Seven	My Father's Death	25
Eight	A Friend	27
Nine	London Calling	31

BOOK II
1888 to 1896

One	The Sailing	41
Two	London, At Last	44
Three	Settling In	47
Four	Student Life	51
Five	Life Beyond Studies	56
Six	Returning Home	61
Seven	To South Africa	66
Eight	Becoming a South African	70
Nine	An Indian Interlude	76

BOOK III
1896 to 1908

One	Back to South Africa	85
Two	Cannons	91

Three	Trying India Out	98
Four	Back in South Africa Again	107
Five	A New Turn	114
Six	1906—A Year to Remember	126
Seven	In London with Mr H. O. Ally and much Hope	136
Eight	Back to Reality	146
Nine	Onward to Gaol	155

Book IV
1909

One	Compromise and an Assault	165
Two	With the Family, Briefly	175
Three	The Struggle Revives	180
Four	Harilal to the Fore	184
Five	Between Home and Gaol	189
Six	Kastur's courage	199
Seven	My Third Imprisonment	206
Eight	Deputed to London Again	215
Nine	Back to Struggle and a New Experiment	228

Book V
1910 to 1913

One	Tolstoy Farm	237
Two	Harilal Revolts	240
Three	Smuts Retreats	249
Four	Professor Gokhale Visits South Africa	256
Five	The Struggle Not Availeth	264
Six	The Last Straw	268
Seven	A Crisis at Home and a Great Loss	276
Eight	Satyagraha Resumed	281
Nine	The Great March	291

Book VI
1913 to 1914

One	Arrest	305
Two	Gaol	311
Three	Negotiations	316
Four	Suspense	321
Five	Agreement	328
Six	Cape Town Capers	333
Seven	Phoenix and a Fast	344
Eight	The Beginning of the End	348
Nine	Farewell	350

Acknowledgements	357
References	361
Index	373

PREFACE

The Story of My Experiments with Truth is famous. It is also famously incomplete.

Beginning at the beginning, Mohandas Karamchand Gandhi's autobiography moves rapidly from his recollections of his early years as a child, youth, husband, student, then enters real time. That is, the events he describes are happening around him as he writes about them. He includes events that are personal and 'out there' in the public sphere, as well as the seemingly small and the obviously momentous. Like two tracks of the many railway lines he travelled on, the events and his descriptions of them move together. And then, like a train that is stopped by the pull of a chain, the narrative stops, abruptly, at year 1920. Gandhi is just fifty-one at that point and his most climactic years—nearly three full decades' long—lie ahead of him.

He brings 'these chapters to a close' at that point because, he says, his 'experiments' are now indistinguishable from the life stories of Congress leaders and propriety requires that he not bring those into the account. 'In fact,' he says in his farewell chapter, 'my pen instinctively refuses to proceed further.'

But the 'self' cannot really disappear. Gandhi continues to speak and write about his life, incidentally, as it were. Plunged in political work, organizing his mass campaigns of satyagraha, undertaking fasts for public and personal reasons, getting imprisoned, freed, imprisoned again, traversing the Indian countryside to spread awareness of his political goal—Swaraj, freedom, for India—and also his 'constructive' work such as hand-spinning, the eradication of untouchability, Hindu–Muslim amity, Gandhi yet finds the time—and the need—to look back to incidents from his life, about his family, himself.

Glimmers about his life, his association with people and with his large and growing family, biological and ideological, slip through his public actions, speeches, letters, and other writings. As do personal observations about his inner struggles, his relationships with people—both famous and not famous. With the same frankness as marks his autobiography, he shares in speeches, recorded conversations, articles, and in letters to the family and close friends, of the years 'covered' in his autobiography and beyond.

Those scattered narrations of his fill in and fill out the before-life, the real-time life, and of his autobiography's story. Alongside *Experiments,* these cameos of his childhood, adolescence, student life, his mature years, show us the son, brother, husband, father, grandfather, mentor, friend in the man who was being hailed as a Mahatma. Starting from his early days, these go right up to what probably is the very last sentence—'I hate being late'—spoken by him (in Gujarati) seconds before his assassin-to-be, Beretta in hand, stands facing him.

His scattered autobiographical references have been utilized by biographers to retell, analyse, and interpret his life. Rajmohan Gandhi has given us a magnificent biography of Gandhi, based very crucially on some of these sources. His *Mohandas* is not going to be surpassed for the veracity of its narration and the fairness of its interpretations. Ramachandra Guha has skilfully woven Gandhi into history's giant mills and history into Gandhi's austere loom. The biographical mill will keep working in this manner. But this autobiographical compilation does what it does for the sole reason that a story as first told is not a story, it is reality. 'Original' footage, howsoever grainy, jerky, starting and ending without notice, has the ring of truth. It is the 'thing' itself, not an image of it. A mint-fresh 'feature' film, for all its vivid fascination, is still a manufactured product. Gandhi's life story in his own words and those of his contemporaries who quote him is heard best when heard directly. It is the organic truth. This book is not *Experiments with Truth* taken further afield, nor is it a foil to the many remarkable biographies of him. It threads *Experiments* into other autobiographical texts including, somewhat unprecedentedly, what he wrote within the fold of his family he so loved but did not privilege. Also, it uses, principally, five sources which reflect Gandhi's life—experiences as observed by or told to five of his contemporaries—Prabhudas Chhaganlal Gandhi (1901–1992), Gandhi's grand-nephew, who ran from Sabarmati Ashram a journal *Madhpudo* (Honeycomb) during Gandhi's lifetime; Joseph J. Doke (1861–1913) his first biographer; Millie Polak (1881–1962), author of *Mr Gandhi, The Man,* a remarkable work of first-hand observation; and the writings of his secretaries, Mahadev Desai (1892–1942) and Pyarelal (1899–1982).

Doke's biography, *M. K. Gandhi; An Indian Patriot in South Africa,* first published in 1909 by The *London Indian Chronicle,* was described by Devadas Gandhi* as 'the first and perhaps the best book' on Gandhi. It contains autobiographical material pertaining to his birth, parentage, adolescence, study, and early years in South Africa, all of which was clearly conveyed in dictation form, as it were, to Doke by Gandhi. It was, later, clearly vetted and checked by Gandhi. Doke carried a notebook with him on his first visit to Gandhi and doubtless did so on subsequent ones as well, filling them with jottings as Gandhi spoke.† Doke told Gandhi that he wanted to write a short book—'bright, graphic, reliable', to make Gandhi's personality real to the people of England. 'You must tell me about your childhood and youth, allow me to picture your personality....' Doke told the then thirty-eight-year-old Gandhi. 'Ah,' Gandhi replied, almost turning the proposal down, 'you have caught me completely.' Doke persevered, saying the book would help further the cause of Indians fighting for civilian rights in South Africa. 'You don't want me to write anything, do you?' asked Gandhi. 'No,' Doke replied, 'just let me question you about the city where you were born, that beautiful home of yours far away in the East....' And, so, as Doke says, 'with a grip of the hand' the bond was

---

*On a slip affixed to his copy of the book's first edition.
†'Once, when he paused longer than usual...I closed my notebook, thinking he had finished.' 'Don't close it,' he said, 'the chief point is yet to come.' (*An Indian Patriot in South Africa,* p. 9)

confirmed and the story was born. The Doke account is in fact Gandhi's first attempt, albeit indirect, at autobiographical writing. I have treated it as such.

Millie Polak, likewise, wrote her memoir of Gandhi's South Africa days in his lifetime and Gandhi, there is no doubt, went through it word by word. Some of the ellipses and name claddings in that narrative point to Gandhi's sensitive engagement with the writing of that book.

And, so, apart from selected borrowings from *Experiments,* mainly from the Gujarati original, Gandhi's own words occurring elsewhere, the narrations of Joseph Doke, Millie Polak, Mahadev Desai, Prabhudas Gandhi, and Pyarelal (both when they quote Gandhi or clearly write to what is almost his dictation) have been incorporated in this text. Notes at the end direct the reader to the specific works and pages where these words appear.

C. B. Dalal's epic *Gandhiji ni Dinavari* (Government of Gujarat publication, 1970) has been invaluable for date alignments and authentications.

This compilation may be said to carry one distinguishing mark: it brings into focus Gandhi's descriptions of his life in its familial aspect. His life in the epic domain of actions for public causes has been and will continue to be written about. His life as lived within the fold of domesticities has had fewer tellings. And that cannot ring truer than in his own and his intimates' words.

The question has often been asked, with understandable reason: Why did Gandhi not concern himself with the cause of South Africa's majority, its African population? The fact is, by Gandhi's standards of respect for things as they are, he did not make the Africans' cause his own. He did not identify with it, nor express himself on it except occasionally and almost incidentally. His priority in South Africa was securing from the British authorities of the union Indian South Africans' rights as British subjects. And going beyond that question, the point is made that Gandhi uses phrases like 'Kaffir' to describe the African people and makes remarks about them that would today be termed racist. Gandhi's words are there for all to see, his descriptions for all to judge. They jar. They are not to be defended or explained away. But they are, in all objectivity, to be seen in the context of the insensitive vocabulary used at that time by the people of South Africa, including the African majority. Nelson Mandela, writing for a 'Gandhi-125' volume said 'All in all, Gandhi must be judged in the context of the time and the circumstances.'

His immediate circle in South Africa did not include Africans but some African contemporaries, notably John Dube, saw his work with unconcealed admiration. And Albert Luthuli (1897-1967), the African National Congress president from 1952 to 1967 and recipient in 1961 of the Nobel Peace Prize for his struggle for justice in South Africa, declared in a talk at Howard University, Washington, DC, in 1948, that he had 'no doubt that [Gandhi's] efforts for his people inspired people such as Dr John Dube and others to concern themselves with seeking human rights for their people'. The words may be seen in Luthuli's hand-written draft of his Howard University remarks, a document now preserved in the Luthuli Museum in KwaZulu-Natal.*

A word is needed on the procedure followed. Except when otherwise indicated in the footnotes, all the material in this work is traceable to the relevant entries in *The Collected Works of Mahatma Gandhi* (CWMG) from the Gandhi Heritage Portal or to the e-book *The Collected Works of Mahatma Gandhi* published by the Publications Division Government of India, New Delhi, 1999, in ninety-eight volumes. Wherever the entries from the CWMG are in the present tense, it has been altered from the present to the past tense in order to accord to an autobiography's retro-narrative manner. In some places, word-connectors have been supplied to link two narrations in the interests of thematic coherence.

Gandhi's autobiography has been used in certain places to contextualize the entries. In the earlier part of the compilation, reliance has been placed on the Gujarati original of the autobiography.

---

*Scott Couper, *Albert Luthuli: Bound by Faith*, University of KwaZulu-Natal Press, 2010, p. 50.

Where this has been done, passages have been translated afresh into English.

The royalties accruing from the sales of this book are, it may be stated for the record, to go to the Navajivan Trust, Ahmedabad.

'Moniya was restless as mercury, could not sit still even for a little while,' Raliyat, Gandhi's sister on her little brother.

Pyarelal, *Mahatma Gandhi,*
The Early Phase, Ahmedabad: Navajivan, 1965, p. 195

Karamchand (Kaba) Gandhi (1822–1885)
Source: Pyarelal, Mahatma Gandhi: The Early Phase

BOOK I
1869 to 1888

This first section says it from where it all began—the protagonist's forbears, his immediate family and its early homes. It contains, crucially, apart from his own words, a narrative by Prabhudas Gandhi on Gandhi's family and his early years in Gujarat. Gandhi had obviously read it and in effect, though not formally, attested to the veracity of his grand-nephew's vivid yet un-embroidered account. Prabhudas Gandhi consolidated the biographical pieces into book form (Jivan nun Parodh—The Dawn of Life), published by Navajivan in 1948).

Separately and much later, Prabhudas Gandhi made another abiding contribution to Gandhi documentation in the meticulous Otabapa no Vadlo *(Otabapa's Family Tree; Ota being short for Uttamchand, Gandhi's paternal grandfather). That 'Tree' lives in this section. Prabhudas is Gandhi's first and most authentic in-house archivist, chronicler, and primary source for dates, sequences, and narrations pertaining to the early years. Gandhi's diligent secretary, Pyarelal, utilized Prabhudas Gandhi's* Jivan *extensively (not always with clear ascriptions) for the* Early Phase *volume of his monumental biography. Pyarelal's excerpts from* Jivan *and his transcriptions of Gandhi's direct descriptions of his personal experiences are utilized in this section.*

~

One

THE GANDHIS

There is a saying that Kathiawaris have as many twists in their hearts as they have in their turbans.

Going by our family name, my early ancestors must have practised the Bania avocation of 'gandhiana', grocering. Over time, however, the Gandhis of Kathiawar left that trade for service in different Kathiawari states. They became, essentially, administrators*.

The princes of Porbandar, who were knit up with our family, traced their genealogy back to Hanuman†. This shows that their records were ancient. These old chiefs must have been unusual characters, strange in their nature and choleric in their manner of functioning.

Porbandar became the home town of the Gandhis. It occupies today the same old spot close to the sea but the city going by that name today is not the Porbandar that I was born and raised in. It was then surrounded by substantial walls, some twenty feet thick, and high in proportion. Although most of the streets were narrow, and the bazaars crowded, the effect was picturesque.

Outside the walls, the sea was almost within stone's throw. It swept around the city so close that it made almost an island of Porbandar, changing the neighbouring fields into a swamp, and necessitating a bridge in later times. Beyond this, and away from the sea, the plain

---

*The family's vadlo (family tree) climbs seven ascending branches up to Lalji Gandhi (1665–1725) who held an administrative position in Kutiyana, the village in the Junagadh state of Kathiawar, which was the Gandhis' mul-gaon (original village). Four of Lalji's descendants were daphtaris in the Porbandar state, that post being equivalent to Home Minister to the Rana Sahib, the ruler of Porbandar who held fifty villages in his vassalage which was regarded as a 'first-class power' in the Kathiawar subprovince of Gujarat.
†The Porbandar royal coat of arms displayed Hanuman at its centre.

spread out unchecked to the distant Barda Hills.

There were few trees in Porbandar. The only green things which were common in the city were the Tulsi plants, in their pots or tubs, before which puja was done.

That old Hindu Porbandar has gone forever.

The houses such as the one we lived in were built chiefly of stone quarried in the neighbourhood. The stone was white and soft, easily worked but hardening under exposure, so that, in time, these buildings became like solid blocks of marble fitted to endure.

One of my earliest memories is connected with the learning and repetition, as a child, of the family pedigree, with all its ramifications, and offshoots, there in the old home within the walled city.

My grandfather, Uttamchand Harjivan Gandhi*, or Ota Bapa as we called him, rose to the higher position of diwan or raj mantri, the equivalent of prime minister, in Porbandar. To be prime minister in the Porbandar court was no sinecure. And it meant at least occasional excitements, and a general sense of insecurity.

Uttamchand Gandhi would be described in Gujarati as tekila, a man of firm purpose. It is said that he was an ajanabahu, long-armed. When standing, his palms would touch his knees. This is believed to be a sign of prowess. His forehead shone, they say, and his eyes had a certain brilliance to them so that men of half-baked intelligence would start to stammer in his presence.

When still a youth, he left Kutiyana for Porbandar to acquire some livelihood skills under the patronage of his uncle, the then daphtari Daman Gandhi. There he began work as a collector of customs in the port town's thriving salt mart but also regularly attended his uncle's office in the royal court of the Rana sahib† of Porbandar. He mastered a daphtari's duties so well and so fast that before long old Daman Gandhi would take it easy resting at home while young Ota Gandhi would dispatch all the business at court. One day when the Rana sent for Daman, the daphtari was away. Ota presented

---

*Uttamchand Gandhi (1786–1852).
†Rana Khimoji (1813–1831).

himself before the Rana in his uncle's stead and, in tones of respect, said the daphtari 'was out' but could he, Ota, not do whatever the Rana needed done?

'I too am your Highness's servant.'

After he had answered some sceptical questioning, Ota was assigned a knotty task which he performed, gaining thereby the Rana's confidence. Taken up by the young man's cleverness, style of speaking, and gutsiness, the Rana sent for him again.

'The matter is not exactly simple, Ota. Do you have the confidence to take it up?'

'Is there a task that cannot be accomplished under your authority?'

The issue pertained to an obstinate contractor in Madhavpur who, with the backing of the stronger neighbouring state of Junagadh, was taking advantage of Porbandar's relative weakness.

'The man has to be sorted out.'

'That should not be difficult to do.'

'How do you propose to go about it?'

'That will be clear once I get down to see the situation on the ground and study the facts.'

Ota Gandhi concluded the negotiations over Madhavpur so well that the Rana placed on his shoulders the mantle of Porbandar's diwan. Having entered that office at a young age, Uttamchand Gandhi displayed keen intelligence, truthfulness, and courage throughout his incumbency. Flattery and yes-manship were never part of his style. His actions were shaped entirely by his sense of what was right and in the public interest.

He was a good rider and would traverse the countryside extensively on his steed.

Rana Khimoji did not live long. His son[*] being a minor at the time of the Rana's death, all power moved to the hands of the Queen Regent[†]. This lady, 'fed' on tales by ladies of the court, became hostile to Ota to the extent of sending an armed party with cannons

---

[*]Vikmatji.
[†]Rupali Ba.

to lay siege on the diwan's fortress-like house. An Arab bodyguard defended Ota during the shelling.

There is a saying that Kathiawaris have as many twists in their hearts as they have in their turbans.

Compelled by intrigues, Ota had to leave Porbandar and seek refuge in neighbouring Junagadh. There, he salaamed the Nawab of Junagadh* with his left hand. Asked to explain the apparent discourtesy, he replied: 'The right hand remains pledged to Porbandar.' The Nawab praised Ota Gandhi's sense of duty in full court and made suitable arrangements for his financial and personal stability in Kutiyana.

---

*Nawab Muhammad Hamid Khanji II (1828–1851).

Two

MY FATHER

I know how turgid Kathiawari politics is.

Ota Bapa had set up two households one after another. That is, he had two wives. The first gave him four sons and the second, two. My father, Karamchand or Kaba Gandhi*, was the fifth and his younger brother, Tulsidas†, the sixth and last. I do not recall having been aware as a child that my four elder uncles were born of another mother.

Both of them came to hold their father's position of Diwan of Porbandar. Kaba Gandhi served Rana Vikmatji. Firm-minded, singularly chaste in morals, keen-sighted, often cruel, so independent that he quarrelled with the British political agent, so niggardly that his dependants were almost starved, and yet with compensating characteristics which won their affection, the Rana was a curious combination of traits not unusual in old India.

After demitting his office in Porbandar, my father moved to Rajkot as diwan and then, for a brief while, was Diwan of Vankaner as well. He was, thus, diwan of three states‡ over a period of four decades. Kaba Gandhi enjoyed a reputation at home and among the public for fair-mindedness. To the state he was uncompromisingly loyal. An officer of the British Raj§ once disparaged the Thakore Sahib of Rajkot in my father's presence. Kaba Gandhi objected to

---

*Karamchand Gandhi (1822–1885).
†Tulsidas Gandhi (1824–1890).
‡Karamchand Gandhi was Diwan of Porbandar from 1847 to 1874, Diwan of Rajkot from 1874 to 1878 and 1879 to 1883. He was Diwan of Vankaner from 1878 to 1879.
§P. S. V. Fitzgerald, Assistant Political Agent and later Agent to the Governor in Kathiawar.

this at once, whereupon the angered official asked him to apologize. My father of course refused to do so. For this effrontery he was held, for a while, in detention. Seeing the diwan's spirit remained unsubdued, the official asked for him to be freed. His stature made him a member of the influential Rajasthanik Court.

At the time of his death at sixty-three, Kaba Gandhi was a pensioner of Rajkot state, having spent nearly all his subsistence, chiefly on charity. It is a marvel that in the enervating atmosphere of an Indian darbar, Kaba Gandhi remained incorruptible. Once when the Thakore of Rajkot pressed him, after long service, to accept a piece of land, urging him to take as much as he desired, he indignantly rejected the offer, thinking it had the appearance of bribery. 'What will you do with your sons?' asked the Rana. 'You must provide for them. Take as much as you need.' He was firm but his relatives bore down his opposition and he accepted a mere strip of ground four hundred yards long. Money had no fascination for him.

Kaba Gandhi had four households in succession. His first and second wives died early*. Each of them gave him a daughter†. The third wife‡ and he had no children together. She was incurably ill and it is said when my father asked for her consent to remarry, 'You may,' she said, 'if you can find someone to offer his daughter's hand to you.' Implied in those words was a taunt about Kaba Gandhi's age but the diwan was not to be put off. 'I could do that within twenty-four hours,' said he and within that space of time did, in fact, get engaged. With all my reverence for my father and perhaps because of that reverence, I have not been able to forgive him for this. It showed that to a certain extent he was given to carnal pleasures, for he was over forty when marrying for the fourth time.

His fourth wife, Putlibai§, and Kaba Gandhi had four children.

---

*At ages twenty and eighteen respectively. Their names are not known.
†Muli (1842–1913) and Pankunvar (1845–1870).
‡Her name is not known. At the time of her death, she was twenty-six.
§Putliba or Putlibai (1843–1891) was from Datrana, Junagadh state.

The first was a son, Lakshmidas*, then a daughter, Raliyat† who was followed by two more sons, Karsandas‡ and I, Mohandas.

Kaba Gandhi and Putlibai formed an ideal householding pair. Being the state's diwan and the head of a large clan did not prevent Kaba Gandhi from lending a hand to his wife in the running of the household. My father loved his family and was devoted to his household, which extended beyond his own children to his brothers, cousins. Lunchtime was 'his hour'. When he sat down to that meal, he did so with at least twenty others, mainly relatives and their staff. On festive days the number could go up to 100 or 150.

In a house with so many to be fed, the stock of vegetables to be washed and diced was not small. He would routinely help cut vegetables. Even when meeting official visitors, his hands would be busy with the vegetable dicer, getting those who were calling on him to join in the exercise. Family functions like betrothals, weddings, and the give and take of customary rituals found Kaba Gandhi in the forefront of all planning and organization. Helping kith in happy matters such as schooling and in distressful situations like illness came to him as to the manner born.

Apart from Kaba Gandhi's five brothers' dependants, others from the extended Gandhi clan invariably sought his help in getting employment. Kaba Gandhi would judge the person's abilities and try set him up in some suitable position in the state's revenue or public works departments or the port. He had no interest in hoarding any money and so left us brothers with hardly anything by way of material possessions or inheritance. When asked why he did not set aside any property for his children, he used to say his children represented his wealth. He spent all that he earned on charity and on the education and weddings of his children.

When my father had to attend the darbar during a governor's visit, our household was turned upside down. He did not wear stockings

---

*Lakshmidas alias Kalidas Gandhi (1860–1914), treasurer in the Porbandar state and later a pleader at Rajkot.
†Raliyat Vrindavandas nee Gandhi (1863–1960).
‡Karsandas Gandhi (1876–1913) studied with Mohandas at Alfred High School, Rajkot.

or boots, then called 'whole boots'. His normal footwear was soft leather slippers. If I was a painter, I could paint my father's disgust and the torture on his face as he put his legs into stockings and his feet into ill-fitting uncomfortable boots. He had to do this.

The Sepoy War (1857) was quelled by means of superior force. Outwardly things quietened down but the hatred against an imposed rule went deep. The British established schools and law courts and Indians took to them with enthusiasm but they could not bear the insult or degradation involved in political subjugation.

Much of my father's time was taken up in mere intrigues. Discussions started early in the morning and went on till it was time to leave for the office. Everyone talked in whispers. I know how turgid Kathiawari politics is.

Kaba Gandhi's education was drawn from his experience of life. Of learning he had something like 'five books' worth'. History and geography were wholly beyond his ken. Nevertheless, his knowledge of the world's ways was extensive and he could, with that practical grounding, unravel the subtlest of questions and get a thousand men to attend their duties. He had not read religious texts but he had that sense of dharma which countless Hindus are able to derive from regular visits to temples and by listening to religious discourses. In his last year, on the advice of a learned Brahmin friend of the family, he had begun to study the Gita and, every day, during his puja, he would recite, in a high pitch, a few slokas from it.

Jaina monks would pay frequent visits to my father and would even go out of their way to accept food from us, non-Jainas. He had besides Musalman and Parsi friends, who would talk about their own faiths, and he would listen to them always with respect, and often with interest.

Three

MY MOTHER

Just like what my mother used to wear.*

I remember her in the flower of her youth. She was not fond of jewellery, and wore comparatively little of it, just the usual nose rings, with bangles of ivory, and heavy anklets just like the 3,000-year-old heavy silver pair that I have seen in the archaeological museum at Taxila.

Though very young, she was remarkably clear-sighted and intelligent. She had an abundance of practical wisdom. 'Darbari' matters were no mystification to her; she knew their ins and outs. The Rajkot princely court had taken a correct measure of her intelligence. She became, in fact, a political influence of no mean importance in the state through her friendship with the court ladies. Child though I was, my mother would take me along on occasion to the court. I still remember some of the conversations she used to have with Bamasaheb, the widowed mother of the Thakore.

My mother would see to the needs of the entire large household. She sat down to her own frugal meal, which comprised very often of leftovers, only after having seen to it that all her daughters-in-law had eaten and every child had been fed. She worried that no one found food falling short.

My mother believed in stern discipline yet, withal, she bore such a strain of tenderness and sympathy in her heart that the children clung to her with boundless affection. She would never allow us to see an eclipse at all, as she was afraid evil would befall us if we did.

---

*On seeing the 3,000-year-old heavy silver pair of anklets in the archaeological museum at Taxila, shown to him by the curator of the museum on a visit to that site, now in Pakistan, on 26 July 1939.

Uka, a child from an 'untouchable' caste used to come to clean the lavatories in our house. My mother said to me, 'You must not touch this boy, he is an untouchable.' 'Why not?' I questioned back and from that day my revolt began.*

While at school I would often happen to touch 'untouchables'. As I would never conceal such a happening from my parents, I would tell my mother of this 'touching' and she would tell me that the shortest way to 'purification' was to cancel that touch by touching any Musalman passing by. And simply out of reverence and regard for my mother I would often do so but I never did so believing it to be a religious obligation.

'When brothers and sisters quarrel with each other,' she once told me, 'they square it out among themselves. If your brother hits you, you can return the blow.' I said he could hit me if he so wanted, I would not hit back. 'Moniya,' she said, 'wherefrom has this come to you?'

She never raised her voice nor spoke to anyone with even the hint of an insult. If there was sickness in the home, she would sit up night after night discharging the duties of nurse. Every morning the old gateway of the house was besieged by twenty or thirty poverty-stricken people who came to receive alms or the cup of whey which was never refused.

A kind of innate nobility marked whatever she did. The impression I have of her is that of a sadhvi, a saintly woman. I have used the word 'saintly' for her instead of 'austere' because austerity implies external renunciation, endurance, and sometimes even hypocrisy. But saintliness is an inner quality of the soul.

Never did I see any frivolity in her or interest in the pleasures of life, nor any recourse to beauty aids.

She was very devout. Going to the haveli† was a daily practice. Sometimes these visits happened four or five times a day, and were never less than two.

---

*Interview with Christian missionaries, before 12 December 1938.
†Vaishnava temple.

There was no question of her having anything to eat before doing her puja. She would take the hardest vows and adhere to them without flinching. Illness was no excuse for relaxing them. She fell ill once when she was observing the Chandrayana vow* but the illness was not allowed to interrupt the observance. Keeping two or three consecutive fasts was nothing to her. I do not recall her having ever missed the Chaturmas†. One Chaturmas she had resolved that she would eat only after a darshan of the Sun God. Now it is well known that during that season of rains, it is difficult to see the sun. The children of the house kept a lookout that Chaturmas for the truant sun and, if we caught as much as a glimpse of it, we would shout out. 'Ba, Ba, look! The sun, the sun!' She would come rushing out but by then the fugitive orb would have run away. 'Oh, well,' she would say, 'I am not meant to eat today,' and would return to whatever she had been doing, with total absorption.

She died at the early age of forty.‡

---

*A fast in which the intake of food is calibrated to the moon's waxing and waning.
†The four-month season of rains when fasts and partial fasts are observed.
‡This is incorrect; she was nearing fifty at the time of her death.

Four

CHILDHOOD

I was a good boy, not a bright boy.

Our family house in Porbandar was reached through a lane opening onto the main street. The two temples, one to Krishna and the other to Rama kept guard on either side. The building can be said to have been made of afterthoughts. Someone long ago purchased the ground adjoining two temples and then built the house on them. New generations added to the ancestral home, and as expansion was impossible, storey was built on storey, until, when the fourth was reached, it was found that the weight of stone would mean disaster, so the last storey was made of wood. A rambling, old, weather-beaten house thus came to be raised, reflecting the collective afterthoughts of a long line of the Gandhis of Porbandar.

It was here that, on day 12 in the dark half of the lunar month of Bhadar in Samvat 1925 or on the 2nd of October of 1869, I made my appearance as the youngest of four children. On the sixth day, according to Hindu custom, a great feast was held under the auspices of Vidhata, the God of Fortune, and I was given the name Mohandas. The family astrologer was more or less responsible for this. He had consulted the signs of the Zodiac, made a reckoning with the stars, and presented my parents with the fortunate letters out of which a name may be made. The letters suggested 'Mohandas' and with that name, I was set up for life.

My horoscope was always kept perfect and up to date but that practice died away with my father. He used to take interest in it and got the yearly forecast from it.

My childhood was spent in Porbandar. I remember having been

taken to a neighbourhood school* by someone. But I remember little of what I learnt there except for some rude words that the children there used to think up to lampoon our teacher. One was a limerick that used the image of a papad. I do not wish to immortalize the caricatured name of the teacher that occurred in the verse.

My mother always got me ready for the school in time and never allowed me to waste my time when I returned home. If I was idle, lazy or listless, she at once pulled me up.

We used coir-string cots in our house. When my mother had to prepare ginger pickle, she used to rub the fresh ginger on them. The skin was not removed with a knife but in this way, by rubbing it against the coir string.†

I roamed about the villages in a bullock cart. As I was the son of a diwan, people fed me on the way with jowar roti and curds and gave me eight-anna pieces. I had to be either playing or roaming about. I used to be restless as mercury, not sitting still even for a little while. My sister used to carry me in her arms when she went out, showing me the familiar sight of streets—cows, buffalos, horses, cats, and dogs. Mother used to worry for me lest my sister dropped me or lost sight of me. I have seen in my childhood in Porbandar cows freely eating human faeces. This appeared to me revolting and the feeling has persisted to this day.

Once I picked up some wild flowers from under a tree and ate them. This caused a burning in my throat. A vaidya was sent for and he administered an antidote and a throat paint. My father thereupon gave strict instructions that I was not to be left unaccompanied at any time. A nurse was engaged especially to look after me. This was Rambhabai.

I used to be in constant fear of thieves, gnomes, and creepy-crawlies. The phobia had me in its complete grip. Going anywhere alone after nightfall was out of the question. I imagined ghosts emerging from one direction, thieves from another, snakes from a

---

*Called dhooli shala or 'dust school', after the wooden board on the dusty surface of which the teacher drew or wrote the lessons.
†Ginger makes a delectable Gujarati pickle in non-Jaina homes.

third. A lamp burned in my room through the night. Rambha saw my fear and suggested, as a remedy for this fear, the repetition of Ramanama. I had more faith in her than in her remedy. She remained with the family till her death which occurred, it seems, due to asphyxiation while preparing dhupel, a scented hair oil over a low fire.

My father knew nothing of what I was doing. When he left Porbandar for Rajkot to take up the diwanship there, I was put into a primary school in that town. As in Porbandar, so here too my studies amounted to nothing much. I must have been regarded as an average student. I was then moved to a suburban school and from there to high school*. I was over twelve by the time I reached high school. At that school, the teachers did not consider me a very bright boy. They knew I was a good boy†, but not a bright boy. I do not recall having made any friends as I was essentially a very shy boy. I minded my work and that was that. I got to school as the bell rang and when school gave over, ran back home. 'Ran back' is deliberately used here for I just did not want to engage in conversation with anyone. What if someone were to make fun of me?

The medium of my study at school was English. As the teacher struggled to make his exposition on geometry understood by us, my head would reel. I know now that what I took four years to learn through English of arithmetic, geometry, algebra, chemistry, and astronomy, I should have learnt easily in one year if I had not to learn them through English but Gujarati. This English medium also created an impassable barrier between me and the members of my family who had not gone to English schools. I could not, even if I wished to, interest my father in what I was doing. He had ample intelligence but he knew not a word of English. I was fast becoming

---

*Alfred High School.
†J. M. Upadhyaya says in his carefully researched work *Mahatma Gandhi as a Student*, Publications Division, Government of India, 1965, pp. 19–20: 'Mohandas's performance at the first terminal examination of standard I...placed him almost at the bottom of his class.... But his failure at the examination was more than made up for by the term certificate (sent to his father) in which his conduct was recorded as "very good".'

a stranger in my own home. I certainly became a superior person.

Rumours of conversions to Christianity found their way into my school and so, into my home. But they were vague. The Presbyterians had a mission in Rajkot and, at one time, our school was deeply stirred by the authentic report that a well-known Hindu had become a Christian. The idea among us of what becoming a Christian meant was not complimentary to Christianity. The schoolboys held the firm conviction that conversion meant eating meat and drinking wine.

Sometimes, on the way to school, we could catch a glimpse of Mr Scott preaching, or hear his voice at a distance. Occasionally I heard of his ill-treatment by the people, but I, at least, never went near him then. Later, I got to know him and to admire him.

Although Rajkot is not so picturesquely situated as is Porbandar, certainly, as an educational centre, it was preferable. Rajkot stands on the bank of the Aji River and, at that time, it too was partly surrounded by a wall. Rajkot is divided into two parts, representing the old and the new, the East and the West. The residents of the old, ruled by the Thakore of Rajkot, were simply under British protection. The new town or 'station' was subject to the Governor of Bombay and was essentially British, with even the customs regulations and the civil courts being distinct as though they belonged to different countries.

Old Rajkot was not so rich in buildings as Porbandar. It had no white glossy plaster and white stones. Our second home was in old Rajkot, close to the palace. At first, we were merely guests in the town. But later a house was built by my father and we became settled citizens. The houses in Rajkot were poor, with peaked tiled roofs. The place had something of the squalor of the Orient. But the 'station' was beautiful. In those days, trees were being planted, gardens beginning to show their flowers, rich bungalows springing into view. Notable among these was the Rajkumar College, with its splendid European appurtenances, and Prince Ranjitsinhji* was already pursuing a course of study there.

---

*Prince Ranjitsinhji (1872–1933) of Nawanagar, brilliant cricketer and later ruler of Nawanagar.

I read nothing outside of my school books. Even storybooks held no attraction to me. Once my eyes fell on a book purchased by my father. It was *Shravana Pitribhakti Nataka*, a play about Shravana's devotion to his parents. I read it with intense interest. There came to our place around that time itinerant showmen*. Shravana carrying, by means of slings fitted from his shoulders, his blind parents on a pilgrimage was one of the pictures painted on glass I was shown. The book and the picture left an indelible impression on my mind. The agonizing lament of the parents over Shravana's death is still fresh in my memory. The tender verse moved me deeply and I played it on a music box† which my father had procured for me. I liked learning to play musical instruments.

At about this time, a translation into Gujarati of *Manusmriti* came into my hands. It was among my father's collection. I studied the Code of Manu in the hope of finding some light on the riddle of life. What I found perplexed me more.[1] The story of Creation and similar things in it did not impress me very much and, on the contrary, made me somewhat incline towards atheism. Reading the work taught me nothing of ahimsa. It also seemed to suggest it was moral to kill snakes, bugs, and the like. And my memory is that during that period of adolescence I dispatched insects and the like imagining that doing so had dharmic sanction.

One belief did take root in me at that time—life on this world stands on a moral principle. And that principle abides in truth.

Time goes on doing its work.

I have remained absolutely free from the habit of masturbation. Even today I am not able to understand it and shiver at the thought of it. I have no doubt whatever that a man who practises it would become weak in body and mind and I know of many such cases. Marriage is no remedy for bad habits.‡

---

*Presumably with the magic lantern or laterna magica using image projectors and painted glass slides.
†The Gujarati original has 'vajo', suggesting a music box or a harmonium. The English version has 'concertina'.
‡Letter to D. B. Khoja, 11 July 1936.

Five

MARRIAGE

My brother's wife* had thoroughly coached me about my behaviour on the first night.... But no coaching is really necessary in such matters. Impressions of the former birth are potent enough....

It is my painful duty to have to record here my marriage at the age of thirteen. It appears that two girls chosen for me had died[†] in turn and, therefore, I infer that I had been betrothed three times. I have a faint recollection that my third betrothal[‡] took place in my seventh year.

It will be remembered that we were three brothers. The first[§] was already married. The elders decided on getting my second brother[¶], who was two or three years my senior, a cousin[**] possibly a year older, and me married. It would be better, they thought, to have all the bother over at one go. My father and my uncle[††] were both old[‡‡]. We were the last children who remained to be married. A triple wedding

---

*Nandkunvar (1861–1925), wife of Lakshmidas Karamchand Gandhi (1860–1914).
[†]Life-threatening serious illness was a regular feature, as was early mortality among females in the Kathiawar of Gandhi's childhood. The names of the two girls Gandhi was betrothed to remain unknown.
[‡]To Kastur Makanji Kapadia (1869–1944), who was born in Porbandar in a home that could be seen from the terrace of that of the Gandhis.
[§]Lakshmidas Karamchand Gandhi aka Kalidas Gandhi.
[¶]Karsandas Karamchand Gandhi (1867–1913).
[**]Presumably Motilal Tulsidas Gandhi (1869–1924), married to Harkunvarba (1867–1905).
[††]Presumably Tulsidas Uttamchand Gandhi (1824-1890), aka Chakan Gandhi, younger brother of Karamchand Uttamchand Gandhi.
[‡‡]They were sixty and fifty-eight respectively, certainly 'old' by the standards of life-expectancy (around thirty years) at birth in nineteenth-century Kathiawar.

was decided upon and months were taken up in preparation for it.

Marriage in the Hindu world is no trifling matter. Parents of the bride and groom cannot undertake the arrangements lightly. They go bankrupt over the celebration, squander their time on them for months on end. New clothes are made, jewels are ordered, expensive feasts are arranged with a sense of competition verging on rivalry. And the womenfolk! Sing they must, whether they can hold a tune or not and they go hoarse in the raucous effort, even falling ill in the process. The neighbours' peace is, of course, broken but those unfortunates can hardly complain for they, when their turn for marriages comes, will be up to the same. And so, with a sigh they endure the din, find their way around the thrown-away leavings of food and all the other forms of garbage that a wedding generates.

My father was Diwan of Rajkot at the time and the threesome wedding was taking place at Porbandar. Diwan that he was, my father was, nevertheless, a servant of the state. And further, being utterly devoted to the state, he was that much less free. The Thakore sahib would not let him leave for Porbandar until the last minute. He did arrange for special stagecoaches to hie my father to Porbandar but only two days before the wedding, when the journey was, ordinarily, a five-day affair. The cart rushed as fast as it could but in its last stage, toppled over. Father was seriously injured. He arrived, all bandaged up, bandage on the hands, bandage on the back. Half of his and, of course, our collective joy vanished. But can nuptials be put off? Can the 'written hour' be spurned? Of course not. My father bore his injuries like the stoic that he was and, tapping his forehead in resignation, sat through the ceremonies with cheer. I still remember the spots where he was seated, where he performed the rituals that a bridegroom's father must. And as for me, within moments, I forgot all about my father's trauma and allowed the razzmatazz to draw me right back into its giddy whorl.

The three of us—brother bridegrooms—knew only from all that was happening around us that something like a marriage was going to envelop us. And as for me, all that the bustle meant was that I would acquire some new clothes, there would be music around, flowerful processions, much feasting. And a stranger in the form of a girl would materialize for me to romp about with. That was about it.

Even today I can picture to myself how we sat on the wedding dais, how we took those 'seven steps', the priestly chanting of mantras, the game of cowrie shells, and how the newly-weds put the sweet kansar into each other's mouths. Carnal thoughts had no place in my mind at the time.

And oh! That first night! My brother's wife* had thoroughly coached me about my behaviour on the first night. But no coaching is really necessary in such matters. Impressions of the former birth are potent enough.

I must say I was passionately fond of her. Even at school I used to think of her and the thought of nightfall when we would be together again was ever haunting me. Separation was unbearable.

In those days there used to be sold—for a paisa or a pie, I forget how much—small four-pagers† or primers dealing with conjugal love, child marriage, thrift, and suchlike. If one of those came my way, I would devour it. What did not appeal to me in those tiny tracts I would let drop out of my mind and what appealed to me, I would decide to carry into practice. Monogamy should be a good husband's dharma was one tenet that got imprinted in my heart. I understood that this meant I would not have relations with any other woman that would make me false to my wife. There was, of course, little scope for faithlessness in a child–husband.

But a problem arose. If I am to be faithful to my wife, the thought came to me that my wife must also be faithful to me. More than 'I should observe the fidelity vow', it became a case of 'I should make her observe the fidelity vow'. And if I am to do that I have to maintain vigil. I had no reason to harbour doubts about her chastity. I had no reason whatever to suspect her faithfulness. But does jealous possessiveness—for that is what it was—wait for reasons? I had to know, just had to know, if Kastur‡ went anywhere, where it was that

---

*Nandkunvar (1861–1925), wife of Lakshmidas Karamchand Gandhi (1860–1914).
†The Gujarati word used is chaupania.
‡Compared to the torrent of letters that he wrote to family, friends, colleagues, strangers,

she went. More, she had to take my permission before she could go anywhere. This became the root of a sad discord between us. To not be able to go anywhere without leave was a kind of imprisonment. But was Kastur one to submit to any such imprisoning? She was not. If she wanted to go somewhere, she just went right ahead and did what she wanted to. She was, of course, completely unafraid of things like serpents. Stepping out in the dark held no terror for her. And step out whenever she wanted to, she did. The more I pressured her, the more she defied me. And the more she defied me, the more I would get riled.

very few letters were written by Mohandas to his wife. And fewer still survive. So there is but slender evidence or indication on the manner in which the young husband addressed his wife of the same age. The form of address used by him in his early letters—all in Gujarati, of course—was 'Vhali Kastur' (Beloved Kastur). And so it would be fair to assume that when young she was called by him, and by others in the family, by the name given to her by her parents—Kastur. By the time his autobiography came to be written, she was already known widely as Kasturba, the 'ba' being a suffix standing for 'Ma' that their children used, as did the many younger members of the family who joined the Mohandas–Kastur family in South Africa. Gandhi refers to her in his autobiography as Kasturba or the more formal Kasturbai. In this compilation, bearing in mind the context of their early years and his referring to her as Kastur in correspondence of that period, the editor has employed 'Kastur' for that early period even when in Gandhi's texts written later, he has referred to her as Kasturba, in keeping with the practice of those, later, times. Kastur gives place go Kasturba as she grows into motherhood and that stature which was so uniquely hers.

Six

A CONFESSION

I wrote it on a slip of paper and handed it to my father myself...
I gave it trembling.

There are some misdeeds that need to be set down.

With a kin of mine, I developed a fondness for smoking. It is not that the two of us saw any particular merit in smoking or any joy in tobacco's smell. It was just that we were drawn to the prospect of blowing tobacco puffs. My uncle* had the smoking habit and it was seeing bidi smoke billowing from his mouth that gave us the thought that we could do the same. We did not, of course, have the money to buy bidis. And so we would steal the stubs that he left behind. But these were not to be found all the time. And in any case the cold castaways did not have much smoke left in them. The house servants always had a few coppers kept knotted into the folds of their attire and when they were not looking, we would steal a couple of those. And with those stolen coins we would buy our bidis.

But more serious than the stealing of stubs and then stealing servants' coppers occurred another theft. The bidi-related thefts took place when I was around thirteen. This other, more serious theft, I committed when I was fifteen. What happened was this: My meatarian brother had run into a small debt of some twenty-five rupees. Both of us pondered ways of discharging the debt. Karsandas had a wristlet made of solid gold. It was not difficult, we reckoned, to pare from it a tola-worth of the precious metal. The wristlet was snipped and the debt cleared.

The consequence for me was unbearable repentance. I decided

---

*Tulsidas Gandhi.

to confess the crime to my father. There was no question of my summoning up courage to speak to him about it. I was, to put it plainly, afraid. I did not fear a thrashing from him, as he had never ever hit any of his children. I was afraid that he would be disconsolate and might strike his forehead in anguish. And yet, I was clear that I should take that risk and acknowledge my crime. I decided, after much thought, to write out a confession and seek his forgiveness. I would never feel clean again, I felt, if I did not confess. I wrote out the confession on a slip of paper and handed it to my father myself. 'So, father,' I said in it, 'your son is now, in your eyes, no better than a common thief.[2] I also urged my father not to take the pain of this crime upon himself and vowed never, ever, to repeat it again.

I gave it with trembling hands. He was bedridden at that time, fighting a painful illness. I sat myself down in front of his wooden cot. He sat up to read the letter. Pearl drops of anguish trickled from his eyes as he went through it, wetting the paper. He then closed his eyes for a moment and then, lying down again, tore it up. I too dissolved in tears. That scene I can picture vividly to this day and if I were an artist, would paint it in the sharpest detail.

 Rama's arrow heals even as it hurts

Only they know this, who have been pierced by it
 My father's tears had pierced me, cleansed me. They had also given me an object lesson in ahimsa.

Seven

MY FATHER'S DEATH

*Ena charane, teno das, Mohandas**

The time of which I am now speaking is of my sixteenth year. My father, as we have seen, was bedridden. A fistula is painful, disabling. It obliges, in its advanced stages, the patient to be virtually immobile. But my father, in true Vaishnava rigour, refused to be cowed into supine dependence. There are ways taught by Western medical practice that enable a patient to attend to all natural functions, including a bath, without leaving the bed or staining the sheets. But my father insisted till the very end to rely on himself. I extolled this at the time as a sign of Vaishnava dharma and sang praises of my father's determination.

But how he suffered. Three of us—my mother, a trusted old servant, and I—were on such attendance as my father permitted. For me, the 'nurse', this comprised cleaning the wound, applying medicines and balms over it. I would massage his legs at night until he told me to go to bed or he himself dozed off. I loved doing this and did not, I think, miss even a day's nursing duty.

That year was one of a double shame for me. I was in high school and conscious, with Shravana as a role model, of duties towards my parents. And yet, carnally obsessed that I was, I had made Kastur, then sixteen, pregnant. Even as I nursed my father, my thoughts would wander off to the bedroom upstairs, to Kastur.

Tulsidas Gandhi, my uncle, who was deeply devoted to my father,

---

*At his feet, his das, Mohandas; when a formal photograph of his father was shown to Gandhi on 29 October 1934 and he was asked to autograph it, he wrote these words on its lower edge.

had come to Rajkot during the time when my father's health entered a critical phase. On the fateful night, which I had no idea would be my father's last, at about ten-thirty or eleven, my uncle said to me 'Mohan, you go now, I will sit beside your father.' I felt relieved and went straight to the bedroom. Kastur, poor thing, was in deep slumber. Would I let her sleep? I woke her. Not more than five or seven minutes would have elapsed when there was a knock on the door. The servant I have written about said to me, 'Get up, Bapuji is very ill'. I immediately understood what 'very ill' meant. Jumping out of the bed, I opened the door.

'Tell me, what is it?'

'Bapuji is no more.'

I doubled down to his room. 'He has left us,' moaned my uncle.

My father had made a sign for pen and paper and written: 'Tayari karo' (prepare for the last rites). He then snapped the amulet on his arm and tore off from his neck a gold chain. The very next moment, his soul had flown.

My shame was that I was lusting during the one moment when I should have been attending to my father. I have not been able to erase that black taint, or forget it. It remains for me to record the fact that the little life that took birth a short time later breathed for some two days or four, no more, and then left us. Could it have been otherwise?

Eight

A FRIEND

He* kept me under his thumb for more than ten years.

At high school I had two close friends, at different times. One of these did not keep up with me for long, though I never moved away from him. He left me because of my closeness to the other friend, Sheikh Mehtab. This forms one of my life's sad passages.

This association lasted for several years. Mehtab was a friend of my middle brother, Karsandas. They were classmates. I could see his many weaknesses but I also saw in him a certain faithful temperament. My mother, my eldest brother Lakshmidas, and my wife, all three, found this association of mine distasteful. My wife's caution I was too proud to heed. My mother I was not inclined to cross, and my brother's wishes I was inclined to comply with. Yet, I argued with them. 'You may find in him the faults that you do,' I dissembled. 'I am not unaware of them. But you do not know the good in him. He is not going to take me down a wrong road. The reason why I am associating with him is that I want to make a better human being of him. I am confident I can do that. I urge you to please have trust in my judgement.' They were not, I think, convinced but they indulged me.

My estimation, I was later to realize, was wrong. It is right to want to reform someone. But in doing so, it is not right to descend

---

*Sheikh Mehtab (1866–1937), Gandhi's best-known classmate from Standard II A of Alfred (or Kathiawar) High School, Rajkot; a strong and persuasive character, swashbuckling athlete, daredevil, later with Gandhi in Durban, South Africa, accommodated in Gandhi's house, from where, having abused Gandhi's hospitality, he was expelled by Gandhi; also a talented versifier and propagandist in Urdu for the Indian cause in South Africa.

into the deep waters oneself. The person being corrected is not to be befriended. Friends are meant to be as one. Friendships augur well and hold when the friends share the right values. Friends impact on each other; where is then room for one correcting the other? Which is why I disfavour intimate friendships. In intimate friendships, wrongdoing is quickly absorbed and imitated, good qualities lag behind in the absorption process.

One who wants God's hand in friendship is better off as a loner in this world. What may appear to be inexplicable actions of mine are really due to inner promptings. It may be a product of my heated imagination. If it is so, I prize that imagination as it has served me for a chequered life extending over a period of now nearly fifty-five years, because I learned to rely consciously upon God before I was fifteen years old.[3] One should be friends not with one or two intimates but with the whole world. Whether there is or there is not any merit in this belief of mine, the fact is that my desire to sustain an intimate friendship failed.

Mehtab told me 'We are a weak people because we do not eat meat. The English rule over us because they are meat eaters. You know how hardy I am and how good a runner I am too. It is because I am a meat eater.' Beside him and my brother Karsandas, I certainly looked feeble-bodied. Mehtab could run long distances and extraordinarily fast. He was an adept in high and long jumping as well. Such was his physical strength that he could take any amount of corporal punishment. He would often display his exploits to me. I would watch entranced. From awe came the desire to emulate. I knew I could not run to save my life. But I said to myself: Wouldn't it be great if I could become as tough as Mehtab, and as venturesome?

Karsandas had already fallen for meat. And now, with my new resolve, I was to follow suit. I was, as I have said, a coward. Mehtab, who knew of my phobias, told me that he could pick up live snakes, feel no fear of robbers and as for ghosts, he did not believe they existed. All this, he went on to assert, was the benefaction of meat-eating. I melted. Eating meat is good, I convinced myself, it will make me strong, and if the whole nation took to it with vigour, all of India would become strong, and we would then defeat the British.

The reader may not appreciate the gravity of this matter. I must therefore explain that my family belonged to the Vaishnava tradition and my parents were thought of as strict and devout Vaishnavas. Temple-going was standard practice. In fact, some temples were regarded as belonging to the family. Then, beyond the confines of the family, the influence of Jainism on Gujarat was strong. It pervaded every place and every activity. And so the eating of meat was opposed, in fact, rejected, in Gujarat by its Vaishnavas and Jainas in a way that could not have been seen anywhere else in India or, indeed, the world. This, then, was my culture. My decision to eat meat therefore was no ordinary matter. It was, as a decision, both fearful and grave.

A day was set for beginning the experiment. It had to be carried out in secret. A lonely spot by the river was chosen and there, for the first time in my life, I saw—meat. There was baker's bread as well. I took to neither. The goat's meat was as tough as leather. It tasted at first nauseous, but worst of all, the memory of it haunted the darkness of the night, and there was no sleep for the sinners. But I got over my dislike of bread and of meat dishes. This went on for about a year. Savoury meat dishes were expensive and I do not know where Mehtab raised the money for them. But raise it he did, for he was bent on turning me into a meat eater. It was not that I was slowly drawn to its taste, no. I was on a 'become strong, become tough' trip. I had to then take the message to others, defeat the British, make India free. In this reformist 'high', I lost my normal wits.

More was to come. Mehtab took me once to the prostitutes' ward. On reaching the selected brothel, the money needed for the transaction was passed and then, giving me suitable instructions on what I should do when inside, Mehtab sent me in. I had some idea that all I would do is talk. But what transpired showed that if God wishes to help someone bent on harming himself, He does. Once in her den-like room, I went up to the woman's bed and just sat. Not one word would come to me. She became furious and heaping choice abuses, showed me the door. Humiliated, I felt my sense of manhood had been destroyed. If the earth had opened up, I would have quietly sunk into it in shame.

I had escaped—escaped from being faithless to my wife by just my good luck. There were to be four other experiences of this kind in my life, in each of which I escaped a fall. But the desire was there in all of them and so must be treated to be no less than the act.

Even after this experience, I did not cease looking at Mehtab as anything but a worthy friend. The realization that he was not was to come much later.

How was I to say anything of my cowardice to the one who slept next to me, my wife, now not so much a child as a young woman? That she was of much firmer purpose than I was something I had understood. And had understood with much embarrassment.

I have written about the role of a husband's jealousy and suspicious nature. Kastur suffered as a result of it. What a terrific quarrel[4] I had with her over my suspicion. I broke her bangles, refused to have anything to do with her and sent her away to her parents. She stayed away from me for a whole year. She showed courage.

How shall I say what other things I did? Sheikh Mehtab was behind this. He kept me under his thumb for more than ten years.

Nine

LONDON CALLING

*I am not a man who would,
after having made an intention, leave it easily.**

The country's and our family's finances were such that if a choice had to be made between appearing for the matriculation examination in one of the two centres, Bombay and Ahmedabad, the choice for a Gandhi would have had to fall on the nearer and smaller venue.

And so I went from Rajkot to Ahmedabad for the examination on what was my first journey to any place alone. The examinations were held over four days, from 21 to 25 November 1887. 'On the advantages of a cheerful disposition' was the subject of the essay in English that I had to write. I passed the matriculation examination, securing 89/200 in English, 45.5/100 in Gujarati, 59/175 in Mathematics and 54/150 in General Knowledge.[5]

It was the desire of elders in the family that, after matriculating, I should move on to some college for higher studies. There was the prospect of joining a college in Bombay or one in Bhavnagar. Again, our finances did the choosing and I enrolled in the Bhavnagar Samaldas College. There I could learn nothing. Everything seemed very difficult. The teachers' lectures I found neither easy nor interesting. The fault was not that of the Samaldas College teachers who were all regarded as being of the first rank; it was that of my immaturity.

While at Bhavnagar, I had a chat with Jayshankar Buch. He advised me to apply to the Junagadh state for a scholarship to study

---

*Gandhi started writing this diary on board the SS *Clyde* that took him to London. The diarist's English is that of a nineteen-year-old Kathiawari who, until this point, had attempted no writing of his own in that language. *London Diary*, CWMG Vol. 1, p. 4.

in London. I do not remember the reply I gave to Jayshankar but I think I regarded the prospect of getting such a scholarship as impossible. From that time the intention of going to London was in my mind. I thought to myself, 'If I go to England not only shall I become a barrister (of whom I used to think a great deal), but I shall be able to see England, the land of philosophers and poets, the very centre of civilization.'

After finishing my first term, I returned on 13 April 1888, for the summer break to Rajkot. Fifteen days into the vacation, my brother and I went to see the Brahmin priest and scholar, Mavji Dave. As an old family friend and adviser, he had kept up with us even after my father's demise. As usual, Joshiji (as we used to call him) asked me how I did and about my study in Bhavnagar. I told him plainly that I hardly had any chance of passing any examination there in that first year. Hearing this he advised my brother to send me as soon as possible to London for being called to the Bar. He said the expense will only be about 5,000 rupees. 'Let him take some urad dal and cook food for himself, whereby there will be no objection about religion.' He suggested that I apply to the Junagadh and Porbandar states for a scholarship and if no help was forthcoming, to sell some furniture to raise the money. He also asked me to meet his son Kevalram, a leading lawyer who had returned from London after becoming a barrister. 'But anyhow,' said Joshiji, 'send Mohandas to London.' We had great faith in Joshiji and my brother promised to him that he would send me to London.

When I met Kevalram he encouraged me to go to London but said I will need 10,000 rupees. This came as a great blow to me. And he added that in London I will have to set aside all my religious prejudices and will have to eat meat and drink wine. 'The more you spend,' he said, 'the cleverer you will be. You are very young. There are many temptations in London. You are apt to be entrapped by them.' He advised my brother to send me to Porbandar to pursue the matter with the state. I was partially dejected by this talk. But I am not a man who would, after having made an intention, leave it easily.

Everything was under the control of my brother and we were all living together. What little my father could leave for me was in the hands of my brother. I proposed that the whole family capital should be devoted to my education. There are very few such brothers in India. He was told that I might prove an unworthy brother after imbibing Western ideas, and that the only chance of regaining the money would be in my returning alive to India, which was very doubtful. But he turned a deaf ear to all these reasonable and well-meant warnings. There was one, and only one condition attached to the consent to my proposal, that is that I should get the permission of my mother and my uncle. May many persons have such brothers as mine!

That very day, the plan was told by my brother and me to my cousin Meghjibhai who agreed with the proposal and agreed to give me 5,000 rupees. When the idea was disclosed to my dear mother she reproached me for being so credulous and said Meghjibhai would never give me the money when the time would come and of course she felt that time would never come.

A day was fixed for my going to Porbandar to meet my uncle and Mr Lely*, the British agent who held that office during the minority of the prince, for some pecuniary help. But an hour before my departure, a serious accident took place. I was always quarrelling with my friend Sheikh Mehtab. On the day of my departure I was quite engrossed in thinking of that quarrel. He had a musical party that night. I did not enjoy it very well. At about 10.30 p.m. the party ended and we all went to see Meghjibhai. On my way I was buried in madcap thoughts of London on one side and on thoughts about Sheikh Mehtab on the other. Amidst these thoughts I came unconsciously in contact with a carriage and received some injury. Yet I did not take the help of anybody while walking. I think I was quite dizzy. On entering Meghjibhai's house I again unknowingly came in contact with a stone and fell flat on the ground and was

---

*Later Sir F. S. P. Lely, official member of the Bombay Legislative Council and author of 'Suggestions for the Better Governing of India', 1906.

not myself for five minutes. And so none would allow me to go to Porbandar at that time.

At length I did get to Porbandar. My uncle was not happy with the idea of my going but did not dissuade me either. He was on the point of going to Benares and such other holy places. After three days' incessant persuasion and arguments I could get the following answer from him: 'I am going on a pilgrimage. What you say may be right, but how could I willingly say "yes" to your unholy proposal? The only thing I can say is that, if your mother does not mind your going, I have no right to interfere.' This was easily interpreted as 'yes'. In meeting Mr Lely I had an interview with an English gentleman for the first time in my life. He said I should graduate first in India and he would then see if he could help me. My having bent deep and salaamed him with both hands went in vain.

On returning to Rajkot, I told the family of all that had transpired in Porbandar, consulted Joshiji. He said I should take out a loan if needed. I told him of my plans to use the jewels in Kasturba's portion. But those would not have fetched more than 2,000 or 3,000 rupees. My brother Lakshmidas took it upon himself to raise the balance somehow or the other. His love for me was like that of my father.*

My mother, meanwhile, had set about enquiring after life in London. She was incredulous. Some had told her that young men go out of control there, become meat eaters. Others had told her that they cannot do without drinking spirits. All this talk she unburdened on me. I told her: 'But don't you have faith in me? I will not let you down. I promise—give you a sacred undertaking—that I will not, when in England, touch women, meat, wine. And if there was such a real danger, how would Joshiji ask me to go?'

Now let me say what happened during my absence in Rajkot. Sheikh Mehtab, full of tricks as always, forged a letter as from me to Meghjibhai asking for 5,000 rupees. The letter actually passed as mine and Meghjibhai, very puffed up, made a solemn promise to give

---

*The family spent about Rs 13,000 on the venture, an amount which James Hunt describes in *Gandhi in London*, Promilla & Co., New Delhi, 1978 as 'the whole capital of the family'.

me the money. Then a day was fixed for my departure from Rajkot for Bombay to set sail. It was the 4th of August. But the matter went to the press and people began asking my brother about it. He now told me to leave off the intention of going but I would not do that.

I met HH the Thakore sahib of Rajkot and Colonel Watson,* the political agent of Kathiawar, for help. All I could get was a photograph from the former and a letter from the latter. When he gave me that trivial note of introduction, Colonel Watson said in a peremptory tone that it was worth one lakh of rupees. Now that really makes me laugh. The fulsome flattery that I had to practise at this time made me quite angry. Had it not been for my credulous and dearest brother, I would not have resorted to such a piece of gross ingratiation.

Kasturba's parents thought of their daughter. Who was to look after her? How was she to manage to spend the three years? Of course, she was to be looked after by my brother. Poor brother! According to my ideas at that time, I should have taken little notice of their legitimate fears and growlings had it not been that their displeasure would have been reflected on my mother and brother. It was no easy task for them to sit night after night with my father-in-law and to hear and successfully answer his objections. But then I was taught the old proverb 'Patience and perseverance overcome mountains' too well to give way.

A farewell address was given to me by my school fellows. I was quite uneasy when I rose up to answer the address. When I had spoken half of what I had to speak, I began to shake.†

When the day of departure from Rajkot to Bombay—the 10th of August—came, my mother was hiding her eyes, full of tears, in

---

*Political agent of the Kathiawar Agency from 1881 to 1889 in Rajkot; came to India at the age of sixteen, served in Poona, Bombay, Ranchi, Kolhapur, Bhavnagar, and Rajkot, a total of nearly thirty-five years working for the British Raj. A museum set up in 1888 in Rajkot in his name (the oldest in Saurashtra) has rich artefacts from the Rajkot region as well as replicas from the Indus Valley sites of Mohenjo-Daro and Harappa.
†The *Kathiawar Times* of 12 July 1888 reported that Gandhi said at the school function: 'I hope that some of you will follow in my footsteps and after you return from England you will work wholeheartedly for big reforms in India.'

her hands but the sobbing was clearly heard. I did not weep though my heart was breaking. Last but not least came the leave-taking with my wife. It being contrary to custom for me to see or talk to her in the presence of friends, I had to see her in a separate room. She, of course, had begun sobbing long before. I went to see her and stood like a dumb statue for a moment. I kissed her, and she said, 'Don't go.' What followed I need not describe. With my mother's leave, and leaving my wife and our son*, but a few months' old, I left Rajkot that day for Bombay.

My brother, Lakshmidas, Sheikh Mehtab, and a couple of others also started with me by the same train.

Meanwhile, my Modh Vania caste fellows tried their best to prevent me from going further. Almost all of them were in opposition. It was my misfortune to have taken up lodgings in the heart of the city of Bombay, where they most abound, so I was hemmed in on all sides. I could not go out without being pointed and stared at by someone or other. At one time, while I was walking near the Town Hall, I was surrounded and hooted by them, and my poor brother had to look at the scene in silence.

The culminating point was reached when a huge meeting of the caste fellows was summoned by the chief representatives. Every member of the caste was called upon to attend the meeting, under pain of forfeiting a fine of five annas. I was seated in the centre of the audience. One of them said to me: 'In the opinion of the caste, your proposal to go to England is not proper. Our religion forbids voyages abroad. One is obliged there to eat and drink with Europeans.' I am helpless, I told them, and cannot alter my resolve. The leader then asked, 'Will you disregard the orders of the caste?' I am really helpless, I repeated, 'I think the caste should not interfere.' The gentleman became incensed. He hurled some abuses at me. I remained unmoved. 'This lad will from now be regarded as an outcaste. If anyone from the caste helps him or goes to see him off, [he] will be questioned by the caste leaders and will have to pay a fine of Rs 1

---

*Harilal Gandhi (1887–1948).

2/5.' This boycott made no impression on me. But would it affect my brother? Luckily for me, he too remained firm and wrote to me that the caste's injunction notwithstanding, he would not impede my going. I was now more confident than ever. In Bombay I got some clothes for myself. Some of the clothes I liked and some I did not like at all. The necktie which I delighted in wearing later, I then abhorred. The short jacket I looked upon as an attire that mimicked nakedness.

The 21st was the day I was supposed to leave Bombay Harbour but people told my brother that the rainy season was dangerous for sea voyages. He got worried and, asking me to leave on a later, safer date, returned to Rajkot.

Bad weather on sea further postponed the departure. But then all on a sudden the sailing was announced for 4 September 1888. I wired my brother for permission to take that boat, and got it. I then went to a family friend and asked for some financial help to buy the steamer ticket. He was kind. He not only advanced the money but also gave me courage and confidence. I learnt that a Junagadh lawyer, Tryambakrai Mazmudar*, was also going on the same boat to become a barrister. Friends got me a berth in that gentleman's cabin, which was good. He was a householder of mature years, I an eighteen-year-old stranger to the world's ways. Many friends came to see me off. Of these Patwari gave me 5 rupees, Shamalji as many, Modi two, Kashidas, Narandas, two.[6] Mr Manshankar† gave me a silver chain and then all of them bade farewell for three years and departed. Mazmudar told them that he would look after me and they should not worry about me. Thus on 4 September 1888, I left Bombay pier on board the SS *Clyde*.

---

*Tryambakrai Trikamrai Mazmudar stayed in touch with Gandhi throughout their stay in England. Rajmohan Gandhi (*The Good Boatman*, Viking, 1999) quotes Mazmudar as saying to Narahari Parekh in 1919 after a meeting with Gandhi: 'We went to England together.... He went on rising and I just sat, doing nothing but eat....'
†Manshanker Ganeshji Anjaria, a neighbour and classmate of Mohandas at the Taluka School and at Kathiawar High School, Rajkot (J. M. Upadhyaya, *Mahatma Gandhi as a Student*, p. 7).

The Houses of Parliament from old Westminster Bridge in the early 1890s
Source: From period stereocard/WikimediaCommons

~

BOOK II
1888 to 1896

This second section is about Mohandas by himself—away from home, from family, friends, the Gujarati society he has known, hurled into an environment he is completely new to—in England. He finds being alone in the cold and alien land dismaying at first, then interesting, and a little later quite fascinating. He grows into his study of the law and of English society on his own terms, of which staying strictly vegetarian and uncompromisingly abstemious are part. He has vowed he will stay away from 'women' and he does, though coming perilously close to breaking his promise.

And then, having been called to the Bar, he goes, after the briefest 'touching base' with home in Rajkot, to a third continent—South Africa. He is something of a dandy, dressed in a knee-length frock coat and turban, as he moves into the highly mixed and yet 'separate' atmosphere of that part-British and part-Boer territory of a people he comes to be among but not become close to—Africans. Racial prejudice, brutally physical and psychological, assails and activates him. He begins to be 'made' as his work extends beyond law to political activism. He becomes a skilful commentator, tractarian, speaker, learning the skills of political articulation— again, on his own terms—from Indian veterans he comes to meet on visits home.

And becoming all that, he finds balancing home and work a demanding cross to bear. Gandhi is, in this phase of his life, a work-in-progress and in no small turmoil.

Drawing from his autobiography, both in its Gujarati original and the English translation, and from entries in the early volumes of The Collected Works of Mahatma Gandhi, *this part opens windows and parts curtains into home, work, and mind.*

~

One

THE SAILING

We do not get water in the English water closets and are obliged to use pieces of paper.

It was for the first time in my life that I sailed in a steamship. I enjoyed the voyage very much. Throughout the voyage I was not at all seasick.

Mr Mazmudar and I were saloon passengers. There was also Mr Abdul Majid* who was a first-class passenger. I liked the arrangements of the steamer very much. When we sat in the cabin or saloons, we forgot they were part of the ship. We sometimes did not feel the motion of the ship at all. There were musical instruments on the ship. I every now and then played on the piano. There were cards, chessboard and draughts on board.

For the first time in my life, I saw in the front of our ship, electric light[†]. It appeared like moonlight. The scene of the sea when the sky is clear is lovely. On one moonlit night, watching the sea, I could see the moon reflected on the water. On account of the waves, the moon appeared as if she was moving here and there. One dark night the stars were reflected in the water. They appeared like so many diamonds.

---

*Abdul Majid, later Khwaja Abdul Majid Sahib, became one of the earliest to join the nationalist movement and take to khadi, becoming vice chancellor of the National Muslim University of Aligarh, which later became the Jamia Millia Islamia of Delhi.
†The first demonstration of electric light in India was in Calcutta on 24 July 1879 by P. W. Fleury & Co. But it was only on 7 January 1897—nine years after Gandhi sailed—that Kilburn & Co secured the Calcutta electric lighting licence as agents of the Indian Electric Company Limited. Power was only thereafter introduced in Bombay with Bombay Electric Supply & Tramways Company (BEST) setting up a generating station in 1905 to provide electricity for the tramway.

For some days I did not speak a word to the passengers. I always got up at 8 in the morning, washed my teeth, then went to the WC and took my bath. The arrangement of the English water closets astonished a native passenger. We do not get there water and are obliged to use pieces of paper.

After enjoying the sea voyage for about five days we reached Aden. All of were tired of the monotony of the voyage and were eager to see land. At about 11 a.m. we anchored at Aden. Some boys came with small boats. They were great swimmers. Some Europeans threw some money in the waters. The boys went deep into the water and found the money. I wish I could do so. This was a pretty sight. I heard that the boys were sometimes injured by sea animals who cut at their arms or legs. But, still, the boys being poor sat on their small boats and came up to the steamers for their money-diving. I must say here that we* simply saw the boys finding out the pieces. We, ourselves, did not throw a single pie.

The construction of the Suez† is indeed marvellous. I cannot think of the genius of the man who invented it. It is quite right to say that he has competed with nature. It is not an easy task to join two seas. The French take a sum of money from every ship that passes through the canal. The income must be very large. Port Said is the terminus of the Suez Canal. We anchored at Port Said in the evening. The construction of Port Said buildings is French. Here we get an idea of French life. We saw some coffee restaurants. On one side we drink coffee or soda or tea or any other drink and on the other side we hear music, with some women playing fiddle. A bottle of lemonade in these cafes, as they are called, will cost you 12 pence, which we will get for a penny in Bombay. Customers are said to hear music gratis. But really it is not so. As soon as the music is finished, a woman with a plate covered with a handkerchief in her

---

*By 'we', Gandhi means the Indians on board the ship.
†The Suez Canal, which had been dug and closed due to silting several times down the centuries, was 'finally' constructed, after a ten-year construction exercise, in November 1869, the year of Gandhi's birth. Ferdinand, vicomte de Lesseps, the French engineer and diplomat, is regarded as its builder.

hand comes before every customer. That means you are obliged to give her something. We gave her six pence.

After three days we reached Brindisi. The harbour there is very beautiful. The steamer just touches the coast and you descend by means of a ladder. Everyone speaks Italian. The streets are sloped and paved with stones. A man came up and asked me: 'Sir, there is a beautiful girl of fourteen, follow me sir, and I will take you there.... The charge is not high....' Your conscience is the best dictator. We left Brindisi in the morning.

Malta is an object of interest. The island is very beautiful. But here we were cheated a great deal. Gibraltar is built upon a rock. It is said that the port being free, smoking in Gibraltar is very cheap.

Two

LONDON, AT LAST

*...with my dark skin and white clothes,
I was in a hopeless minority.*

We reached* London in the afternoon. With Mr Mazmudar and Mr Majid, I went to Hotel Victoria. Mr Majid told the porter in a dignified air to give our cabman the proper fare. Mr Majid thought very highly of himself but let me write here that the dress he had put on was worse than that of the porter.

On the steamer I had worn dark-coloured clothes. Friends had got me a white flannel suit as well. Thinking that suit would be a most becoming costume on landing in London, I disembarked wearing that. In those final days of September, no one else was in flannels and with my dark skin and white clothes, I was in a hopeless minority. I was chafing over my clothes in the hotel. My boxes had been entrusted to the Grindlays' Co clerks for delivery at the hotel. But this being the weekend, the delivery was not to be expected before Monday. So I could not change into anything else either. My clothes and my colour drew the attention of passers-by and I felt courtesy and refinement were not features of London life.

I was quite dazzled by the splendour of the hotel. I had never in my life seen such pomp. My business was just to follow the two friends in silence. Then we were to go to the second floor by a lift. I did not know what that was. The doors opened and I thought that was a room in which we were to sit for some time. But to my great surprise we were brought to the second floor.

---

*The date was 29 September 1888; Gandhi has given an incorrect date, both in the autobiography and in the *London Diary*.

The hotel was costly. I had brought with me four letters or character-certificates from India. They were addressed to Dr Pranjivan Mehta*, Dalpatram Shukla†, Prince Ranjitsinhji‡ and Dadabhai Naoroji§. I had telegraphed Dr Mehta on reaching England and he came to the hotel that very evening. He smiled at my being in flannels. As we were talking, I casually picked up his top hat and, trying to see how smooth it was, passed my hand over it the wrong way and the disturbed fur stood up. Dr Mehta looked somewhat angrily at what I was doing and stopped me. But the mischief had been done. The incident was a warning for the future. This was my first lesson in European etiquette.

We had come in to the hotel on Saturday and decided to leave for cheaper lodgings on Monday. My recollection is that my portion of the bill came to three pounds. At Dr Mehta's behest I moved into the lodgings in Richmond of a friend of his. I was welcomed there as a brother would be. There was nothing that was wanting by way of hospitality.

But the loneliness! I thought of home incessantly. My mother's love would appear before my mind's eye in her human form. And come nightfall, the eyes would well up. Different recollections of home and family made sleep impossible. I could not talk about this pain to anyone. In any case what would that avail? I did not know what remedy could be found for the situation. People seemed strange, lifestyles weird. Even homes seemed peculiarly fashioned, as the ways in which they functioned. And the food that I could eat seemed dry and tasteless. My condition at that time was that of a

---

*Dr Pranjivan Mehta (1864–1932), medical doctor and lawyer, became one of Gandhi's closest friends and lifelong well-wisher and benefactor.
†Dalpatram Bhavanji Shukla (d. 1938), a Kathiawari from Morvi; joined the Inner Temple on 13 November 1886, and was called to the bar on 3 July 1889. He and his 'English family' were welcoming of Gandhi in their Richmond home, to which he moved.
‡Prince Ranjitsinhji, cricketer and later ruler of Nawanagar, was based in Cambridge during Gandhi's years in London and does not seem to have met Gandhi there.
§Dadabhai Naoroji (1825–1917), Parsi by birth, pre-eminent Indian statesman and British parliamentarian, inspired Gandhi in London and was in guiding correspondence with him during Gandhi's years in South Africa.

betel nut in a nut-splicer. England I did not take to, home I could not return to. I saw that I had come for three years and for three years I would have to stay. And that was that.

I had the privilege to see Dadabhai Naoroji shortly after reaching London.[7] A friend of my father's had given me a letter of introduction to him and it is worth noting that this friend was not at all acquainted with Dadabhai. He however took it for granted that anyone from the public could write to such a saintly person. I found that Dadabhai came in contact with all students. He was their leader and attended their gatherings. My first acquaintance with the extent of Indian poverty was to come through Dadabhai's book.[8]

Three

SETTLING IN

*'...I am comfortably settled and have fairly begun my studies...
English life is very expensive.'*

On 6 November 1888, that is, a little over five weeks after reaching London, I formally applied for admission to The Honourable Society of the Inner Temple as 'Mohandass* Karamchand Gandhi, aged 19, the youngest son of Karamchand Uttamchand Gandhi, deceased, of Porbandar, India.'

Three days later I wrote to my brother informing him of my application and asking him why his weekly letters to me had slowed down. If I do not get letters every week, I feel very worried, I wrote, and urged him to please drop a postcard every week. I said the cold was now very bitter but I felt no need for meat or liquor, which fact filled my heart with joy and thankfulness.

A month later I penned the draft of a letter to Mr Lely telling him of my having joined the Inner Temple and asking him for a grant of 400 pounds as the 666 pounds that my brother had raised for me would not suffice for my needs. And I sent it to my brother asking him to hand it in person to the agent. I also wrote on similar lines to Colonel Watson, who had given me a letter of commendation. Telling him that I had comfortably settled and had fairly begun my studies, I said life in England was very expensive and asked him also for some substantial help to prosecute my studies.

Getting the right food had become an issue for me, a big issue.

---

*It is noteworthy that Gandhi spells his first name here—perhaps the earliest sample of his name written in the Roman script by himself—using the double 'ss', perhaps consistently with the way clerkdom in British India (mis)spelt it.

Vegetables cooked without spices or salt I could not abide. What could the landlady cook by way of my needs? The morning's daily fare of oatmeal porridge did fill me up somewhat but by the afternoon and evening I would be famished. The friend would try every day to persuade me to give up my no-meat restriction. I would cite the vow and say nothing more. For lunch I would subsist on bread with marmalade and a green vegetable slop. The same or similar would comprise dinner. I could see that of the bread I was expected to take no more than two or three slices. To ask for any more would be unseemly and embarrassing. Now I was used to eating heartily. My appetite was robust and demanding. There was no milk to be had at lunch or dinner time. Seeing my predicament, he one day asked me: 'When back home you had no need to eat meat you tell me you did eat it; now when you really need to do so, you are starving yourself. How strange!'

Dr Mehta and Bhai Dalpatram Shukla had me move shortly thereafter to new lodgings in the West Kensington home of an Anglo-Indian widow. She was apprised of my dietary quirks and was very understanding. But the hunger pangs stayed! The landlady had two daughters. They would urge me at table to 'take a bit more of the bread'. Little did they know that what my growling stomach really wanted was the whole loaf. A wandering hunt for a vegetarian eating place started then in right earnest. My landlady said she knew such places did exist in London, but was not sure where they were. I would walk some ten to twelve miles looking for them, and fill my stomach with bread bought at some poor eating house. 'Send me some mashala and fine-ground saalam,' I wrote home, 'in tin-plated light-weight containers.'[9] One day my wandering feet reached Farrington Street and lo! there it was, a sign that said 'Vegetarian Restaurant'. I was as a child that had found its heart's desire. Buying a book called *A Plea for Vegetarianism* by Henry Salt for one shilling, I walked into the precincts to sit down for what was my first proper meal in England. God had saved me from hunger at last.

Honouring the word given to my mother was now not a matter of stern vow-keeping alone. It acquired the grace and fullness of joy.

What remained now was becoming an English gentleman.

I had brought 'western' clothes with me but a Bombay cut is only a Bombay cut. That would not do in English society. And so I went to the Army and Navy Stores where a chimney hat to be sat on my head was bought for nineteen shillings. And then on to Bond Street, no less, where the elite had their clothes tailored. There, putting a hissing matchstick on full ten pounds, I got myself an evening suit. And as if this was not enough, I wrote to my brother to send to me a chain that would hold a pocket watch. My brother's innocent and princely nature moved to do so at once and a heavy chain of pure gold arrived at this fop's doorstep from home. It was long enough to work its way into not just the one pocket on the three-piece's jacket, but two.

This was about appearances. What of culture? A cultured man about town must know to dance. He should be able to speak French, the lingua franca of all of Europe—which I wanted to tour. And he should be able to give a speech, fluently. So, I enrolled in a dance class. The first term cost three pounds. Over some three weeks, I took about six lessons. But the feet would not follow the beat. The piano would sing but I could not follow what it wanted me to follow. 'One, two, three,' it said, but at its own pace which was not mine. And so, what was I to do? A cat, says the proverb, must be got to catch the rat. I added to the accoutrements of culture. I started to learn to play the violin just so that I could get a sense of notes and beats. Three pounds went into the purchase of a violin and some more on its learning.

To learn the art of elocution, I went in search of my third teacher in gentlemanship. He cost me a guinea. I bought and started to read Bell's *Standard Elocutionist*. It was when reading it that a 'bell' rang in my mind's ears. Was I going to spend the rest of my life in England? How was my dance-learning going to help me back home? The violin I can learn to play when I return. I am here as a student. I should acquire but one asset: learning. I wrote to my elocution and dance teachers of my thinking. I took my violin to my violin teacher. She was most understanding. She said she would try to sell the violin for whatever value it fetched. She and I had got to know each other and so I told her of my realization that learning dance and music was a kind of delusion with me. She understood and appreciated what I said. The desire to be a gentleman had held me in its grip for some three months. The fascination with apparel lasted much longer. But I had at last become a student in London.

Four

STUDENT LIFE

Question papers were easy and examiners were generous.

A student in India is half student and half householder. He may be married too. In that case, he has to think of his wife, perhaps children, in addition to household cares, which an Indian student is generally saddled with. While, in England, he is alone, no wife to tease or flatter him, no parents to indulge, no children to look after, no company to disturb. He is the master of his time. So, if he has the will, he can do more.[10]

I used to suffer from headaches and nosebleeds in India. I could not read for three or four hours at a stretch during the summer months without getting a headache. Now I was entirely free from both and this I ascribe mainly to the cold and invigorating climate of England. The invigorating climate in England is by itself a stimulant to work, the enervating climate of India is a stimulant to idleness. Who has not passed idle hours on a summer noon? Who has not wished he had nothing to do in summer but to sleep? Of course, persons are there who never cease to work in India. In fact, the hardest working students are found in India. But that work is against the will. In England, you like the work for the sake of it. You cannot help working. I have heard it said of a very learned professor that he read as much in three years in England as he would have in nine years in India. That amount of work which tells upon one's health in India can be gone through with ease in England. An instance is at our very doors. Do we not work more in winter than in summer? So, then, it will not be doubted that a person willing to work will do more in England than in India.

After staying with the friend I have mentioned for a month who treated me very kindly and taught me how to behave and how to use the fork and the spoon, I moved to a family where I had to pay 30s per week for board and lodging. Thus, my board and lodging cost me only 6 pounds. I was told, however, that living on 12 pounds per month would be considered very economical. I therefore managed somehow or other to spend 12 pounds per month. For lunch they gave me bread and butter and cheese invariably. For tea, bread and butter and tea and cake sometimes. All this did not cost them more than 7 shillings per week. Thus, it will be seen that I paid 30s not because the cost of giving board and lodging was so much or even half so much, but because of the privilege of being allowed to enjoy their company. It is generally thought desirable to live with families in order to learn the English manners and customs. This may be good for a few months, but to pass three years in a family is not only unnecessary but often tiresome. And it would be impossible to lead a regular student's life in the family. This is the experience of many Indians. If you live in a family, you must—it is only fair—sacrifice some time for them. I was to spend at the most 8s for one room per week, 6d breakfast, supper and one shilling at the most, for dinner.

I knew every nook and corner of London and somewhat of Oxford and Cambridge and Manchester too. In those great palaces called public houses in London, people went in as sober men and came out dead drunk. About the same time I met a good Christian from Manchester in a vegetarian boarding house. I narrated to him my Rajkot recollections. He said, 'I am a vegetarian, I do not drink. Many Christians are meat eaters and drink, no doubt; but neither meat-eating nor drinking is enjoined by scripture.'

My landlady in London used to say: 'Whenever I am down, there is nothing like a glass of stout to pick me up.'[11]

Of course, it is another thing altogether when you have to dine or take tea outside because you have to go far for some business and it would be a waste of time to return home for tea. Again, while living in the family, you are supposed to be punctual. They have fixed times for all the meals and they do not or are not expected to wait for you. So, if you are outside and if you think that you would not reach in time for your meal, that would be a case of dining outside. These occasions are rare and do not at all prove costly, though one who would live on 4 pounds per month cannot afford to do these things. He cannot even get into a good family for 1 pound per week. The food they used to provide for dinner was third-rate. This was no fault of the family, I was the first vegetarian boarder with them. Vegetable soups and a vegetable, mostly potatoes, and some fresh fruit was my portion. For breakfast they gave me bread and butter and jam and tea and I had porridge occasionally.

A suggestion was thrown out by somebody that I would be considered to be stingy if I took all meals every day in the family and tea very often. Following up this suggestion, I used to lunch outside at least once a week and take tea only thrice a week. Thus, I paid for all this in the family; I spent about 10 shillings in the lunching and taking tea outside. I used to spend unnecessarily a great deal also in travelling. It need hardly be said here that taking your meals or tea outside purposely to show that you are not stingy or that you are rolling in wealth is anything but gentlemanly and entirely unnecessary.

But those only can live on that sum who 'eat to live', not 'live to eat'. If you must have the luxuries, if you cannot sit at the table without company, if you must entertain friends pretty frequently to sumptuous dinners, if you must live like a gourmand, then for you ten times the sum may not be sufficient. But if you would live frugally and happily and not luxuriously, 9s per week would be more than sufficient.

As nothing tells like illustrations, I would first cite illustrations in support of the contention that one pound a week is sufficient for a person of frugal habits and not born in the lap of luxury or rather not addicted to a luxurious mode of living. There are thousands of commercial gentlemen living on one pound a week in England. I had a chat with an Anglo–Indian here who said that he was living on one pound a week. There is a gentleman who is an M.A., B.E.L., Barrister-at-Law, who lived on 10 shillings a week and has yet been living on less than one pound a week. He is the editor of a newspaper and I have seen him work at the rate of sixteen hours or more per diem. He was, when I saw him last, living on bread, figs, and water. There are Irish MPs living on one pound per week. And some of them are the best debaters. The late Mr Biggor, MP, I believe, lived on one pound a week.

In ordinary houses no bathrooms can be found. In such cases very many visit the public baths weekly which cost 6 pence or 4 pence. But it is possible to have a daily bath without any expense wherever you go. You can take a sponge bath with two or three tumblers of hot water always to be supplied at your request by the landlady in the morning. You can pour water into your basin, dip a sponge in it and rub hard with the sponge twice or thrice and then rub the body with a dry towel, and you have taken a very nice bath which gives a glow to the body and keeps it clean. Even the sponge may be left out and the hands only used.

Later, renting a single room, investing in a stove, I was able to keep all expenses within 4 pounds a month. It was possible to live on one pound a week in London and many have lived on less. I may say that I tried the experiment successfully and was never happier than under the 4-pound living. While I was living on 4 pound per month, I had to work the hardest.

It is always best, whenever possible, in London, to walk so that you may have exercise at the same time that you save money. Nothing can be better. Many do this purposely in England, not so much for the sake of saving a few pence, as for the sake of exercise. Walking three or four miles is a pleasure in the cold climate of England. Indeed, whenever it is possible in the cold weather, a brisk walk should be preferred to a ride in a train or a bus. Very often the latter proves injurious. I was once literally stiff in a bus. Even the bus conductors recognize the danger. At intervals they run with the bus and get into it when they are warm.

In addition to lectures at the Inner Temple, I joined a private class for the purpose of taking the London matriculation examination. I kept count of every little item such as omnibus fares or postage or a couple of coppers spent on newspaper, entered it in a diary and struck the balance every evening.

Latin was one of the subjects of study for the matriculation. This was good because when for my Bar examination, I had to study Justinian's Roman Law in Latin, I stood to advantage. And later in South Africa, where Roman Law was the vogue.

Among the books that I read for the Bar was Lavater on Physiognomy. I read up what he had to say about Shakespeare's face but I could just not master the skill of identifying Shakespeares walking up and down the streets of London. I liked reading Tudor's *Leading Cases* and learnt much from it, and *Snell's Equity* was engaging but tough to plod through. Goodeve's *Personal Property* was a good read, but it was Williams and Edwards' *Real Property* that I went through as I would a novel.

I used to read in the Inner Temple library and would often attend Dr Parker's* sermons in the Temple Church. When I had to study hard, I used to spend no more than half an hour all told for preparing my morning and evening meals. In the morning I used to make porridge which took exactly twenty minutes. If I prepared something in the evening, it would be a soup, which required only a little watching and no stirring. So the only time I spent after the soup would be for mixing the ingredients, put the mixture on the stove. While sitting by its side to watch it, I would read some book.

---

*Joseph Parker (1830–1902), congregationalist and pastor in the City Temple, London, who 'converted to Christ' while walking from church one summer evening. His Thursday noon service was celebrated.

Five

LIFE BEYOND STUDIES

To my room I went quaking and trembling and with beating heart like a quarry escaped from the pursuer.

I came in contact with those who were regarded as pillars of vegetarianism and began my own experiments in dietetics. I stopped taking the sweets and condiments I had got from home. The mind having taken a different turn, the fondness for condiments wore away, and the boiled spinach that in Richmond I had found tasteless, I now relished, cooked without condiments. Many such experiments taught me that the real seat of taste was not the tongue but the mind.

Brighton is a seaside resort I visited. I was told that there was a vegetarian restaurant in Brighton. On reaching Brighton, it was after some difficulty that I could get a good room. The landladies could not be persuaded to believe that the room would not be spoiled by my cooking in my room. One of them said: 'No, I cannot give the room even for 20 shillings. The whole carpet would be spoiled by stain of grease and no one else after you leave would take my room.' I however assured her that her ideas were associated with mutton and that by allowing me to cook, her room would not be spoiled as I simply wanted to prepare porridge or boil the milk and I told her also that, if her carpet was spoiled, I would pay for the spoiling. She after some hesitation accepted my proposal and I took her room for 8 shillings per week. After leaving my luggage in the room, I went out in search of a vegetarian restaurant. I could not find it. And I thought my experiment would fail.

This gloomy outlook was rendered gloomier still when I found that no restaurant-keeper would arrange to provide me a dinner consisting of vegetable soup, and bread and butter for one shilling. All thought they could not undergo the bother for one man. I thought the task was hopeless and that I would be obliged to pay 2 or 3 shillings merely for a dinner. I was quite tired by this time and very hungry, but I did not give up. I knew that I was to take rest and was not to read much during my stay in Brighton. So I said to myself that if I should cook two meals, why not cook three? As soon as the idea flashed in my mind, I caught hold of it, went to a grocer and bought the necessary things and went to my place. On reaching the house, I told the landlady that, although the arrangement was to allow me to cook only two meals, I would have to cook three. She was angry and would have driven me out of the house, had I not offered to raise the rent from 8 to 10 shillings. I then set about to work. The first evening I prepared porridge and stewed fruit and I liked it very much. The next morning I had the same. For dinner I had haricot soup which proved to be very nourishing and nice. I thus arranged my meals for the [four] weeks. For breakfast I had bread and milk and stewed fruit and bread and butter (3 d), for dinner I had soup (11/2), strawberries (2 d) and bread (1d). For supper I had porridge (1 1/2), bread and butter and fruit (2). Thus I spent only 11d or 1 shilling per day at the most for food in Brighton. With the 10s rent, 3 shillings for washing, the whole expenses for board and lodging for four weeks amounted to £3-10-0. And it cost me £4-8-5 for fares to and from Brighton.

Thus I was able for four pounds to go to live for four weeks in and return from Brighton. I found out during the last week of my stay in Brighton that there was a vegetarian home where I could have got board and lodging for 14s per week. The house is situated near the Preston Park. The weekly rent was 5s, breakfast 4d, dinner 9d, and supper 4d. Had I found the house a little earlier, I could have lived in Brighton yet more cheaply and more comfortably; but I would not have learnt how to cook with facility. It may be said that the cooking did not take much time. The breakfast took only 10 minutes to be ready. For there was only milk to be made hot. The supper took nearly 20 minutes and the dinner 1 hour. Thus encouraged by success on reaching London, the first thing for me to do was to go on in search of a suitable bed-sitting room. I selected a room in Tavistock Street for 8s a week. Here I cooked my breakfast and supper and dined outside. The landlady supplied me with plates, spoons and knife, etc. The breakfast almost always consisted of porridge, stewed fruit and bread and butter (3d) so then the expenses for board and lodging in England were, during the last 9 months of my stay, only 15s and even 14s latterly when, in the same house, I took up a 7-shilling room.

But there is one experience from Brighton that needs to be set down.

In a restaurant in Brighton, I was struggling with the menu card that was in French. A kindly lady, who I found later was a London-based widow, took pity on me and helped me out with the search for things I could eat. We got talking and she invited me to visit her in London every Sunday for a vegetarian meal. I took up the kindly offer only to find that the good lady had got into her head that I could do with some appropriate female company. There was a lady who lodged with her and I was introduced to her and I must say over a few visits I began to enjoy the company and conversation.

Now, it is to be noted that Indian students coming to England to study are often married men. Mostly, these Indian students, out of shyness but perhaps also out of opportunism, conceal the fact of their being married. If they do not, how are they going to get the pleasing chance of female company?

I thought about my situation with the old lady and her friend. And though I had established very comely relations with them, I decided to write to the lady the factual situation and to say that, with this knowledge, if she wished to cut me out of her consideration, I would understand. Prompt came a letter from her saying she and her friend had had a hearty laugh over the matter and that the revelation had made no difference to their warm feelings for me and that I was expected the next Sunday to their place when they would want me to tell them more about my child marriage and that as to our friendship, as far as they were concerned, remained as strong as ever.

Thus did the poison of untruth in me get purged and after that

I never hesitated to speak about my marriage, being a father, and so on, to anyone.

In 1890, there was a Vegetarian Conference at Portsmouth to which an Indian friend* and I were invited. Portsmouth, a seaport, has many houses with women not exactly prostitutes but, at the same time, not very scrupulous about morals. We were put up in one of these houses. After dinner we sat down to play a rubber of bridge, in which our landlady joined. Every player indulges in innocent jokes as a matter of course but here my companion and our hostess began to make indecent ones as well. It captured me and I also joined in. Just as I was about to go beyond the limit, leaving the cards and the games to themselves, my good companion uttered the warning, 'Whence this devil in you, my boy? Be off, quick!' I fled from the scene. To my room I went quaking and trembling and with beating heart like a quarry escaped from the pursuer. I recall this as the first occasion in which a woman, other than my wife, moved me to lust.

I did not then know the essence of religion or of God.

'Why not accept Christianity?' Dr Josiah Oldfield† once asked me. 'I would not care to study Christianity,' I said, 'without having studied my own religion first.'

Theatres are a national institution in England and as some suppose, a seat of education and amusement combined. They moreover portray the modern habits and customs of England. No one would return to India without visiting the theatres. Theatres do not cost much. Gallery seats are one shilling each and pit 2 or 3 1/2d each. The last seats are used by respectable middle-class persons and frequently patronized by Indians‡.

---

*Tryambak Mazmudar.
†Dr Josiah Oldfield (1863–1953), editor of *The Vegetarian*, a journal of the London Vegetarian Society, who remained a steadfast friend of Gandhi.
‡*Guide to London*, CWMG, Vol. 1, p. 110. The principal theatres in London at the time were Drury Lane, Covent Garden, and the Lyceum, the leading actors of the time being Henry Irving (1838–1905) who was staging Shakespeare plays to acclaim, playing Macbeth in *Macbeth* (supported by incidental music created by Arthur Sullivan) with Ellen Terry (1847–1928) playing Lady Macbeth. Gandhi is likely to have seen that as also *The Dead Heart* by Watts Phillips (1889) and Walter Scott's *Bride of Lammermoor*

During the last nine months of my stay in England I enjoyed the best of health. I used to walk about 8 miles every day and in all I had three walks daily, one in the evening at 5.30 p.m. for an hour and the other for 30 or 45 minutes before going to bed. I never suffered from ill-health except once when I suffered from bronchitis. I got rid of it without having to take any medicine. The good health I enjoyed in England is attributable only to vegetable diet and exercise in the open air. Even the coldest weather or the densest fog did not prevent me from having my usual walks. And under the advice of Dr Allinson, the champion of open air, I used to keep my bedroom windows open about 4 inches in all weathers.

And when there were only 5 months left for the final examination, I had to work very hard if not the hardest.

I passed my examination*, was called to the Bar on 10 June 1891, and enrolled in the High Court on the 11th. On the 12th I sailed for home.

Who, I have been asked, should go to England?

All, I have said, who can afford should go to England. Next to India, I would rather live in London than in any other place in the world.

(1890), again featuring Irving, at the Lyceum.

*The Bar Finals, taken after nine terms, were sat for between 15 and 20 December 1890.

Six

RETURNING HOME

My legs were trembling as I stepped out of the boat in Bombay.

I could not make myself believe that I was going to India until I stepped into the steamship *Oceana*, of the P & O Company. So much attached was I to London and its environments, for who would not be? London with its teaching institutions, public galleries, vegetarian restaurants, is a fit place for a student and a traveller, a trader and a 'faddist'—as a vegetarian would be called by his opponents. Thus it was not without regret that I left dear London.

Bombay-bound passengers transhipped into the *Assam* at Aden. There were English waiters on the *Oceana*, always neat, clean, and obliging. On the other hand, the waiters on the *Assam* murdered the Queen's English and were the reverse of clean and also sulky and slow. We beguiled our time chiefly in eating and drinking. The rest of the time was passed either dozing or chatting, at times in discussing, playing games. But after two or three days, the time between meals seemed to hang heavy despite discussions and cards and scandals. Some of the passengers thought it fit to get drunk every evening. On this particular evening this was followed by a fight of words culminating in a fight of blows. The captain reproved these pugilist gentlemen and ever since then we had no more rows.

After two days, the ship passed by but did not touch Gibraltar. This caused much disappointment among smokers who wanted to get tobacco duty-free in Gibraltar. The next place we reached was Malta, a coaling station, where the ship stopped for nine hours and all passengers went ashore. Malta is a beautiful island without the London smoke but what a wretched place for beggars! You cannot go along a road quietly without being pestered by dirty-looking beggars. After Malta we reached Brindisi which is a good harbour but that is all. After Brindisi we reached Port Said. Of course there is nothing to be seen in Port Said. Unless you want to see the dregs of society. It is full of rogues and rascals.

The Indian Ocean is generally calm, so during monsoon it is stormy with a vengeance. We had to pass five days more before we reached Bombay. The second night brought the real storm. Many were sick. If I ventured out on the deck, I was splashed with water. There goes a crash; something is broken. In the cabin you cannot sleep quietly. The door is banging. Your bags begin to dance. You roll in your bed. You sometimes feel the ship is sinking. At the dinner table your forks and spoons are in your lap, even your cruet stand and soup plate; your napkin is dyed yellow. One morning I asked the steward if that is what he would call a real storm. 'No sir,' he said. 'This is nothing,' and, waving his arm, showed me how the ship would roll in a real storm.

What a human cargo was on the *Oceana* and the *Assam*! Some were going to make fortunes in Australia in high hopes; some having finished their studies in England were going back to India in order to earn a decent living. And some were adventurers who having been disappointed at home were going to pursue their adventures, God knows here. Were the hopes of all realized? That is the question. How hopeful, yet how disappointed is the human mind! We live in hope.

Thus tossed up and down we reached Bombay on 5 July. It was raining very hard and so it was difficult getting ashore. My legs were trembling as I stepped out of the boat. My dear brother had come to meet me at the dock. I was pining to see my mother. I did not know that she was no more in the flesh to receive me back into her bosom. My brother had kept me ignorant of her death. I did not give myself up to any wild expression of grief. I could even check the tears, and took to life as if nothing had happened.

My mother had tied a kanthi—necklace—of Tulsi beads around my neck as a prasadi, a protective blessing. Years later, an English

Quaker in Pretoria, Michael Coates* saw it on my neck. He thought it to be a sign of superstitious belief and offered to break it. I refused to let him do so. 'I do not know its mysterious significance,' I said to him. 'I do not think I should come to harm if I did not wear it. But I cannot, without sufficient reason, give up a necklace that my mother put around my neck out of love and in the conviction that it would be conducive to my welfare.' I also told him that when, with the passage of time, it wore away and broke of its own, I shall have no desire to get a new one. 'But this necklace,' I made it clear to him, 'cannot be broken.' After I had worn it for some years in South Africa, it left me, that is, it snapped. And I did not replace it.

Dr Pranjivan Mehta of London was in Bombay and insisted on putting me up in his house. Thus the acquaintance which had begun in England continued in India and ripened into a permanent friendship between the two families. Dr Mehta introduced me to his brother Shri Revashanker Jagjivan with whom grew a lifelong friendship. But the introduction that I need to particularly take note of was to the poet Raychand† or Rajachandra, the son-in-law of an elder brother of Dr Mehta. He was not above twenty-five then. He was a partner in the family firm of jewellers. My first meeting with him convinced me that here was a man of great character and learning. He was a shatavadhani—having the faculty of remembering or attending to a hundred things simultaneously. I exhausted the vocabulary of all the European tongues I knew and asked the poet to repeat the words. He did so in the precise order in which I had given them. I envied his gift without however coming under its spell. The thing that did cast its spell on me was his wide knowledge of the scriptures, his spotless character, and his burning passion for self-realization. I never saw him lose his equipoise. He was a connoisseur of pearls and diamonds. But these things were not the centre around which his life revolved. That centre was the passion to see God face to face.

---

*An English-born Quaker in Pretoria, about seven years older than Gandhi.
†Rajachandra (1867–1901) or Raychand, now venerated as Srimad Rajchandraji, Bombay-based son-in-law of Dr Pranjivan Mehta's second eldest brother, Popatbhai Jagjivan Mehta, whose daughter Zabakben was married to him.

Before taking me home to Rajkot, my brother took me to Nasik where I had a sacred bath and then gave a caste dinner in Rajkot. I mechanically acted as he wished and thus practically ended the trouble over readmission to the caste. He had assumed that I should have a swinging practice.[12]

On 16 November 1891, I sent a formal application to the Prothonotary and Registrar of the High Court at Bombay stating that I had been called to the Bar in England on 10 June and intended to practise in Bombay Practice.

Ranchhodlal Patwari, whose father had helped me with funds to go to England and to whom I owe more than obligation, advised me to go abroad to practice law but my brother was very much against it. He thought I need not despair about getting a decent livelihood in Kathiawar and that, without directly taking part in khutput.* And since my brother was entitled to my consideration, I decided to follow his advice.

My relations with my wife were still not as I desired. Even my stay in England had not cured me of jealousy, squeamishness, suspiciousness in respect of everything. I had decided that she should learn reading and writing and that I should help her in her studies but my lust came in the way and she had to suffer. I planned reform in the education of the children at home. My brother had children and my own child† was now a boy of nearly four. I succeeded more or less. With the necessity for 'food reform', tea and coffee found their place in the house. I completed the Europeanization by adding European dress. Expenses thus went up.

Friends advised me to go to Bombay. And so I did, starting a household in Bombay with a cook as incompetent as I. He was a Brahmin. He would pour water over himself but never wash. His dhoti was as dirty as his sacred thread. So I began to run the kitchen and we went on merrily together.

---

*The term according to Hobson-Jobson (1994 edition) '...is a native slang term in Western India for a prevalent system of intrigue and corruption'. *CWMG*, Vol. 1, p. 9 and 56.
†Harilal Gandhi (1888–1948).

Once in Bombay, Raychandbhai and I were discussing the path of compassion. The point was whether one may use leather. In the end we both agreed that we cannot do without leather. However we should refrain from wearing anything on the head that contains leather. I have always been a man who would not miss a chance for a jest. I asked him to examine the cap on his head. He was ever wrapped in contemplation and never thought about what he wore and how he covered himself. The fact that there was a leather strip in his cap had entirely escaped him. But as soon as I pointed it out, he tore the strip off.

I began in Bombay my study of Indian law and developed some liking for the Evidence Act but had not the courage to conduct a case.

So I thought I might take up a teacher's job. I came across an advertisement in a paper: 'Wanted, an English teacher to teach one hour daily. Salary Rs 75'. This was in the middle of 1892. I applied and was called for an interview which went like this:

School Principal: Are you a graduate?

G: No. But I have matriculated from London University.

Principal: Right enough, but we want a graduate.

G: I had Latin as my second subject.

Principal: Thank you, this will do. Now you can go.

In the meantime, a Memon firm from Porbandar with business in South Africa wrote to my brother about 'a big case' over a claim for 40,000 pounds, saying I could be useful to them and to myself. This was how a servant, not a barrister goes but I wanted somehow to leave India. I closed with the offer.

Another baby* had been born to us since my return from England and leaving my wife this time, I felt the pang of separation. 'We are bound to meet again in a year,' I said to her by way of consolation and left Rajkot for Bombay.

---

*Manilal Gandhi (1892–1956).

Seven

TO SOUTH AFRICA

The Magistrate...asked me to take off my turban.
This I refused to do and left the court.

The Port of Natal is Durban. I reached there towards the close of May 1893. My dress marked me out from the other Indians. I had a frock coat and a turban, an imitation of the Bengal pugree*.

Abdulla Sheth† was there to receive me. He was practically unlettered but I could see that he had a fund of experience. On the second or third day of my arrival he took me to see the Durban Court. The magistrate kept staring at me and finally asked me to take off my turban. This I refused to do and left the court.

The Natal Advertiser reported on 26 May 1893 in a report under the heading 'An Unwelcome Visitor': 'An Indian entered the Court House yesterday afternoon and took a seat at the horseshoe...without removing his head covering or salaaming and the Magistrate looked at him with disapproval...' I wrote a letter to the newspaper's editor the same day saying: 'I am very sorry if His Worship the Magistrate looked at me with disapproval. It is true that on entering the Court I neither removed my headdress nor salaamed but in so doing I had not the slightest idea that I was offending His Worship or meaning any disrespect to the Court. Just as it is a mark of respect amongst

---

*The nativity of the 'Bengal pugree' as Gandhi describes it could have come to him only from the headgears worn famously by two Bengalis known outside Bengal at the time—Raja Rammohun Roy (1772–1833) and Bankim Chandra Chatterjee (1838–1894).
†Abdulla Hajee Adam Jhaveri (1854–1912), proprietor of Dada Abdulla & Co., Durban, in connection with whose lawsuit Gandhi had gone to South Africa. He was one of the leading lights of the Durban Indian Committee, which protested against the discrimination the community was suffering from, by submitting petitions and lobbying prominent politicians.

the Europeans to take off their headdress, in like manner it is in Indians to retain one's headdress.... As to bowing or salaaming, as you would call it, I again followed the rule observed in the Bombay High Court....' But through that letter I begged His Worship's pardon if he was offended by what he considered to be my rudeness.

The case that had brought me to South Africa was mainly about accounts. I purchased a book on bookkeeping and, studying it, understood the case and prepared to go to Pretoria for it. And that was to give me one experience that changed the course of my life. That fell to my lot seven days after I had arrived in South Africa.

When I came to South Africa, I knew nothing about the country. I was bound to my client only. I had come on a purely mundane and selfish mission. I was just a boy returned from England wanting to make some money. Suddenly, my client Abdulla Sheth asked me to go to Pretoria to meet his lawyer. That was also where his cousin and adversary in the case, Tyeb Sheth, lived.

It was not an easy journey. There was the railway journey as far as Charlestown and then the stagecoach to Johannesburg. For the train journey I had a first-class ticket. At Maritzburg the guard came and turned me out and asked me to go to the van compartment. I would not go and the train steamed away leaving me shivering in the cold. I was afraid for my very life. I entered the dark waiting room. There was a white man in the room. I was afraid of him. What was my duty, I asked myself. Should I go back to India or should I go forward with God as my helper and face whatever was in store for me? I decided to stay and suffer. My active non-violence began from that date. And God put me to the test through the rest of that very journey. I was severely assaulted by the coachman on the journey to Johannesburg for my not moving from my seat.[13] So, within seven days of my coming I had found that I had to deal with a situation too terrible for words.[14]

On 15 September of that year, 1893, *The Natal Advertiser* carried a leading article that described the Asiatic trader in South Africa as 'wily' and 'wretched' and alleged that he has 'driven out the small European trader'. And it asked for their expulsion. I wrote a letter to the editor of the newspaper on 19 September asking if the greater competency of the Indian trader in commerce was to be reason for his expulsion. 'They are not a political danger to the government,' I said, 'since they meddle very little if at all in politics. They are not notorious robbers. I believe there is not a single case of an Indian trader having suffered imprisonment or even been charged with theft, robbery or any of the heinous crimes. Their teetotal habits make them exceptionally peaceful citizens.' And, I added, 'They are British subjects.' I ended the letter on *The Advertiser*'s call for Indian traders' expulsion with: 'Is this Christian-like, is this fair play, is this justice, is this civilization?'* On 19 September—the very day that I sent my letter—the newspaper set forth a programme for an anti-Asiatic League which was to concern itself about 'the coolie vote swamping the European vote' and the fitness of the Indian to vote. A property qualification was required to make one eligible to vote. I pointed out that the Indians in South Africa were divided into two classes, traders and labourers, that some of the former have the property qualification but would not care to vote and the latter who live on starvation wages can never dream of having the qualification. But beyond property qualifications, what *The Advertiser* was out to say is that Indians were 'not civilized enough to be fit for voting'. They were, in the newspaper's eyes, 'semi-barbaric'. So, 'I may,' I wrote, 'be allowed to point out that they enjoy these privileges in India' and added that 'an Indian has been the acting Chief Justice of the High Court of Calcutta, an Indian is a judge of the High Court at Allahabad, and an Indian is a Member of the British Parliament'. I drew attention to Akbar the Great and Todurmull, the great financier, of whose land system the one now in vogue in India is a copy with but few modifications. 'If all this,' I wrote, 'is the outcome not of civilization but of semi-barbarity, I have yet to learn what civilization means.'

My interest in a vegetarian diet and physical exercise remained active with me during this time in South Africa.

---

*Echoes in this line from Shylock's famous courtroom defence in Shakespeare's *Merchant of Venice*, Act 3 Scene 1 are unmistakable: 'He hath disgraced me, and hindered me half a million, laughed at my losses, mocked at my gains, scorned my nation....'

In April 1894, a grand convention of Keswick Christians was held in Wellington, South Africa. I attended it in the company of some dear Christians. They had a boy, six or seven years old. He came out with me for a walk one day during this time. I simply talked to him about kindness to animals and we discussed vegetarianism. Ever since that time, I was told, the boy did not take any meat. He had watched me, before this conversation, taking only vegetables at the dinner table and had questioned me why I did not take meat. The boy and I became thick friends.

In May or June 1894, I wrote to Raychandbhai asking him questions that were occupying me, such as what is the soul, what is God, what is moksha*? I asked him what will finally happen to the world? And also a very practical question: If a snake is about to bite me, should I allow myself to be bitten or should I kill it?

Meanwhile, I saw that the case that had brought me to South Africa, if it were persisted in, would ruin the plaintiff and the defendant. Lawyers' fees were rapidly mounting and mutual ill-will was steadily increasing. I approached Tyeb Sheth and advised him to go for arbitration. I strained every nerve to bring about a compromise. At last Tyeb Sheth agreed and though the Arbitrator ruled in favour of Dada Abdulla Sheth, he agreed to let Tyeb Sheth pay the sum of 37,000 pounds in moderate instalments. My joy was boundless. I had learnt the true practice of law—to unite parties riven asunder.

---

*Raychandbhai's detailed answers are given as Appendix I to *CWMG*, Vol. 32.

Eight

BECOMING A SOUTH AFRICAN

I had established a good practice. I had got to know the people and they had got to know me.

The case having been concluded, I began to make preparations for my return home. At a farewell party that Abdulla Sheth gave to me, whilst turning over the sheets of some newspapers, I chanced to see a paragraph under the caption 'Indian Franchise'. This was with reference to a bill before the House of Legislature, seeking to deprive Indians of their right to elect members of the Natal Legislative Assembly.

I told Abdulla Sheth: 'This bill is the first nail into our coffin. It strikes at the root of our self-respect.' One of the guests then said, 'You cancel your passage, stay here a month longer, and we will fight as you direct us.' I agreed provided I got help with men and funds. The farewell party turned into a working committee.

After a hurriedly called meeting of the community which decided that the proposed bill is to be opposed, I drafted a petition addressed to the Speaker and Members of the Natal Legislative Assembly, urging them to appoint a committee to examine the fitness of Indians to exercise the privilege of exercising franchise, before passing the bill. The twenty-four paragraph-long petition sought to make the Honourable Assembly see that 'the exercise of the franchise [by the Indians] is no extension of a new privilege they have never before known or enjoyed'. It drew attention to Maine's *Village Communities in the East and West* in which the eminent jurist pointed out that India has been familiar with representative institutions from time immemorial.

The petition said that there were, in 1891, 755 municipalities and 892 Local Boards in India, with 20,000 Indian members. 'The State of Mysore,' it said, 'has at the present moment a representative Parliament called the Mysore Assembly, on the exact model of the British Parliament.' Newspapers published it with favourable comments and it made an impression on the Assembly which, nevertheless, passed the bill. It was then decided to send a monster petition to the Secretary of State for the Colonies, Lord Ripon. I took considerable pains over drawing up this petition. Ten thousand signatures were obtained for this petition, volunteers going across the whole province to not just collect signatures, not taking a single signature without making the signatory fully understand the petition. A thousand copies of the petition were printed and distributed. India came thus to be acquainted with the condition of Indians in Natal.

I also wrote to Dadabhai Naoroji urging him to use his influence in London in this matter. 'I am inexperienced and young,' I said in my letter to him, 'and therefore quite liable to make mistakes.' I said I was the only person available to handle the question and requested him to guide me as a father would a child. On 27 July, I wrote another letter to him, marked 'Confidential' in which I gave him what I regarded as the main reason for the disenfranchising: 'They do not want the Indians to elect white members—2 or 3—who may look after their interests in Parliament.' I ended by urging him to 'give hints as to the way of [my]working'.

It was now impossible for me to leave Natal. About twenty merchants gave me retainers for legal work and Dada Abdulla purchased furniture for me in lieu of the purse that was to have been given to me on my departure. And so I settled in Natal.

The Natal Mercury, meanwhile, came out with a leader on 7 July 7 1894, contesting Maine's allusion to India's village communities, saying that these had nothing to do with political representation and arguing further that village community life was primitive and proved the backwardness of its people. I wrote to the newspaper's editor saying it was natural that Maine's theories and conclusions be contested but gave him further details of contemporary Indian representation through facts about Mysore where all landholders and all non-official university graduates from anywhere in India ordinarily residing in Mysore could elect and be elected to the Mysore Assembly.

The Natal Indian Congress came to be established in August 1894 as a public organization of a permanent character. I recommended that it should be called by that name. I knew the name was in bad odour with the Conservatives in England and yet the Congress was the very life of India. The proposal for the organization and its name received the enthusiastic approval of all present at the meeting held in Dada Abdulla's spacious room. Abdulla Hajee Adam was named its chairman and I, its honorary secretary. The Congress's constitution was simple, the subscription heavy. Its seven objectives included one to induce the community 'to study Indian history and literature relating to India' and another 'to inquire into the conditions of indentured Indians and to take proper steps to alleviate their sufferings'. And the rules included: 'No smoking shall be allowed at any committee meeting' and 'If two members get up simultaneously to speak, the chairman shall decide who is to speak first.'

The Times of Natal published a leader on 22 October 1894 titled 'Rammysammy'. I had to and did immediately send a response. Maintaining that the leader betrayed contempt for the Indian, I wrote: 'You in your wisdom would not allow the Indian or the Native the precious privilege [of franchise] under any circumstances because they have a dark skin. You would look to the exterior only. So long as the skin is white it would not matter to you whether it conceals beneath it poison or nectar. To you the lip-prayer of the Pharisee, because he is one, is more acceptable than the sincere repentance of the publican and this, I presume, you would call Christianity. You may; it is not Christ.' I ended with, 'Sir, May I venture to offer a suggestion? Will you read your New Testament?'

I had, in the meantime, become agent for the Esoteric Christian Union and the London Vegetarian Society and as such placed an advertisement in *The Natal Mercury* in November 1894 announcing the availability in my office of books for sale by Anna Kingsford and Edward Maitland, which included *The Perfect Way* (7/6) and *The Bible's Own Account of Itself* (1/-). *The Mercury* carried it on 28

November. While sending the advertisement I also sent to the same newspaper a letter which it carried six days later in which I said that the sale of the books advertised was not for a pecuniary concern but to help answer the question humanity has always and everywhere asked itself: 'Whence come we? Where are we? Whither go we?' I also pointed out that in the books 'there is no reviling Mahomed or the Buddha in order to prove the superiority of Jesus' and that 'on the other hand, it reconciled the other religions with Christianity'.

Though my family was still in India, by now I was householding in Durban, that role being no new experience for me. But this time, part of the expense on maintaining a home establishment was solely for the sake of prestige. I thought it should be in keeping with my position as an Indian barrister in Natal. So I acquired a nice little two-storeyed house* in Beach Grove, a prominent locality. It was also suitably furnished. I used to invite English friends and Indian co-workers. Some of my office clerks boarded and lodged with me. And there was a cook who had become a member of the family. Sheikh Mehtab who had come from Rajkot to Durban was staying with me[†]. This set up had a fair amount of success but Mehtab became jealous of a clerk who stayed with us and wove a tangled web around him so that I suspected the clerk who, possessed of a temper of his own, left both my home and my office.

One day at about twelve o'clock a temporary cook who was filling in for my cook who had gone on leave came panting to my office[‡]. 'Please come home at once,' he said, 'there is a surprise for you.'

'How can I leave the office at this hour to go and see it?'

'You will regret it if you don't.'

---

*'An un-pretentious semi-detached double-storeyed building with an iron front gate, a side entrance with a passage and a verandah under the balcony.' (Pyarelal in *Mahatma Gandhi: Early Phase*, p. 493.) Gandhi lived in this house from 1894 to 1901.

†Pyarelal writes in *Mahatma Gandhi: Early Phase*: 'Gandhiji's multifarious activities left him hardly a moment to attend to his domestic affairs.... To free himself from such cares he, therefore, invited his boyhood friend, Sheikh Mehtab, who came from Rajkot and was installed in his house.'

‡326-8, Smith Street, Durban (1894–1895) and then 374, West Street, Durban. (Paul Tichman, *Gandhi Sites in Durban*, The Local History Museum, Durban, 1998.)

I felt an appeal in his persistence and accompanied by a clerk went, the cook leading us. He took me straight to upper floor, pointed to Mehtab's room and said, 'Open this door and see for yourself.'

I saw it all. I knocked at the door. No reply! I knocked heavily so as to make the very walls shake. The door was opened. I saw a prostitute inside. I asked her to leave the house, never to return. To Mehtab I said, 'From this moment I cease to have anything to do with you. I have been thoroughly deceived and have made a fool of myself. That is how you have requited my trust in you.' Instead of coming to his senses, Mehtab said he would 'expose' me.

'I have nothing to conceal,' I said. 'Expose whatever I may have done but you must leave me this moment.' This made him worse. I said to the clerk standing downstairs to inform the police superintendent that I shall be much obliged if police help can be sent to me. This unnerved Mehtab. He apologized and entreated me to not inform the police and agreed to leave the house which he did.

But for the new cook I should never have discovered the truth. I had known Mehtab was a bad character and yet had believed in his faithfulness to me. In the attempt to reform him I was near ruining myself. I had disregarded the warnings of kind friends. Infatuation had completely blinded me. This was not the first time that the woman had been brought to my house. She had come often before but no one had the courage of this cook. For everyone knew how blindly I trusted Mehtab. The cook had, as it were, been sent to me just to do this service for, saying, 'I cannot stay in your house, you are too easily misled,' he begged leave of me that very moment. I let him go.

By now I had been three years in South Africa. I had established a good practice. I had got to know the people and they had got to know me. In 1896, I asked permission to go home for six months, fetch my wife and children, and return to settle out there. I also saw that if I went home I would create more interest there in the Indians of South Africa.

Thirty-eight members of the Indian community signed a formal statement titled *The Credentials* saying they '...hereby appoint M. K. Gandhi, Esq. of Durban, Advocate, to represent grievances Indians are labouring under in South Africa before the authorities and public men and public bodies in India.'

Shortly before I left Durban, a reporter of *The Natal Advertiser* called on me to ascertain my views on the state of affairs with Indians in the colony generally. 'What will your future programme be?' he asked. 'The Congress will continue', I replied, to 'resist any attempt to introduce colour distinctions in the legislation for the Indian community for these, if introduced might be used in other colonies and other parts of the world'.[15] The day before I left Natal, the son of an Indian gentleman, spotlessly dressed, was walking along the pavement in the principal street in Durban. Some Europeans pushed him off the pavement without any reason but to amuse themselves.

Nine

AN INDIAN INTERLUDE

The editor of Bangabasi* *would not as much as look at me. But I was not discouraged.*

I sailed out on the SS *Pongola* on 5 June 1896.

It had two English officers, with one of whom I played chess for an hour daily. I found out among the deck passengers an Urdu munshi and I and the English officer made good progress in our Urdu studies. I often found it difficult to decipher Urdu letters and brought more perseverance to bear but could never overtake the officer who would never forget a word after once he had seen it. The ship's doctor gave me a *Tamil Self-Teacher,* a well-written book, with which I made fair progress. I had hoped to continue these studies even after reaching India but that was impossible.

At the end of the pleasant voyage and admiring the beauty of the Hooghly, I reached Calcutta on 4 July and left for Bombay the next day. Without halting at Bombay I went straight to Rajkot and began to make preparations for writing a pamphlet on the situation in South Africa titled 'The Grievances of The British Indians in South Africa: An Appeal to the Indian Public'. I started the text with 'This is an appeal to the Indian public on behalf of the 100,000 Indians in South Africa' and went on to give proof of the grievances, citing my own testimony and that of others who have undergone the grievances personally. This work took a month. The publication had a green cover and came to be known as *The Green Pamphlet*. Ten thousand copies were printed and sent to all the papers and leaders of every party in India. A summary of it was cabled by Reuter to England

---

*First published on 10 December 1881, with Jnanendralal Roy as editor.

and a summary of that summary, no longer than three lines in print, was cabled in turn by Reuter's London office to Natal. To get these ready for posting, preparing wrappers, was no small matter and expensive too. So I gathered together all the children in my locality and asked them to volunteer two or three hours' labour of a morning when they had no school. They willingly agreed and gave them as a reward, used postage stamps which I had collected. Two of those little friends were to become my co-workers later.

While busy in Rajkot with the pamphlet, I paid a flying visit to Bombay during which I met Justice Ranade* and Justice Badruddin Tyabji†. Both advised me to meet Sir Pherozeshah Mehta‡, who had earned the popular titles of 'Lion of Bombay' and 'Uncrowned King of the Presidency'. The 'king' met me as a loving father would his grown-up son. He carefully listened to me and said, 'Gandhi, I see that I must help you. I must call a public meeting here' and a date was settled for it.

During this stay in Bombay I called on Raliyat, my sister and her husband, Vrindavandas§, who lived in Bombay. My brother-in-law was lying seriously ill. He was not a man of means and my sister was not equal to nursing him and so I took both of them home to Rajkot. The illness went on for longer than I expected and though Vrindavandas could not survive, I had the consolation of having

---

*Mahadev Govind Ranade (1842–1901) scholar, social reformer, judge, author, and one of the founding members of the Indian National Congress. B. R. Ambedkar, in a speech in Poona on 18 January 1943, said of Ranade: 'Nobody can question that Ranade had intellect of a high calibre. He was not merely a lawyer and a judge of the High Court, he was a first-class economist, a first-class historian, a first-class educationist, and a first-class Divine. He was not a politician. Perhaps it is good that he was not. For, if he had been, he might not have been a Great Man.'
†Badruddin Tyabji (1844–1906) lawyer, activist, and politician, the first Indian to practise as a barrister of the High Court of Bombay; third President of the Indian National Congress.
‡Sir Pherozeshah Merwanjee Mehta (1845–1915) politician and lawyer from Bombay, Municipal Commissioner of Bombay Municipality in 1873 and its President four times (1884, 1885, 1905, and 1911), one of the founding members and President of the Indian National Congress in 1890.
§Vrindavandas (1860–1896).

nursed him night and day during his last days. As I had to keep awake for part of the night through that period, I got through some of my South Africa work whilst I was nursing him. This experience also led to my aptitude for nursing develop into a passion that was to often make me neglect my work.

The very next day after Vrindavandas died, I had to go to Bombay for the meeting that Sir Pherozeshah Mehta had organized.* This was the first meeting of the kind in my experience. My voice could reach only a few. I was trembling as I began to reach my speech. Sir Pherozeshah cheered me up continually by asking me to speak louder and louder. Far from encouraging me this made my voice sink lower and lower. 'Every Indian without exception,' I said, 'is a coolie in the estimation of the general body of the Europeans [of South Africa]...notable among whom is Mr Rustomji of Durban who in his generosity would do credit to Sir Dinshaw [Petit]. No poor man goes to his door without having his hunger satisfied. No Parsi lands on the Durban shores but is sumptuously treated by Mr Rustomji. And even he is not free from molestation. Even he is a coolie....'[16]

Sir Pherozeshah liked my speech. I was supremely happy.

From Bombay I went to Poona. First, I met Lokamanya Tilak. He said: 'I am at your disposal.' This was my first meeting with the Lokamanya. It revealed to me the secret of his unique popularity. Next, I met Professor Gopal Krishna Gokhale. With him too this was my first meeting and yet it seemed as though we were renewing an old friendship. I found him on the Fergusson College grounds. His manner immediately won my heart. Sir Pherozeshah had seemed to me like the Himalaya, Lokamanya like the ocean. But Gokhale was as the Ganges. It was a joy to be on it with a boat and an oar.

During all this period I also remained very busy with domestic matters.[17] Towards the middle of October, I went to Madras. It was wild with enthusiasm.

The Natal Indian Congress had advanced me 75 pounds towards

---

*On 26 September 1896 at the Framji Cowasji Institute, presided over by Sir Pherozeshah. The *Times of India* and *Bombay Gazette* carried Gandhi's speech in extenso.

my expenses in India. So I maintained during this time a day by day statement of accounts in rupees, annas, and pice for being tendered to the Natal Indian Congress. On the day I reached Madras, for instance, my expenses were like this:

October 14:

Railway Station, Madras 0-4-0
Guide 0-4-0
Porter 0-2-0
Carriage (whole day) 4-2-3
Trickman 0-0-6
Papers and envelopes 2-10-0
Carriage for station 1-8-0

News had come meanwhile from the Australian Colonies of legislation being enacted there to restrict 'the influx of Indian immigrants'. I sensed that there would soon be an end to Indian enterprise outside India. From the Buckingham Hotel, in Madras, where I stayed, I wrote a letter to Professor Gokhale on October 18, urging that '... our great men should without delay take up this question...in the Imperial Council* in Calcutta and the House of Commons'.

A meeting was called by the Mahajana Sabha in Pachaiyappa College's hall in Madras on 26 October. 'Every Indian without distinction,' I said in my speech, 'is contemptuously called a "coolie". He is also called "Sammy" or "Ramasammy", anything but "Indian"...There is a very respectable firm of Madras traders by name A Colandeveloo Pillay & Co. They have built a large block of buildings in Durban; these buildings are called "coolie stores".' The audience listened to every word with attention. I ended by saying: 'Being under the yoke of oppression we can only cry out in anguish. You have heard our cry. The blame will now lie on your shoulders if the yoke is not removed from necks.'

The meeting ended with a resolution calling for the relief of South

---

*The Viceroy's Executive Council of which Gokhale was a member.

African Indians. The secretaries of the Madras Mahajana Sabha had worked unremittingly to organize the meeting and making the cause their own. Madras's public had rallied round the cause admirably. There was a scramble for copies of *The Green Pamphlet*. It sold like hot cakes. I will not easily forget that scene.[18]

From Madras I went to Calcutta. I knew no one there. Reaching there on 31 October, I took a room in The Great Eastern Hotel. My expenses on that day were:

October 31:

Tea and bread on way to Calcutta 0-9-0
Breakfast 1-15-0
Tiffin 0-7-0
Paper 0-2-0
Porter at Station 0-6-0
Porter at Asansol 0-2-0
Porter at hotel 0-4-0
Carriage to hotel 1-0-0
Carriage & Theatre 4-12-0

On 1 November, I was invited by Mr Ellerthorpe, a representative of *The Daily Telegraph* to meet him at The Bengal Club. He did not realize then that an Indian could not be taken to the Club's drawing room. He expressed his sorrow and apologized. I had of course to see Surendranath Banerjee, the 'Idol of Bengal'. He said people will 'not take interest in your work as our [own] difficulties here are by no means few'. I called at the office of the *Amrita Bazar Patrika**. The gentleman whom I met there took me to be a wandering Jew. The editor of *Bangabasi* would not as much as look at me. But I was not discouraged.

On 7 November I saw a play† on a 4-rupee ticket.

---

*First published as a Bengali weekly on 20 February 1868 with Sisir Kumar Ghosh as editor, later an English weekly and daily. Closed in 1991.
†It could have been any of the following plays showing in Calcutta on 7 November 1896:

I kept on seeing editors of other papers. *The Statesman** and *The Englishman*† realized the importance of the question. On 10 November, a reporter of *The Statesman* asked me: 'What then, is the cause of all this trouble, Mr Gandhi?' I answered: 'Simply, trade jealousy.' He then asked 'Suppose you succeed in having the legal disabilities removed, what about the social disabilities?' To this I said, 'We hope that when the legal disabilities are removed, the social persecution will gradually disappear.'

Mr Saunders,‡ editor of *The Englishman*, placed his office and paper at my disposal. He subjected me to a searching cross-examination before he began to sympathize with my cause, and he saw that I had spared neither will nor pains to place before him an impartial statement of the case even of the white man in South Africa. What Mr Saunders liked in me was my freedom from exaggeration. *The Englishman*'s reporter asked me: 'What has been the attitude of the [South African] Indians?' I explained: 'Politically speaking, the Indian does not want the vote; it is only because he resents the indignity of being dispossessed of it that he is agitating for its restitution.'

The unexpected help from Mr Saunders had begun to encourage me to think that I might succeed after all in holding a public meeting in Calcutta when I received the following cable from Durban: 'Parliament opens January, return soon.' I wired to the Bombay agent of Dada Abdullah & Co to arrange for my passage by the first possible boat to South Africa.

Prabhas-Milan and *Mohashel* by Biharilal Chattopadhyay (Royal Bengal Theatre, 9 Beadon Street), *Madhabi*, author not cited, and *Behadda Behaya* by Kedarnath Mandal (Emerald Theatre, 68 Beadon Street), *Kalapahar* by Girish Chandra Ghosh (Star Theatre, 75/3 Cornwallis Street), *Abu Hosain* and *Aladin* both by Girish Chandra Ghosh (Minerva Theatre, 6 Beadon Street).
*Started as The *Indian Statesman* in 1875, its founder Robert Knight having purchased William Carey's Serampore-based *The Friend of India* (founded 1818) a little earlier.
†Founded in 1818, merged with *The Statesman* in 1934.
‡John O'Brien Saunders (1852–1905) succeeded his father in about 1878 in the management and running of *The Englishman*.

Kastur with her sons and Gandhi's nephew, in Durban (1898).
L to R: Gokuldas (son of Gandhi's sister, Raliyat), Manilal (seated), Kastur, Ramdas (seated) and Harilal.
Gandhi carried this photograph with him to London when he went there in 1906 on a deputation, sending it to a Mrs Freeth who, it would appear, asked for a photograph of his family. (See letter reproduced on p. 145)

Courtesy: Sabarmati Ashram Preservation and Memorial Trust, Ahmedabad.

~

BOOK III
1896 to 1908

Two major theatres of battle draw Gandhi into their fold: The Anglo–Boer War (1899–1902) and the Bambatha Rebellion (1906). He shows to himself, to his community, and to the South African authorities his extraordinary skills in mobilizing mass support, chiefly by the strength of his personal courage in the face of danger and, in these two cases, death.

He wins laurels and medals but not without much agonizing self-doubt about where political ethics lie, where ethnic morality dwells in all that he is doing. But in the context of where he is and what he is, Gandhi sees himself now not as an Indian working for a living in South Africa and lobbying for his fellow Indians' dignity but as an Indian South African who must work, full-time, for his rights and those of his fellow British subjects, as is their entitlement in this colony. The Asiatic Law Amendment Ordinance, which he finds is worse than the law it seeks to amend, requires that not only traders but every Indian now resident in the Transvaal must be registered and carry a pass in spite of the fact that they are already in possession of permits which authorize them to reside there and while they also hold registration certificates for which they have each paid 3 pounds.

This phase also sees Gandhi make crucial observations about two leaders of the African community—John Dube (who ran the weekly Ilanga lase Natal*) and Tengo Jabavu (founder of* Black Opinion*).*

If white South Africa has demeaned Indian South Africans as a community, the South African regime is now destroying their basic rights, politically and legally. The barrister in him, the thinking and strategizing politician in him sets to work—a two-member deputation goes to London to argue the Indians' case. He meets, among others, someone history is going to set opposite him—young Winston Churchill. Prospects for the community seem momentarily to brighten during that voyage, only to splinter on the twin rocks of imperial hubris and colonial duplicity.

Householding seems, meanwhile, to offer both sweets and bitters, not always in balance. Kasturba is devoted to him but is not to be taken for granted, no sir! She may not know English, nor the law or politics but her Gujarati is as strong as her will is and knows enough to spell dissent in her own idiom. And when she does assent—as in her husband's seeking celibacy—she has made it clear that she counts.

Introduced to Ruskin's and Tolstoy's philosophies, Gandhi initiates two of the most pivotal experiments of his life—he sets up what in effect is his first attempt at founding and running an ashram, in Phoenix, near Durban, and a journal—Indian Opinion. The political scene turns grim and after a major act of resistance, Gandhi has his first experience of jail or, as he writes in Oscar Wilde's style, gaol.

~

One

BACK TO SOUTH AFRICA

When I held on to that bar, I was mentally prepared for death. If, however, I had lost hold of the bar...I would have struggled on, would perhaps have slapped or bitten the man and would have resisted till death.

Dada Abdullah had just purchased the SS *Courland*. He insisted on my travelling on that boat with my family, free of charge. I gratefully accepted the offer and, in the beginning of December, set sail for South Africa, the second time now. Another vessel, the SS *Naderi* had left the Prince's Dock in Bombay on 28 November 1896 for Natal and the SS *Courland* on 30 November.

I had with me my wife, our two sons, Harilal, eight, Manilal, four, and Gokuldas, the nine-year-old son of my widowed sister*.

Kastur was pregnant. I determined that she wore the Parsi sari, the boys the Parsi coat and trousers. Of course, no one could do without shoes and stockings. The shoes cramped their feet, the stockings stank with perspiration and the toes often got sore. They agreed to the changes and, with even more reluctance, adopted the use of knives and forks. As though to warn us of the real storm on land, a terrible gale overtook us whilst we were only four days from Natal. All became one in face of the common danger. 'His will be done' was the only cry on every lip. At last the sky cleared, the sun made its appearance and with the disappearance of the danger disappeared also the name of God from their lips. The fear of death was gone and earnest prayer gave place to maya.

The two ships landed on 18 December but we were not to

---

*Gokuldas (1887–1908), son of Raliyat and Vrindavandas.

disembark before 13 January and were quarantined owing to a mild form of bubonic plague having raged in certain districts of Bombay at the time of the ships' departure. While the passengers were on board, an agitation was being got up in Durban to prevent the passengers from landing. A reporter of *The Natal Advertiser* came on board the *Courland* and interviewed me. 'What is your plan of campaign?' he asked. I replied: '...resist the passing of any laws that restrict the freedom of Indians coming to the colony. There is absolutely no danger of the colony getting swamped. The law of supply and demand regulates the inflow and outflow of passengers.' The reporter, as he left, advised me, for my sake, to be exceedingly careful in regard to disembarking.[19]

Mr Harry Escombe, the attorney general, sent word to the captain that as the whites were against me and my life is in danger, my family and I should disembark at dusk. But the shipping company's advocate Mr Laughton, a fearless man, came on board and said everything was quiet now and advised that while my wife and the children be driven to Mr Rustomji's house, he and I follow them on foot. As I went ashore with Mr Laughton, some youngsters recognized me and shouted, 'Gandhi, Gandhi....' A mob followed us. With every step we took, it became larger and larger. A man of powerful build caught hold of Mr Laughton and tore him from me.[20] Then they pelted me with stones, brickbats, and rotten eggs. Someone snatched away my turban whilst others began to batter and kick me. A burly fellow came up to me, slapped me in the face and then kicked me. I was about to fall down unconscious when I held on the railings of a house nearby. But I remember well that even then my heart did not arraign my assailants.

When I held on to that bar, I was mentally prepared for death. If, however, I had lost hold of the bar, I could not have inflicted any serious injury on my assailant [but] I would have struggled on, would perhaps have slapped or bitten the man and would have resisted till death.[21] The wife of the police superintendent*, who knew me,

---

*Richard Charles Alexander from Suffolk, an orphan, joined Prince Albert's Own

happened to be passing by. The brave lady came up, opened her parasol and stood between the crowd and me. This checked the fury of the mob. The police superintendent, R. C. Alexander, sent a posse of men to ring me round and escort me safely to my destination.

The Indian community, wanting to express its appreciation of this, sent to him a gold watch with a suitable inscription in grateful recognition and a sum of 10 pounds for distribution among those of his force who assisted him.[22] And to Mrs Alexander also it sent a gold watch with a chain and a locket with a suitable inscription: 'As a token of our appreciation of the way in which you defended one whom we delight to love...at no small risk to yourself'. The letter added that her act 'will ever be a pattern of true womanhood'.

Joseph Chamberlain, Secretary of State for the Colonies cabled the Government of Natal to prosecute the assailants but I told Harry Escombe, the attorney general, that I did not want it. Escombe then asked me to put that in writing. I at once obtained some blank paper from him, wrote out the desired note: 'I do not wish that any notice should be taken of the behaviour of some people towards me last Wednesday which, I have no doubt, was due to misapprehension on their part as to what I did in India with reference to the Asiatic question.'[23]

On behalf of the Indian community in the colony a petition was sent to the Natal Legislative Assembly on 27 March 1897—which had before it three bills restricting the rights of Indians in Natal—to institute an enquiry to ascertain whether the presence of the Indian population is detrimental to the colony at large before considering those bills. Strange as it may appear, the three bills did not mention by name the population—Indians—that they affected. The petition said: '...such a mode of procedure is un-British'.

Meanwhile a great deal was being said about me and much as I would have liked to avoid it, it became necessary for me to say

---

Light Infantry. At twenty-three, he was a young sergeant-major in the British Army, was also a fencing instructor, spent four years in India with his regiment and learnt Bengali, then applied for a police post in Durban in 1876 when his regiment was stationed in Pietermaritzburg. His wife's name was Jane.

a few words in the matter. So in a letter to *The Natal Mercury* on 13 April, I said: 'I have no political ambition whatever. Those who know me personally know well in what direction my ambition lies. I do not aspire to any parliamentary honours whatever. I receive no remuneration for the public work I am doing. I am here not to sow dissensions between the two communities but to endeavour to bring about a reconciliation between them.' The 60th anniversary of Queen Victoria was coming to its completion.[24] The Indian community of Natal sent to her an address saying: 'We are proud to think we are your subjects...and the confidence of security of life and prosperity which enables us to venture abroad are due to that position.' The address inscribed on a silver shield bearing twenty-one signatures, including mine, was presented to the Governor of Natal for being conveyed to her.

None in the community, fortunately, ever insulted me by calling or regarding me as 'sahib'. Abdulla Sheth refused to address me as 'Gandhi'. He hit upon a fine appellation—'bhai', i.e., brother. Others followed and continued to address me as 'bhai', until the moment I left South Africa. There was a sweet flavour about the name when it was used by the ex-indentured Indians. My office clerks had made themselves thoroughly at home with me.

We did not always have a cook.[25] The last cook we had left because I would not let him use chillies. After that we managed without a cook. Cooking, washing clothes, cleaning the lavatories, grinding grain—everything was done by members of the family. We had a hand mill made of steel which cost 6 pounds. It could be worked by two persons. Working at it was the first thing I did in the morning and I would take anyone who was available as my fellow worker. We had to stand as we worked. In a quarter of an hour, we had sufficient flour for the day, fine or coarse just as we pleased.

Our Beach Grove home was built after the Western model and the rooms had no outlets for dirty water. Each room had therefore chamber pots. Rather than have these cleaned by a servant or a sweeper, my wife or I attended to them. The clerks staying with me would naturally clean their own pots. Vincent Lawrence*, a panchama† by birth, was a newcomer and it was our duty to attend to his bedroom. To clean his pots seemed to my wife to be the limit and we fell out. Her eyes were red with anger and pearl drops streamed down her eyes as she descended the stairway, pot in hand. Far from being satisfied by her merely carrying the pot, I would have her do this cheerfully. Raising my voice, I said, 'I will not stand this nonsense in my house.' The words pierced her like an arrow. 'Keep your house to yourself,' she shouted back, 'and let me go.' I forgot myself. I caught her by the hand, dragged the helpless woman to the gate with the intention of pushing her out. 'Have you no sense of shame?' she cried. 'Must you forget yourself? Where am I to go? For heaven's sake, behave yourself.' I put on a brave face but was really ashamed and shut the gate. If my wife could not leave me, neither could I leave her.

There can hardly be a task more difficult than to conquer one's passion in regard to one's own wife.[26] Ramdas‡ and then Devadas§ were born to us even after I had made up my mind and was persevering in that effort.

We had decided to have the best medical aid at the time of her delivery but if the doctor and the nurse were to leave us in the lurch at the right moment what was I to do? So I studied Dr Tribhuvandas's book *Ma Ne Shikhaman* (Advice To A Mother). Ramdas was delivered at home on 4 May, 1987.

Over the January and February of 1898, I was in correspondence with B. N. Bhajekar, a High Court pleader in Bombay about the possibility of a religious preacher coming from India to South Africa.¶

---

*Gandhi's Roman Catholic confidential clerk hailed from South India.
†Meaning a 'fifth', coming after the four traditional categories of Hindu society and at that time regarded as 'untouchable'.
‡Ramdas Gandhi (1897–1969).
§Devadas Gandhi (1900–1957).
¶As quoted in Marie Louise Burke, *Swami Vivekananda in the West: New Discoveries: The World Teacher*, Vol. 4, Advaita Ashram, Mayavati, India, 1985, pp. 507–09: '...from a young Indian barrister who was then living in Durban, Natal, and championing the rights of his people. His letter...was forwarded to Swami Vivekananda, then in

The wandering monk Swami Shivananda, or Taraknath Ghosal as he was before he met Sri Ramakrishna, was thought of, but I put it to Mr Bhajekar that there should be no haste in the matter and that a religious preacher working on European lines would not work in South Africa or, for that matter, anywhere amongst the orthodox Hindus.

'Could not Swami Vivekananda himself be induced to pay us a visit?' I asked Mr Bhajekar. 'I shall do everything I can to make his mission a success.' Asking him to place my letter before the Swami if he so wished to, I said, 'He can work both among Indians and Europeans. I take it he moves freely among the Indians, the highest and the lowest.'

I was sure that if Swami Vivekananda were to come, he would do one thing: 'Electrify the Europeans by his eloquence and possibly hypnotise them into linking the "Coolies" in spite of themselves.' I added, 'Though the Europeans here are very obstinate, they are not so as to never listen to reason.'

Kashmir.... The Swami could not go—even as he could not go to China, Japan, or Russia to spread his Master's message.'

Two

CANNONS

'...there should be very little said by the Indians themselves of their work in connection with the war...their part was merely to do without speaking.'

When towards the middle of October 1899 hostilities were clearly pending between the Imperial government and the Two South African Republics—Transvaal and Orange Free State—my personal sympathies were with the Boers but I believed then that I had yet no right to enforce my individual convictions.*

About 100 English-speaking Indians of Durban met at a few hours' notice to consider the advisability of offering unreserved and unconditional services to the Natal or the Imperial government. A list was made of those among them who volunteered to offer that service and I forwarded the names to the Colonial Secretary at Maritzburg. All of them were put through a rigorous medical examination.

The services were offered without pay. 'We do not know how to handle arms,' I said in my letter of 19 October, 'but it may be there are other duties to be performed on the battlefield.' I went on to specify 'field hospital' and 'commissariat'. I got a reply of thanks and appreciation which also said '...should the occasion arise the government will be glad to avail itself of those services'.

---

*The Second Boer War (1899–1902), by the Transvaal and Orange Free State against Britain, had at its root, Britain's eyeing of the gold under the Transvaal soil. President Kruger and the Boer government refused to countenance British demands and war resulted. Indians were divided on the issue, being ill-treated by both Boer and Briton. Gandhi pondered the dilemma, deciding to side with the British through his Ambulance Corps as a sign of loyalty while his 'personal sympathies were all with the Boers'. The war ended with the annexation of the two republics by Britain.

When, by December, we had still not been called, I sent a wire to the Colonial Secretary in Maritzburg: 'We have made arrangements to start at a moment's notice, being eager to render whatever service we can without pay. May mention some of us have been taking lessons in hospital work. It would be a great disappointment if after all arrangements government will not accept us.'

The Boer showing more pluck, determination, and bravery than expected, our services came ultimately to be needed. The Indian Ambulance Corps was 1,100 strong, comprising mostly indentured men. Harry Escombe invited me and leaders of the Corps to his Beach Grove home for a farewell gathering.[27] I was asked to speak. Our dream has been realized, I said, and hoped we would discharge our duties—which were offered unconditionally and absolutely without payment in any capacity—well. We were not trained in the use of arms, I said, but if the Goorkhas or Sikhs had been here, they would have shown what they could do in the way of fighting.

In the event we were asked, though not bound to do so, to venture inside the firing line to fetch the wounded from the field.

Major Bapty, secretary to Colonel Gallwey, the principal medical officer attached to General Buller's troops, addressed us thus: 'Gentlemen, you have been engaged to work without the range of fire. There are many wounded men to be removed from the field hospital. There is just a chance, though very remote, that the Boers may drop a shell or two on the pontoon. If you are prepared to cross the bridge in spite of the little risk—and you are at liberty to say no—I shall be glad to lead you.' These words were spoken with such earnestness and so kindly and gently that the leaders and men with one voice offered to follow the gallant leader.[28]

The Corps had the honour of carrying some officers of note—Major General Woodgate being one among them. It was freely remarked each time 'the light-footed, elastic-stepped' bearers covered the whole distance of 25 miles with their charge under a trying sun and over a difficult road, that they alone could perform the feat. When Lieutenant Roberts received a mortal wound at Chieveley camp, we had the honour of carrying the body from the field.

The day of that march was sultry, we were all thirsty for water. There was a tiny brook on the way but who was to drink first? We proposed to come in after the tommies but they would not begin, and urged to do so.

If Sir George White's testimony is correct, Ladysmith was saved from passing into the Boers' hands, even temporarily, to some extent, be it ever so small, owing to the work of a single Indian, Parbhu Singh. At the peril of his life, he sat perched on a tree, and gave a warning by sounding a gong each time a gun from the Umbulwana Hill was fired. The work done by Parbhu Singh was considered sufficiently important to merit special mention by Sir George and a special recognition on the part of Lady Curzon who sent a choga to be presented to Parbhu Singh publicly in Durban.[29]

In the Boer War, I myself served wine to the stone-breakers in my Corps and served bidis to others. Discretion is very necessary in doing all such things. Generosity to others is as necessary as strictness with oneself.*

The Corps was disbanded after six weeks of service. Our humble

---

*Vere Stent (1872–1941), war correspondent, theatre critic, playwright, and author who represented the Reuters News Agency during the Siege of Mafeking from 1899 to 1900, described the work of the Indians in the *Illustrated Star of Johannesburg*, July 1911, as follows: 'My first meeting with Mr M. Gandhi was under strange circumstances. It was on the road from Spion Kop, after the fateful retirement of the British troops in January 1900. The previous afternoon I saw the Indian mule-train moved up the slopes of the Kop carrying water to the distressed soldiers who had lain powerless on the plateau. The mules carried the water in immense bags, one on each side, led by Indians at their heads. The galling rifle-fire, which heralded their arrival on the top, did not deter the strangely-looking cavalcade which moved slowly forward, and as an Indian fell, another quietly stepped forward to fill the vacant place. Afterwards the grim duty of bearer corps, which Mr Gandhi organised in Natal, began. It was on such occasions the Indians proved their fortitude, and the one with the greatest fortitude was the subject of this sketch [Mr Gandhi]. After a night's work, which had shattered men with much bigger frames, I came across Gandhi in the early morning sitting by the roadside—eating a regulation Army biscuit. Every man in Buller's force was dull and depressed, and damnation was heartily invoked on everything. But Gandhi was stoical in his bearing, cheerful, and confident in his conversation, and had a kindly eye. He did one good.... I saw the man and his small undisciplined corps on many a field during the Natal campaign. When succour was to be rendered they were there.' (E. S. Reddy, 'India and the Anglo-Boer War', 29 July 1999, *CWMG*, Vol. 63, p. 379.)

work was at the moment much applauded and the Indians' prestige was enhanced.

Towards the end of December, I was back in Durban. On the 27th, I was near the entrance to my office on Mercury Lane when Harry Escombe saw me from across the road. Crossing over for a word, he recalled the attack on me of January 1897 and said he was really sorry about that. He added he did not realize there was 'so much Christian charity locked up in the Indian heart'. Three hours later, on my returning home, a servant from Escombe's home (which was next door) hurried in to report that Escombe had just dropped dead.[30]

By January, the Indian Ambulance Corps' work was widely appreciated. *The Natal Advertiser* asked me to contribute notes on the work being done. My reply[31] took time as beside taking charge of stretchers we had to look after the provisioning etc. of the Corps, getting hardly any time to sleep or eat. I wrote to the editor: '... there should be very little said by the Indians themselves of their work in connection with the war and that their part was merely to do without speaking.'

By 1 March, with the relief of Ladysmith, I could send a wire[32] on behalf of the Corps to the Colonial Secretary saying: 'Respectful congratulations to General Buller on brilliant victory.'

When the hostilities ceased with British victory, a public meeting was called in Durban on 14 March 1900 at which three resolutions were passed congratulating the three British generals who had led Britain to victory—Field Marshal Lord Roberts on his securing the relief of Kimberley and, after a stubborn fight, having captured General Cronje and his commando, General Sir Redvers Buller upon his having, undismayed by temporary reverses, effected the relief of the beleaguered garrison at Ladysmith, and General Sir George White on his having sustained British honour and prestige. Speaking at the meeting, I said Indians took joy in the British victory provided they did not become too conceited. And I said Indians had a special interest in the proceedings because Lord Roberts, the 'hero of Kandahar'* who was at the head of the forces, and Sir George White who had conducted the siege at Ladysmith with gallantry had both been for some long time commanders-in-chief in India. All three generals individually acknowledged the felicitations.

I had a feeling that the volunteers had enlisted partly out of regard for me and to that extent I was beholden to them. I wrote to the leaders of the Corps that whilst I cannot compensate them in terms of money, I offer them and their friends the gift of my legal services without any fees to the extent of 5 pounds for a year.[33] And to each of the stretcher bearers themselves I sent a cyclostyled letter and a personal present.

On 21 May, I drafted and sent a felicitatory cable to Queen Victoria on the monarch's 81st birthday, asking the Natal government to forward it to London, not forgetting to remit 1 pound as transmission charges.[34]

At this time Kastur was pregnant and about to deliver. The travail came on suddenly. As in Ramdas's case, Devadas's birth, at home, on 22 May 1900 put me to the severest test. The doctor was not immediately available and some time was lost in fetching the midwife. Even if she had been on the spot, she could not have helped delivery. I had to see through the safe delivery of the baby.

By the end of the year, Lord Roberts was appointed Governor of Natal. I thought we should present him with an address[35] of welcome, citing his brilliant career in South Africa. But we took care to see that no reference was made in it to his loss of his son in the war or make any political reference.

When news came on 22 January 1901 of the death of Queen Victoria, we British Indians in Natal sent a cable to the royal family '...bewailing the Empire's loss in the death of the greatest and most loved sovereign on earth'.[36] On the weekend following, a great procession was taken out in Durban from West Street to

---

*Lord Roberts had commanded in 1889 the long march from Kabul to Kandahar, then the capital of Afghanistan.

her statue and a wreath placed there, M. H. Nazar and I carrying the wreath on our shoulders. In March, an address on the reign of Queen Victoria was delivered to Indian children in the Town Hall, Durban, and a memorial was distributed to each of them.[37] This comprised a photograph of the late Queen and an extract from her Proclamation to the people of India of 1858 at the top, six dates in her life from her association with India at the bottom, a map of India (1901) showing it as a British possession and her remark 'I will be good' when she was informed at the age of twelve that she was the future Queen of England.

On 30 March, a kind friend sent me an extract from General Buller's dispatch wherein among the officers mentioned was my name. I wrote at once to the Colonial Secretary to say '…if I am entitled to any credit for having done my duty it is due in a greater measure to Dr Booth, now Dean of St John's and to Mr Shire, who spared no pains in making the Corps a success.'[38] And I requested him to bring this to the notice of the military authorities.

Cases of individual distress continued to come to me. On 6 May, an Indian named Kara Trikam was robbed in broad daylight on West Street of 40 pounds by some Europeans. One of them was caught and tried and released on bail. On 21 May I applied for 40 pounds out of the bail for Trikam and offered to provide proof as to my client's possession of that amount.[39]

I got news through a letter that month of the passing away of Raychandbhai.[40] I found it hard to believe the news and could not put it out of my mind. I wrote to Revashanker Zaveri*: 'There is very little time in this country to dwell on any matter. I got the letter while I was at my desk. Reading it for a minute I plunged immediately into my office work. Such is life here. Rightly or wrongly I was greatly attracted to him and I loved him deeply too. All that is over now. So I mourn out of selfishness. What consolation can I give you?'

Sir Mancherji M. Bhownaggree MP was at this time taking a

---

*Raychandbhai's uncle-in-law.

warm interest in the South Africa question. His influence with the authorities and his willingness to work made me write to him on 22 June: '...no man in England is more capable of doing justice to this matter than yourself'. But I cautioned him: 'But may I ask you not to mar the sterling work you are doing there by precipitating a hot debate unless you are sure of success.'[41]

Their Royal Highnesses the Duke and Duchess of Cornwall and York visited South Africa in August. King Edward VII had asked them to visit Australia and other parts of the Empire. India was not on their itinerary. And so for the British Indian community in Natal it became a double duty incumbent on it to pay homage to them. We presented them an address on 13 August, with an engraved silver shield and four pictures—of the Taj Mahal, the Karla Caves of Bombay, the Bodh Gaya temple and of indentured Indians working in Natal sugar estates. The address, signed by Abdul Kadir, M. C. Camrooddeen & Co, and sixty others, said: 'It is because we are in the folds of the all-embracing Union Jack that we have a footing outside India.'

The manner in which representatives of the Indian community were chosen for the presentation of the address led to a Protest Meeting being organized, which I chaired. I was not at all in sympathy with the two resolutions adopted at it but, having chaired the meeting and because ventilation in the press of grievances is the best safety valve, I forwarded them to *The Natal Mercury*. The first of the resolutions said: '...only Mohammedans were apprised of the meeting, thus depriving the other Indians from participating in it'.

On 11 September, I had to go to Ladysmith to appear for Abarrah, a barber, who had been booked under the Pass Law for being out 'after 9 p.m.' and 'failing to produce a pass from his employer'. How could he, I argued, produce such a pass when he was his own employer? He was discharged.[42]

Three

TRYING INDIA OUT

The Gandhis were and are a big family.

With the war over, I began to feel that my work was no longer in South Africa but in India.[43] And that my main business might become merely money-making. Friends at home were also pressing me to return. After very great difficulty, my request was conditionally accepted by my co-workers, the condition being that I should be ready to go back to South Africa if, within a year, the community should need me.

The farewell was overwhelming. Gifts included things in gold and silver. There were articles of costly diamond as well. One of the gifts was a gold necklace worth fifty guineas, meant for my wife. But even that gift was given because of my public work. I decided I could not keep these things. I drafted a letter creating a trust of them in favour of the community. My children readily agreed to my proposal.

'You may not need them,' said my wife. 'Your children may not need them. Cajoled, they will dance to your tune. I can understand your not permitting me to wear them. But what of my daughters-in-law? They will be sure to need them. And who knows what will happen tomorrow?' And thus the torrent of argument went on, reinforced by tears.

'And what right have you to my necklace?'

'But is the necklace given to you for your service or for my service?'

'I have toiled and moiled for you day and night. Is that no service?'

These were pointed thrusts and some of them went home. But I was determined to return the ornaments. I somehow succeeded in extorting a consent from her.

In a letter to Parsi Rustomji, Honorary Secretary of the Farewell Address Committee I wrote on 18 October 1901: 'Neither I nor my family can make any use of the costly presents. They are too sacred to be sold by *me* or by *my heirs*, and seeing that there can be no guarantee against the last contingency, in my opinion, the only way in which I can return the love of our people is to dedicate them all to a sacred object. And since they are in reality a tribute to the [Natal Indian] Congress principles, to the Congress I return them.'[44]

We sailed for India on 18 October, disembarking in Port Louis, Mauritius, on 30 October. The Indian community gave us a reception on 13 November at which I said the sugar industry in the island owed its unprecedented prosperity to Indian immigrants.[45] *The Standard* and *Le Radicale* reported my speech on 15 November, including my exhorting the community to acquaint itself with happenings in the motherland. While in Mauritius we spent a night with the India-born Governor of Mauritius, Sir Charles Bruce*, a scholar of Sanskrit and sympathizer of the cause of Indian emigrants.

We reached India in the middle of December. I wrote to the Editor of the *Times of India* on 19 December on the South Africa question: 'Sir Mancherji Bhownaggree has been rendering a most useful service to the cause of the sufferers. In season and out of season, within the House of Commons and without, with pen and voice, he has been asking for, not without success, a redress of our grievances....

---

*Lord Charles Bruce, the present owner of that title and name, writes (June 2020) to the editor of this volume: 'Sir Charles was a member of the Bruce of Arnot family—a branch of the main line—but his Christian name is a popular choice in the family. Like many Scottish families, I believe his father was serving in the East India Co. in Bengal, where Charles was born in 1836. After attending Harrow School and Yale he studied Oriental languages in Germany, ultimately contributing to von Bohtlingk and von Roth's *Sanskrit Worterbuch* (St Petersburg 1855-75). Other publications included *Die Geschichte von Nala* (1862) and *The Broad Stone of Empire* (1910). His colonial career started in 1868 when he was appointed Rector of the Royal College, Mauritius. He returned in 1897 as governor—when he met Gandhi—and in between he served in Ceylon, British Guiana, and the Windward Islands. In some respects, this career was typical of well-educated Scots of this period, but he seems to have avoided the ICS. I'm not sure why he was drawn to Germany to study Sanskrit—a chair had been established in Oxford in 1832.'

The [Indian National] Congress has been passing resolutions year after year, sympathizing with us. But, in my humble opinion, something more is required. I have been asked by the leading Indians in South Africa to suggest a representative delegation to the viceroy.'[46]

Making a brief halt at Porbandar, we went home—to Rajkot. The two older boys, Harilal and Manilal, and my nephew, Gokuldas, were not strangers to it but Ramdas, then about 4, and Devadas, just one and a half, were seeing India, Bombay, Porbandar, and Rajkot for the first time. All of them needed to be taught our traditional texts apart from whatever they could learn at school. I also engaged a clerk to help me—Mehtaji. My nephew Chhaganlal,* was asked by me to see to it that he was paid his due salary during my absence, for which Chhaganlal was to take the required amount from my wife.

Gokuldas and Harilal started studying in Standard IV of the secondary school. Manilal began studying privately, not having joined any specific standard at school.

I had to leave for Calcutta almost immediately to attend the Congress session. I stayed there at India Club.

From there I wrote on 23 December to Chhaganlal, who was a teacher, to see to it that Gokuldas and Harilal had stories read out to them from *Kavyadohan*, a collection of story-poems based on the Mahabharata, *Bhagavata* and other works. I asked him to particularly read out and explain the stories of Sudama, Nala, and Angada. The story of Harishchandra I asked him to narrate or read out from the book. It was not necessary, I said to Chhaganlal, to read out to the boys English plays as they would not be interested in them. Moreover there was not so much moral to be drawn from English poets as from our story-poems. But study apart, it was important that the boys behaved well in class and did not pick up bad habits of any kind. And he was to see that besides attending to studies they took adequate exercise.[47]

The boys were getting fever by turns. On 25 January, I requested my old friend from London days, Dalpatram Shukla,[48] now settled

---

*Chhaganlal Khushalchand Gandhi (1881–1970).

in Rajkot, to keep visiting our home now and then.⁴⁹

At the Congress camp, I made friends with a few volunteers. I told them things about South Africa and they seemed to understand. They were clashing against one another. You asked one of them to do something. He delegated it to another and he in turn to a third. The delegates were of a piece with the volunteers. They would do nothing themselves. 'Volunteer, do this', 'Volunteer, do that', were their constant orders. There was no limit to insanitation. Pools of water were everywhere. There were only a few latrines, and the recollection of their stink still oppresses me. I pointed it out to volunteers. They said point blank: 'That is not our work, it is the scavenger's work.' I asked for a broom. The man stared at me in wonder. But that was for myself. I saw that if the Congress session were to be prolonged, conditions would be quite favourable for the outbreak of an epidemic.

Moving a resolution on the condition in South Africa, I spoke at the Congress on 27 December. 'If our worthy President were to go to South Africa,' I said, 'I am afraid, he too would be classified as a coolie, a member of the semi-civilized races of Asia.' And I reminded the delegates: 'The Congress is, I believe, meant among other things to testify to our ability to stand side by side with the other civilized races of the world in foreign enterprises and self-government.'

I walked up and down the streets of Calcutta. On my way to the Kali temple, I saw a stream of sheep going to be sacrificed to Kali. Rows of beggars lined the lane leading to the temple. That very evening I had an invitation to dinner at a party of Bengali friends. There I spoke about this cruel form of worship. He said: 'The sheep don't feel anything. The noise and drum-beating there deadens all sensation of pain.'

It was impossible to be satisfied without seeing Swami Vivekananda. So with great enthusiasm I went to Belur mostly or may be all the way on foot. I loved the sequestered site of the Math. I was disappointed and sorry to be told that the Swami was at his Calcutta house, lying ill, and could not be seen.

I then ascertained the place of residence of Sister Nivedita and met her in her Chowringhee mansion. I was taken aback by the splendour that surrounded her* and even in our conversation there was not much meeting ground. I spoke to Gokhale about this and he said he did not wonder that there could be no point of contact between me and a person like her. He used a word to describe her that I cannot recall. But I put it down in my *Autobiography* (written in Gujarati in serialized form for *Navajivan* and *Young India* in 1927) as tej. This was translated by Mahadev Desai as 'volatile'. I cannot disassociate myself from its use because as a rule I revise these translations and I remember having discussed the adjective with him. We both had doubts about the use of the adjective being correct. The choice lay between volatile, violent, and fanatical. The last two were considered too strong. Mahadev chose volatile and I passed it. *The Modern Review* said (July 1927): 'We do not know if Mr Gokhale spoke to Mr Gandhi in English and actually used the word "volatile" to describe her; for what has appeared in *Young India* is translated from the Gujarati *Navajivan*. But whoever is responsible for the use of the word "volatile" has wronged her memory.' I have a full recollection of the conversation between Sister Nivedita and myself. But I do not propose to describe it. No fault in the translation of the original can possibly damage the memory of one who loved Hinduism and India so well.[50]

I met her again in Mr Pestonji Padshah's place[†]. I happened to come in just as she was talking to his old mother and so I became an interpreter between the two. She made a remark which I still remember: 'Tell her that having abandoned her own faith she is not in a position to expound my faith to me.'[51]

---

*Margaret Noble (1867–1911), charismatic Irishwoman who met Swami Vivekananda in London in 1895 and took the name of Nivedita on becoming his disciple, was the guest of Mrs Ole Bull and Miss Josephine MacLeod at the American Consulate. Her own simple residence was in Bosepara Lane, Baghbazar.

†Pestonji Padshah (1866–1909) was a Parsi contemporary of Gandhi in London, noted for his erudition and for his vegetarianism; a barrister in London, he met Gandhi in London at various times between 1888 and 1891; rejected Gandhi's appeal for admission as an advocate of the High Court of Justice, Bombay, in 1891; advised him against working in South Africa as 'there was so much to do in India'.

As I had to meet various people in connection with work in South Africa, I stayed in Calcutta for a month. Gokhale invited me to stay with him. From the very first day he made me feel completely at home. He arranged to see that I got everything I needed. Fortunately my wants were few. He would introduce me to all important people that called on him. This is how he introduced Professor (now Sir) P. C. Ray: '…having a monthly salary of Rs 800, keeps just Rs 40 for himself and devotes the balance for public purposes. He is not and does not want to get married.'

Gokhale, I saw, used to have a horse carriage. I remonstrated with him: 'Can't you make use of the tramcar? Is it derogatory to a leader's dignity?'

'I envy your liberty to go about in tramcars but I am sorry, I cannot do likewise. When you are the victim of as wide a publicity as I am, it will be difficult if not impossible for you to go about in a tramcar. I love your simple habits. I live as simply as I can….'

I could see that he was slightly pained by what I had said.

Writing to him on my journey out of Calcutta on board the SS *Goa* for Rangoon on 30 January, I apologized: 'I had no right to question your taste on Monday evening. I was too presumptuous. Had I known that I would cause you thereby the pain I did cause, I should certainly never have taken the liberty. I trust you will forgive me for the folly.' It so happened that I myself used the coach for my journey from Mr Gokhale's home to the pier. But I failed to observe due etiquette and so in the letter said to my host: 'I forgot to pay the coachman a gratuity. Will you kindly ask Mr Bhate to pay him a rupee and the groom half a rupee?'

I travelled through north and northwest India on my return journey, alighting in Benares, Agra, Jaipur, and Palanpur. In each city I stayed one day and put up in dharamsalas or with pandas. In Benares I went to the Kashi Vishvanath temple for darshan. The approach was through a narrow, slippery lane. Quiet there was none. The swarming flies and the noise made by the shopkeepers and pilgrims was perfectly insufferable. When I reached the temple, I was greeted at the entrance by a stinking mass of rotten flowers.

The floor was paved with marble which was, however, broken by some devotee innocent of aesthetic taste who had set it with rupees, serving as an excellent receptacle for dirt.⁵²

The Central Hindoo College in Benares seemed to me to be not a bad institution, the 'dream in marble' in Agra certainly worth a visit.

On getting back home in Rajkot, I had the children with me. But everything was undecided. Plague was raging in Rajkot. I intended settling down in Bombay if I could afford it. It was difficult to do public work from Rajkot. The future alone would decide it.⁵³ I got down to work on my typewriter which was quite different from the one I used in Professor Gokhale's home in Calcutta.⁵⁴

Meanwhile, a cablegram in *The Times* announced the death of the uncrowned king of South Africa.* However much we may have disliked Rhode's policy, it is impossible now that the man is gone to withhold a tear; that he was a true friend of the Empire, it would be very difficult to gainsay.

Funds from Natal amounting to over 3,000 rupees having come to me, I decided on settling in Bombay and took up a room from Payne, Gilbert, Sayani, and Moos opposite the High Court for office. I was thus free to lounge about the High Court to let solicitors know of an addition to the ranks of the briefless ones.⁵⁵ I can recall the case of Mr Hasam, a poor man from Porbandar who came to see me. He had been deprived of his ancestral land worth about 100 rupees. I asked him not to risk losing 500 rupees in order to get back land worth only 100 rupees. 'It is my ancestral land,' he said. 'I shall recover it at any cost. I shall never allow the title deed to be nullified.'⁵⁶

Helping the plague-stricken remained an engagement with me and my brother wrote to me bitter letters of imprecation telling me that if I were to die in the process, the responsibility for supporting Kastur and the children would fall on him. And, so, though I was against

---

*Cecil John Rhodes (1853–1902), British statesman, imperialist, mining magnate, believer in white supremacy, describing Anglo–Saxons as 'the first race in the world', died on 26 March 1902. Served as Prime Minister of the Cape Colony from 1890 to 1896 when he was forced to resign after the raid—the Jameson raid—he ordered on Kruger's South African Republic (The Transvaal).

insurance as a concept, I took out an insurance policy in her favour.

I had hired chambers and a house in Girgaum, but God would not let me settle down. My ten-year-old son, Manilal, had a severe attack of typhoid, combined with pneumonia, the temperature going up to 104 degrees. At night he would be delirious. The doctor,* a very good Parsi, said medicines would have little effect but eggs and chicken broth might be given with profit. Religion, as I understood it, did not permit me to use meat or eggs and so I proposed to try some hydropathic remedies which I happened to know. I asked Manilal his opinion. 'Do try your hydropathic treatment. I will not have eggs or chicken broth.' What right had parents to inflict their fads on their children? My mind was torn. It was night. I was in Manilal's bed, lying by his side. I decided to give him a wet sheet pack. The whole body was burning like hot iron, with absolutely no perspiration. I got up, wetted a sheet, wrung the water out of it, and wrapped Manilal in it. Then, leaving him in his mother's charge, went out for a walk on Chaupatty to refresh myself. Very few pedestrians were out. I scarcely looked at them. 'My honour is in Thy keeping, oh Lord, in this hour of trial,' I repeated to myself. Ramanama was on my lips. My heart beating within my breast, I returned home after a short time.

No sooner had I entered the room than Manilal said: 'You have returned, Bapuji?'

'Yes, darling'.

'Please pull me out. I am burning.'

'Are you perspiring, my boy?'

'I am simply soaked'.

I felt his forehead. It was covered with beads of perspiration. The temperature was going down. I thanked God. I undid the pack and dried his limbs. We then fell asleep in the same bed, each like a log. Today Manilal is the healthiest of my boys.

I prospered in my profession better than I had expected. Like other

---

*Most likely Dr Dadibarjor, the now Bombay-based doctor who had been retained by Abdullah Sheth for his company and had treated Gandhi in Durban on 13 January 1897 after the assault on him.

fresh barristers I made a point of attending the hearing of cases in the High Court more, I am afraid, for enjoying the soporific breeze coming straight from the sea than for adding to my knowledge. I was not the only one to enjoy this pleasure.

Gokhale peeped in at my chambers twice or thrice every week.

But when I was feeling that I had just settled down in Bombay, a cable came from Natal asking me, with funds being sent, to come at once: 'Committee requests fulfil promise. Remitting'.[57] Whether Kastur would accompany or not, I was clear that I would leave Gokuldas and Harilal in Rajkot as soon as it was free of the plague. I would put them in the Kathiawar High School and keep a trustworthy paid man who would look after them. I wrote to my Rajkot-based friend Dalpatram Shukla to help me find such a man if I failed to do so.[58] And also to look after the boys, to look them up now and then, and induce them, if he had no objection, to use his tennis court.

'I wish I could meet you before my departure,' I wrote to Gokhale 'but that seems impossible. And I urged him to: 'keep an eye on the Indian question in South Africa'.

I kept our Bombay bungalow and left Kastur and the children there in the care of Chhaganlal. The separation from wife and children, the breaking up of a settled establishment, and the going from the certain to the uncertain—all this was for a moment, painful but I had inured myself to an uncertain life.

I took with me to South Africa four or five enterprising youths, one of who was Maganlal Gandhi* and another Anandlal†. The Gandhis were and are a big family. I wanted to find out all those who wished to leave the trodden path and venture abroad. My father used to accommodate a number of them in some state service. I wanted them to be free of this spell. I neither could nor would secure other service for them; I wanted them to be self-reliant. But as my ideals advanced, I tried to persuade these youths also to conform their ideals to mine and I had the greatest success in guiding Maganlal Gandhi.[59]

---

*Maganlal Khushalchand Gandhi (1883–1928).
†Anandlal Amritlal Gandhi (1878–1943).

Four

BACK IN SOUTH AFRICA AGAIN

I built up a decent practice and could pick and choose.

I reached Durban not a day too soon. I had been called by the community to lead a delegation to the visiting Secretary of State for the Colonies, Chamberlain. On 28 December, we met him in Durban. We met him again in Maritzburg. It was my intention to remove one or two of his misapprehensions when he received our deputation in Maritzburg. But I was asked not to discuss any matter. So I simply endorsed what had been said in Durban and Mr Chamberlain repeated what he had said to us there.[60]

He had come to get a gift of 35 million pounds from South Africa, and to win the hearts of Englishmen and Boers. So what could he give to the Indian question? He gave us a cold shoulder.

We said in the petition presented to him in Durban: 'Ours is not, after all, a question that affects only a few thousand Indians but it is that of the status of His Majesty's subjects.' And we reminded him of what Lord Ripon had said in one of his dispatches: 'It is the desire of Her Majesty's government that the Queen's Indian subjects should be treated upon a footing of equality with all Her Majesty's other subjects.'

Chamberlain was travelling across South Africa, from Durban to Cape Town, a distance of 1,100 miles. We sought to meet him in the Transvaal as well. I had obtained a permit to enter the Transvaal but on reaching Pretoria, I was first summoned to see the head of the Transvaal's Asiatic Department*. I went with Sheth Tyeb Haji Khanmahomed.

---

*W. H. More, formerly of the Ceylon Civil Service.

No seats were offered.[61]

'What brings you here?'

'I have come here at the request of my fellow countrymen to help them with my advice.'

'But don't you know you have no right to come here? The permit was given you by mistake. You must go back. You shall not wait on Mr Chamberlain. You may go.'

I smarted under the insult, but as I had pocketed many such in the past I had become inured to them. George Godfrey, an Indian barrister, led the delegation.

A commission from the Natal government, meanwhile, set out to India to see to it that indentured Indians did not have an opportunity to settle in the Natal. In other words, to secure the termination of Indian indenture. On 30 January 1903 I apprised[62] Dadabhai Naoroji of the position and with others from the community sent a petition[63] to Lord Curzon, the Viceroy of India, about this situation which amounted to sending indentured Indians back. We quoted the late Harry Escombe's words: 'A man is brought here, in theory with his consent, in practice very often without it. He gives the best five years of his life, he forms new ties, forgets the old ones, and he cannot, in my view of right and wrong, be sent back.'

'It is at your instance that the community helped in the [Boer] War and you see the result now,' I was taunted by some people. 'In taking part in the war, we simply did our duty,' I said. 'Let us think of the task before us.' And I decided that instead of returning to India or carrying on my work from Natal, I ought not to leave the Transvaal. I should get enrolled in the Transvaal Supreme Court, practising in Pretoria or Johannesburg, and help the community refuse to put up with the veritable dog's life that we were expected to lead. The Law Society did not oppose my application and the court allowed it. And L. W. Ritch, a manager in a commercial firm there, helped me secure suitable rooms for my office on Rissik Street in the legal quarters of Johannesburg.

During a few months of my opening an office, I built-up a decent practice and could pick and choose. My public work, however, was of an exacting nature and caused me very great anxiety. I worked from nearly a quarter to nine [in the morning] to ten o'clock at night, with intervals for meals and a short walk. It was a time for exertion and worry with no prospect for the work, in the near future, to slacken. I saw that it was impossible for me to get away for several years.

The question then was my promise to Kastur. I had told her that I should return to India at the end of the year or she should come here by that time. I was most anxious to fulfil that promise. How to do that was the difficulty. In any case, I was not to think of returning for three to four years. Will she consent to remaining in India for all that time? If not, then, of course, she must come here by the end of the year. It will however be a terrible thing to establish a new home here in Johannesburg and then to break it up as I did in Durban. If there were great difficulties about it in Natal, they will be greater in Johannesburg.[64]

By February, Maganlal and Anandlal, another nephew, had opened a shop in Tongaat. And I had told Maganlal that if he so preferred, he could come to Johannesburg where there was a good chance to secure him a job. Manilal, I learnt from Chhaganlal, had been withdrawn from a class where he was learning instrumental music in Bombay. I wrote to Chhaganlal this was wrong, though it was Kastur's, not his fault. As for me, I told Chhaganlal, life in Johannesburg was no bed of roses.[65]

Johannesburg, the city of gold, is a city where people do not walk but run and no one has the leisure to look at anyone else.[66] Earning a living in South Africa is not a prospect to build hopes on. Except the mealie meal, a South Africa produce, every necessity of life is dear. There is everywhere a great pressure of population, the number of unemployed is very great, business dull, and people did not know what would happen if the mining labour problem was not solved in the near future.[67]

Chhaganalal was to come to South Africa at this time and I sent a cablegram saying Harilal should also come with him. Harilal had been very ill and I was glad to learn by the middle of June that he was out of danger. He was looked after by Haridas Vora* and his family in Rajkot. Along with Revashanker Jhaveri, Haridasbhai had supplied my place to Harilal. This kindness of friends was for me, in my self-imposed exile, overwhelming. I said to Haridasbhai that the cold weather would have passed by the time Harilal comes and he will benefit by the change of climate and greater regularity of habits. Haridasbhai believed in nature cure and I told him that I shall see so far as possible that Harilal does not receive any drugs while here.[68]

Kastur had very little of my company in Durban. She would have less in Johannesburg. However, I wished to be guided by her entirely and placed myself in her hands. If she must come, she must make preparations, I sent word, in October and start in November.[69]

I wrote to Chhaganlal to try to convince her that it would be best for her to remain in India but that if she wants to come, to come with her, Harilal, Ramdas and Devadas by the first available boat in November, leaving Manilal and Gokaldas behind, making proper arrangements for their accommodation and education. If Manilal was not willing to stay behind to bring him also. It would be good, I said, for Gokaldas to continue with his studies in Bombay, consulting his mother about it. I wrote all this to Chhaganlal in a great hurry and asked him to read it out to his aunt and to Revashankerbhai carefully.[70]

I wrote to Professor Gokhale on 23 February, saying I was in the thick of the fight and the struggle was far more intense than I expected.[71] By May I was able to tell him I had settled in Johannesburg under very difficult circumstances and that the Indian question had assumed a very serious aspect, requiring very close attention.[72]

The Immigration Restriction Bill was passed without an amendment. Both the Houses had pre-judged the issue and made up their minds about it. At the time of introducing the disfranchising bill, Sir John Robinson had declared that the rights of the disfranchised

---

*Haridas Vakhatchand Vora, a leading lawyer of Kathiawar, based in Rajkot; his daughter, Chanchal aka Gulab, was to marry Harilal.

would be justly guarded. Well may the Indians say 'Save us from our guardians'.[73]

Around the middle of August 1903 Lord Milner, the governor, proposed a change of the Indian location in Johannesburg on the grounds of insanitation.

Socially and popularly, the Indian is a pariah in South Africa—in some places less so than in others. Popular prejudice has portrayed him as a 'filthy being' without any virtue. The struggle seems to be the fiercest in the Transvaal.[74] If a European commits a crime or a moral delinquency, it is the individual. If it is an Indian, it is the nation. An Indian saw fit to let houses taken by him on lease for immoral purposes. For conduct such as this there is absolutely no defence. But it is one thing to condemn the individual and another to justify and advocate restrictions on a whole nation. And let it not be forgotten that it is a European landlord who had leased the premises to the Indian in question.[75]

Madanjit Vyavaharik, who had been a school teacher in Bombay, had been loaned some money by me in 1899 to start the International Printing Press in Durban. Early in 1903, he approached me with the idea of using his press for running a weekly called *Indian Opinion** to be published in four languages—English, Gujarati, Tamil, and Hindi. I approved of his proposal and the journal was launched with Mansukhlal Nazar as editor. But I became virtually responsible for it. I soon discovered it could not go on without my financial help. Ultimately I was sinking all my savings in it.

On 11 February 1904, I had to write to Dr C. Porter, the Medical Officer of Health, Johannesburg, regarding the shocking conditions in the Indian location: 'From what I hear, mortality in the location has increased considerably and it seems to me that, if the present

---

*Established in 1903 in Durban, it ran from 1904 until 1915 from Phoenix and, on Manilal Gandhi's return to South Africa in 1917, was revived and run by him and after 1920 edited by him, assisted by his wife, Sushila, who became a Gujarati compositor in the press, attended to correspondence, managed the finances of the newspaper, taking over its editorship after Manilal's death in 1956, changing its name to *Opinion* in 1957. The paper closed in 1961.

state of things is continued, the outbreak of some epidemic disease is merely a question of time. I know you are very great on sanitary reform. May I therefore ask you to be good enough to pay a personal visit? I shall be pleased to accompany you.' Dr Porter did visit the site and I wrote thanking him. He asked me to suggest remedies. The location had stands from which stand-holders carried out business. I suggested that each stand should be let on a short lease and the lessee made responsible for the stand's sanitation, with inspectors visiting daily and coming down on defaulters with a heavy hand.[76]

On 18 March, I received a pencil note from Madanjit Vyavaharik, who had come from Durban canvassing subscribers for *Indian Opinion* and realizing subscriptions, to say that there has been a sudden outbreak of the black plague and asking me to come immediately. 'Otherwise,' it said, 'we must be prepared for dire consequences.' I cycled to the site—Brickfields—where Madanjit had opened the lock of a vacant house where all the twenty-three patients were put. They had all been working in a gold mine in the vicinity of Johannesburg. They had returned from the mines to their quarters one evening with an acute attack of the plague. Dr William Godfrey, who was practising in Johannesburg, ran to the rescue.[77] A temporary hospital was set up. I had at that time four Indians in my office. I decided to sacrifice all four—call them clerks, co-workers or sons. One of them, Kalyandas,* had been entrusted to me by his father. I have rarely come across anyone more obliging and willing to render implicit obedience than Kalyandas. In years he is still a child, but in our experience we have seldom come across a youth so tender of heart, so scornful of money, so regardless of his own body, but at the same time so solicitous of the welfare of others.† There was no need to consult Kalyandas. The others expressed readiness as soon as they were asked. 'Where you are, we will also be,' was their short and sweet reply.

The Town Clerk informed on 19 March that he was unable to

---

*Son of Jagmohandas Mehta of Bombay, Kalyandas returned to India in 1907.
†In a letter to his brother Lakshmidas Gandhi on 27 May 1906, Gandhi wrote: 'Young Kalyandas, Jagmohandas's son, is like Prahlad in spirit. He is therefore dearer to me than one who is a son because so born.' *Indian Opinion*, 11 May 1907.

take charge of the patients or incur any financial responsibility until after the 21st beyond giving the Government Entrepot to be used as a temporary hospital. This was originally a Customs Depot. Thirty volunteers were put on to it. The place was thoroughly cleaned and voluntary Indian nurses worked night and day, taking charge of all the patients that were being received. Every bed, all the medical comforts, food and everything were supplied entirely by the Indians. It is but fair to state that the Town Council since paid the expenses incurred.[78]

The municipality lent the services of a nurse, a kindly lady, who wanted to attend to the patients but rarely allowed her to touch them lest she should catch the contagion. We had instructions to give the patients brandy. The nurse asked us to take some ourselves, as a precaution just as she was doing herself. But none of us would touch it. I had no faith in its beneficial effect even for the patients. With the permission of Dr Godfrey, I put three patients who were prepared to do without brandy under the earth treatment. Two of these survived. The other twenty died. In the course of a few days we learnt the good nurse had had an attack and immediately succumbed.

Those who had witnessed the scenes at this hospital and had carefully attended to the patients crowded into the small rooms would never forget the sight at once ghastly and inspiring—ghastly because of the grim tragedy and inspiring because the event showed the ability of the community to rise to the occasion and to organize. At last plague was declared. It required the ocular demonstration of poor men dying like flies for the Town Council to rise up to the scratch. And yet no one individual is to blame. It is the soulless bulky corporation wound up in red tape and nurtured on theory that must be held blameable for the ghastly tragedy.[79]

I wrote to Dadabhai Naoroji: 'All honour to it (the Johannesburg Municipality) that after the situation was realized, it spent money like water in dealing with the calamity, but that work could never undo the past.... The thing is now finished. The Indians have suffered undeservedly....' Dadabhai then quoted the bulk of my letter in a communication he addressed on 22 November to the Secretary of State for India.

Five

A NEW TURN

...it were better for a man to lose millions than that he should lose a good name.

The plague taught the British Indians of South Africa lessons which we trust will not be forgotten. We have a homely saying in India that it were better for a man to lose millions than that he should lose a good name. What is true of individuals is equally true of communities. The French have a name for the artistic, the English for personal bravery, the Germans for hard-headedness, the Russians for frugality, the Colonies in South Africa for gold hunger; similarly the Indians in South Africa have, rightly or wrongly, got the evil reputation of being insanitary and ignorant of the first principles of hygiene. In the Transvaal the inhabitants of the late Indian location are being treated practically as prisoners. Even dogs, cats, and other animals found in the location have been killed—lest their contact with the Indians may have conveyed to them the plague germs! A name once lost is not so easily regained. It is well for us to protest against exaggerated charges. It is our duty to strain every nerve to prevent legislative measures based on them. But we hold it to be equally our duty to examine those charges critically, admit the partial truth in them, and strive to correct the evil that may be in us. It is thus and only thus that we can rise in the estimation of our neighbours.[80]

In a letter to the Johannesburg press I said, 'I admit that the poorer of my countrymen do not observe the laws of sanitation, except under supervision. But I do submit they are not the keepers of public health. They are defaulters as individuals and have suffered as such. It is the Public Health Committee which has to enforce obedience to such laws.'[81]

This letter secured me Mr Henry Polak,* and Mr Albert West,†
who used to visit two vegetarian restaurants‡ that I used to have my
meals in. Mr Polak, a young man, sitting a little way off my table
at The Alexandra, sent me his card. So I invited him to join me at
my table. He was a subeditor at *The Critic*; he said. 'When I read
your letter to the press about the plague, I felt a strong desire to
see you.' His candour drew me to him. The same evening we got
to know each other. We seemed to hold closely similar views on the
essential things of life.

Albert West, a partner in a small printing firm, used to have his
meals in another restaurant I used to have meals in. He too had
read my letter and one day, when I was busy nursing the patients,
not finding me in the restaurant, had got worried lest I should have
contracted the disease. So he decided to come and make sure. 'Well,'
he said 'here I am at your disposal. I am ready to help in nursing
the patients.'

'I will not have you as a nurse,' I said, 'but...there is one thing.'

'Yes, what is it?'

'Could you take charge of the *Indian Opinion* press at Durban?'

After thinking it over that night, he agreed. Salary was no
consideration for him. The very next day he left for Durban by
the evening mail. And Polak, believing he can freely express his
feelings against oppression in *Indian Opinion*, informed his chief at

---

*Henry Solomon Leon Polak (1882–1959) born in Dover, England, to Jewish parents;
went over to South Africa in 1903 for a health cure and after working as a journalist
in *The Transvaal Critic* at Johannesburg, worked with Gandhi as a close colleague in
the cause of Indians in South Africa and was one of the leaders of the Indian Passive
Resistance Movement; on becoming a lawyer, served his articles with Gandhi before
setting up his own legal offices in Johannesburg; edited *Indian Opinion*, Durban;
sentenced to three months' imprisonment by the Volksrust Magistrate in Natal, for his
advocacy of the cause of Indians; delegate to India from the Transvaal and the Natal.
†Albert West, Theosophist by conviction and printer by trade, became a founder–settler
in Phoenix and played an active role in the 1913 Satyagraha. His wife, mother-in-law,
and sister also joined him at the settlement.
‡West met Gandhi for the first time at Adolf Ziegler's establishment. The other
establishment, the Alexandra Tea Room, where Polak met Gandhi for the first time,
was of Miss Ada M. Bissicks, West's sister.

The Critic of his intention to resign and join *Indian Opinion* at the beginning of 1905.[82]

In early November, we received from London a circular from the Edwin Arnold Committee asking if any our readers would send subscriptions for endowing a scholarship or scholarships, or found prizes at the University of Oxford for proficiency in Oriental literature in his memory. The committee included the names of the Right Honourable Lord Brassey as chairman, His Highness the Aga Khan, Sir M. M. Bhownaggree, Sir George Birdwood, the Right Honourable Joseph Chamberlain, the Viscount Hayashi, Mr Rudyard Kipling, and others. A notice was put out in *Indian Opinion* at once, saying, 'The services of Sir Edwin to the East and West have not yet been fully appreciated. Time alone will show the measure of those services. *The Light of Asia* alone has left on the Western mind an indelible impression for good. It has been said that he missed the Poet Laureateship because of the Oriental turn of his mind.'[83]

Indian Opinion was, meanwhile, getting more and more expensive. Towards the end of May 1904, West wrote to me: 'The books are not in order. There are heavy arrears to be recovered.... But I remain on....' On receipt of West's letter, I left for Natal. Polak came to see me off. I had taken him into my fullest confidence. He left me with a book to read during the journey which he said I was sure to like. It was Ruskin's *Unto This Last*.

The book was impossible to lay aside once I had begun it. It gripped me.

The teachings of the book I understood to be:

1. The good of the individual is contained in the good of all.
2. A lawyer's work has the same value as a barber's.
3. A life of labour, i.e., the life of the tiller of the soil and the handicraftsman is the life worth living.

Johannesburg to Durban was a twenty-four-hours journey. I could not get any sleep that night. I arose with the dawn, ready to reduce these principles to practice. I determined to change my life according to the ideals of that book.

Ruskin has said that man as an economic factor is not to be studied simply as a machine but is to be taken with all his mental attributes. I wrote in *Indian Opinion* on 5 November 1904 that considered as such, the Indian is the most efficient labourer in the world. He may be puny, he may be slow, he may be weak but he is most sober, uncomplaining, patient, and long-suffering.[84] This was the first book of Ruskin's I had ever read. *Unto This Last* brought about an instantaneous and practical transformation in my life.[85]

I advertised for a piece of land in the vicinity of Durban and an offer came in respect of Phoenix. Within a week we purchased twenty acres of land. Adjacent to it was a piece of eighty acres which had many fruit trees and a dilapidated cottage. We purchased this too, the total cost being 1,000 pounds.

The area was full of snakes of different varieties. It was not unusual for one to across five or six of them in a single day. Some of them were non-poisonous but there were others which were deadly. There were innumerable kinds of birds. The place was quiet except for the chirping of these birds and the voices of some Zulus crossing over from the Phoenix railway station to Inanda at the time trains arrived and went. In the evenings, one could see a few dim lights coming from the scattered huts of Zulu families and one or two Indian homes who had settled on agricultural farms. Sometimes when there were quarrels among the Indian families, we could hear their raised voices.

It was in this desolate place that we made our homes.[86]

The plan was shortly this: If a piece of ground sufficiently large and far away from the hustle of the town could be secured for housing the plant and machinery, each one of the workers could have his plot of land on which he could live. This would simplify the question of living under sanitary and healthy conditions, without heavy expenses. The workers could receive per month an advance sufficient to cover their monthly expenses. And they also could have the option of buying out their plot of land at the actual cost price.[87]

On returning to Johannesburg, I informed Polak of the important changes I had made. His joy knew no bounds when he learnt that the loan of his book had been so fruitful.

Living under such conditions and amidst the beautiful surroundings which have given Natal the name of the Garden Colony, the workers could live a more simple and natural life and the ideas of Ruskin and Tolstoy combined with strict business principles.

By December, *Indian Opinion* had begun to appear from Phoenix. Chhaganlal kept the accounts and looked after the Gujarati section of the journal, Maganlal did the composing and other jobs becoming proficient at them. The shed for the press was large enough to hold the cases for English, Hindi, Gujarati, and Tamil types and stools for nearly a dozen compositors. Special arrangements were made for the English and Gujarati sections and I had a room made for my use. All the machinery, equipment, and furniture were fitted up neatly in the shed which was well lit and ventilated. With the help of a couple of carpenters, all the staff members were able to construct one room houses for each made of corrugated iron sheets. All these were on a higher level and 50 to 200 yards of one another. After the settlers had cleared the wild grass from around their houses, planted gardens around them and levelled some area to be used as a courtyard, the houses took on the appearance of a neat little colony. When the houses were set up, I asked Chhaganlal and Maganlal to send for their families.[88]

I informed Dadabhai of this and of our intention of having a weekly of fortnightly letter from England on matters of general interest and on the India–South Africa question. I requested him to recommend a person who would undertake the work.

Although this journal supplied a real want, what may be termed a commercial demand had to be created. In other words, the paper had not only to find its matter, it had to find its readers also. Moreover, the sending of over five hundred copies was a great drag.[89]

In the January of 1905, I wrote to Professor Gokhale about Phoenix. 'It is also my intention,' I wrote, 'if my earnings continue, to open a school on the grounds, which would be second to none in South Africa for the education primarily of Indian children who would be resident boarders. And a sanatorium.' I also asked him for:

1. At least two or three graduates who have an aptitude for teaching, bear a blameless character and who would be prepared to work for a mere living.
2. A letter of encouragement to be sent to the editor of *Indian Opinion* for publication.
3. Whenever he can spare a few moments, to write and send an article, be it ever so small, for publication in it.
4. Honorary or paid correspondents who would write Notes for it in English, Gujarati, Hindi, and Tamil.[90]

To my regret although I started the settlement at Phoenix, I could stay there only for brief periods. My original idea was to retire from practice, go and live on the settlement, earn my living by manual work there. But it was not to be.

With signs of plague reappearing in Johannesburg, I wrote in *Indian Opinion* on 16 January 1905:

> Once again the dark clouds are gathering. It will be to the great benefit of our people if they bear in mind the following rules; otherwise there would be immense harm. What is more, it might be used as an argument for enacting more severe laws against us:
>
> 1. No one should think that the government will harass the patient after removing him to the hospital.
> 2. The government should be immediately informed in case of a sudden attack of fever or asthma.
> 3. A doctor should be immediately consulted.
> 4. Everyone should stay where he is without becoming panicky.
> 5. Those who might have come in contact with a plague patient should not try to conceal the fact but should come forward to have their clothes etc. disinfected.
> 6. One should not, under any circumstances, have one's bedroom attached to the shop to save money.
> 7. One should not stock any goods for sale in one's house.
> 8. One should keep one's house scrupulously clean.
> 9. Every house or room should be well lighted and well ventilated.

10. One should sleep with the windows open.
11. The clothes worn by day as well as those used during the night should be kept clean.
12. The food taken should be light and simple.
13. Lavish dinners and feasts should be stopped.
14. Dry earth or ashes should be provided in latrines where buckets are used; and everyone should after easing himself cover the night soil thoroughly with these so that no flies sit thereon.
15. Lavatories and urinals should be kept clean.
16. The floors and other parts of the house should be washed clean with disinfecting fluid mixed in hot water.
17. No article from an infected place should be used elsewhere.
18. More than two persons should not sleep in a room of normal proportions.
19. One should not sleep in the kitchen, dining room or the larder.
20. Walls should be plastered with cement in order to keep out rats. Care should, most of all, should be taken to see that foodstuffs are kept beyond their reach.
21. Those who always work indoors should go out into the open air and walk a couple of miles daily for exercise.

Towards the end of March, the thought occurred to me: We make plans of how best to use our spare time; but whenever we get a few stray minutes of spare leisure we men and women—particularly women—allow them thoughtlessly to pass away. We go on cherishing dreams of the many things we would do if and when we have the time and yet we idle away the stray minutes which put together would make a whole day, just as stray shillings make a bank note. By making regular daily use of such minutes a lady succeeded in learning Italian. Another was able to collect an astonishingly large sum of money in a year by knitting for charity during such moments of leisure. And so I wrote in *Indian Opinion* to that effect.[91]

Himalayan India was shaken by an earthquake in such a way that the divine wrath will not be forgotten for years. Many an old historic monument, numerous villages, palatial buildings in large cities, the simple huts of the poor, and tented camps of the army were all devastated. Several families in Dharamsala, the Kangra Valley, Palanpur, and Mussoorie were wiped out. Subscriptions were opened in India and we did too, through *Indian Opinion*.[92]

Some time ago there was a rebellion in Russia and one of the chief participants was Maxim Gorky*. This man was brought up in extreme poverty. At first he was apprenticed to a shoemaker who discharged him. Afterwards he served as a soldier for some time. He then served under a lawyer and finally served as a hawker at a baker's. The very first book he wrote in 1892 was so excellent that he soon became famous. All this time he was educating himself through his own efforts. Thereafter he wrote many things, all of them with a single purpose, to stir up people against the tyrannies they were labouring under. He writes with such vehemence and bitterness that the authorities keep a stern eye on him. I wrote a short piece on Gorky in *Indian Opinion* on 1 July 1905.[93]

From cables received in South Africa a little later, it appears that the Czar of Russia had given effect to his promise to his people regarding the introduction of a constitution based on the elective principle. This constitution resembled very little the more democratic constitutions of modern times which give wider power to the people. It made imperative the assent of the Czar to whatever laws were passed by the elected National Council. Nevertheless, it cannot be denied that the new constitution was a step which would enable the people to make greater efforts in the future.[94]

Tolstoy was still writing with great energy. Though himself a Russian, he had written many strong and bitter things against Russia concerning the Russo–Japanese war. He addressed a very pungent and effective letter to the Czar in regard to the war. Selfish officers viewed him with bitterness but they and even the Czar feared and respected him. Such was the power of his goodness and godly living that millions of peasants were ever ready to carry out his wish no sooner than it was spoken.[95]

---

*Maxim Gorky (1868–1936), writer and political activist.

Abraham Lincoln can be said to be still alive for the changes he made in the American constitution are still in force. And Lincoln's name will be known as long as America endures.[96]

Around the same time my attention was drawn to a comment made by Dr Hutchinson on the salt tax in India. He said it was a shame that the British government levied it when Japan had abolished it. He called the salt tax 'a barbarous practice'. I noticed his important observations in *Indian Opinion* on 8 July 1905.[97]

On 22 June 1905, the world prepared to celebrate the birth centenary of Joseph Mazzini. I wrote a tribute to the remarkable Italian who was so broad-minded as to be regarded as the citizen of every country.[98] As Mazzini was under orders of banishment, he used to enter his country in disguise. Once when the police went to arrest him, he opened the door for them as if he were an usher and gave them the slip. There are very few instances in the world where a single man has brought about the uplift of his country by his strength of mind and his extreme devotion in his own lifetime.

Maintaining the family in India caused me to write to Revashankerbhai on 18 July 1905 to send Harilal to me in South Africa. The burden on me was so heavy that it was becoming difficult for me to meet the expenditure there and so I said, 'It is quite necessary to reduce to the utmost the expenditure that is being incurred there.'[99]

News came around this time that the Viceroy Lord Curzon was considering partitioning Bengal into two parts and merging one of them into Assam. Meetings were held in almost every village of Bengal with people of all communities participating in them. These were so impressive that reports reached us in far-off South Africa. It appears to have been suggested at these meetings that if the government did not take heed, Indian merchants should stop all trade with Great Britain. If the people really act accordingly there would be nothing surprising if our troubles came to a speedy end. 'But,' I asked in an article in *Indian Opinion*, on 19 August 1905 'will our people in Bengal maintain the requisite unity? Will the merchants suffer for the good of the country? If we can answer both the questions in the affirmative, India can be said to have truly woken up.'[100]

Some members of the British Association in England were, at this time, visiting South Africa. They were all scientists, and possessed great knowledge. When they were in Natal, the Hon'ble Mr Marshall Campbell* took them to his residence at Mount Edgecombe. Here these people were introduced to educated Kaffirs†. Addressing them, Mr Dube‡, their leader, made a very impressive speech. Mr Dube is a Negro of whom one should know. He has acquired through his own labours over 300 acres of land near Phoenix. There he imparts education to his brethren, teaching them various trades and crafts and preparing them for the battle of life. In the course of his eloquent speech, Mr Dube said that the contempt with which the Kaffirs were regarded was unjustified. The educated among them were better than the uneducated ones, for they worked more, and since they had higher standards of life, they offered more custom to the merchants. It was unfair to burden the Negroes with taxes; also, it was like cutting down the very branch one was sitting on. The Kaffirs understood and performed their duties better than the whites. They worked hard and without them the whites could not carry on for a moment. They made loyal subjects, and Natal was the land of their birth. For them there was no country other than

---

*Sir Marshall Campbell (1848–1917) was a pioneer of the sugar industry in the Colony of Natal, became a member of the Natal Legislative Council, later being appointed senator for Natal. In 1915, he received a knighthood for services to the country.

†A term used in the nineteenth and early twentieth century to denote 'native' Africans, it is now universally regarded as derogatory and offensive, in the same category if not worse than 'Sammy' for Indian South Africans. Gandhi uses 'Kaffir' in his writings of the early 1900s routinely. Though explicable in terms of early twentieth-century practice, including among Africans, it cannot but strike modern readers as jarring. Its use by Gandhi has led to his being accused of racist bias. Nelson Mandela is worth quoting here: 'All in all, Gandhi must be judged in the context of the time and the circumstances.' (*Mahatma Gandhi 125 Years*, ICCR, New Delhi, 1995.) Mandela however substitutes 'Kaffir' with 'Native Africans' in the quotes from Gandhi in his article. This editor cannot exercise such editorial privilege. He has retained the word wherever Gandhi has used it, knowing that Gandhi himself would want him to be judged not by the norms of a changing vocabulary but by his perspectives of the human condition.

‡John Langalibalele Dube (1871–1946), founder of the Ohlange Institute near Phoenix, of the newspaper *Ilanga Lase Natal* and of the South African Native National Congress.

South Africa; and to deprive them of their rights over lands, etc., was like banishing them from their home. Mr Dube's speech produced a very good impression on the whites, and he suggested to them that, if they sympathized with the Negroes, they might help him to start a smithy on his farm. The members of the British Association subscribed 60 pounds on the spot and presented the sum to him.[101]

I also noticed at this time that a considerable amount of enthusiasm had been evoked by the movement that was initiated some months earlier by Mr Tengo Jabavu, editor of *Imvo Zabantsundu*, with the object of creating an Inter-State Native College with the Lovedale Institute as its nucleus.[102] Both Mr Jabavu and Mr K. A. Hobart Houghton, organizing secretary of the movement, had been touring South Africa—their purpose being the threefold one of enlisting the sympathetic co-operation of the various South African governments, creating a healthy native opinion on the subject by means of careful explanation and illustration, and, perhaps, most important of all, the collection of funds to enable serious work to be commenced in the near future. It was proposed to develop the work to be undertaken by the new college on the same lines of industrial training as in the American Tuskegee Institute of Booker T. Washington. All this can do nothing but good, and it is not to be wondered that an awakening people, like the great native races of South Africa, are moved by something that has been described as being very much akin to religious fervour. To them undoubtedly the work must be sanctified and hallowed, for it opens up a means to advancement of thought and gives a great impetus to spiritual development. The enormous sum of 50,000 pounds is in contemplation of collection from the natives, apart altogether from subsidies from the various states and the different religious bodies interested. British Indians in South Africa have much to learn from this example of self-sacrifice. If the natives of South Africa, with all their financial disabilities and social disadvantages, are capable of putting forth this local effort, is it not incumbent, I asked.

I had promised Kastur that I would return home within a year.* The year had gone without any prospect of my return, so I decided to send for her and the children. On the boat bringing them to South Africa, Ramdas, my third son, broke his arm while playing with the ship's captain. The captain looked after him well and had him attended to by the ship's doctor. Ramdas landed with his hand in a sling. The doctor had advised that, as soon as we reached home, the wound should be dressed by a qualified doctor. But this was the time when I was full of faith in my experiments in earth and water treatment.

What was I to do with Ramdas? He was just eight years old. I asked him if he would mind my dressing his wound. With a smile he said he would not mind at all. It was not possible for him at that age to decide what the best thing for him was but he knew very well the distinction between quackery and proper medical treatment. And he knew my habit of home treatment and had faith enough to trust himself to me. In fear and trembling I undid the bandage, washed the wound, applied a clean earth poultice, and tied the arm up again. This sort of dressing went on daily for about a month until the wound was completely healed. There was no hitch, and the wound took no more time to heal than the ship's doctor had said it would under the usual treatment.

---

*In preparation for the family's return to South Africa, Gandhi wrote to his Johannesburg landlord to effect repairs in the house and, in view of the fall in the rents in the city, to reduce the rent as well. But, in the event, Gandhi rented a two-storey house with a garden in Johannesburg's upscale Troyeville. Though this home where Kastur, Manilal, Ramdas, Devadas, and Gandhi lived for about two years was fair-sized, modern and in an enviable location, life inside was drastically simple 'in the light of Ruskin's teaching'. There was a servant in the house, living 'as a member of the family', and 'the children used to help him in the work'. A municipal sweeper removed the night soil from the house but Gandhi and the family, rather than the servant, cleaned the toilet. Bread was not bought at the baker's. Unleavened wholemeal bread was baked at home according to Dr Kuhne's recipe, made from flour ground at home by two males, one of them invariably being Gandhi, working at a hand mill that Gandhi purchased for seven pounds.

Six

1906—A YEAR TO REMEMBER

*Great changes, I saw, were likely to take place in
South Africa during the coming years.*

I met Hermann Kallenbach* quite by accident. At our very first meeting he asked searching questions concerning matters of religion. He incidentally talked about Gautama Buddha's renunciation. I was startled at his love of luxury and extravagance. At that time, he was single and expending 1,200 rupees monthly on himself over and above house rent.

I had as many as four Indian clerks who were perhaps more like my sons than clerks. But even these were not enough or my work. It was impossible to do without typewriting which, among us, if at all, only I knew. I taught it to two of the clerks but they never came up to the mark because of their poor English.

But a permanent stenotypist was now added—Miss Schlesin†, introduced to me by Mr Kallenbach. She was about seventeen when she came to me. 'This girl has been entrusted to me by her mother,' he said. 'She is clever and honest but she is very mischievous and

---

*Hermann Kallenbach (1871–1945), a German architect practising in Johannesburg, met Gandhi in 1905 and became a trusted friend and associate, helped him found Tolstoy Farm on a 1,100-acre plot near Johannesburg that he purchased for Gandhi's project of self-reliant community, and lived among the families of satyagrahis. He taught the inmates there carpentry, gardening, and sandal-making which he himself learnt from a Trappist monastery. Differed in later life from Gandhi's support to Palestine and opposition to the formation of the post-WW II political state of Israel.

†Sonja Schlesin (1888–1956) of Russian–Jewish descent joined Gandhi's office in Johannesburg as a stenotypist. Making herself very useful to the Indian cause in South Africa, she was also involved in the production of *Indian Opinion*. After Gandhi's departure from South Africa, Schlesin became involved in school education.

impetuous. Perhaps she is even insolent. You keep her if you can manage her. I do not place her with you for mere pay.'[103]

Some of her idiosyncrasies were at times too much for Mr Kallenbach and me. Colour prejudice was foreign to her temperament. She would not hesitate even to the point of insulting a man and telling him to his face what she thought of him. Her impetuosity often landed me in difficulties. I have often signed without revision letters typed by her as I considered her English to be better than mine.[104] Miss Schlesin in her folly started smoking a cigarette in my presence. I slapped her and threw away the cigarette. For the first time she cried before me and wrote to me afterwards saying she would never do such a thing again and that she had recognized my love.[105]

Henry had been engaged to Millie Downs whom he had known from his days in London. Millie came to South Africa towards the end of 1905 and I told them they must get married, which they did and moved over to our home, becoming part of the family. She was to say of the house (and of me): 'The little house to which I was taken was devoid of any pretence of beauty or of the things that I had been accustomed to look upon as necessities. There were no carpets or rugs to cover the bare deal boards of the floor, no curtains to the windows, only some ugly yellow blinds to keep some suggestion of privacy. Of course, there was not a picture on the yellow-washed walls, and only furniture of the simplest was installed in the house.... I said to Mr Gandhi that I wanted some curtains, some floor-covering and a few other things to make the little house "home".'[106]

She soon began to teach my three sons, in simple English, reading and writing, arithmetic, composition, and elementary grammar. And a few key English words to Kastur as well.

A beautiful framed picture of Christ adorned the wall in front of my desk in my office. When Millie first noticed it, she said, 'How beautiful it is!' 'Yes,' I told her, 'I love to have it there. I see it each time I raise my eyes from my desk. It is indeed beautiful.'*

---

*Other pictures on Gandhi's office walls in Johannesburg included those of Annie Besant, Sir William Hunter, Justice Ranade, and of the Indian contingent in the Boer War.

On 20 January 1906, we lost Mansukhlal Harilal Nazar, who had been editing *Indian Opinion*.[107] It was in the dark days of 1896 that he landed in Durban, a perfect stranger. He wanted to live a quiet life but a patriot of his type was not able to sit still when he saw his countrymen needing the help of a guiding hand during those trying times. Mr Nazar placed the public cause before his own; his dream of leading a private life was never realized, and though people were never allowed to know it, for the cause of his countrymen, Mr Nazar has died a pauper. For days together he used to live away from Durban, in a secluded home in Sydenham, existing on nothing but a little milk and some biscuits.

Without him *Indian Opinion* would never have come into being. In the initial stages of its struggle, Mr Nazar took up almost the whole of its editorial burden and if it is known for is moderate policy and sound views, the fact is due, to a very large extent, to the part Mr Nazar played in connection with it.

Chhaganlal was responsible for the management of *Indian Opinion*. He used to send to me all letters to the editor that the journal received for publication. I used to approve all of them. But on 19 February, I decided to discontinue the practice setting out the rules that should govern the selection of letters for publication. These were:

1. We should as a rule publish all letters against us;
2. We should be chary of long harangues;
3. We should consider who the correspondent is. If we feel that his contribution must be accepted, it should be abridged, if lengthy;
4. We should take letters giving local news.[108]

The last arose from a matter of interest to the people of Dundee where an Indian barber, while giving an Indian merchant a shave, left off in the middle to attend to a European customer whereupon the Indian community decided to boycott the barber.

Harilal and Gokuldas having gone to India, I asked Kastur and the children to move to Phoenix and be with Chhaganlal and Maganlal and their families in the house on the settlement that had been set apart for us and was known there as 'the big house'. She had the company of Kashi, Chhaganlal's wife, and Santok, Maganlal's wife, and the children, Manilal, Ramdas, and Devadas had besides each other, Chhaganlal's son Prabhudas, a year and a half younger than Devadas, to play with. I spent some days with the family after it had moved to Phoenix. The entire group would gather in our house in the evenings when Kashi would sing. This started the tradition of a daily evening prayer at home. I gathered that Kastur and these two ladies would spend hours in home chat.[109]

The rising in revolt, in March 1906, of the Kaffirs of Natal against the poll tax and the killing of Sub-Inspector Hunt and Trooper Armstrong by them were events the effects of which would not be forgotten for many years. Martial law was declared in Natal and twelve Kaffirs were condemned to death and blown up at the mouth of a cannon. Kaffirs from neighbouring areas and their chiefs were invited to witness the execution on 29 March. Great changes, I saw, were likely to take place in South Africa during the coming years.[110]

As this revolt of the Zulu and the response to it were taking form, I got a letter from my brother Lakshmidas. I did not know what to say in reply to it. I could see that he was prejudiced. On 27 May, I wrote a reply to him in which I said:

> I have no idea of distancing myself from you.
> I claim nothing there.
> I do not claim anything as mine.
> All that I have is being utilized for public purposes.
> It is available to relations who devote themselves to public work.
> I could have satisfied your desire for money if I had not dedicated my all for public use.[111]

And I assured him that in case he passed on before me, I would cheerfully assume the burden of supporting the family but at the same time said that I was not in a position to send him the money he desired. I was, I said, engaged in activities essential to life. If I have to face death while thus engaged, I said I would face it with equanimity. I am, I said a stranger to fear.

My brother had mentioned Harilal's wanting to marry. It is well, I said, if Harilal is married; it is also well if he is not. For the present, at any rate, I have ceased to think of him as a son.* I like those who are pure of heart. Young Kalyandas[112], Jagmohandas's son, is like Prahlad in spirit. He is therefore dearer to me than one who is a son because so born.

The rebellion, meanwhile, instead of being quelled, gathered strength. The small party of soldiers that went on the trail of Bambata, the Kaffir chief, was encircled and defeated, some of them killed. The dead included those who had executed the twelve Kaffirs. Such is the law of God. The executioners met their death within two days. What was our duty during those calamitous times?† It was not for us to say whether the revolt of the Kaffirs was justified or not. We were in Natal by virtue of British power. It was our duty to render whatever help we could.[113]

A Stretcher Bearer Corps was formed in July, comprising twenty Indians to help in the operation against the natives. Of these six were Mohammedans, fourteen Hindus. Geographically, five belonged to the Bombay Presidency, twelve to the Presidency of Madras, two to the Punjab, one to the Presidency of Bengal. According to status, thirteen of the men had been under indenture in Natal and were now working in the capacity of gardeners, domestic servants, etc., two were engine drivers, one a goldsmith, three were agents and bookkeepers and one—myself—a barrister.[114] We had to march with the whole of our kit on and as the experience was new to most of us and as the marching was mostly uphill, it was severely felt by some. All were

---

*Gulab alias Chanchal, seventeen, was the daughter of Gandhi's lawyer friend in Rajkot, Haridas Vakhatchand Vora. Gandhi knew and was fond of Gulab but he did not warm to the idea of Harilal and Gulab getting married at so young an age. Lakshmidas, as the elder uncle, went ahead with arrangements and the wedding took place on 2 May 1906. Gandhi did not know this detail when he wrote his reply.

†The South African leader John Dube, on his part, expressed the view (during the Zulu Rebellion) that while the Zulus had serious grievances, 'at a time like this we should all refrain from discussing them, and assist the government to suppress the rebellion'. Quoted from Andre Odendaal, Vukani Bantu, 1984, p. 70, in E. S. Reddy, *Gandhiji: Vision of a Free South Africa*, New Delhi: Sanchar, 1995, p. 21.

mounted men whom we had to follow. Men in the rear were to guard us. We were all unarmed. As the troops galloped away in front us, we were quickly out-distanced. However we marched on, trying, as far as possible, to overtake the column, but it was a hopeless task. There was no prospect before us except of running after the troops or of being assegaied by the rebels. The Corps was disbanded after six weeks of service and I could confidently assert that the little band was capable of carrying out any work entrusted to it.

We were to dress the wounds on the backs of several natives who had received lashes.[115] We found that the wounded Zulus would have been left uncared for unless we had attended to them. No European would help to dress their wounds. We had to cleanse the wounds of several Zulus which had not been attended to for as many as five or six days and were therefore stinking horribly. We liked the work. The Zulus could not talk to us but from their gestures and the expression of their eyes they seemed to feel as if God had sent us to their succour.[116]

I shall never forget the lacerated backs of Zulus who had received stripes and were brought to us for nursing because no white nurse was prepared to look after them. It is reasonable to suggest that but for our services some of them would have died. I cite this experience not to justify my participation however indirect it was. I cite it to show that I came through that experience with greater non-violence and with richer love for the great Zulu race. And I had an insight into what war by white men against coloured races meant.[117] And yet those who perpetrated these cruelties called themselves Christians. This was no war but a manhunt.

Marching with or without the wounded, I often fell into deep thought. I pondered over brahmacharya and its implications and my convictions took deep root. What, I asked myself, should be my relation with my wife? Did my faithfulness consist in making my wife the instrument of my lust? So long as I was the slave of lust my faithfulness was worth nothing. To be fair to my wife, I must say she was never the temptress. I could not live both after the flesh and the spirit. Even after my conscience had been roused in the matter I failed twice. I failed because the motive that actuated the effort was none of the highest. My main object was to escape having more children. On the present occasion, for instance, I should not have been able to throw myself into the fray had my wife been expecting a baby.[118]

Kastur, away from me in Phoenix, worried for me. Chhaganlal would take time from his work in the press to go to her and give her the latest news, how far the Zulu rebels had reached and what they had done. Phoenix being in a Zulu area, it could have been attacked by Zulus there and destroyed. But that never happened.[119]

When, with the rebellion crushed, the Corps was disbanded and I went to Phoenix. I consulted Kastur about my resolve. She raised no objection. And I broached the subject with Chhaganlal, Maganlal, West, and others as well.[120] That done, I at once returned to Johannesburg, eager for the vow and even more for action. A *Gazette Extraordinary* of the Transvaal government had been issued at the instance of a young official in the Asiatic Department called Lionel Curtis. This contained a draft law written by Curtis for amending existing laws and proposing new legislation. I was staying at Kallenbach's house in Orchards but took a copy of this *Gazette* to a hill near the house to study the draft. It required every Indian who was eight or older, male or female, to obtain a new certificate of registration, providing fingerprints and other marks of identification. Failure to comply would invite a fine, imprisonment, and/or deportation. I saw hatred of Indians in the proposed law and explained its provisions the next day to a few leading Indians who were as shocked as I.[121]

The *Transvaal Government Gazette Extraordinary* unsettled the Indian mind as no other measure in South Africa had ever done before. It threatened to invade the sanctity of home life. It required the holder of every permit of registration certificate to appear before the Registrar of Asiatics and satisfy that official that he is lawful holder. Women and children do not possess any documents. Will they, I asked, be banished from the colony and torn from their husbands or parents?[122]

A correspondent asked, 'What is the difference between Russian rule and British rule a la Transvaal?' I answered: 'In Russia, when it suits the authorities, they do not hesitate to murder people openly and directly. In the Transvaal because they wish to do away with Indians but cannot do so openly and honestly, instead of resorting to the direct way of murdering them or banishing them from the colony, they intend to kill them by inches.'[123]

What then were we to do? If the government enforces the ordinance, I said, Indians will not abide with it; they will not (re-) register themselves, nor will they pay the fines; they will rather go to gaol.[124] A mass meeting was held in Johannesburg on 11 September at which I said: 'It will not do to be hasty, impatient or angry. But God will come to our help if we calmly think out and carry out in time measures of resistance....'[125]

At a meeting held in Empire Theatre, Hajee Habib proposed that we take a solemn oath to oppose the ordinance. I supported the suggestion but cautioned the gathering of about 3,000 that if we took the pledge and offered resistance we might have to endure every hardship that we can imagine; we might have to go to gaol where we may be insulted, go hungry and suffer extreme heat or cold, have hard labour imposed on us, be flogged by rude warders, be fined and have our property attached and held up to auction. Some of us might fall ill and even die. But so long as there is even a handful of men true to their pledge, I said, there can only be one end to the struggle and that is victory.

I added a word about my personal responsibility. Even if everyone else flinched leaving me alone to face the music, I said, I am confident that I would never violate my pledge.

Five resolutions were passed, the fourth saying:

> Should the Legislative Council, the local and Imperial governments reject the humble prayer of the Indian community against the Asiatic Ordinance, every Indian present at this meeting solemnly and sincerely resolves that, rather than submit to thus tyrannical law, and abide by its un-British provisions, he will prefer to go to gaol, and will

continue to do so until it pleases His Majesty the King-Emperor to grant relief.

Even as Mr Hajee Habib rose to move this fourth resolution, the audience greeted him with cheers. When Mr Hajee Ojer Ally stood up to second the resolution, the whole theatre resounded with prolonged cheers which took some time to subside.

There arose later that September the case of Punia who was arrested at Volksrust for being without a permit though in the company of her husband, Mangare. The reason given by the authorities was that '...women are being taken in as wives who were nothing of the kind but often of indifferent character'. This was a wicked libel on Indian womanhood. I challenged the immigration official who is said to have given this reason to publish the name of even one such woman.[126] It is a thousand times better, I wrote in *Indian Opinion*, for a man to suffer imprisonment than to suffer such a law.[127]

After deleting the clause affecting women, the Legislative Council passed the ordinance practically as it was first drafted. The royal assent to measures adopted by it was not a mere formality. I submitted to the community that a deputation could go to England and boldly inform the Secretary of State for India and the Secretary of State for the Colonies about the resolve of the community. The greatest difficulty however was encountered in selecting the personnel of the deputation. I flatly declined to go alone, but who would go with me? There was no Hindu–Muslim problem in South Africa but my advice was that there must be a Mussalman gentleman going with me and that the personnel should be limited to two. But the Hindus at once said that as I represented the Indian community as a whole, there should be a representative of Hindu interests. Some even said there should be one Konkani Musalman, one Memon, one Patidar, one Anavala and so on.[128]

At last all understood the position and Haji Ojer Ally and I comprised a two-member delegation to go to England to meet Lord Elgin, the Secretary of State for Colonies and urge that the ordinance not be given royal assent. We sailed from Cape Town by the SS *Armadale Castle*. Mr Ally was feeling exhausted owing to overwork and feeling ill and restless. He had rheumatism. Pain started on the train from Johannesburg to Cape Town. I pressed and massaged his joints and did whatever I could. But that gave no lasting relief. Mr Ally took the food he had brought with him and also some coffee. I went to the saloon for meals and took boiled potato and peas with bread. I then did my writing. Mr Ally went to bed at ten. I retired at midnight after finishing my writing, Mr Ally spent a restless night. When he got up, he had a severe pain and a slight fever and bronchitis.

Seven

IN LONDON WITH MR H. O. ALLY AND MUCH HOPE

All we claim is fair and honourable treatment for British Indians residing in the Transvaal.

The steamer was as big as a small town, with about a thousand persons on board. But there was no noise, no disorder. On board the steamer, for the first two days, Mr Ally felt obliged to stay in bed. During those two days he took the pills he had brought with him and got me to rub in soap liniment. But the pain did not stop altogether. I then recommended Dr Kuhne's treatment. He then took hot and cold baths and did without the morning meal. As a result he felt better. He was hungry at 1 p.m. and constipation and indigestion did not trouble him. He did not even smoke till 1 p.m. At one he would take fish and potatoes, pudding and coffee and ginger ale. He had a cup of tea at four in the afternoon. And at 6.30 p.m., fish and green vegetables, ginger ale, pudding, and coffee. If the reader is curious to know what I ate, I may say that for three days I had three meals a day. But finding these unnecessary I began taking milk, bread, soda water or ginger ale, stewed fruit and cream at 1 p.m., cocoa at 4, potatoes, boiled vegetables, stewed fruit and soda water or ginger ale at 6.30 in the evening. I did not eat bread, raw fruits and nuts for the only reason that a loose molar had been hurting me. I felt quite satisfied with this diet and could do a lot of work. The main reason for this is that the stomach had rest till 1 p.m. Food on an empty stomach never does harm.

I sent to my son, Ramdas, a picture postcard* showing the

---

*This has to be the first letter that Gandhi addressed to his third son. Sent from a

12,973-tonne United Castle Line steamer[129] with a horse power of 12,500 cruising the high seas, with just a line to say that I will be expecting letters from him, from home. Signing off, as Mohandas, I addressed it:

Ramdas Gandhi
Indian Opinion
Phoenix
Natal

Mr Ally read Justice Ameer Ali's *The Spirit of Islam*, and Washington Irving's *Mahomet and His Successors*. I studied Tamil and read Forbes's *Rasamala Or A History of Gujarat*. We had very little contact with other passengers. Other passengers spent the day in much merriment. Sports went on—deck-cricket, ring tennis, egg-and-spoon race etc., and subscriptions were collected for awarding prizes and we had to part with a guinea each. The band played twice a day and at night the passengers danced.

When I saw all this I asked myself: Why is it that the English rule? I find that the Englishman is not just 'full five cubits tall, a host in himself, a match for five hundred', but capable in every other way. When he chooses to enjoy wealth and power, he excels in doing it and he makes the best of poverty, too. He alone knows how to give orders and knows, too, how to take them. In his behaviour he is great with the great and small with the small. He knows how to earn money and how to spend it. He knows how to converse and move in company. He lives in the knowledge that his happiness depends on the happiness of others. The Englishman I observed during the war seems to be an altogether different person now. Then he did all his work himself, trekked over long distances, and felt happy with dry bread. Here on board the ship he does not do any work. He presses a button and an attendant stands before him. He must have nice dishes of all kinds to eat. Every day he puts on a new dress.

---

port en route some day before 20 October 1906, it bears a clear Pietermaritzburg postal stamp dated 2 November.

All this becomes him but he does not lose his balance. Like the sea, he can contain all within himself.

Why indeed should such a people not rule?

The ship reached Southampton on 20 October 1906 and we were met by Albert West and his sister, Ada. I sent a cable to Johannesburg about our arrival, as Mr Ally had promised his wife that we would.[130] To a representative of *The Tribune* who interviewed me on board the ship about the purpose of the deputation, I said: 'All we claim is fair and honourable treatment for British Indians residing in the Transvaal.'

At Waterloo station later the same day, immediately I got on to the platform, J. H. Polak, the brilliant father of Henry Polak, met us.[131] He introduced us to a representative of *The Morning Leader* who interviewed me, I said:

> The only thing the Boers did was to deprive British Indians of Burgher rights and land ownership and to pass the Law 3 of 1885 under which those desiring to settle as traders in the country had to be registered and pay a fee of 3 pounds. Under the British system we are still debarred from the privilege except in locations, the idea being to reproduce the system of Jewish ghettos. But other disabilities have been added. There are, for example, difficulties about travelling in trams. In Johannesburg British Indians are only allowed to travel in trailer cars. In Pretoria they are not allowed to travel in trams at all. Under the Law 3 of 1885 passed by the Boers, Indians settling in the country for purposes of trade had to register themselves. But the Legislative Council has now carried an amending law—the Asiatic Law Amending Ordinance—which is worse than the law it seeks to amend. By virtue of that ordinance, not only traders but every Indian now resident in the Transvaal must be registered and carry a pass in spite of the fact that they are already in possession of permits which authorize them to reside there and while they also hold registration certificates for which they have each paid 3 pounds.

Ritch had arranged for us to stay at India House and so we went there. We ate our meal and went forthwith for the meeting of the

London Indian Society where we had the good fortune of paying our respects to the Grand Old Man, Dadabhai Naoroji. And the same day, we set to work. I met Pandit Shyamji Krishna Varma that night at India House which he has founded at his own cost. Our conversation went on till 1 in the morning.

We were very well looked after there but as India House is rather remote, we were obliged to move to Cecil Hotel at great expense.[132] For reasons of health Mr Ally slept in the home of my old friend, Dr Josiah Oldfield.

The Johannesburg correspondent of *The Times* sent a cablegram in connection with our deputation which the paper carried on 22 October. He said in it: 'The present ordinance provides for the complete registration of all Asiatics in such a way that personation, in which the Asiatic is a past master, would be made impossible.' Hajee Ojer Ally and I sent a jointly signed letter to the editor of the newspaper the same day denying that there had been any personation and stating emphatically that the existing certificates held by British Indians entirely prevent personation.[133]

We were utilizing every single minute of our time in London. The sending of a large number of circulars etc., could not be done single-handed and we sorely needed outside help. Fortunately for us, we had many volunteer helpers. Many an Indian youth in England for study surrounded us and some of them helped us day and night without any hope of reward or fame. But there was an English friend named Symonds who cast all these into the shade. I first met him in South Africa. He had been in India. He was perfectly free from any race or colour prejudice. He believed that the truth is always with the minority. He was an expert stenographer. He happened to be in England when we were there. The noble Englishman found us out. 'I will work as a servant if you like,' he said, 'and if you need a stenographer, you know you scarcely come across the like of me.' This Englishman toiled for us day and night without any payment.

I spent a day with J. H. Polak and wrote to A. H. Gool, the son of Hamid Gool of Cape Town, asking him to call at the hotel between 9 and 9.30 a.m. any morning. I explained to him that my arrangements did not allow of my paying friendly calls at present. The day, I told him, was occupied by paying visits in the line of the deputation's work and I was never sure when I would be in.[134] Office copies of all such typewritten letters were kept by me.

At the Polak home, I met Henry's unmarried sisters and as I wrote to him, if I was unmarried, or young or believed in mixed marriages, he—Henry—knows what I would have done! Henry's mother though suffering from severe indigestion, welcomed me very warmly. I mildly proposed an extended Jewish fast but I am afraid the proposal did not wash. I also pushed in the claim for earth bandages and she said she was open to suggestions. Henry's father prepared the soup for which he thought out all the ingredients etc. I was unable to see Millie Polak's sister as I had more work than I had bargained for and had not a moment to spare for friendly calls.[135]

Yuk Lin Lew, the Chinese consul general in the Transvaal and L. M. James, specially deputed by the Chinese community in the Transvaal, had sailed with us on the same boat to present a petition on their behalf to the Chinese Ambassador in Britain. Their deputation had also been occasioned by the same ordinance, from the perspective of the Chinese in the Transvaal. I drafted for them, on board the steamer, the draft for a representation as from the Chinese Ambassador to His Majesty's Foreign Office. To discuss relevant matters I had fixed up a lunch appointment with James but he failed to turn up and I was sorry he did not. So I wrote to him to suggest we meet up some other time.[136] I took the opportunity to return to him a handkerchief that he had kindly lent me.

By this time, Mr Ally had to be admitted to St Margaret's Hospital in Bromley for his rheumatism. I called on him on 25 October and found him chatting away hilariously and so was very much pained to hear the next day—26 October—that he had passed a very bad night. I wrote to him to say I am superstitious enough to say it was because of the cigar he smokes. Convalescence can be retarded by even one deadly puff of nicotine. I beseeched him to stay completely away from cigars though, I said, he could have as much as he liked of the hubble-bubble. I asked him to pardon me if I was mistaken.

'All I want,' I wrote to him, 'is to find you hale and hearty.'[137] And I requested Dr Josiah Oldfield to visit him in hospital every single day, expense being no consideration.[138]

Two things were being widely discussed in England at the time. One was the decision of soap manufacturers, like their American opposite numbers, to combine and resolve to raise the price of soap. Dealers in soap and the public naturally did not relish the decision. But they did not approach the government for help; neither did they appeal to manufacturers; they resorted to direct action. They notified the manufacturers that they would not buy their soap. The result was that Lever Brothers of Sunlight Soap fame restored sixteen ounces of soap (from fifteen) for the cake costing one pound.

The second is the movement in England for women's right to vote, which the government was unwilling to concede. The women sent petitions, wrote letters, delivered speeches. They went to the House of Commons and demanded the right to vote. They caused some damage also for which they were prosecuted and sentenced to furnish a security of 5 pounds each. On their refusing to do so they were sentenced to imprisonment. Some persons regarded these women as insane; the police used force against them; the magistrate looked upon them with a stern eye. They are bound to succeed and gain the franchise. If even women display such courage, will the Transvaal Indians fail in their duty and be afraid of gaol? Or will they regard the gaol a palace and readily go there? When that time comes India's bonds will snap of themselves.[139]

In the midst of all this I had to write to Dr Oldfield about my own sorrows. I told him that when I was in Bombay I lost my sense of smell and as my doctor put it I was suffering from chronic ozaena. I have chronic catarrh. I was not sure whether he had made a specialization of throat diseases and so I requested him, if necessary, to put me on to a specialist. When I was carrying on a fruit-and-nuts experiment I had damaged two molars. Thinking, while on board, that I was going to lose one of them, I tried hard to pull one out but did not succeed. So I asked Dr Oldfield if he would see those or give me the name of a dentist and if so, please a reliable one.

And, finally, friends though we were I urged him to attend to these complaints professionally. I knew that whatever he received went to a humanitarian purpose.[140]

From Johannesburg, Mr Kallenbach wrote to me and replying to him on 2 November, I said: 'I am working under greater pressure than in Johannesburg. Except for one night I have not gone to bed before one o'clock. At times I have sat up till 3.30 in the morning—and I do not know when I shall retire tonight. It is now 10.15. I shall look forward to your letters every week. If I don't write again from here, you will know why.'[141]

Visitors came by unexpectedly to the hotel. I did not know all of them. One such was a Mrs Reide. She seemed to be very ill. I was unable to follow all she said and as she appeared very nervous, I did not put any question to her. She gave the name of Albert Cartwright, later editor of *The Transvaal Leader*. So I wrote to him saying this lady needed some assistance.[142]

Tanzi, a waiter in our hotel, The Cecil, had been suffering for three months from rheumatism in the left hand. I sent him bearing a letter[143] from me to Dr Oldfield, urging the doctor to charge him the poor fee, letting me know of it. Mr Ally, meanwhile, much recovered from his rheumatism, came back to the hotel.

Lord Elgin, the Secretary of State for the Colonies, appointed Thursday, 8 November, 3 p.m. to receive the Transvaal Indian Deputation at the Colonial Office. I then drew up the representation to be given to Lord Elgin. This gave the background to the deputation, described the members thereof, gave a profile of the population of British Indians in the Transvaal, the Law 3 of 1885, then the situation under the British, a comparison of the Law 3 of 1885 and the new ordinance, and suggested that the least that is due to the Indian community is the appointment of a strong and impartial commission to investigate the allegations as to the unauthorized entry of British Indians into the Transvaal.

The deputation was led by Sir Lepel Griffin and included among others Sir Mancherji Bhownaggree and Dadabhai Naoroji apart from the two of us. Lord Elgin heard us with attention, expressed his sympathy, referred to his own difficulties and yet promised to do for us all he could.[144] In addition to the representation we presented to him a memorial which ended with these two lines: 'We have been asking all these years for bread but we have received stones in the shape of this ordinance. We have therefore every reason to hope that Your Lordship will not countenance the legislation above described.'

Lord Elgin began by saying, 'My sentiments would all be in favour of doing anything I could in the interests of British Indians.' Sir Lepel then said, 'Under this ordinance every single Indian in the Transvaal, whether an adult male, whether a woman or whether a child, and even babes in arms will be obliged to be registered under such conditions as ordinarily apply only to convicts in a civilized country. And evasion or ignorance or even forgetfulness on this point is punished by crushing fines, by imprisonment with hard labour, expulsion and by ruin. You, my lord, who have been Viceroy of India, and whose sympathy is with the country must know that legislation of this sort is unheard of under the British flag.' He said, 'Those who have seen India will never tolerate the refuse of Europe that has collected in the Transvaal tyrannising the Indians there.'[145] And he concluded with, 'My lord, we ask you to propose the vetoing of this ordinance.' And he said graphically, 'The toad under the harrow (alone) knows where and whether he is hurt.'[146]

I said that under the ordinance we shall be branded as criminals. The least that is due to the British Indian community is to appoint a commission.... It is a time-honoured British custom that whenever an important principle is involved, a commission is appointed before a step is taken.

Mr Ally, his voice choking with emotion, said, 'We have not asked for and we do not now ask for political rights. We are content that the white man should be predominant in the Transvaal; but we do feel that we are entitled to all the other ordinary rights that a British subject should enjoy.'

Mr Dadabhai Naoroji said the British government would stand disgraced if the oppression of Indians continued.[147]

Lord Elgin said he did not regard the demand for a commission unreasonable. The matter deserved consideration he said and would respond after giving it sufficient thought.

It was said that such a strong deputation had never before waited upon Lord Elgin.

Mr Morley, Secretary of State for India, met us on 22 November. Mr Dadabhai Naoroji, Sir Mancherji, and Sir Henry Cotton were among others who joined us. 'It is not merely prejudice of colour,' Mr Morley said, 'it is not a prejudice of racial inferiority because that would be absurd when there are as we know Indians in the Transvaal pursuing professions and so forth who are not only not inferior but greatly superior in many of the elements that make a civilized being to many of those who are not excluded from the Transvaal.... Nobody occupying my position could do anything less than promise you not only the sympathy...but as much support as I find myself able to give....'

On the subject of a commission, Mr Morley said '...a serious difficulty in the way is that in May next the Transvaal will be under responsible government. Now it would be a serious matter if a conflict arises between the new government and the commission's recommendations.'

Mr Ally and I met Winston Churchill, Under Secretary of State for the Colonies at the Colonial Office, Downing Street, on 27 November at 12 noon. He spoke nicely. He asked both of us whether we were not afraid of responsible government in case the ordinance was refused assent. What if a worse Act were to be passed by the new government? We replied that we could not imagine an Act worse than the present ordinance and that we had asked for refusal of assent leaving the future to take care of itself. He then asked us to send him a brief note covering, say, a foolscap sheet of all we had to say on the question as a whole. He would read it and let us know. Mr Ally then reminded him that he was the same person who had received him and had been present at the Point to receive him on his return from the war. And it was with the same Mr Churchill he now pleaded for redress on behalf of the Indian community. Mr Churchill smiled, patted Mr Ally on the back and said he would do all he could. This answer added to our hopes.[148]

I had brought on this journey a photograph, one of Kastur and our sons. When a lady asked me for a photograph of my family, I sent it to her saying: 'I send you the photograph I promised. To Mrs Gandhi's right is the only son of my widowed sister.'*

On 29 November, Mr Ally and I hosted all those who had helped us to a farewell breakfast in the banqueting room of Hotel Cecil. A hundred covers were laid. Sir Mancherji was among those who attended. Mr Dadabhai Naoroji could not as he was at that very time leaving England for India to preside over the forthcoming session of the Indian National Congress. It was my misfortune that I was therefore also unable to pay him my respects at the station.[149] I thanked Sir Mancherji for having helped and counselled us in the House of Commons and outside the House as to how we should go to work.[150] Speaking at the occasion I said our difficulties—whether the ordinance be passed or not—had only just commenced and expressed the hope that the support of our friends in London will be maintained.

---

*In a letter to Mrs Freeth dated 14 November 1906:

Dear Mrs Freeth,

I am exceedingly sorry that I shall not be able to be with you on Sunday evening. If you are free some other evening next week I should like to accept it provisionally.

    I send you the photograph I promised. To Mrs Gandhi's right is the only son of my widowed sister.

Yours sincerely...

CWMG (PD 1999), Vol. 6, p. 86.

Eight

BACK TO REALITY

The whole white population of the Transvaal is of one mind in the matter—Smuts

We left Waterloo station on 1 December. Sir Mancherji was among those who saw us off. We sailed out on SS *Briton*. When we reached Madeira, two cables were received, one from London and the other from Johannesburg. Both said the ordinance had been refused assent by Lord Elgin. This was more than we had hoped for.

When we reached Cape Town, we had as many as thirty messages of greetings from Durban in addition to a few from Mafeking. As it was difficult to write to all of them individually, I acknowledged them through the columns of *Indian Opinion* saying it was God who had to be thanked, the delegates having only done their duty.[151]

Replying to a welcome address in Durban on 1 January 1907 I said: 'We should not be elated by our success. Our struggle has only just begun. Now it is up to us to retain the victory. We have to explain things to the politicians here.'[152]

Returning to the columns of *Indian Opinion* with comments on matters of general interest, I devoted a paragraph in the issue of 5 January to the subject of smoking. Quoting an address to schoolboys in Liverpool by Major General Baden-Powell of Mafeking, I wrote '…many of the world's best men were non-smokers—Bassett the football player, Grace the cricketer, Henlane the great rower, Weston the walking champion, Tej the golf-star, Taylor the great hunter, Celloo the famous hiker, are all of them, non-smokers. When Baden-Powell's stock of tobacco ran out, the soldiers at Mafeking addicted to tobacco became absolutely useless, for they were helpless if they could not smoke. Thus smoking makes of man a slave.'*

Aspects of the working of *Indian Opinion* came to my notice. Many subscribers wrote saying they did not get it regularly. Another wrote saying he got two copies, one wrapped inside the other. As he returned the second one intended for someone else with the stamp on it un-defaced, I sent it to Chhaganlal asking him to reuse it.[153] I could see that packing the copies and wrapping them was being done carelessly.

My second son Manilal was studying in Phoenix under Chhaganlal's guidance. I asked Chhaganlal to let me know what Manilal was reading and if that was enough.[154] Manilal asked for a Sanskrit book which I sent without quite knowing what he proposed to do with it. He was also doing some work in the *Indian Opinion* press.

My occasional comments in *Indian Opinion* on general themes included, on 2 February, a piece that I titled 'Nausea'. To some, I wrote, the sight of blood or pus is nauseating, to others the smell of kerosene. Similarly an Englishman is averse to certain things. Once an Indian and some Europeans were at dinner table. During the meal the Indian started belching. An English lady at the table almost fainted and could not eat at all that day. It is necessary for us to show consideration for the feelings of others. With that end in view I listed some 'Don'ts' in that issue:

1. Avoid as far as possible, blowing your nose or spitting on swept or paved walks in front of others. On hygienic grounds also this rule is worth adopting. Doctors say that sometimes serious diseases are caused by contact with the nasal and oral discharge of another, Dr Murison has said that we often spread tuberculosis through our habit of spitting anywhere.
2. One should not belch, hiccup, break wind or scratch oneself in the presence of others. By practice one can learn to check one's instinct to do any of these things.

---

*The comment is likely to have been triggered by Gandhi's thoughts in the weeks preceding on H. O. Ally's smoking habit. The novelist Keshava Guha points out that 'Tej' seems to be a misprint, while Celloo remains unidentified. *CWMG*, Vol. 6, p. 270.

3. If you want to cough, one should do so holding a handkerchief against the mouth. If one's spittle gets blown on to others, it annoys them and if one has any disease, the spittle carries it to them.[155]

The election to the new Parliament ended with results that nobody had foreseen. The Dutch won a victory leaving all the other parties well behind. This means that in political affairs the Dutch have won back what they had lost in the war. General Botha is likely to be the prime minister. That is to say he will be as good as President. One may hope the Dutch will do the Indian community some measure of justice.[156]

In just two days in March the new Transvaal Parliament passed the ordinance exactly as it stood in September last. On the 20th the ordinance was introduced in the Assembly and the same day within two hours it went through all the three readings and was immediately sent to the Legislative Council where, at the instance of Mr Martin, it was postponed to the 22nd so that members would have time to study it. But this was merely a pretence. How were the members to digest it in one night? The Legislative Council passed it in on the 22nd.[157]

No one ever dreamt that the bill would be passed in this manner.

Speaking on the bill, Mr Smuts, the Colonial Secretary said the whole white population of the Transvaal is of one mind in the matter. Indians, he said, come in large numbers and should be stopped. The British Indian Association in the Transvaal sent cables to the Secretary of State for the Colonies Lord Elgin and to the Secretary of State for India, Mr Morley to say that memorials will be presented to them and urging that a decision on the royal assent to the enactment be withheld until then.

A mass meeting was held at Gaiety Theatre on 29 March 1907 at which a resolution was passed that said that since the government argues that it cannot have an effective check (on illegal immigration) with the existing permits, we will agree to take out permits in a form acceptable to us and without the compulsion of law.[158] We proposed that they give up the idea of passing the law and we voluntarily take out fresh permits and they withdraw the law. I argued at the meeting that anything voluntarily agreed by us cannot be regarded as humiliation. The ultimate remedy, I said, was of course was gaol-going.

A deputation travelled on 4 April from Johannesburg to Pretoria to wait upon Mr Smuts and place before him the resolution passed at the mass meeting. Mr Smuts listened carefully to us for more than three-quarters of an hour. He said that he had heard some things for the first time and these he said he would inquire into and send us a written reply. But he said this should not be interpreted to mean that they would accept the resolution proposing voluntary registration in return for a withdrawal of the law.[159] Mr Smuts's reply said, 'I regret to have to say that the suggestion made by the deputation about fresh registration cannot be accepted.' It added: 'I am sorry to find that in your meeting and speeches people have been advised to disobey the law by not registering themselves. In your own interests, I expect you will not advocate a course of action that will make it impossible for us to grant special concessions to your community.'[160]

'Now,' I asked the community through the columns of *Indian Opinion*, 'what is to be done?'[161] The association, reflecting on Mr Smuts's reply, urged the government to give the Indians' proposal a trial before the law is enforced.

Harilal, now married, came with his wife, Chanchal, to South Africa in April. While he stayed with me in Johannesburg, she went on to Phoenix to be with the larger family there. He spent time with me daily in my office where Polak, too, worked. I taught him for an hour a day and urged him to read newspapers even if for a few minutes every day. If he came across a word he did not understand he should I said turn immediately to the dictionary or to me or to Mr Polak.[162]

Household concerns over the Phoenix establishment were, meanwhile, causing me intense dissatisfaction.[163] Seeing the monthly accounts I found they seemed to have spent money lavishly, though there was very little in the detail that I could object to. A piano had been procured without a debit to me and so I increased the amount expended by another 10 pounds.

My nephew Gokuldas, I understood had been betrothed with 2,000 rupees being paid in order to bring it about. Was it over jewellery? I had but meagre details and so I asked Chhaganlal about it.

My brother sent me an angry letter in April 1907 in which he reminded me of my duties, mainly financial, to my family, by which he meant the sons of Karamchand Gandhi and their progeny. I had to send him an answer with the utmost calmness. 'I fail to understand,' I wrote to him, 'what you mean by the word "family". To me the family includes not only the two brothers but the sister as well. It also includes our cousins. Indeed, if I could say so without arrogance, I would say that my family comprises all living beings: the only difference being that those who are more dependent on me because of blood relationship or other circumstances get more help from me.'[164]

I assured him that if by any chance he was to die before me, I would serve as 'an insurance policy' for his wife and children. But as to his asking me for 100 rupees a month I told him I had neither the means at present nor saw the need for it. And I also told him that I ran the Phoenix press on borrowed money and that I may have to go to gaol in the course of the struggle here against the new ordinance in which case I may become poorer still.

He had mentioned Harilal's situation. I said if Harilal and Gokuldas had gone astray I was not responsible, the pernicious atmosphere there was. Harilal's coming over to South Africa had improved him, whereas Gokuldas's leaving had spoilt him. Harilal and Gokuldas getting married, I said, was because of the sensual atmosphere there. Fortunately, I said Manio, Ramo, and Devo* were with me in South Africa and growing up in a healthy atmosphere. If they were to die unmarried, I shouldn't be sorry but rejoice instead. However, if when they come of age they wish to marry, they will, I am sure, find suitable brides.

And I had to say:

---

*Manilal, Ramdas, and Devadas.

1. I would remind you that between you two brothers I have already paid 60,000 rupees.
2. I have cleared all the debts while I was there and you told me no more money was wanted.
3. It was only after this that I began spending money here.
4. I handed over all my savings in Natal to you.
5. I have not kept a penny for myself either from that account or from my subsequent earnings.
6. I have paid back much more than the 13,000 rupees spent on me during my stay in England.

I added that in saying this I did not mean to imply that I had done him a favour, only stated the bare facts to pacify his anger. If I regard all living beings as equal both from the practical and moral points of view, it is in the fitness of things that those who are more dependent on me have a greater claim on me. That is to say I should help my wife and sons first and then those who are helpless and have therefore a claim on me.

Hariyo* was with me as I wrote this letter and I asked him to make a copy to be sent to my brother lest he have difficulty reading my hand. I also wanted Hariyo to understand how I have answered my brother's angry letter and learn whatever he can from it according to his karma.

I received on 21 April a letter from Kastur in Phoenix to say Chhaganlal's wife† had delivered another son‡ and that both mother and child were well. I wrote to Chhaganlal to ask how much his two sons weighed and to particularly advise him that the child's bed and linen be kept clean. A cradle, I put it to him, rather than a hammock should be used. How are you feeling in your mind, I asked Chhaganlal. Apart from his responsibilities at the press, and at home, he was at that point considering going to England to study law. I asked him what he thought about that plan.[165]

---

*Harilal.
†Kasi.
‡Krishnadas, younger brother of Prabhudas.

Harilal also moved to Phoenix to join Chanchal and the rest of the family. Once there, he helped with the printing of *Indian Opinion*, and tried to involve himself in the settlement's other activities: carpentry, shoemaking, tailoring, cooking, gardening, and farming. He also attended the school improvised there. Harilal also took turns with my nephew Gokuldas in playing with and looking after seven-year-old Prabhudas. They took him on their bicycles to the Phoenix station and back, seating him on a little cushion tied to the cycle's bar.[166]

At about this time I came across the text of a letter that the new Governor of Pondicherry* had written to the people in France's three bases in India just prior to his arrival and to his meeting them. 'A representative of the Republic is bound to regard all citizens as equal and there is only one thing between us, viz. the laws and I shall explain their limitations to you quite clearly.... You are engaged in your agricultural work. I have also many jobs to attend to. So we have no time to meet in a grand hall and receive garlands of roses and jasmines. Believe me when I say that I shall come to see you without pomp and show. And I shall be glad if I meet you in simplicity.'[167]

Reading this I could not but say: How can people with such officials be unhappy?

In early May of 1907 came a cable saying the Imperial government had assented to the Transvaal Act. Every one asked 'What can avail us now?' I replied: 'This is not an Act designed for our enslavement, but for the loosening of our chains. We must not submit to it but go to gaol instead. We should treat it as a blessing that the Act has been passed.'[168]

Indian Opinion announced a one-pound prize on 1 June for the finest poem in Gujarati or Hindustani (Urdu or Hindi) composed in support of the gaol resolution. The conditions included the citing of modern and ancient examples of bravery, Muslim and Hindu, with any others as well.[169] Twenty competed, of who three seemed to have

---

*Gabriel Louis Angoulvant (1872–1932).

equal merit and it was somewhat of a problem to decide which poem should be placed first. The poem of Mr Ambalal Mangalji Thakar, President of the Natal Sanatan Dharma Sabha, was ultimately found to be worthy of the first place. The poems could have been still better if their writers had taken more pains in composing them. None of the poems revealed any special poetic power or art.

I had been asking myself: Should the British be thrown out of India? And can it be done even if we wish to do so? On the same day that the journal announced the poetry prize, it also carried this reflection of mine on British Rule: We stand to lose by ending British rule and even if we wanted to, India is not in a position to end it. Whatever the motives of the British in coming to India, we have much to learn from them. They are a brave and considerate people and on the whole honest. Blind where self-interest is concerned, they give unstinted admiration for bravery wherever found. They are a powerful nation and India enjoys not a little protection under them. It is not, therefore, desirable that British rule in India should disappear.

Should we then, I asked, repudiate such men as Lala Lajpat Rai? That, too, is not possible. They are patriots and endure hardship for the sake of the country. To that extent they command our respect. However, they appear to be in error in so far as they want to eliminate British rule.

The Asiatic Act, as notified in the Transvaal *Gazette* came into effect on 1 July 1907. On 30 June, a mass meeting was held in Pretoria in which the community asserted its resolve to stand together and to not submit to the law.[170] Volunteers from the community in Pretoria then went on to defend the honour of the community, even at the cost of neglecting their own business by going round the Permit Office by turns to courteously persuade any Indian going to register, to turn back.[171]

Mr Kallenbach wrote to *The Star* a letter in which he said: 'I shall consider it a privilege to visit my Indian friends in the gaol and to do my utmost to redress the hardships of prison life which they are prepared to undergo.'[172] A white gentleman, Mr Van Weenan, wrote to *The Star*: 'To me the fault of the Indians appears to be that they are diligent. The fact that indolent whites should want to oppress them can be understood. Like Mr Kallenbach I too have found among the Indians men worthy of esteem.'[173]

During the struggle excellent work was done by the 'volunteers' or 'pickets' or 'missionaries' or 'watchmen' or whatever other name is used for them. The real credit for the struggle goes to the pickets in Pretoria. Ordinarily we shall feel contempt for any Indian seeking to soil his hands (by seeking a permit). But it will be better to show pity rather than contempt.[174]

A watchman's duty is to watch, not assault. We have not the slightest hesitation in saying that if anyone in Johannesburg seeking registration is assaulted, our success will turn into failure. Our duty is to reason with those who are doing wrong, to entreat them, to beg of them. If in spite of this they wish to court slavery, they ought to have the freedom to do so. For we do not see any gain in freeing them from the yoke of the law in order to subject them to our own yoke.[175]

Pretoria put up a good show but Pietersburg was beyond praise. Not a single black sheep was found there. The Permit Office was sent back as hungry as it had come.[176]

Having been asked at the Permit Office to give his fingerprints, Bakhtawar, an Indian from Calcutta refused to comply. Then he was asked to apply under the new law. This too he refused to do. Every Indian ought to have such courage.[177]

General Smuts sent us a message: 'If the resistance of the Indians residing in this country leads to results which they do not seriously face at present, they will have only themselves and their leaders to blame.' One can send a score or two to prison. But however brave, General Smuts cannot have the courage to punish thousands of men.[178]

I was served a notice, on 28 December, to leave the colony within forty-eight hours.

Nine

ONWARD TO GAOL

A time may come when every vestige of support may be withdrawn from us.

The Transvaal Immigration Restriction Act (TIRA) came into force on 1 January 1908.

A huge meeting was held that day at the Surti Mosque, Fordsburg, Johannesburg, to protest against TIRA and the Transvaal Asiatic Registration Act (TARA). It was attended by at least 2,500 persons, all full of enthusiasm. Sonja Schlesin, my twenty-year-old stenotypist, after getting her parents' permission, asked to speak at it. She said: 'Now that the struggle has reached its culminating point, I who have followed it with the closest attention almost from its inception… implore you not to flinch from the hardships which now confront you, not to falter at the shoals ahead but to continue steadfast.'[179]

We had invited through the columns of *Indian Opinion* suggestions from readers for a Gujarati equivalent for 'passive resistance'. We received one from Maganlal Gandhi that was not bad, though it did not render the original in its full connotation—sadagraha. I thought satyagraha was better than sadagraha. Though the phrase does not exhaust the connotation of 'passive', we shall use satyagraha till a word is available which deserves the prize.[180]

Satyagraha, then, was at high tide, getting worldwide publicity.

I wrote in *Indian Opinion* on 10 January, 'Let no one look to the others; let each depend on his own strength so that even if in fear a few Indians submit to the outrageous law, others will not be tempted to do likewise.'[181] A meeting was called in the Newtown Mosque, Johannesburg at 11 a.m. It was known that I and others who had been served notices to leave the colony and had not done so, were to appear in court that afternoon for sentences. Despite the short notice for the meeting there was a large gathering. A platform had been erected on the grounds for the speakers and for the audience serviceable paraffin tins had been scattered in the thousands. I spoke first in Hindustani and then in English. I said those going to gaol today were not at all afraid. On the contrary it was a fit opportunity given by the government to show that they were men, not dogs.

About the law, I repeated for the thousandth time that it was not a question of giving a wife's name or a mother's name or giving a thumb impression or a ten digits' impression although these things were undoubtedly to be considered when they were compelled to give these things, but the sting lay in the spirit itself—the condemnation of the whole of the Indian community.

It was drizzling as I walked towards the court in Government Square. The public entrance to the court was blocked. The magistrate Mr Jordan also walked through the crowd near the entrance which was cordoned off by mounted and foot police. A few minutes after 2 p.m., 'silence' was called and I was asked to come forward. I at once pleaded guilty to the charge of disobeying the order to leave the colony in forty-eight hours. On being asked if I had any questions to ask, I said, 'No, sir'. I then asked leave to make a short statement, on receiving which I said a distinction should be made between my case and those that were to follow. I said I had learnt that in Pretoria my compatriots had been sentenced to three months with hard labour and fined a heavy amount in lieu of which they would get another three months with hard labour. If these men, I said, had committed an offence, I had committed a greater one and so I asked the magistrate to award me the heaviest penalty.

'You asked for the heaviest penalty which the law authorizes?' asked Magistrate Jordan.

'Yes, sir.'

'I do not feel inclined to accede to your request which is six months' hard labour with a fine of 500 pounds. That appears to me to be totally out of proportion to the offence you have committed—contempt of court for disobeying the order of 28 December.

This is more or less a political offence and if it had not been for the defiance set to the law I should have thought it my duty to pass the lowest sentence which I am authorized by the Act. Under the circumstances I think a fair sentence to meet the case would be two months imprisonment without hard labour.'

On the sentence being pronounced I was at once removed to custody and was then quite alone. The policemen asked me to sit on a bench for prisoners, shut the door on me and went away. I was somewhat agitated and fell into deep thought. Home, the courts where I practised at the Fort Prison, the public meeting—all passed away like a dream.

I was now a prisoner.

What would happen in two months? Would I have to serve the full term? If the people courted imprisonment in large numbers, there would be no question of serving the full term. But if they failed to fill the prisons, two months would be as tedious as an age. How vain I was! I began to laugh at my own folly. I began to think of what kind of imprisonment would be awarded to them and whether they would be kept with me in the prison.... The police officer opened the door and asked me to follow him, which I did to the prison van. I was driven to Johannesburg jail.[182]

In jail we were first taken to the reception room as the room used for measuring and dressing prisoners is called. There we were weighed and totally undressed. We were given non-labour clothing to wear consisting of trousers, shirt, jumper, caps, socks, and closed sandals. We were all required to give our digit impressions and marched to our cell with eight ounces of bread for our evening meal.* There our clothes were stamped with the letter 'N', which meant that we were being classed with the natives. We were all prepared for hardships but not quite for this experience. It was however well that we were classed with the natives. It was a welcome opportunity to study the treatment meted out to natives, their conditions of life in gaol and their

---

*This experience of being stripped was also that of Nelson Mandela whose first jail term in 1954 was also, coincidentally, in the same prison. Mandela writes in *Long Walk to Freedom* (1994) '...we were taken to an outdoor quadrangle and ordered to strip completely and line up against the wall.' CWMG, Vol. 8, pp. 120–21.

habits. It did not seem right to feel bad to be bracketed with them.

I knew that convicts were made naked in jail. We had all decided as satyagrahis voluntarily to obey all jail regulations so long as they were not inconsistent with our self-respect or with our religious convictions. The clothes which were given to me to wear were very dirty. I did not like putting them on at all. It was not without pain that I reconciled myself to them from an idea that I must put up with some dirt. After the officers had recorded my name and address, I was taken to a large cell and in a short time was joined by my compatriots who came laughing and told me how they had received the same sentence as myself and what took place after I was removed. I understood from them that when my case was over, the Indians, some of whom were excited, took out a procession with black flags in their hands. The police disturbed the procession and flogged some of the members. We were all happy at the thought that we were kept in the same gaol and in the same cell. Leung Quinn, leader of the Chinese community, and Thambi Naidoo were among my cell mates.

The cell door was locked at 6 o'clock. The door was not made of bars but was quite solid, there being high up in the wall a small aperture for ventilation so that we felt we had been locked up in a safe.[183] I was told these cells were the best ventilated of all the prisons in the Transvaal. Galvanized iron sheets served for walls with glazed apertures at three places, half an inch in diameter, through which the gaolers could watch the prisoners while remaining unobserved themselves.[184] There was electric light in the cell but the only light in it was not strong enough to do any reading with any degree of comfort. The light was switched off at eight o'clock in the evening and was spasmodically switched on and off at night. A bucket of water and a tin tumbler was our ration of water for the night. For natural convenience a bucket in a tray with disinfectant fluid in it was placed in a corner. Our bedding consisted of wooden planks fixed to three-inch legs, two blankets, and an apology for a pillow and matting. At our request the governor placed a table and two benches in the room for writing.[185]

There was no provision for privacy in the bath or latrine. It often happened therefore that two or three prisoners sat down in a row. The arrangements for bathing were similar.[186] From the second or third day, Satyagrahi prisoners began to arrive in large numbers. They were most of them hawkers. They had taken the lead. It was easy for them to be arrested. They only had to refuse to show their licences and that was enough.

Ten days after we were locked up, on 21 January I wrote to the Director of Prisons saying that of the twenty-one of us, eighteen were British Indians and three Chinese and that none of us was used to the mealie meal, without salt, that we were given for breakfast and most were suffering from constipation, probably due to eating mealie meal. And I asked for 'European scale or such other diet as may be suitable for keeping body and soul together and may be consistent with our national habits or habits formed by prolonged residence in South Africa.'[187]

When we asked the prison medical officer for some condiments, he said sternly to us, 'This is not India, there is no question of taste about prison diet.' Our warder was a good man and he allowed us, upon or asking, a morning drill in the small yard in the front of our cells. This was in the nature of a merry-go-round. When the warder finished the drill and went away, we could continue with a Pathan compatriot of ours named Nawabkhan. He rendered 'Stand at ease!' as 'Sundlies'. We could not for the life of us understand what Hindustani word it was until it dawned on us that it was no Hindustani word but only Nawabkhani English.

I mentioned earlier that the governor had allowed us a table. We were also given pens and an inkpot. The gaol had a library which lends books to prisoners. I borrowed some of Carlyle's works and the Bible. From a Chinese interpreter who used to visit the place I borrowed a copy of the Koran in English, Huxley's lectures, Carlyle's biographies of Burns, Johnson, and Scott, and Bacon's essays on civil and moral counsel. I also had some books of my own; these included an edition of the Gita with a commentary by Manilal Nabhubhai, some Tamil books, an Urdu book presented by Maulvi Saheb, the writings of Tolstoy, Ruskin, and Socrates. Most of these books I either read [for the first time] or reread during my stay in gaol. I used to study Tamil regularly. In the morning I read the Gita and in the afternoon portions of the Koran.[188]

There is a rule that every prisoner sentenced to two months [or more] must have his hair cropped close and the moustache shaved off. In the case of Indians, the rule was not enforced rigorously. Should a prisoner object, his moustache was spared. In this connection I had an amusing experience. I knew very well that prisoners had to have their hair cropped. I also knew that the rule about having the prisoner's hair and moustache removed was really for his own convenience and not to humiliate him. Personally, I believe that it is a very useful rule. In gaol there are no combs or other means for keeping the hair tidy. If the hair is not groomed, there is the risk of scabies. On hot days, hair makes one feel extremely uncomfortable. Moreover, the prisoners are not given a looking-glass. There is the danger, therefore, of the moustache remaining unclean. As there is no serviette for use at meals and the wooden spoon is rather awkward to handle, food is apt to stick in the moustache. It was my intention to go through all the experiences of a prisoner. I therefore asked the chief warder to have my hair cropped and my moustache shaved off. He told me the governor had strictly forbidden that. I said I knew that he did not wish to force me [to observe this rule], but that I myself wanted it. He suggested that I might apply to the governor. The next day, permission was received from him. But he said that since two days out of my two-month period had elapsed, he now had no right to order the cropping of my hair and moustache. I said, I knew the rule but wanted this of my own free will and for my own convenience. He smilingly demurred. I learnt later that the governor had felt a little apprehensive. So I offered to state in writing that I had myself requested the cropping [of my hair]. This allayed the governor's suspicion, and he ordered the chief warder to give me clippers and a pair of scissors. My fellow prisoner, Mr P. K. Naidoo, was a master of the tonsorial art. I, too, knew something of it. When the others saw me cropping my hair and moustache, they saw the point of it, and followed suit. Some of them had only their hair cropped. Mr Naidoo and I, between us, spent two hours each day clipping the Indians' hair. I believe this made for better health and convenience. The prisoners looked the smarter for it.[189]

When the officials came to inspect the prisoners, the latter had all to line up. As the official approached, they had to take off their caps and salute him. All the prisoners wore caps, and it was not difficult to take them off, for there was a rule that they must be taken off, and this was only proper. The order to line up was given by shouting the command 'fall in' whenever an official came. The words 'fall in' therefore became our daily diet. They meant that the prisoners should fall in line and stand to attention. This happened four or five times a day. One of these officials, who bore the designation of Assistant Chief Warder, was somewhat strict. The Indian prisoners therefore nicknamed him 'General Smuts'. He often came early in the morning, and sometimes in the afternoon as well. The doctor came at half-past nine. He appeared to be a kind and well-meaning person. He made solicitous inquiries about our health.

Under the Gaol regulations, every prisoner had to undress himself in public for examination by the doctor. But the doctor did not insist on the observance of this rule. Moreover, when the number of Indian prisoners increased, he asked them if anyone had eczema or similar infection, so that he might examine the person in private. The governor and the chief warder used to come at half-past ten or eleven. The governor appeared to be firm, fair-minded and quiet-tempered. He always had the same questions to ask: 'Are you all well? Is there anything you want? Have you any complaints?' He listened to a request or a complaint patiently and granted every request which was reasonable; if there was a [genuine] grievance, he set matters right. The deputy governor also came sometimes. He, too, was a kindly person. But the kindest among them all, the most gentle and sympathetic, was the official known as the chief warder, who was especially charged with looking after us. He was a very devout man; we were not the only ones to whom he was nice and courteous in every way; [for] the other prisoners were also very warm in their praises of him. He was anxious to respect the prisoners' rights. He would condone any minor offence on their part. He was particularly kind to us because

Dadabhai Naoroji, 1889; a pre-eminent Indian statesman and British parliamentarian, he inspired Gandhi in London and was in guiding correspondence with him during Gandhi's years in South Africa.
Source: Wikimedia Commons

BOOK IV
1909

This section shows Gandhi at his truest—physically tough, intellectually vibrant, politically daring, and spiritually questing. Also conflicted at home between what he wants to do according to his lights and what he wishes to leave his dependents to do according to theirs. He is evolving in every department of his life, every theatre of his activity, and not always to the satisfaction of those near and dear who are observing him. And so these pages also show him vulnerable, physically, intellectually, politically, and—domestically.

Satyagraha is to the fore as is his eldest son Harilal in that struggle. Father and son share for the first and last time in their lives a mutuality of purpose and action, a concordance which is almost too good to be true, certainly too good to last. Both see life in prison at its most demanding, most debilitating, and both emerge from the experience strangely strengthened.

Gandhi has experienced brutal physical assaults from atypical representatives of all three major sections of South Africa's population—the ruling European, the majority African, and the minority Asian. This has helped his belief in non-violent struggle for truth glow like an ingot in the furnace of South Africa's complex society and even more complex polity. It has been smelted both in the heat of imprisonment and that of negotiation. And that 'truth' as he has come to see it finds utterance in his remarkable 'first' publication—Hind Swaraj, unique in its content and unusual in its structure—a conversation, his, with an unnamed 'reader' who is none other than Dr Pranjivan Mehta, his friend from the time he was a student in London.

~

One

COMPROMISE AND AN ASSAULT

Seeing that the assault was committed by...Mohammedans, the Hindus might probably feel hurt.... Rather let the blood spilt today cement the two communities indissolubly—such is my heartfelt prayer. May God grant it.

On 21 January, I had an unexpected visitor.[191] Mr Albert Cartwright, editor of *The Transvaal Leader*, had himself suffered imprisonment for reasons of conscience and was as broad-minded as he was able. He had remained indefatigable in his support of the Indian cause. He and I had become good friends. When he came, after securing special permission to do so, he and I discussed the whole issue and we agreed that the law should be repealed during the following session of Parliament and the Indian community should immediately take out registers voluntarily. We put this agreement down in writing. He then met leaders of his party, the Progressive Party who, while accepting the suggestions, asked that the Indians should write a letter from gaol volunteering to register.

Mr Cartwright then brought the draft letter to me on 28 January. It had either been drafted or approved by General Smuts whom he met and found to be welcoming of his mediation. He then met Indian leaders who told him they would ratify any arrangement that I accepted. Its substance was that Indians were to register voluntarily and not under any law and that if the majority of Indians underwent voluntary registration, the government would ensure that on them the Act be not applied. But I found that it did not, however, say categorically that the new law would not apply to those who registered voluntarily. And it was moreover on behalf of the Indians alone, leaving out the Chinese some of whom, including their leader Quinn, were in gaol

165

with me. It did not furthermore safeguard the interests of those who were outside the Transvaal at present and included children under the age of sixteen. I proposed changes on both these points. The draft Mr Cartwright brought also said '...the penalties of the Act be not applied'. I suggested that this be amended to '...the Act be not applied'.

On Mr Cartwright appearing hesitant, I said to him that if these changes were not accepted, the Indians would prefer to remain in gaol. He was visibly touched and said, 'Well, you must make whatever changes you want. You are fighting for truth. The changes you propose are reasonable and necessary for your self-respect. If Mr Smuts does not accept them, I shall myself oppose him and I also hope to turn the Progressive Party against him.' After these changes had been made, Mr Quinn and Mr Naidoo were called in. They both approved the letter and signed it at 12.30 p.m. and I handed it to Mr Cartwright who left for Pretoria by the 2.30 train the same day.[192] At five in the afternoon he rang up to say General Smuts had accepted the draft with one suggestion for alteration which we accepted.

There are some things that can be put down in writing and for others one has to rely on oral understanding. That is what happened with this compromise as well. It was conveyed to the government through Mr Cartwright that efforts should be made to reinstate all Indians who had been relieved of their posts in the government and that the Indian community should be consulted about the form of the new registration certificate. Mr Cartwright informed us over the telephone that General Smuts would not commit himself on the question of reinstating government servants but that he had agreed to do his best. As for the form of the register he agreed to consult the Indian community. The proposed voluntary registration would not be under the law.[193]

On 30 January, Mr Vernon, the Superintendent of Police, Johannesburg, took me to Pretoria to meet General Smuts. A meal on the way had been arranged for me. Everything was to be confidential. So the train was actually stopped before it reached Pretoria for me to alight lest I be noticed by the ever vigilant pickets of Pretoria. I went to the Colonial Office accompanied by General Smuts's secretary,

Mr Lane, and Superintendent Bates.[194]

With General Smuts I had a good deal of talk. He said to me: 'I could never entertain a dislike for your people. You know I too am a barrister. I had some Indian fellow students in my time. But I must do my duty. The Europeans want this law and you will agree with me that these are not mostly Boers but Englishmen. I accept the alteration you have suggested in the draft. I have consulted General Botha also and I assure you that I will repeal the Act as soon as most of you have undergone voluntary registration.'

So saying, General Smuts rose. I asked him 'Where am I to go? And what about the other prisoners?'

The general laughed and said, 'You are free this very moment. I am phoning the prison officials to release the other prisoners tomorrow morning. But I must advise you not to go in for many meetings or demonstrations, as in that case the government will find itself in an awkward position.'

I assured him there would be not a single meeting for the sake of it but that I will have to explain to the community how the settlement was effected, what its nature and scope is and how it has added to our responsibilities.[195]

It was seven o'clock in the evening. I had not a single farthing in my pocket. General Smuts's secretary gave the railway fare to Johannesburg. There was only one more train for Johannesburg and I was able to catch it.[196]

Watchful pickets who had come to know had surrounded the Colonial Office, guarding all the exits. I met them as soon as I came out. I told them that every Indian would be set free the next day and asked them to inform others.[197]

Immediately on my return, a representative of the *Rand Daily Mail* met me and levelled questions at my head:

Q: Honourable to both sides, Mr Gandhi?

A: Absolutely, the honour of the colony has not been affected in the least, and the feelings and scruples of the Asiatics have received the fullest consideration.

Q: Then it is no climbdown?

A: Absolutely not—satisfactory to all parties concerned.

Noticing my head closely cropped and my moustache cut, he asked me if I was subjected to regulations usually applied to criminals. 'No,' I said 'this is all my doing.'

I then went straight to the mosque at Fordsburg for a hurried meeting called of a number of my compatriots though it was past midnight. I explained the terms of the settlement with General Smuts and asked those present to register voluntarily because the opposition was to compulsion, not to registration. As I finished, Mir Alam, one of the Transvaal's fifty or so Pathans, fully six feet in height and of a large and powerful build, stood up and asked if they had to give ten fingerprints. Those with difficulties of conscience need not, I replied.

'What will you do yourself?'

'I have decided to give ten fingerprints. It may not be for me not to give them myself while advising others to do so.'

'It was you who told us that ten fingerprints were only required from criminals. It was you who told us the struggle centred round the fingerprints.'

'Even now I say that in India fingerprints are required from criminal tribes. But circumstances have now changed. I say with all the force at my command that what would have been a crime against the people yesterday is in the altered circumstances of today the hallmark of a gentleman. If you require me to salute you by force and I submit to you, I will have demeaned myself. But if of my own accord I salute you as a brother or fellow man, that will be counted in my favour before the Great White Throne.'

'We have heard you have betrayed the community and sold it to General Smuts for 15,000 pounds. We will never give the fingerprints nor allow others to do so. I swear with Allah as my witness that I will kill the man who takes the lead in applying for registration.'

'One may not swear to kill another in the name of the Most High. However that may be, it is my clear duty to take the lead in giving fingerprints. To die by the hand of a brother rather than by disease cannot be for me a matter for sorrow.'

A Pathan's anger becomes particularly uncontrollable when he has to deal with anyone whom he takes to be a traitor. When he seeks justice, he seeks it only through personal violence. Pathans fully participated in the satyagraha struggle; none of them submitted to the Black Act. The single suggestion—why should I ask them to give fingerprints if I was not corrupt?—was enough to poison the Pathans' ears.[198]

On the next day all the incarcerated Indians numbering 220 were released. I was inundated with telegrams of congratulations on what the senders considered to be a victory for the Indian cause. I replied through the columns of *Indian Opinion* that we can only consider a victory for truth. I added that we should be prepared—should the occasion arise again—to undergo imprisonment or any other hardship for the sake of Truth, Honour, and Self-respect.[199] I also saw this as a victory for satyagraha.[200]

Maganlal wrote to me from Phoenix about the reactions in Durban to the compromise settlement. I told him it was good he sent me a full account. The discontent in Durban, I told him, did not affect me in the slightest degree though I did not expect it to come in such vehemence. A time may come, I said, when every vestige of support may be withdrawn from us. That time has not come, I told him, but those who are prepared for the worst can always take philosophically the intermediate stages. 'You should,' I wrote, 'hear these things and let them pass away from your mind as water off a duck's back.'[201]

Answering those who felt 'what victory is there to talk about, here we are yielding on the question of giving digit impressions' I said, 'The giving of fingerprints is not in itself a disgraceful thing. There is no humiliation in polishing a friend's shoes as a gesture or of our free will. But polishing shoes out of fear when ordered to do so would amount to demeaning ourselves as menials. In other words, whether a particular thing is good or bad depends on the context.'[202]

A large meeting was called on 2 February of Indians and sympathizers at the Masonic Lodge, in Johannesburg. The gathering overflowed the confines of the hall, crowding up the doorway and porch. After the meeting was over, I came down [from] the platform, talked with a few people, and walked out of the hall together with Millie, Henry Polak's wife. As we reached the outer door, she and I noticed a man standing in the shadow of it. I walked up to him directly and linked my arm with his. As we spoke in a low voice, Millie could not hear us and in any case could not have followed us for we were talking in a language that she did not understand. After I had finished the man hesitated for a moment, turned and walked away. Millie observed all this from the other side of me and then she and I stepped onto the street. At the end of the street the man came back and handed me a knife that he had been carrying. The following conversation then ensued between Millie and me:

M: What did the man want—anything special?

G: Yes, he wanted to kill me.

M: To kill you? To kill you? How horrible. Is he mad?

G: No, he thinks I am acting traitorously towards our people, that I am intriguing with the government against them and yet pretending to be their friend and leader.

M: But that is all wicked and dreadful. Such a man is not safe. He ought to be arrested. Why did you let him go like that? He must be mad.

G: No, he is not mad, only mistaken. And you saw after I talked to him, he handed over to me the knife he had intended to use on me.

M: He would have stabbed you in the dark. I....
G: Do not disturb yourself so much about it. He thought he wanted to kill me but he really had not the courage to do so. If I were as bad as he thought I was I should deserve to die. Now we will not worry any more about it. It is finished. I do not think that man will attempt to injure me again. Had I had him arrested I should have made an enemy of him. As it is, he will now be my friend.[203]

I was staying at Kallenbach's home at this stage. One day when I picked up my coat before going out I noticed something that looked like a revolver in the pocket of his coat that was also hanging on the same coat stand. It really was one. I asked him why he was carrying one. Obviously embarrassed, he first gave an evasive reply. He said it just happened to be in his pocket.

'Have Ruskin or Tolstoy ever suggested in their books that one should carry revolvers in one's pockets just for the fun of it?'

'I have heard that some rascals are planning to attack you.'

'And you want to protect me from them?'

'Yes, that is why I follow you about.'

'Well, now I need not have any fear. You have taken over from God the responsibility of protecting me. As long as you are there, I can consider myself invulnerable.'

Kallenbach was touched to the quick. 'The Almighty is there to protect us,' I said. Putting the revolver away, he said, 'I have acted wrongly. I shall now no longer be anxious on your account.'[204]

On 10 February, some of us got ready to go out and take out certificates of registration. When I reached my office, I found Mir Alam and his companions standing outside the premises. He was an old client of mine and used to seek my advice in all his affairs. He was a manufacturer of straw or cotton mattresses. Although his eyes met mine, he refrained from saluting me. I saluted him and he saluted me in return. I noticed his angry eyes and took a mental note of the fact. I thought that something was going to happen. I entered the office. Mr Yusuf Mian and others arrived and at 10.30 a.m. we set out for the Asiatic Office. Mir Alam and his companions followed us. I did feel there would be an attack on me. Not more than three minutes' walk from the Registration Office, I became surer. Mir Alam accosted me and asked, 'Where are you going?'

'I propose to take out a certificate of registration, giving the ten fingerprints. If you will go with me I will first get you a certificate with an impression of only two thumbs and I will then take one for myself, giving the fingerprints....'

I had scarcely finished the last sentence when a heavy cudgel blow descended on my head from behind. I do not remember the manner of the assault but people say that I fell down unconscious with the first blow which was delivered with a stick and they also kicked me. Thinking me dead, they stopped. I have an impression that as the blows started I uttered the words 'Hey Rama'. I have no notion of what followed.[205] When I regained consciousness I saw Mr Doke bending over me.

'How do you feel?'

'I am all right but there is pain in the teeth and ribs. Where is Mir Alam?'

'He has been arrested along with the rest.'

'They should be released.'

'That is all very well.... The police are ready to take you to hospital but if you will go to my place, Mrs Doke and I will minister to your comforts as best as we can.'

'Yes, please take me to your place. Thank the police for their offer but tell them I prefer to go with you.'

Mr Doke was not exactly a friend. I had met him barely three or four times before then. It was thus a stranger he was taking into his home. His son's room was put at my disposal and the son himself slept on the floor in the library. Mr Doke took the sanitary part of the duties on himself while I looked helplessly on. The work of bandaging me and of washing the bandages was taken on by Mrs Doke.[206]

I learnt later that Mir Alam and his companions had given me more blows and kicks some of which were warded off by Yusuf Mian and Thambi Naidoo. When I came to somewhat, I had been picked up and carried into Mr J. C. Gibson's private office opposite which I had been attacked. I was attended to by Mr Lew, the Chinese consul general in the Transvaal and Mr Gibson Junior.

I was taken in a carriage to this good clergyman's residence on Smit Street and a doctor was called in. Mr Chamney, the Registrar of Asiatics, too now arrived on the scene. I said to him:

'I have to now request you to bring the papers and allow me to register at once.'

'Where is the hurry about it? Please rest.'

'I am pledged to take out the first certificate if I am alive and if it is acceptable to God. I insist....'

Upon this Mr Chamney went away to bring the papers.

Dr Thwaites came in and examined me and stitched up the wounds on the cheek and on the upper lip and enjoined silence upon me so long as the stitches were not removed.

I then had a wire sent to the attorney general that I did not hold Mir Alam and others guilty of the assault and did not wish them to be prosecuted. Mr Chamney returned with the papers and I gave my fingerprints but not without pain. I saw that tears stood in Mr Chamney's eyes. I had often to write bitterly against him but this showed me how man's heart may be softened by events.

Mr Doke and his good wife were anxious that I should be perfectly at rest and peaceful. They were therefore pained to witness my mental activity after the assault. They removed all persons from near my bed. I made a request in writing that in order that I might lie down quietly, their daughter, Olive, who was then only a little girl, should sing for me my favourite hymn, 'Lead Kindly Light'. Mr Doke called Olive by signs and asked her to stand at the door and sing the hymn in a low tone.[207]

Though I was under the care of a physician, the treatment consisted entirely of home cure methods. For the first two days I had nothing to eat or drink. That had the effect of keeping the fever down. On the third day I had no temperature. I started on a diet of a quarter pound of milk and gradually added to it grapes, pears, and other fruit. Then I began taking bread dunked in milk once a day.

Mr Doke received nearly forty telegrams of thanks from different parts of the colony and some Indians sent him fruits and other gifts as a mark of their gratitude.

On reflection, I feel we fear death unnecessarily. I believe I have not known such fear for a long time now. And I have grown more fearless after this incident.[208]

I thought I should write a general letter to friends through *IO*. Writing the same day, I said:

I am well in the brotherly and sisterly hands of Mr and Mrs Doke. Those who have committed the act did not know what they were doing. They thought that I was doing what was wrong. They have had their redress in the only manner they know. I therefore request that no steps be taken against them.

Seeing that the assault was committed by a Mohammedan or Mohammedans, the Hindus might probably feel hurt. If so, they would put themselves in the wrong before the world and their Maker. Rather let the blood spilt today cement the two communities indissolubly—such is my heartfelt prayer. May God grant it.

I then added that the promise of the repeal of the Act against voluntary registration having been given, it is the sacred duty of every good Indian to help the government and the colony to the uttermost.[209]

Two

WITH THE FAMILY, BRIEFLY

Hip Hip Hullah Lamdas!

When I was assaulted in Johannesburg my family lived in Phoenix and was naturally anxious about me. But it was not possible for them to spend money on the journey from Phoenix to Johannesburg. It was therefore necessary for me to see them after my recovery. From the Natal friends I learnt that in Natal too the settlement had been grossly misunderstood. And I had received a sheaf of correspondence addressed to *Indian Opinion* in which adverse criticism was passed on the settlement. The Transvaal struggle was not merely a local affair and the Indians in Transvaal were really fighting the battle on behalf of all the Indians in South Africa. I therefore felt I must go to Durban and remove the misunderstanding prevalent there. So I took the first opportunity to run up to Durban.[210]

Leaving on 5 March, I addressed a public meeting organized the same evening by the Natal Indian Congress in Durban. Some friends had warned me beforehand that I would be attacked at this meeting and that I should therefore not attend it at all or at least take steps for defending myself. But neither of the two courses was open to me. The meeting was held at 8 o'clock in the evening. The proceedings were nearly over when a Pathan rushed to the stage with a big stick. The lights were put out at the same time. I grasped the situation at once. Sheth Daud Mahommed, the chairman, stood on the chairman's table and tried to quell the disturbance. Some of those on the platform tried to surround me to defend my person. One of them had a revolver and he fired a blank shot. Meanwhile Parsi Rustomji who had noticed the gathering clouds went with all possible speed to the police station and informed Superintendent

Alexander, who sent a police party. The police made way for me and took me to Parsi Rustomji's place.

The next day Parsi Rustomji brought all the Pathans of Durban together in the morning and asked them to place before me all their complaints against me. I tried to conciliate them but with little success. They had a preconceived notion that I had betrayed the community and until this poison was removed it was useless reasoning with them.

I left Durban for Phoenix the same day. The friends who had guarded me the previous night would not leave me alone and informed me that they intended to accompany me to Phoenix. 'But Phoenix is a jungle,' I told them. 'That won't frighten us,' one of them replied.

'And what will you do if the only dwellers there do not even give you food?'

'Who is there to prevent us from robbing your pantry?'

We thus made a merry party for Phoenix.[211]

As Phoenix learnt I was coming they tidied up the press and the homes. The children, as I learnt later, had decided to welcome me in their own way. At Ramdas's suggestion they decided to build a tiny hut with branches of trees to show to me. They covered the roof with grass and flowers and the floor with paper they got from the press. And they kept it just high enough for me to enter it. But I got there only late at night by which time the children had all fallen asleep.[212]

The leader of the self-appointed guard accompanying me was Jack Moodaley, a Natal-born Tamilian well known among the Indians as a trained boxer. He and his companions believed that no man in South Africa, whether white or coloured, was a match for him in that branch of sport. In South Africa I had for many years been in the habit of sleeping in the open at all times except when there was rain. I was not prepared now to change the habit and the self-constituted guard decided to keep watch all night. Though I had tried to laugh these men out of their purpose, I must confess that I was weak enough to feel safer for their presence.

Early in the morning, after having his bath and wearing clean clothes, seven-year-old Prabhudas, Chhaganlal's son, presented himself. I was talking to someone, looking across a grassy stretch, when he came quietly and stood by me. He was to say much later that I was wearing a half-sleeve white shirt of 'thin gauze-like material' and a pair of white trousers. But what caught his eye particularly were the coverings 'shining' over two of my lower teeth. Prabhudas says he took them to be made of gold and that Devadas had to tell him they were made not of gold but platinum. He noticed too that I 'laughed more often than anyone else in Phoenix *in spite of being such an important person*'![213]

Soon, other children also collected there and, after finishing my conversation, I began playing with them, carrying each one of them on my shoulders by turn and then dropping them on the sloping garden to roll down. They would return to me again and again to be rolled down again and yet again. This boisterous fun continued for about half an hour after which I took all of them on a round of the settlement.[214] With the children following me, I called at each house to find out how they were faring. Not finding Ramdas, Prabhudas called out: 'Lamdas Kaka!' I asked him to say the name again, getting the 'R' right but, no, it was 'Lamdas' and again 'Lamdas'. So I got all of them together to shout 'Hip hip hurrah' which they did, except Prabhudas who was stuck with his 'L'. I asked him to slowly repeat his 'hurrah' by himself and it was only when after many attempts I got him to say 'Hurr-Rrraamdas', that he was let off.

A primary school had started functioning at the settlement which Ramdas, Devadas, and Prabhudas attended as did two or three children of non-indentured labourers from outside the settlement. They walked a mile or more from the hillocks facing Phoenix where they lived. Hindi was the language that these children learned to speak with the settlement children. Chhaganlal taught them arithmetic, Maganlal Gujarati, and Mr Cordes* gave lessons in English.[215]

Whenever I visited the settlement, I made it a point to go to the school not to give a class or to see to the lessons as much as

---

*A German theosophist who was attached to Gandhi and later moved to India; died at Sevagram in 1960.

to its cleanliness. Prabhudas remembers that I once saw his ears were unwashed and told him to be careful when bathing so that no dirt got left behind anywhere. On another occasion I saw boils all over his body and went to his house to tell his mother Kashi about my remedy for them: tomatoes—not red ripe ones but raw ones to purify the blood.[216]

I encouraged the eating of groundnuts and there used to be sackfuls of them in the house. Devadas used to fill his pockets with them. Harilal once caught Devadas stealing groundnuts. He lay in siege for Devadas outside the door of the room where they were stored. As Devadas dipped his hands in the sack, the door opened and in came Hari to take him by the arm, feigning anger. The rattle of the nuts was what he had waited behind the door to hear.[217]

Discussing with me, on this visit, the attack by Mir Alam, Harilal asked me what he should have done had he been present: should he have watched me being assaulted, or run, or hit the attacker? I answered that unless he saw a non-violent way of defending me, he should have used force.[218]

I stayed with the family in Phoenix until 27 April, more than one and a half months. In those days I used to relish good food. Special dishes were made by Kastur, now known in the settlement as a whole as Ba, or by Chhaganlal's and Maganlal's wives. Sometimes the meals would be had in our house, sometimes in those of Chhaganlal's or Maganlal's.[219]

Friday nights were important for the weekly *Indian Opinion* was dispatched by Saturday. The material would be composed by the afternoon of Friday. It was evening by the time the paper would go to press. We had no servants, peons, or other labour. All of us—'press workers'—had to ourselves print the paper, fold it, paste addresses on the wrappers, make the bundles and take them to the station. That work would take up the whole of Friday night and there would still be something left to do after daybreak. Along with the others I would stay up the whole night. And we would all get some kheer at midnight.[220]

Shortly after this happy reunion, a letter came from Rajkot to say that my nephew, Gokaldas, who had only then got married, had died. Within fifteen days of his marriage, the young man was gone, leaving a younger widow with my widowed sister. What could one do? I wrote to my cousins Meghjibhai and Khushalbhai: 'Gokaldas is gone. We are helpless. Our relations were such that I feel like crying even as I write this; but the ideas that I have been cogitating for a long time have now become stronger and more emphatic. I find that we are all engrossed overmuch in the affairs of this world. I see that the whole country is in the same predicament in which our family finds itself. I express here only those ideas which are now uppermost in my mind. Out of a false sense of prestige or mistaken notions of affection, we think of marrying off our boys and girls at a very early age. We spend a lot of money doing so and then look on sadly at the young widows. I do not suggest that people should not marry at all. But surely we should observe some limits. We marry off little boys and girls and make them miserable.'[221]

On 9 May, *Indian Opinion* concluded its series of excerpts from the Life of Socrates. It closed with the following words of the great soldier for truth:

> Now, my last request: If, when my sons grow up, if they begin to care for riches or for any other thing before virtue, if they think they are something when they are nothing at all, warn them, censure them, punish them, just in the same manner as I have warned you against these things and reproached you with the love of them. If you can do this I will consider that you have been kind to me and to my sons. Now the time has come and we must go hence, I to die, you to live. God alone can tell which is the better state, mine or yours.

Three

THE STRUGGLE REVIVES

If I have to give my life for a cause which I consider to be good, what better death can there be?

At the annual meeting of Het Volk, a Dutch society in the Transvaal, held in April, General Smuts declared that a municipal bill, which, he hoped, would solve the question of coloured persons living among whites, would be introduced during the next session of Parliament. He did not elaborate the point further. True satyagrahis, I said to my compatriots, need not be frightened at such moves; only, they must remain vigilant. This should serve as a warning particularly to those who feel that satyagraha once has been enough.[222]

In May came news that a white woman in Muzaffarpur, Bihar, had been killed by an explosion.* The cablegram suggested that the intention [of the assailant] was to kill a magistrate but an error on his part led to the death of an innocent woman. I wrote at once in *Indian Opinion* that it is likely that the easy and straightforward methods of campaigning for one's rights will be gradually eschewed and, in the end, the methods which we imagine we would use only against foreigners will be used against ourselves. This has ever been so. There was, I said, therefore not the slightest reason for Indians to gloat over this incident. At the same time, the government, too, cannot be absolved wholly from blame. Had there been no oppression, the people would not have even dreamt of using dynamite.

On 12 May, I received a wire from the Registrar of Asiatics saying

---

*At Muzaffarpur, on 30 April 1908, Khudiram Bose intended to fling a bomb at Kingsford, the district judge, as an act of political reprisal. The bomb, however, hit a coach carrying two Englishwomen, Mrs and Miss Kennedy. Both the women and the syce were fatally wounded. Khudiram Bose was subsequently sentenced to death.

that all Asiatics who at the time of the compromise were outside the colony and who are now coming in, or came after 9 May, will have to apply under the Act. This created panic and I tried to telephone General Smuts and on not getting through wrote to him to say that I am sure he did not mean this at all.[223] He replied the next day through his secretary, E. F. C. Lane upholding the Registrar's position.

I responded at once to Lane. 'But the essence of the compromise is that, the undertaking of the Indian community being fulfilled, as I claim it has been, the Act should be repealed. Voluntary registration should go on in connection with those who may arrive until the Act is repealed.' I also had to say '…it is within the General's knowledge that I very nearly lost my life, and this arose because, in the opinion of some of my countrymen, I had sold them, by reason of having agreed to the principle of ten fingerprints. Were the proposed registration under the Act of new arrivals persisted in, not only will suspicion be accentuated, but it will be justified, and I cannot help saying that those who may feel irritated against me will be entitled to my life.'

And I wrote to Mr Cartwright to say that he—the Angel of Peace—may have to be requisitioned again and I pointed to 'the danger of trusting'.[224] General Smuts's was a frightful reply, and suggested foul play. It was not in itself a serious matter that a score or so of Indians who had recently returned from home were not to be allowed to take out certificates voluntarily. That would not be a sufficient cause for panic. The roots of this went much deeper. The obnoxious law, I saw, had to be repealed now. But General Smuts's brief reply to my letter merely announced that my demand would not be accepted. And nothing was said about whether or not the law would be repealed.[225]

I met General Smuts in Pretoria during this time, reiterating our position. On one morning when I was to leave for Pretoria I berated Kallenbach for something he had omitted to do.

K: It is no use your wasting your time over domestic trifles when you must be thinking of the interview you are going to have with General Smuts.

G: No, these little things are to me of as much importance as the big ones. They touch the very core of our life and truth is one whole, it has no compartments.[226]

The more the government rebuffed us and the more the Act's repeal seemed to become unlikely, the harder grew the anger of those who felt I had betrayed them.

All this naturally was dismaying to the family in Phoenix. I reassured Maganlal who had written expressing great anxiety for my safety, my life: 'You need not worry about me. I think I shall have to sacrifice myself. I do not believe that Smuts can play foul to the end. But it gives an opportunity to those who have reached the limits of their patience and are ready to strike at me. If that should happen, we need not be unhappy. If I have to give my life for a cause which I consider to be good, what better death can there be? If God found it fit to take away Gokaldas, why should the idea of death make us sorrowful? This world is transient. If, therefore, I leave this world, why should one be worried on that account? It should be enough to wish that nothing improper is done by me as long as I live.'

If the struggle was to be revived, satyagraha would be put to the test again. But I could see that it would be all the more impressive and, if the Indian community proved resolute, a wonderful spectacle to watch.[227]

I called on General Smuts on 13 June and followed up our conversation with a letter: 'I ask you to recognize the very great service rendered by the Indian community in giving fingerprints in the face of enormous odds.... But I may state that they will never accept, so far as I am aware, anything in the nature of compulsion....'

On 16 June, I had to admit in *Indian Opinion* that the collapse of the settlement with Smuts was drawing nearer each day. When, after repeated communications and meetings, it became clear that the Act would not be repealed and that the terms being offered to us were demeaning, a mass meeting was called to consider the situation. It was held on 24 June. I said to the large gathering:

'I believe that, in seeing General Smuts as I saw him, I acted correctly and in accordance with my conscience, but time has shown that I need not have gone to General Smuts as I did. What I did was simply and solely to accept voluntary registration that was placed before him for over a year by the whole Indian community. I felt that I was yielding nothing, not a single new principle, not a single concession, in accepting this voluntary compromise. I believed that I had full instructions from my countrymen to do so, but I believed too much.

'I state most emphatically and definitely that General Smuts did promise that he was going to repeal the Act, in the presence of the Registrar of Asiatics....'

A new spirit was now infused into Indians throughout South Africa. We should congratulate and thank the government upon having, perhaps unconsciously, assisted us in doing this wonderful thing.[228]

In July, Sorabji Shapurji Adajania was sentenced to a month's hard labour. We took this to be the conferment of an honour on him. A time was coming when, to ascertain the number of titles a man holds, we shall have to enquire of him how often he has been to gaol. Sorabji went to gaol exclusively for his country's sake, and in defence of educated Indians' rights.[229]

Four

HARILAL TO THE FORE

I want every Indian to do what Harilal has done.

Harilal was among those who courted imprisonment.* He was among six Indian hawkers who appeared in court before Mr P. C. Dalmahoy on 28 July, charged with hawking without licences. The others included Thambi Naidoo, who had been to prison in January last with me and who was sentenced to four days' imprisonment the previous week for hawking without a licence. Harilal was arrested some days earlier at Volksrust for failing to register and had been warned to appear at Pretoria to apply for a registration certificate. He came to Johannesburg and immediately commenced hawking fruit, when he was arrested. In Magistrate Dalmahoy's court, Mr Cramer prosecuted, while I appeared for the defence. The first to be charged was an Indian named Hera Mariji. Formal evidence as to the accused's having been hawking within the municipality without a licence was given, and the accused, who pleaded guilty, was fined 1 pound, with the alternative of seven days' imprisonment with hard labour. The next to be placed in the dock were Harilal Gandhi, Thambi Naidoo, and Govindasamy Kistnasamy, who were all described as Indian hawkers. They pleaded guilty. A sergeant of police gave evidence that he had arrested the accused, who were hawking fruit in Bellevue East without licence: Naidoo, Harilal Gandhi, Hera Mariji, Kistnasamy, Pillay, and Naiker.

---

*Harilal Gandhi spent a total of 577 days in South African prisons for his political activities: 27 July to 3 August 1908 in Johannesburg, 18 August to 17 September 1908 in Johannesburg again, 10 February to 9 August 1909 in Volksrust and Pretoria, 1 November 1909 to 30 April 1910 in Pretoria, 23 June 1910 to 22 September 1910 in Johannesburg and, finally, 10 October 1910 to 9 January 1911 in Johannesburg. He thus bettered by far his father's South Africa gaol tally of 188 days.

I said in court that I had had a long conference with the prisoners at the gaol, and Harilal had been requested to ask for the severest penalty. If a light sentence was imposed, as soon as they came out, they intended to repeat the action. It would be a saving of time to give them a long sentence, and it would be better for the sake of their health if they had a sustained term. Thereupon Naidoo was fined 2 pounds, with the alternative of 14 days' imprisonment with hard labour, Harilal and Kistnasamy were fined 1 pound [each], or seven days' imprisonment, with hard labour. Two other British Indians, named Sinnappa Rangasamy Pillay and Soopa Veerasamy Naiker, were then charged. They pleaded guilty, and were fined 1 pound, or seven days' imprisonment, with hard labour. In each case the accused elected to go to prison.[230]

I received enquiries from many quarters as to why I sent Harilal, my son, to gaol. I replied to them through *Indian Opinion*: 'I have asked every Indian to take up hawking. I am afraid I cannot join as I am enrolled as an attorney. I therefore thought it right to advise my son to make his rounds as a hawker. I hesitate to ask others to do things I cannot do myself. I think whatever my son does at my instance can be taken to have been done by me. I want every Indian to do what Harilal has done. Harilal is only a child. He may have merely deferred to his father's wishes in acting in this manner. It is essential that every Indian should act on his own as Harilal did [at my instance] and I wish everyone would do so.'[231]

Maganlal wanted to court arrest as well but I dissuaded him. 'I get no time these days to write to you or to anyone else,' I wrote to him shortly after Harilal's arrest. 'I know that you want to join the struggle. But you need not think as if you were doing nothing by remaining there. It was necessary for Harilal alone to come over. I think he did a very good thing by coming here and going to gaol. Since I could not go, I could be happy only if Harilal went. I think it has been a very good experience for Harilal himself.'

The Chairman of the Transvaal British India Association, Mr Essop Mia, applied for a hawker's licence to give a stimulus to the movement and to forgo the protection afforded him by his voluntary registration certificate and trade licence.²³²

On 4 August, Mr Thambi Naidoo's wife suffered a miscarriage. Mr Naidoo, serving a jail term for hawking, could not know this. The community's obligation to him mounted. He had left his wife's side at a difficult time and deliberately gone to gaol for the sake of the community, and this is what has happened meanwhile. I had seen Mrs Naidoo on the same day on which he went to gaol. She was in a pathetic state. There is hardly another woman so spirited who would face with courage a second term of imprisonment for her husband. In any case, that cannot be expected of a woman in Mrs Naidoo's condition.²³³

My cousin, Khushalbhai, father of Chhaganlal and Maganlal, was getting increasingly concerned from his distance in India. I felt obliged to say the following to him:

> Revered Khushalbhai, I write this letter in the middle of the night. There is no time to write at length. You ask me to look after 'myself', but we have been taught that the self does not die, neither does it kill nor cause anyone to be killed. If you mean by 'self' the body and ask me to take care, I would then point out to you that this has been dubbed moha by the Lord. What then shall I look after? I shall take care of the self only, that is, I shall try my utmost to realize it. One must cultivate the strength to sacrifice one's body in the process if need be. I feel obliged to write this because, after much thought, I find some of our sayings and current precepts irreligious. The very book that we consider the supreme scripture, we reject altogether in practice. I therefore propose to use all the strength at my command against this way of living.²³⁴

They swooped down on Harilal again on 11 August. He was arrested on the charge of being in the Transvaal without a register. The case was heard at 2 o'clock. I asked for only twenty-four hours' notice to be given to him since he [Harilal] had no preparations to make and had made up his mind to go to gaol. But the magistrate gave him seven days' notice. I said I hope that after seven days we shall find him engaged in hard labour. Gaol life is good education for anyone who accepts it in full knowledge of what it means. It is an important part of children's training that they should be taught to bear hardships from their earliest years.

The afternoon of 16 August witnessed such a scene as, it is to be hoped, may never need to be re-enacted in this country. Some 3,000 British Indians gathered together purposefully, intent only upon consigning [the registration certificates] to the flames. The whole of the space looking westwards from the Fordsburg Mosque, Johannesburg, within the fence was packed with members of the Indian community. It was a wonderful display of national unity, and one that the mother country might well be proud of. On the platform were the Congress leaders, various prominent Transvaal Indians, Mr Leung Quinn, Chairman of the Chinese Association, and I. Mr Essop Ismail Mia presided over this vast gathering. Beyond that, a sea of upturned and expectant faces, with determination and a bitter merriment stamped deep. In the front row a dozen representative Chinese leaders grimly sat, awaiting the fateful moment. Briefly, the chairman, first in Gujarati, and then, through the medium of Mr N. A. Cama, detailed in measured accents the reason for calling the meeting together. Then in my address I said, 'I ask you this afternoon to burn all these certificates.' The response to this was with spontaneous cries of: 'We are ready to burn them.'[235] After which the voluntary registration certificates were thrown into a large cauldron, saturated with paraffin, and set ablaze by Mr Essop Mia in the name of the community. Mr S. Haloo who had registered under the Act, now publicly burnt his badge of slavery, and poured oil upon the flames.[236]

Harilal continued in jail and some Indians saw him on 24 August. They told me that he was looking perfectly healthy. He walked with a firm step, and, on seeing them, he smiled several times which showed that he was not languishing.[237]

Information came that the prisoners undergoing hard labour were breaking stones in the public streets and that raw meat was supplied to them as prison food, which they refused to eat. I told a public meeting in Johannesburg on 10 September that I considered what seemed degrading work as really an honour. This statement was greeted with applause. The reason for their suffering, I said made me proud of my countrymen. It was a disgrace, however, that their government should act thus—it reflected no credit on the local or the British or the Indian government.[238]

Harilal's sentence was ending on 17 September. And anxious to see him, I called on the official concerned for information about Harilal's release. I sensed that the authorities would want there to be no demonstrations of welcome or congratulation for him upon his release. And Harilal would comply. But the official said to me that he had heard nothing about the plans for Harilal and would let me know the following day, the day of the release. When I presented myself at the gaol the next day, I was informed that Harilal had been taken away under escort at seven o'clock. When Harilal's train reached Jeppe Station, the carriage windows were shut. They were also kept shut at Germiston. I telegraphed him, on release, to re-enter the Transvaal and break the law again. He did that on 19 September when the case against him was withdrawn.[239]

Five

BETWEEN HOME AND GAOL

The two exchanged obscene jokes, uncovering each other's genitals. Both these prisoners had charges of murder and larceny against them. Knowing this, how could I possibly sleep?

I was in Natal from 26 September to 6 October and was able to spend some time with the family at Phoenix. The settlement was now observing a simpler style of living in the matter of food and dress. Spicy foods and special meals in the individual homes were given up for common eating of simple meals brought to the Orchards from the different homes. Some sons of those who had been imprisoned in the Natal and Transvaal satyagrahas were being housed with each of the families in Phoenix. I went from house to house getting the consent of the family units to keep two or three such children with them, treating them as their own children. It was not easy for the settlers to look after these young guests. The hard-worked housewives in those dwellings had to find time to cook for them. There was always the danger of difficulties arising over the cleaning of their plates and the washing of their clothes. Even though the guests were modest and good-natured, for them staying in Phoenix was an entirely new experience. For them the change meant coming from the life of the cities, at their parents' instance, to a forest dwelling without any shopping areas to walk about in and spend money on.[240]

Chhaganlal and Kashi put up three children, two Muslim and one Parsi, all from well-to-do Gujarati-speaking families. I learnt later that Kashi and Maganlal's wife, Santok, both from orthodox Vaishnava homes, used to 'purify' utensils used by my Muslim guests by turning them over a fire. And if Chhaganlal got over his difficulty in eating with them it was only because he had surrendered himself to my ideals. But I put Ba to an even severer task: She had to host boys from South Indian Christian families who were aggressive by nature.[241]

The number of children at Phoenix was small. There was no school building as such. Mr Cordes, the German teacher helping us offered the use of his own residential building for classes. The teaching was done through both Gujarati and English. Attention was paid to the simultaneous development of mind and body. Special emphasis was laid on strengthening the moral character of pupils. Our chief object was to provide education to those children only who may live in Phoenix. For it is not good for children to have one standard of behaviour in the school and another at home. Some who heard of this school expressed a desire to send their children to Phoenix. But, for want of residential and school accommodation facilities we were not in a position to meet their request. And we did not have the resources for putting up the required buildings. Buildings need money. We therefore invited the views of those among our readers who believed that a school along the lines indicated above should be established. If they offered us monetary help, we would be prepared to put up a building for the school as also a hostel.[242]

Cordes lived in a thatched mud house surrounded by a beautiful garden. He was very particular about maintaining his house spotlessly clean and orderly. He had his own methods of teaching. To teach the children calligraphy, he got them two-foot long pencils of half an inch diameter. If any of them did not hold the pencil exactly as he wanted them to, he would be there in a second to take the pencil and hit the offender's knuckles with it. And he got them to drill in a soldierly fashion. Even the slightest slackness would not go unpunished. At one hint from him, the children had to climb trees with the swiftness of monkeys and then jump down to the point he would indicate. None of the elders liked this and I did not quite approve either but everyone acknowledged the German teacher's devotion to duty and discipline and his emphasis on physical fitness.[243]

In early October we learnt from Syed Ali, who had just returned from gaol after seven days' imprisonment at Boksburg, that he had

had no end of suffering to put up with. He had been sentenced to hard labour. He was made to carry closet buckets. He was made to stay in cold water for a long spell. He was kicked. How was one to bear this? But we will carry buckets and suffer kicks. We will regard this as an expression of our nobility. Our bonds will be loosened when we enjoy carrying buckets. Only then may we claim that we understand the meaning of satyagraha. True victory will consist in cultivating the ability to bear with all this.'[244]

On my return journey to Johannesburg on 7 October, I was arrested at the border town of Volksrust with seventy-five other satyagrahis for failing to give my thumb and finger impressions upon demand and was lodged in the prison there. I called it King Edward's Hotel.[245]

On 14 October, the day sentence was to be pronounced, I wrote to Kallenbach from Volksrust Prison: 'Not a single day has passed on which I have not thought of you. We know each other so well that we talk to each other without talking and see without seeing. I feel that the punishment I shall receive today will be trivial. No serious charge seems to be pending. I must be content with even little.'[246]

I appeared before the Volksrust court on that day, where I pleaded guilty. I said on being asked on 7 October to produce documents, and to furnish means of identification as required by Regulation 9, I had refused. Giving evidence, I further said: 'In connection with my refusal to produce my registration certificate and to give thumb impressions or finger impressions, I think that, as an officer of this court, I owe an explanation. There have been differences between the government and British Indians whom I represent as Secretary of the British Indian Association, over the Asiatic Act, No. 2 of 1907, and after due deliberation, I took upon myself the responsibility of advising my countrymen not to submit to the primary obligation imposed by the Act.'

The magistrate, Mr Mentz, thought that as I had admitted my crime to be greater than that of the others and asked that the heaviest penalty (100 pounds or three months with hard labour) should be awarded, he found me guilty. He felt very sorry, he said, to see me in that position today, but he sentenced me to pay a fine of 25 pounds or go to jail with hard labour for two months. Of course, no fines were paid, and all went smilingly to jail, I being especially happy.[247] Through *Indian Opinion*, I sent this message to my compatriots: Keep absolutely firm to the end. Suffering is our only remedy. Victory is certain.[248]

The incarcerated Indians were so happy in gaol that one could think of it only as a palace. It was well built, too, constructed of stone with large cells. Ventilation was satisfactory. There was an open courtyard in the middle, with a flooring of black stone. For bathing there were three showers. Water poured out of these in large quantities, enabling one to have a very good bath. The courtyard was covered with a barbed-wire netting. In spite of strict arrangements, two Negroes once escaped by breaking through the tin roof. Hence, a strong iron ceiling had been put in place.

The Muslim month of Ramzan having set in, all the Muslim prisoners among us duly observed the Ramzan fast and diet timings. All of them were particular about the namaz, and passed the time cheerfully. Those who were observing roza and other Indians as well were being given very little work for the present such as cleaning the cells or such other miscellaneous work, which they did not find hard or difficult in any way. If anyone was found to be ill, he was totally exempted from work. All the officers, including the gaoler, behaved well. One did not take off one's cap, only salute. This was a mere trifle. I am reporting this just to show that even in a matter like this, the officers did not harass anyone. Orders had been issued permitting the Parsis among us to wear their customary shirt and sacred thread as well as their own cap.[249]

The batch which included me was assigned the task of maintaining cleanliness in the gaol garden and looking after its cultivation. Our work was mainly to sow maize seeds, clear the potato bed, and dust the potato plants. And then, for two days, they took us to dig a municipal tank. Our work there consisted of digging, piling up the earth, and carrying it away in barrows. This again was hard work. We had a taste of it only for two days. I had a swollen wrist, which was cured when treated with earth. The place being at a distance of four or five miles, we used to be taken there in a trolley. We had to cook our meal near the tank, so that we also carried with us the necessary provisions and fuel. After making us work on the tank for two days, they gave us some other work. Hitherto they used to take out mostly such Indians as were strong enough for work. Now, however, they were formed into groups. Some of them were sent to dig out the weeds that had shot up round the soldiers' tombs. Others were sent to clean the graveyard. This arrangement continued for some time. During the remaining period, we were assigned work in the garden. This included digging, reaping, sweeping, etc. This cannot be considered to be heavy work; rather, it was conductive to vigour of health. Apart from the work described above, it was the duty of the men in every cell to carry the bucket for urine, etc., placed in it. I observed that our people are unwilling to do such work. In fact, there is no reason why one should mind it. It is wrong to think of any work as humiliating or degrading. Moreover, those who have offered themselves for imprisonment cannot afford to stand on prestige thus. I saw that sometimes there was some argument as to who should carry the urine bucket.[250]

A fellow prisoner Hassan Mirza had been suffering from a very bad disease of the lungs. He was delicate of health. All the same, he gladly took upon himself whatever work fell to his lot from day to day. Furthermore, he gave no thought to his health. Once, asked to clean the chief warder's privy, he instantly started doing so. As he had never done such work, he vomited. He was not upset by this. I felt great affection for him. Another time, the chief warder wanted to find two Indians to clean the latrines specially set apart for the Indians. I thought I was the best person for such work, and so I went myself. Once one of us was locked up in a cell by himself for refusing to do such work. Of course, I see nothing wrong in our having to submit to any kind of sentence. But, in this particular case, the penalty could have been avoided. It is, moreover, not proper that we should hold ourselves back from such work. When I set out to attend to the work, the warder began to scold others and urged them to come forward. This spread the news about the order and forthwith Mr Omar Osman and Mr Rustomji ran to my help; the work was very light, though. If we are hurt by the nature of the work assigned to us, we cannot take part in any fight worth the name.[251]

All the Indians set to work with great energy. But only a few of them were used to hard work, so that we were all quite exhausted with the exertion.[252]

Among us was Ravikrishna, son of Babu Talevant Singh. I was much disconcerted to see him work, and yet the energy with which he went about it gladdened my heart. As the day advanced, we found the task quite hard. The warder was rather sharp of temper. He shouted at the prisoners all the time to keep on working. The more he shouted, the more nervous the Indians became. I even saw some of them in tears. One, I noticed, had a swollen foot. I was sorely distressed at this. However, I went on urging everyone to ignore the warder and carry on as best he could. I too got exhausted. There were large blisters on the palms, the lymph oozing out of them. It was difficult to bend down, and the spade seemed to weigh a maund. For myself, I was praying to God all the time to save my honour, so that I might not break down, and to give me strength to keep doing the work as well as I should. Placing my trust in Him, I went on with the work. The warder started rebuking me. He did so because I was resting. I told him that there was no need to shout at me, that I would do my best and work to the utmost limit of endurance. Just then, I observed Mr Jhinabhai Desai fainting away. I paused a little, not being allowed to leave the place of work. The warder went to the spot. I found that I, too, must go, and I ran. Two other Indians also followed me. Water was sprinkled over Jhinabhai. He came to. The warder sent away the others to their work. I was allowed to remain by his side. After plenty of cold water had been poured over Jhinabhai's head, he felt somewhat better. I told the warder that Jhinabhai would not be able to walk down to the gaol. Hence a cab was sent for. I was ordered to take him in it to the gaol. As I splashed cold water over Jhinabhai's head, I thought to myself, 'A great many Indians have been going to gaol at my word. What a sinner I would be if I had been giving wrong advice! Am I the cause of all this suffering on the part of Indians?' As I thought thus, I sighed deeply. I considered the matter afresh, with God as witness and, after being plunged in reflection for some time, I collected myself with a smile. I felt I had given the right advice. If to bear suffering is in itself a kind of happiness, there is no need to be worried by it. This was only a case of fainting but even if it were to be death, I could have given no other advice. Seeing that our sole duty was to break free from our fetters by enduring every hardship rather than remaining bound for life, I felt light in heart and tried to instil courage in Jhinabhai.

On 25 October, I was removed from Volksrust Prison to the Fort Prison in Johannesburg in connection with a case in which I was required to give evidence. Carrying my prisoner's knapsack I walked to the Volksrust station and likewise from the Johannesburg station to the Fort Prison. The incident provoked strong comments in newspapers. Questions were asked in the British Parliament. Many persons felt hurt. Everyone thought that, being a political prisoner, I should not have been made to walk the distance, dressed in gaol uniform and carrying a load.[253]

It was evening when we reached Johannesburg. I was given a bed in a cell of the prison where there were mostly Kaffir prisoners who had been lying ill. I spent the night in this cell in great misery and fear. I became quite nervous. I felt extremely uneasy, but I resolved in my mind that my duty required me to bear every suffering. I read the Bhagavad Gita which I had carried with me. I read the verses which had a bearing on my situation and, meditating on them, managed to compose myself. The reason why I felt so uneasy was that the Kaffir and Chinese prisoners appeared to be wild, murderous, and given to immoral ways. I did not know their language. A Kaffir started putting questions to me. I felt a hint of mockery even in this. I did not understand what it was. I returned no reply. He asked me in broken English why I had been brought there in that fashion. I gave a brief reply, and then I lapsed into silence. Then came a Chinese. He appeared to be worse. He came near the bed and looked closely at me. I kept still. Then he went to a Kaffir lying in bed. The two exchanged obscene jokes, uncovering each other's genitals. Both these prisoners had charges of murder and larceny against them. Knowing this, how could I possibly sleep? Thinking that I would bring this to the notice of the governor the next day, I fell asleep for a while late in the night. Real suffering lies in this. Carrying luggage and such other troubles are nothing very serious. Realizing that the experience I have had must also sometimes be that of other Indians, and that they too would feel the fear that I did, I was happy that I had suffered in the same way as others. The experience, I thought, would impel me to agitate against the government all the more tenaciously, and I hoped that I might succeed in inducing prison reforms in regard to these matters. All these are indirect benefits of satyagraha. As soon as we rose the following day, I was taken to where the other prisoners were lodged, so that I had no chance to complain to the governor about what had happened.[254]

I had one further unpleasant experience in the Johannesburg gaol. In this gaol, there were two different kinds of wards. One ward is for prisoners sentenced to hard labour. The other is for prisoners who are called as witnesses and those who have been sentenced to imprisonment in civil proceedings. Prisoners sentenced to hard labour have no right to go into this second ward. We slept in it but we could not use its lavatory as of right. In the first ward, the number of prisoners wanting the use of the lavatory is so large that a visit to it is a great nuisance. Some Indians find this a source of great inconvenience. I was one of them. I was told by the warder that there would be no harm in my using a lavatory in the second ward. I therefore went to one of the lavatories in this ward. At these lavatories, too, there is usually a crowd. Moreover, the lavatories have open access. There are no doors. As soon as I had occupied one of them, there came along a strong, heavily-built, fearful-looking Kaffir. He asked me to get out and started abusing me. I said I would leave very soon. Instantly he lifted me up in his arms and threw me out. Fortunately, I caught hold of the door frame, and saved myself from a fall. I was not in the least frightened by this. I smiled and walked away; but one or two Indian prisoners who saw what had happened started weeping. Since they could not offer any help in gaol, they felt helpless and miserable. I heard later that other Indians also had to go through similar tribulations.[255]

While in Johannesburg, I was taken to the court three or four times. I was allowed to see Mr Polak and Harilal there. Others also came sometimes. I was even free, when in the court, to have food brought to me from home and accordingly Mr Kallenbach used to bring bread, cheese, etc., for me. When I was in this gaol, the number of satyagrahi prisoners in it mounted very high. At one time, there were more than fifty. Many of them were asked to pound gravel with a small hammer, sitting on a stone. About ten men were employed in mending torn clothes. I was given the work of stitching caps with a [sewing] machine. I learnt sewing for the first time here. It was not difficult work and therefore I learnt it in no time.[256]

When prisoners first come to this gaol, they are examined by the physician. This is done in order to find out if any of them suffers from a contagious disease and, if anyone does, to give him treatment and isolate him from the others. For this reason, the prisoners are examined with great care. Some of the prisoners are found to suffer from diseases like syphilis, and therefore everyone of them has his genitals examined. For this purpose, the prisoners are totally undressed, while being examined. Unlike the others, Kaffirs are kept standing undressed for nearly fifteen minutes so as to save the physician's time. Indian prisoners are made to lower their breeches only when the physician approaches them. The other garments have to be removed in advance. Almost every Indian resents having to lower his breeches, but most of them do not create any difficulty in the interest of our movement, though at heart they feel ill at ease. When in the presence of men only, there should be no need to conceal any parts of our anatomy. There is no reason to believe, moreover, that others will keep staring at the parts which we generally hide. Formerly, Indian prisoners were not examined by the physician at all. But once two or three Indians were interrogated. They replied that they had no disease. The physician examined them nevertheless, having felt somewhat suspicious, and found that they had not spoken the truth. He decided thenceforth to examine even Indian prisoners. We can thus see that whenever we are in some trouble, it is generally of our own making.[257]

I was taken back to Volksrust on 4 November. This time, too, I was accompanied by a warder. I was dressed in the prisoner's uniform, but on this occasion, instead of being made to walk, I was taken in a cab. All the Indians were happy to find me back in Volksrust. I was locked up in Mr Dawad Mahomed's cell for the night, so that we kept awake till a late hour narrating our experiences to each other.

While serving this term in Volksrust, I became the cook for the other Indian prisoners as only I could adjudicate on the conflicting claims of the ration supplied. My companions took without complaining the half-cooked porridge without sugar that I gave them, thanks to their love of me.[258] On 15 October, I reported for road-making work at Volksrust's Market Square and when asked by a Reuter's representative how I felt, said quite frankly that I was the happiest man in the Transvaal. I gathered that the next day the Transvaal British Indian Association and the Natal Indian Congress sent cables to London protesting against my being made to do road-work. A meeting too was called in London, with Sir Mancherji Bhownaggree presiding at which Lala Lajpat Rai and Bipin Chandra Pal spoke, criticizing my imprisonment. On the other hand, Kastur, I learnt, was congratulated on my imprisonment by many and she expressed her thanks to them.[259]

Six

KASTUR'S COURAGE

As she was extremely emaciated, the operation had to be done without chloroform.

Halfway through my imprisonment, on 9 November, I received a telegram from Albert West in Phoenix saying Kastur was suffering from haemorrhage and her condition was grave. He asked me to seek release and come. I replied: 'Your telegram to hand. It cuts me but does not surprise me. It is impossible for me to leave here unless I pay the fine which I will not. When I embarked upon the struggle I counted the cost. If Mrs Gandhi must leave me without even the consolation a devoted husband could afford, so be it. Please do what you all can for her. I am wiring Harilal to go there. I expect from you or someone a daily bulletin—not that I can help thereby. Please let me know by wire what the disease is exactly. I am writing to her. I hope she will be alive and conscious to receive and understand the letter. The authorities will allow me to receive the letters daily. The enclosed is for Mrs Gandhi. Let Manilal read it to her.'

To her I wrote: 'Beloved Kastur, I have received Mr West's telegram today about your illness. It cuts my heart. I am very much grieved but I am not in a position to go there to nurse you. I have offered my all to the satyagraha struggle. My coming there is out of the question. I can come only if I pay the fine, which I must not. If you keep courage and take the necessary nutrition, you will recover. If, however, my ill luck so has it that you pass away, I should only say that there would be nothing wrong in your doing so in your separation from me while I am still alive. I love you so dearly that even if you are dead, you will be alive to me. Your soul is deathless. I repeat what I have frequently told you and assure you that if you do succumb to your illness, I will not marry again. Time and again I have told you that you may quietly breathe your last with faith in God. If you die, even that death of yours will be a sacrifice to the cause of satyagraha. My struggle is not merely political. It is religious and therefore quite pure. It does not matter much whether one dies in it or lives. I hope and expect that you will also think likewise and not be unhappy. I ask this of you. Mohandas.'

Learning of some satyagrahis' resolve weakening, I was able to send on 5 December a message from gaol: 'My only desire is that everyone should remain steadfast and ever refuse to violate his pledge, however long the struggle lasts, whether eight days or eight months or eight years, or even longer. We ought not to bring any pressure on those who may yield and desert the movement. If anyone does, I shall believe that he does not understand the nature of the movement. If the struggle has become drawn out so long, we are ourselves the reason for that. If we make a conscious effort to remove the causes, everything can be over even today.'[260]

I was set free, after nine weeks of imprisonment, on 12 December. As I was leaving, I gave to Nelson, a warder, a copy of Tolstoy's *The Kingdom of God is Within You*, with this inscription: 'To Mr G. Nelson for his many acts of kindness within the law during my incarceration at Volksrust. M. K. Gandhi.'[261]

When the stationmaster at Volksrust congratulated me on my release, I told him also that it was really on that day that I found myself in prison, and that I was now facing much heavier tasks than those assigned to me while in gaol.[262] On my way from Volksrust to Johannesburg, I was interviewed by the press at Germiston station and asked about my time in the prison.

G: I enjoyed every minute in gaol.

Q: Was there ill-treatment?

G: I was very well treated in gaol. My complaint is against the gaol regulations. The officers only did their duty in enforcing the regulations.

A large number had gathered at Johannesburg station to welcome me back. Speaking to them I said: 'God is present everywhere; He sees and hears everything. I am sure that we shall be free when that God stirs our opponents' conscience. We do not sacrifice as much as we should. The moment we do so, our fetters will fall away. I thank all the friends who have assembled here today. I want them to inscribe my words in their hearts and to pray to God that He may make everyone feel the same as I do.'

The Hamidiya Islamic Society arranged a big public reception the next day. 'There were 75 prisoners with me in the Volksrust Gaol,' I recounted, 'among them all I observed Sorabji to be the mildest, the most even-tempered and steadfast. He put up with everything that people said to him. Living with him, I have very well realized his worth. Next, from among the Imam sahib, Moosa Essakji and the two Madrasis who had received six weeks' imprisonment, I spent more time with the Imam sahib. I used to feel concerned how he would be able, with his poor health and physique, to withstand the strain. But I saw that he endured all difficulties and performed every task. The Hamidiya Islamic Society and the community are fortunate that the society has a chairman like him. Once, when the gaoler asked for some men to go with him to mow grass, no one responded. Imam sahib felt that it was our duty to go. When he got up, others started remonstrating with the gaoler, saying that he was an Imam and should not be put to work. They all rather felt ashamed on this occasion. Such habits of ours are also responsible for our struggle being prolonged. After the release of others, a few of us were left behind. Moosa Essakji took charge of cooking. The Imam sahib agreed to help him. They used to get up at three o'clock in the morning and start the cooking. Because the community has such men among it, I believe that it has come out victorious.'[263]

When I was garlanded by the organizers I could only say: 'I take this to be a diamond necklace, offered not out of respect merely but out of love. It is with that feeling that I thank you.'

The Tamil community of Johannesburg extended the same honour to me the following day and I could again only say: 'This garland has in fact been earned by the Tamil community which has given such as excellent account of itself. Hence what you have offered to me I offer in turn to your chairman. I have nothing more to say.'

I was in Phoenix with the family in the first week of January when Kastur took seriously ill again, with frequent attacks of haemorrhage. Surgery was advised and she agreed after some hesitation. As she was extremely emaciated, the operation had to be done without chloroform. It was successful but she had to suffer much pain. She however went through it with wonderful bravery. Dr R. M. Nanji and his wife who nursed her were all attention. This was in Durban. The doctor gave me leave to go to Johannesburg, saying I need have no anxiety about the patient.

In a few days however I received a letter to the effect that she was worse, too weak to sit up in bed and had once become unconscious. Dr Nanji phoned me at Johannesburg for permission to give her beef tea. I said I could not grant the permission but that he could consult her and she was free to do as she liked. He refused to consult her and asked me to come myself. I took the train for Durban the same day. When I met the doctor he quietly said, 'I had already given Mrs Gandhi beef tea before I phoned you.' I said to him I would call that a fraud. 'No question of fraud in prescribing medicines or diet for a patient,' Dr Nanji said. 'In fact we doctors consider a virtue to deceive patients or their relatives if thereby we can save our patients.'

Kastur was too weak to be consulted. But I thought it my painful duty to do so. 'I would far rather die in your arms than pollute my body with such abominations,' was her resolute reply. I pleaded with her. I told her she was not bound to follow me. She was adamant and wanted to be moved to Phoenix at once. I was delighted. I told the doctor. 'What a callous man you are!' he said.

'Nothing will happen to me,' she said. 'Don't worry.' I got a rickshaw to enable me to take her by the next available train.

She was skin and bone, having had no nourishment for days. As the rickshaw could not be taken inside the station platform, one had to walk some distance before reaching the train. So I carried her in my arms and put her in the compartment. From Phoenix station we took her in a hammock to the settlement where she slowly picked up strength under hydropathic treatment. I do not think she suffered in transit. She started having cold hip baths and sitz baths. But the haemorrhages returned. Hydropathy by itself did not answer. Kastur did not have much faith in my remedies, though she did not resist them. She certainly did not ask for outside help. So, when all my remedies had failed, I entreated her to give up salt and pulses. She would not agree, however much I pleaded with her. At last she challenged me, saying even I could not give up these articles if I were advised to do so. I was pained and delighted—delighted in that I got an opportunity to shower my love on her. I told her that I was giving those two things up for a year. She was rudely shocked. 'I should not have provoked you,' she said. 'I promise to abstain from these things, but for heaven's sake take back your vow. This is too hard on me.' I cannot retract a vow, I told her, 'It will be a test for me and a moral support to you in carrying out your resolve.'

'You are too obstinate,' she said, giving me up. 'You will listen to no one,' she said, seeking relief in tears. After this Kastur began to pick up quickly—whether as a result of the saltless and pulseless diet or of the other consequent changes in her food or as result of the mental exhilaration produced by the incident, I cannot say. But she rallied quickly and the haemorrhaging completely stopped. And I added somewhat to my reputation as a quack.[264]

Kastur could not bear my leaving her bedside for a single minute. Like a baby she would cling to me and hug me. So much so that I feared my scheduled departure for Johannesburg would send her to the grave. This posed a great conflict of duty for me. At that time Kastur absorbed my attention to the exclusion of everything else. Yet there was no doubt in my mind that I must leave her the following week and accept the king's hospitality.[265]

On 16 January 1909 when I was returning from Phoenix to Johannesburg, I was arrested at Volkstrust and released. I wrote to Harilal's wife, Chanchal, who was taking care of our household in Phoenix: 'I was arrested, deported, again arrested and am now released on bail. I shall now proceed to Johannesburg. You will know more from Manilal. I feel unhappy that I was not able to have much talk, rather any talk, with you. But such is my plight.'[266]

Harilal was also in and out of gaol at this time. And both he and Chanchal were worried about their future together or in different places. I wrote to Chanchal: 'Be sure that if you give up the idea of staying with Harilal for the present, it will do good to both of you. Harilal will grow by staying apart and will perform his other duties. Love for you does not consist only in staying with you. At times one has to live apart just for the sake of love. This is true in your case. From every side, I see that your separation is for your benefit. But it can be a source of happiness only if you do not become restless owing to separation. I think Harilal will have to stay at Johannesburg till the struggle is over. Considering your stage of life, I do not intend to treat you as a child. I wish you and Manilal take charge of the household. You two have to look after everything in the house, keep Rama and Deva in proper form, take care of their belongings, and teach them to do so themselves, see that they are clean and their nails are well trimmed. None can say when Ba will completely recover. Even when she is fully restored, your role will not be affected. You have to behave as mistress of the house. Do not forget that we are very poor.'

I wrote to her on 28 January on hearing from her that her mind was restless: 'I would always want to know your inner feelings. Do not hide them thinking that I shall be unhappy. It is not right that you should think you are away from your father's house. I consider you to be my daughter, not a daughter-in-law. I must on no account behave in a way that may cause any harm to you or make you unhappy. There have been innumerable women in India who saw their ultimate good in separation from their husbands. Damayanti became immortal on account of her separation from Nala. Taramati separated from Harishchandra and that separation led to the good of both. Draupadi's separation from the Pandavas proved a blessing to them and the entire Hindu nation sings the praises of her resoluteness. Do not think that these instances have not taken place. Lord Buddha left his wife and became immortal and so did his wife. This is an extreme case. By these examples I only want to show you that your separation is not going to do you any harm. That it would cause you mental agony is quite natural. That is a sign of love. But that does not necessarily mean that it will do you harm. Weal and woe depend on the purpose behind separation. My separation from Ba was almost involuntary; that is, it was not of my choice and yet it proved to be a blessing for us both. By giving these examples, I do not want to impress upon your mind that you have to live in separation for ever. I write this so that you are not unhappy over your separation during the struggle. I shall hardly be a cause of your separation after the struggle is over. My effort, however, is to change your mental attitude. That also will be effected after you understand and get used to it. Preserve this letter. Read it again and again. Ask me whatever you do not understand. Do both of you read it. My object in writing this is your welfare. I am always eager to promote it. But I do not insist that you should accept my ideas. My only desire is that both of you should grow with your own effort.'

The Transvaal struggle was now entering its third phase. Some Indians were now giving in. It also appeared that there were rifts among them. This, I said to the community, need not depress us. It is so in every conflict. It is very difficult to climb the last steps. Not all horses remain on the course till the end—they cannot. Some of them just stall. Some others get exhausted. Some die while running; only a few reach the destination. The same thing happens in the history of every community. There was, therefore, no cause for disappointment in the developments mentioned above. In a campaign which produced thousands of Indians who have held out with determination for two years, there are, I knew, bound to be some who will reach the goal.

The main object of this fight was that we should learn to be men, to be a nation, to cease being the goats that we are and be lions, and to show to the world that we are one people, that we are the children of India ready to lay down our lives for her.[267]

Seven

MY THIRD IMPRISONMENT

*No other Indians can equal the performance of
the Tamils in this fight.*

Harilal was sentenced to imprisonment for six months on 10 February. I was arrested soon thereafter with Polak and was to be in gaol again with hard labour—my third imprisonment—from 25 February to 24 May. I was first kept in Volksrust, where Harilal also was. When, on 25 February, I was sentenced to three months' imprisonment with hard labour and I embraced my fellow prisoners and Harilal in the Volksrust Gaol, I did not imagine that I would have much to say or write about this pilgrimage to gaol. But my expectation, like many other expectations of man, proved false. My fellow prisoners—elderly and prominent Indians—and my son—were all serving a six months' term each, so that I wanted the officers' wish to be fulfilled. However, since I had been charged under the regulations framed under the Act, I was afraid that three months would be the utmost I might get, and that is what happened. After the sentence had been passed, it was a pleasure to join Mr Dawad Mahomed, Mr Rustomjee, Mr Sorabji, Mr Pillay, Mr Hajurasingh, Mr Lalbahadursingh and other veterans. Except ten of them, all were provided with beds in tents pitched on the ground in front of the gaol. The scene had therefore the appearance of an armed camp rather than a gaol. Everyone liked sleeping in a tent. Arrangements for food were satisfactory. As on previous occasions, cooking was in our own hands. It was therefore possible to prepare food to our taste. In all there were about seventy-seven (satyagrahi) prisoners. Those who were taken outside for work were set a rather difficult task. They had to build a road in front of the magistrate's court.

This required quarrying out stone, digging into heaps of stones that had been piled up, and carrying them in loads. After the work on the road was over, they were set to uproot the grass in the school compound. But, on the whole, everyone worked cheerfully. I also went with the gangs for three days to join in this work. There was a telegram meanwhile that I should not be taken for work outside. I was rather disappointed, for I liked going out. It improved my health and kept me fit. Ordinarily, I have two meals a day, but on account of this exercise, the stomach insisted on my having three meals while in Volksrust Gaol. I was now assigned only the work of sweeping. That kind of work, I thought, would do me no good. And then came a time when I was denied even this.

I wrote to Chanchal from there saying, 'Be sure that Harilal and I are quite well', and that we were happier there than she was in Phoenix. I asked her to read the letter out to Kastur and read out good writings and poems to her.[268]

On 2 March, I heard that my removal to Pretoria had been ordered. I was asked to get ready the same day. It was raining, the roads were bad; despite this, my warder and I were obliged to leave, with my luggage on my head. I was taken by the evening train the same day in a third-class carriage. Some thought that this might possibly mean a settlement; others felt that the intention was probably to harass me by isolating me from the rest. Some also thought that the object might be to keep me in Pretoria and give me more freedom and better facilities so as to prevent a discussion in the House of Commons. I did not like leaving Volksrust. Happy during the day, the evenings too we passed in cheerful conversation. Mr Hajurasingh and Mr Joshi, especially, asked a number of questions, which were in no way flippant but were quite instructive. Which satyagrahi would like to leave a place where conditions were so happy and where the largest number of Indians were congregated? But man would not be man if things always happened as he wished. And so I left. On the way, Mr Kajee saluted me. The warder and I found ourselves huddled up in a compartment. It was cold, and it rained the whole night. I had my overcoat with me, which I was allowed to put on.

I felt a little better after that. I had been given bread and cheese to eat on the way. I did not touch them, since I had had my meal before starting. They were consumed by the warder.

I reached Pretoria on the 3rd. Everything appeared unfamiliar. Even the gaol is of recent construction. The men were strangers. They gave me something to eat, but I had no appetite. They placed before me mealie meal porridge; I tasted a spoonful, and left it off. The warder was surprised. I told him that I was not hungry. He smiled. Then I passed on to the charge of another warder. He said: 'Gandhi, take off your cap.' I did so. He then asked me: 'Are you Gandhi's son?' 'No,' I replied, 'my son is serving six months in Volksrust.' I was then locked up in a cell. I began pacing up and down. Before long, the warder peeped through the watch-hole, saw what I was doing and shouted: 'Gandhi, stop walking about like that; my floor is being spoiled.' I stopped, and stood in a corner. I had nothing even to read. I had not yet received my books. I must have been locked in at eight. At ten, I was taken to the physician. He asked me if I suffered from any contagious disease, and dismissed me. Was locked in again. At eleven, I was removed to another small cell. It was in this that I spent the rest of my term. It was a cell of the kind intended for one prisoner at a time. It measured, I believe, ten feet long and seven broad. The floor was covered with black pitch. The warders were constantly engaged in keeping it shining. For ventilation, it had a very small glass window, with iron bars. It was provided with an electric light for keeping a watch on the prisoner during the night. The light is not meant for the prisoner's use, for it is not powerful enough to read by. Standing close to it, I could read a book printed in large type. The light was put out exactly at eight. But it was switched on five or six times in the night when the warders have a look at the prisoner through the watch-hole mentioned above. After eleven, the deputy governor came. I asked for three things from him: books, permission to write to my wife who was ill, and a small bench to sit on. As to the first, the reply was: 'I shall see'; as to the second: 'Yes'; as to the third: 'No'. When, however, I wrote in Gujarati, the letter was returned to me with the remark that I should write in English.

I said in reply that my wife did not know English, that my letters served as medicine for her, that they contained nothing of special significance. In spite of this, however, I did not get the permission. I refused to avail myself of the permission to write in English. The same evening my books were handed over to me. When the midday meal arrived, I had to eat it in the cell standing, with the doors shut. At about three, I asked permission to take a bath. The spot for bathing must have been at a distance of about 125 feet. The warder replied: 'All right. Undress (make yourself naked) and go.' I asked him if this was necessary, suggesting that I could place my clothes on the screen. He then gave his permission, but asked me to be quick. While I had yet to wipe my body after bath, the gentleman shouted: 'Are you ready, Gandhi?' I said I would not take long. I hardly ever got an opportunity to see an Indian face. When it was evening, I was given a blanket, with half a piece in addition, and a coir mat by way of bedding; there was no pillow or bed-board. Even when I went for evacuation, a warder stood by to keep watch. If by chance he did not know me, he would shout: 'Sam, come out now.' But Sam had the bad habit of taking a long time for evacuation; how could he get out so soon, and if he did, how would he feel easy in the bowels afterwards? Sometimes a white warder, and sometimes a Kaffir would thus stand by, and keep peeping over or shouting to the refrain of 'get up, get up'. The next day, I was given the work of polishing the floor and doors. The latter were made of varnished iron. What was the point of polishing them every day? I often spent three hours at a stretch on polishing one door. But I could not observe the slightest difference. Yes, it did make some difference to the floor. There were some Kaffirs working with me. They would sometimes talk in broken English of how they had come to be imprisoned, and ask me questions about my imprisonment. One asked me whether I had committed theft, and another whether I had been imprisoned for selling liquor. When I explained the correct position to one of the intelligent Kaffirs, he exclaimed, 'Quite right.' 'Amlungu bad' (The whites are bad). 'Don't pay fine.' My cell bore the description 'isolated'. I saw five other cells adjoining mine bearing the same description. My neighbour was a

Kaffir who had been serving a term of imprisonment for attempted murder. The three next to him were convicted of sodomy. It was in the company of such men and in such surroundings that I commenced my experience in Pretoria Gaol.[269]

The Pretoria prison authorities would not grant permission for me to write to Kastur in Gujarati. She wanted to read my own writing. I was told that even if a letter in Gujarati were passed, it would take quite ten days before it could be transmitted. Since it is more dignified not to take advantage of a privilege grudgingly given, I did not press for permission. I asked West on 4 March to write to me, or for Manilal to do so in English on how she was progressing from day to day and also about Harilal's wife. I asked him to please tell Kastur that I was all right and not to worry about me. For the sake of the children, I said she should help herself to get better, should have the bandages regularly and add hip baths if necessary and should adhere to the diet that I used to give. She ought not to start walking till she is quite restored. I also told West that Chanchal who had all the directions should follow them. She ought on no account to omit sago and milk in the morning, with Manilal watching that she takes it. And Rami* should have the breast yet for a month and can only be gradually weaned.'[270]

Four days later, I was summoned as a witness in Mrs Pillay's case. I was, accordingly, taken to the court. I was handcuffed on the occasion. Moreover, the warder locked up the handcuffs rather tight. I think he did this unintentionally. The chief warder saw this. I had obtained his permission to carry a book with me to read [on the way]. Thinking probably that I felt ashamed of the handcuffs, he asked me to hold the book with both hands, so that the handcuffs might not be seen. I was rather amused at this. To me the handcuffs were a matter of honour. It happened by chance that the title of the book which I was carrying, if rendered in Gujarati would be: Khuda-no Darbar Tara Antar-man Chhe†. I regarded this as a wonderful

---

*Harilal's and Chanchal's infant daughter.
†*The Kingdom of God is Within You* by Tolstoy.

coincidence. Whatever the difficulties that pressed on me from outside, so long as I kept my heart worthy of God's presence in it, what need had I to mind anything else? I was taken on foot in this fashion. For the return journey, a truck was sent from the gaol. Indians must have come to know that I was to be brought [to the court]; some of them were, therefore, present there.

I had a great many benefits in the course of these three months. One of the most important, to be sure, was that I got an opportunity for reading. I must admit that during the earlier part [of my imprisonment], I often found myself lost in thought and felt dejected. The moment I had succeeded in withdrawing my mind from an unpleasant thought, it would again wander off like a monkey. In such circumstances, men often go mad. My books saved me. Thanks to them, I did not feel much the absence of contacts with Indian friends. Every day I had three hours for reading. I had an hour to myself in the morning, which could be spared [for reading] because I went without a breakfast. It was the same about evening. At noon, I read while eating. Besides, in the evening, I continued reading even after the light was switched on, if I was not too tired. On Saturdays and Sundays, I had plenty of time on hand. I read over thirty books during this period, and reflected on some of them; among these, there were books in English, Hindi, Gujarati, Sanskrit, and Tamil. Notable among the English books, I would say, were those by Tolstoy, Emerson, and Carlyle. The first two were on religious subjects. Along with these, I also borrowed a copy of the Bible from the gaol. Tolstoy's writings are so good and simple that a man belonging to any religion can profit by them. Moreover, he tries to put into practice what he preaches, so that, by and large, they command greater confidence. There is a forceful book by Carlyle on the French Revolution. I realized after reading it that it is not from the white nations that India can learn the way out of her present degradation. It is my belief that the French people have gained nothing of value through the revolution. Mazzini also thought the same way. I came across many instances of satyagraha even in this history. The books in Gujarati, Hindi, and Sanskrit which I read were *Veda-Shabda-Sangna*, sent by Swamiji, the Upanishads received from Bhatt Keshavram, the *Manusmriti* received from Mr Motilal Diwan, the Ramayana printed in Phoenix, *Patanjal-Yoga-Darshan, Ahnika-Prakasha* prepared by Nathuramji, and *Sandhya-ni Gutika,* given by Professor Parmanand, the Gita and the writings of the late worthy poet Raychand. All of them gave me much food for thought. The Upanishads proved a great source of peace to me. One statement in them has made a deep impression on my mind; in substance, it means that everything one does must be done for the welfare of the soul. The thought is expressed in words of great beauty. There is much else in it worthy of attention. But it was the writings of the poet Raychand which proved the most satisfying. So far as I can judge, they should appeal to all. His way of life was noble, like Tolstoy's. I memorized a portion of his writings and of the book on Sandhya. I would repeat them over and over again in my mind whenever I happened to wake up at night, and every morning I spent half an hour meditating on them. I would recite most of what I had memorized, and this kept me cheerful all the time. If ever I gave way to despair, I would smile with happiness again the moment I went back in thought to what I had read, and would be filled with gratitude to God. On this subject, too, I have a great many thoughts which I should like to place before the readers. But this is not the occasion to do so. I shall only say this, that in these days, good books partly make up for the absence of good men with whom we can cultivate contacts, and that, therefore, every Indian who wants to be happy in gaol must form the habit of reading good books.

No other Indians can equal the performance of the Tamils in this fight. It therefore occurred to me that I should read Tamil with close attention, if for no other reason than to tender sincere thanks to them at least mentally. Accordingly, the last one month was devoted mostly to the study of Tamil. The more I learn it, the better I appreciate the beauties of this language. It is a very fine and sweet language, and from its structure and from what I have read in it, I find that the Tamils have produced, and still produce, a large number of intelligent, thoughtful and wise men. Moreover, since India is going to be one country, some Indians outside Madras should also learn Tamil.[271]

The Director of Prisons paid a visit, and made kind inquiries about myself, and, when he asked me whether I had any complaints, I pointed to some. A bed-board, felt mattress, nightshirt, and handkerchief were issued to me, and I was allowed the use of pencil and notebook, which had been hitherto denied to me. I would also mention here gratefully that I was allowed an unrestricted use of books, which to me were a source of the greatest consolation. The tailoring work in my cell, which required bending to it for nearly seven hours per day, began to tell upon my health. I, therefore, requested that I should have more active work, or, at least, that I should be allowed to do the tailoring in the open. Both the requests were at first rejected. I suffered, I believe, owing to this close confinement in the cell, from violent neuralgia for nearly ten days, and I developed symptoms, too, of chest disease. On repeating my request, I was allowed to do the tailoring work in the open air.[272]

And then the bench which had been refused to me was later sent by the chief warder of his own accord. Meanwhile, I received from General Smuts two books on religion, and I inferred from this that it was not under his orders that I had been subjected to hardships, but that it was the result of his negligence.[273]

I had a number in this prison—777. That figured at the top of the regulation paper on which I needed to write my letters. On 25 March, I wrote on one of those to Manilal: 'What can be better than that you should have the opportunity of nursing mother and cheerfully bearing her ill temper, or than looking after Chanchi and anticipating her wants and behaving to her so as not to make her feel the want of Harilal or, again, than being guardian to Ramdas and Devadas? If you succeed in doing this well, you have received more than half your education. In your lessons you should give a great deal of attention to Mathematics and Sanskrit. The latter is absolutely necessary for you. Both these studies are difficult in after life. You will not neglect your music. You should make a selection of all the good passages, hymns and verses, whether in English, Gujarati or Hindi and write them out in your best hand in a book.

The collection at the end of a year will be most valuable. All these things you can do easily it you are methodical, never get agitated and think you have too much to do and then worry over what to do first. This you will find out in practice if you are patient and take care of your minutes. I hope you are keeping an accurate account, as it should be kept, of every penny spent for the household.... With love to all and kisses to Ramdas, Devadas, and Rami.'[274]

On removal from Volksrust, Sorabji, Medh, and Harilal were handcuffed together, and marched from the gaol to the station, a distance of over a mile. They were, in spite of the handcuffs, made to carry their own bundles, which were fairly heavy, as they contained, in addition to their personal clothing, books also, and they had to carry things belonging to the warder in charge and one blanket each. They were marched from Park Station to the Fort in the same manner.[275]

On my discharge, at a meeting in Johannesburg on 25 May, I said it was not with any degree of pleasure that I had come out of gaol. The reason was obvious. Some of the best men in the Indian community were still in one or other of the Transvaal gaols, and some of them were elderly men. My own eldest son was also still in gaol. Some of them had still two to two-and-a-half months to do. Some of them had worked with me as friends, and some had gone to gaol simply out of love and regard for me. Could I, as a human being, derive any pleasure from my freedom when all those men had a restraint placed on their liberty? I could not be happy under such circumstances. So long as justice, which was their due, had not been done to them, they could not take food and rest. When that justice was to come, God only knew, but that it was bound to come, they did know. During the last three months, I said I had found much consolation in reading the book of the prophet Daniel in the Bible. Daniel was one of the greatest passive resisters that ever lived, and they must follow his example. The laws of Generals Botha and Smuts, I said, were not for them (Indians) if they were in conflict with their consciences. They must sit with their doors flung wide open and tell those gentlemen that whatever laws they passed were not for them unless those laws were from God.[276]

Eight

DEPUTED TO LONDON AGAIN

...the British were preoccupied with their own affairs.

In June it was decided by leaders of the community that a deputation should be sent to England to place before the authorities and the British public the true situation with regard to the present Asiatic struggle and the British Indian view of the coming Union of South Africa. The deputation was to consist of Messrs A. M. Cachalia, Hajee Habib, V. A. Chettiar, and myself. Simultaneously Messrs N. A. Cama, N. Gopal Naidoo, E. S. Coovadia, and H. S. L. Polak were appointed as a deputation to proceed to India to place before the authorities and the Indian public the true situation with regard to the present Asiatic struggle in the Transvaal. A sudden and unwarranted arrest of Messrs Cachalia, Coovadia, Cama, and Chettiar followed. The government was called upon to release them in order to fulfil their mission under approved security as to their return after completion of their mission, and undergo the sentence passed upon them by the court.[277]

In the event I went with Mr Hajee Habib. But I advised the community that there was no guarantee that by going to England we shall succeed in getting our demands accepted—demands whose rejection has led already to hundreds of Indians going to gaol. It may also happen, I said, that Lord Crewe will refuse to receive the deputation, saying that he cannot meet men who have been defying the law. Those who are sending the deputation must realize, I urged, that in sending a deputation, we were only making an experiment.[278]

Park Station was crowded with Indians seeing us off. About 500 Indians must have assembled. The police had made special arrangements. They were not seen shoving the people about.

A number of Indians were made to stand quite at the back. There were many who had brought bouquets and garlands. This at least could be observed, that every face was lit up with the hope that the deputation might meet with success. Mr Kallenbach, his partner Mr Kennedy, Mr MacIntyre, Miss Olive Doke, Miss Schlesin and Mr Polak were also there. The train started exactly at 6.15 p.m. On the way, Mr Hajee Habib suffered from some infection in the left eye. It had been with him from before he left Johannesburg. The eye was a violent red and watered profusely. A wash with hot saline water gave him relief, but not much. We had to consult the physician on board the ship, RMS *Kenilworth Castle*. I put eye drops every day twice or thrice, in addition to which ice-cold compresses were also being applied. The physician was very solicitous.[279]

Mrs Olive Schreiner, a prominent South African lady, and Mrs Lewis came on board the ship specially to shake hands with us. Both the ladies appeared to have great sympathy for our cause. We saw that the satyagraha movement had won a place in their hearts. Mr Cachalia sent in a cable a rousing and stirring call to the deputation to do its duty. It read as follows: 'Happy to know both going. Suffering in gaol for country's sake preferable to going with you. Wish you success.' Mr Ebrahim Coovadia sent the following telegram at the time of his arrest: 'On way to gaol, wish the deputation success. Can serve the community best through gaol.' I was aware that there could be nothing but empty bubbles where we were going, whereas those who were in gaol at that moment were assuredly serving the community. I was convinced that whatever the deputation may be able to achieve will be nothing as compared to the value of the gaol-goers' service. Mr Cachalia, Mr Coovadia, and other prisoners demonstrated the new spirit of the Indian community. Those who have pinned their hopes on the deputation would, I knew, be disappointed, if we returned empty-handed. Therefore, I advised everyone to expect nothing from the deputation.[280]

As in 1906, I sent Ramdas a picture postcard showing the steamer we were on.[281] It is far better to be in prison than travel first class on a ship. Another passenger, Bhikhubhai Dayalji Malia was travelling third class. Mr Habib and I saw him every day. That gave us some experience of what third-class travel means. I am of the opinion that the freedom and comfort available in the third class are not to be found in the first class. But even that cannot match what is available in gaol. The servants in a ship are happier—if only they knew it—than the passengers. First-class passengers are looked after by servants as though they were so many babies. There is something to eat every two hours. We cannot even lift a glass of water with our own hands. At the table it is considered beneath one's dignity to reach out one's hand for a spoon lying at some distance. As for work, first-class passengers have hardly any, so that they are growing altogether delicate and soft. It vexed me to observe the state of my hands and compare it with what they were like in gaol. I envied the servants at their work. Here on board I had neither the peace nor the freedom I enjoyed in gaol. On the contrary, I had to live hedged in on all sides. My prayers lacked the depth, the serenity, and concentration they had when I was in gaol. Prayers do not come easily in an atmosphere of luxuries. Even if we do not ourselves share the luxuries, we cannot escape their natural influence.[282]

I had known Mr Hajee Habib for the last fifteen years. But I never had any opportunity of living with him as I had on board this ship. Hajee sahib is a man of strict religious principles. He kept the namaz hours punctually. He carefully followed the religious injunctions about food and drink. He allowed me to decide for him the menu for every meal. I knew what would prove acceptable to him. In the morning he had porridge, eggs, and tea. At noon, boiled potatoes, sometimes fish, a vegetable called lettuce, much like the moola, some variety of pudding, fruit and coffee, and in the evening some leafy vegetable, pudding, fruit, and coffee. The ghee and pickles given to him when he started the journey, he passed on to Mr Bhikhubhai. It was a constant thought with him how to make the deputation a success, and we frequently came together to apply our minds to the problem. The passengers on board the ship seemed to think that we were brothers.[283]

I, as usual, had two meals a day. I avoided the pudding as it contained eggs. I also avoided tea and coffee as far as possible, since they are the produce of slave labour. In other respects, my diet was the same as Mr Habib's, except for fish. I am growing more convinced every day, as my body hardens, that I can do with still simpler food. On this voyage I did not feel a craving for delicacies as I did on the previous occasion. Most of the day was spent in reading. The statement to be submitted in England had already been drafted, and approved by Mr Habib. He made some suggestions, which were incorporated.[284]

With Habib's help, I read a book named *Kasassul Ambia*. In it I read how it was commanded of Azazil that should he fail, after 600,000 years of prayers to God, to bow to Him even on a single occasion, all his prayers would be as though they had never been. The point is, first, that it is what we do when we reach the last stage which will provide the test of our sincerity. Second, we can make no conditions with God. We must live as He may order us. If, having gone to gaol ten times, we refuse to do so on the eleventh occasion, the ten previous terms of imprisonment will have been in vain and we shall be laughed at.[285]

We arrived at Southampton on 10 July. South African leaders were also in London at the time, Mr Botha and General Smuts among them, to discuss the unification of South Africa. We were met by a Reuter representative. We gave him a brief statement of facts, and the report appeared in most newspapers. In that we said, 'We feel we must take this opportunity when so many South African statesmen are in this country to see whether something cannot be done to relieve the very acute suffering which British Indians in the Transvaal have been undergoing for the past two-and-a-half years. Our mission does not seriously affect the question of unification except that every Indian feels that the Imperial government should take full guarantee regarding the status of British Indians in South Africa under the Union.'[286]

We reached London at about 10.30 a.m. After conveying our luggage to Hotel Cecil, we set to work the moment we had had our lunch. We, the two 'brothers', accompanied by Mr Abdul

Caadir, Mr Ritch and Mr Hussain Dawad, called on Sir Mancherji Bhownaggree and wrote to Lord Ampthill, former acting viceroy and governor general of India and at that point heading the London Committee for British Indians in South Africa.

And so the round of interviews began that was to go on for nearly four months. The whole day was taken up in interviewing people and writing letters, and we kept working even at night. Being free, Maud Polak, Henry's sister, was entrusted with typing work.

Before long we had met Lord Ampthill, Sir Richard Solomon, Miss Winterbottom, Mr Surendranath Banerjea, Mr Cotton, Mr Justice Ameer Ali, and others. I was able to see that everyone approved of our having courted imprisonment and that, if anything counts, it is the fact that so many Indians have gone and are still going to gaol.[287]

But this was a very bad time to seek interviews with public figures in London. Everyone was out of town on a holiday, so that we were not likely to get help from many people. Moreover, the British people were preoccupied with their own affairs. The new budget had raised a storm in Parliament. Also, the visit of South African statesmen made a heavy demand on people's time. Considering all this and looking at the circumstances around us, I was inclined to believe that, should the private moves that are underway at present fail, nothing was likely to be achieved by our visit.[288]

The terrible tragedy about Sir Curzon Wyllie and Dr Lalkaka* had complicated the situation. The assassin, Madanlal Dhingra, was courageous in inviting death but it was the result of intoxication. It is not merely wine or bhang that makes one drunk; a mad idea also can do so.[289]

Mr Hajee Habib worked splendidly. He always kept me up to the mark and did not let me forget anything at all. We worked in perfect harmony. His eye which had caused him trouble throughout

---

*William Curzon Wyllie, political aide-de-camp to Morley, Secretary of State for India, was shot dead on 1 July 1909 by an Indian student, Madanlal Dhingra, at a reception held by the National Indian Association at the Imperial Institute in South Kensington, London. Dr Cawas Lalkaka, a Parsi doctor from Shanghai, was fatally wounded while trying to save Sir Curzon Wyllie.

the voyage soon became much better, though a slight inflammation persisted.

On 15 July, we received a cablegram saying that the struggle had taken its first victim. A young Indian, Sammy Nagappen, sentenced on 21 June last to be imprisoned for ten days with hard labour in connection with the struggle, was discharged on 30 June in a dying condition, and died on 6 July. The allegations according to the cablegram are that it was bitterly cold, the blankets supplied were insufficient, the native warders were brutal, and medical attendance was not forthcoming. There are at present about 100 Indians in the Transvaal gaols and during the struggle over 2,500 Indians have passed through them.[290]

On 23 July, Madanlal Dhingra's case came up for hearing. We were not permitted to be present in the court. Since Mr Dhingra did not put up any defence, the case did not take much time. He only stated that he had done the deed for the good of his country, and that he did not regard it as a crime. The presiding judge sentenced him to death. Mr Dhingra's statement, according to me, argues mere childishness or mental derangement. The assassination was at a tea meeting of the National Indian Association in the Jehangir Hall of the Imperial Institute. Such meetings are arranged with the object of bringing Indian students into contact with Englishmen, who therefore attend as the guests of Indians. Sir Curzon Wyllie was [thus] a guest of the assassin. From this point of view, Mr Madanlal Dhingra murdered his guest in his own house, and also killed Dr Lalkaka who tried to interpose himself between them. Those who incited him to this act will be called to account in God's court, and are also guilty in the eyes of the world. I must say that those who believe and argue that such murders may do good to India are ignorant men indeed. No act of treachery can ever profit a nation. Even should the British leave in consequence of such murderous acts, who will rule in their place? The only answer is: the murderers. Who will then be happy?[291]

As advised by Lord Ampthill, we requested Lord Crewe and Lord Morley to fix time for interviews with them. The more experience I had of meeting so-called big men or even men who are really great, the more disgusted I felt after every such meeting. All such efforts were no better than pounding chaff. Everyone appeared preoccupied with their own affairs. Those who occupied positions of power showed little inclination to do justice. Their only concern was to hold on to their positions. We had to spend a whole day in arranging for an interview with one or two persons, write a letter to the person concerned, wait for his reply, acknowledge it and then go to his place. One may be living in the north and another in the south. Even after all this fuss, one could not be very hopeful about the outcome. If considerations of justice had any appeal, we would have got long before. Far better to submit to still further suffering than exhaust ourselves in such efforts and waste so much money on them.

Dhingra was awarded the death penalty. Some whites tried to secure remission of the death penalty. They argued that he acted out of foolishness. Moreover, they added, the act was not inspired by any personal motive and, therefore, should not be treated as ordinary murder.[292]

Lord Ampthill asked me if our movement in South Africa was in any way connected to the extremist groups in India. I replied on 4 August: 'I am fully aware of the allegation that we are acting in co-operation with the Extremist Party in India. I however give Your Lordship the emphatic assurance that the charge is totally without foundation. Indian passive resistance in the Transvaal had its rise in that colony and has been continued absolutely independent of anything that is being said or done in India; indeed, sometimes, even in defiance of what has been said or written to the contrary in India or elsewhere. Our movement is absolutely unconnected with any extremist movement in India.'[293]

On 10 August, I wrote to Manilal to say there was little hope of any settlement. He was, I knew, wanting to know of life in London and of prospects of study and work here. I said to him: 'The more I observe things here, the more I feel that there is no reason to believe that this place is particularly suited for any type of better education. I also see that some of the education imparted here is faulty. However, there is a constant desire in my mind that each of you should be able to come and stay here for a while at least. If we go on doing our duty properly, we need not worry about the future. Your studying there earnestly would be your preparation for coming here.'[294] On another subject on his mind—marriage—I advised: 'Thinking of the state of affairs in the country, I believe very few Indians need marry at the present time. The significance of marriage is also very deep. A person who marries in order to satisfy his carnal desire is lower than even the beast. Do not be scared by this and think that I want to bind you not to marry even after the age of twenty-five. I do not want to put undue pressure on you or on anyone whatever. I just want to give you advice.'

Polak meanwhile was touring India and met Professor Gokhale. Polak wrote to me on 14 August about Gokhale: 'He is not hopeful, but is putting the whole of his energies and organization at my disposal. Agrees to necessity of meeting. Promises to work on Sir Pherozeshah Mehta who is holding back. Maps out itinerary—Bombay, Poona, Surat, Baroda, Ahmedabad, Madras, Calcutta, UP etc., etc. Will arrange everything for the future. Wonderful man, has most accurate knowledge of facts and principles. Huge admirer of yours. Is worn out with overwork, worry, and malaria fever.'[295]

Such was the prevailing misconstruction about our movement and the cult of assassination that I had to again write to Lord Ampthill on 29 July: 'I know of no Indian, whether here, in South Africa or in India, who had so steadily, even defiantly, set his face against sedition—as I understand it—as I have. It is part of my faith not to have anything to do with it, even at the risk of my life. Most people, that is most Indians and Anglo-Indians, express their detestation of bomb throwing and violence in words or in unreasonable action. The movement in the Transvaal, with which I have identified myself is an eloquent and standing protest in action against such methods. The test of passive resistance is self-suffering and not infliction of suffering on others. We have, therefore, not only never received a single farthing from 'the party of sedition' in India or elsewhere, but even if there was any offer, we should, if we were true to our principles, decline to receive it. We have hitherto made it a point not to approach the Indian public in India for financial assistance. The accounts of the British Indian Association are open to the world.'[296]

Harilal was, meanwhile, released on 9 August only to be rearrested. I wrote to him on 2 September, care the Johannesburg Prison: '...Henceforth the struggle will be very sharp. I see father and son spending a lifetime in gaol. On my part, I am prepared for it, but I would like to know your state of mind about this. I pray to God that you be afforded all the energy required...I keep feeling it is good that you and I be together in gaol....'[297]

Correspondence with Kallenbach was maintained. On 9 October, a day after I had spoken at Emerson Club to a good audience on the ethics of passive resistance, I told him: '...I failed to find a response. Could I, when I said that if a robber robbed me I should not offer violence or physical resistance even if I was capable of using it? However it set the friends thinking....' [298]

And on 12 October, I had to confess to him: '...My feet are rotten for having to have boots on from 8 a.m. or 9 a.m. to 12 or 2 midnight....'[299]

And by 5 November, I was telling Polak about Harilal in gaol: 'I am itching to join him.'[300] Harilal went to Phoenix on his release but had to return to Johannesburg shortly thereafter to rejoin the struggle.

A meeting to bid farewell to Hajee Habib and me on the eve of our departure for South Africa was held at Westminster Palace Hotel on 12 November. Letters were received from Lord Ampthill, Lord Curzon, Lord Prince Duleep Singh, and other gentlemen expressing their inability to attend. Sir Charles Bruce wrote as follows: 'Although the cause they represent is passing through a dark hour, I am not discouraged. In the history of the human race, it has been darkest before the dawn.... Never did the cause of the Negro seem more hopeless than during the years that preceded the abolition of slavery.... The Saviour of the world deemed Himself lost in the moment that brought our redemption. And so I join you in spirit in wishing Godspeed to Messrs Gandhi and Hajee Habib.'

Sir William Markby wrote: '...I hear that they have not obtained the small measure of justice which they came to this country to ask. No one disputes the reasonableness of their claim. It is for political reasons only that the government refuses to interfere. It is not pleasant to see again and again the British government showing its inability to enforce the just claims of its subjects.' The function was attended, among others, by Princess Sophia Duleep Singh, Sir Raymond West, Mr Ameer Ali, Sir Frederick Lely, Dr Rutherford, Sir Muncherji Bhownaggree, Major Syed Hussain Bilgrami, Miss Winterbottom, Mr and Mrs Dube, the Hon'ble Mr Daaji Abaji Khare, Mrs Khare, Mr Motilal Nehru, Mr and Mrs Marnham, Mr and Mrs Ratcliffe, Mr Ritch, and Mr Ismail Ise.

Speeches were made by Sir Raymond West and Sir Frederick Lely besides me. I said: 'If you, at this meeting, think that the ideals that had led the passive resisters cheerfully to experience these sufferings appeal to you, then you should send that little community of passive resisters your encouragement and sympathy and a word of cheer. At the conclusion of the meeting, the following resolution was unanimously passed: "That this meeting desires to express its earnest sympathy with the Transvaal British Indians in their peaceful and selfless struggle for civic rights and to offer its warmest encouragement to them in this struggle."'[301]

Hajee Habib and I sailed on the SS *Kildonan Castle* on 13 November.

My old friend Dr Pranjivan Mehta who had, characteristically, come to England when I was there, had found a typed copy of Count Leo Tolstoy's *Letter to a Hindoo* circulating in Indian circles and gave me it to me. I liked the letter. I sent it to Tolstoy and sought his permission to publish it, asking him at the same time whether the letter was in fact written by him. The permission having been received, I commenced the translation into Gujarati for publication in *Indian Opinion*. To me Tolstoy's letter is of great value. Anyone who has enjoyed the experience of the Transvaal struggle would, I could see, perceive the letter's value readily enough. A handful of Indian satyagrahis have pitted love or soul-force against the might of the Transvaal government's guns. That is the central principle of

Tolstoy's teaching, of the teaching of all religions. Khuda–Ishwar has endowed our soul with such strength that sheer brute force is of no avail against it. We have been employing that strength against the Transvaal government not out of hatred or with a view to revenge, but merely in order to resist its unjust order. Tolstoy gives a simple answer to those Indians who appear impatient to drive the whites out of India. We are [according to him] our own slaves, not of the British. This should be engraved in our minds. The whites cannot remain if we do not want them. If the idea is to drive them out with firearms, let every Indian consider what precious little profit Europe has found in these.

In translating [the letter], I endeavoured to use the simplest possible Gujarati. I was mindful of the fact that readers of *Indian Opinion* prefer simple language. Moreover, I wanted Tolstoy's letter to be read by thousands of Gujarati Indians, and knew that difficult language could prove tedious reading to such large numbers.

I also wrote a Preface to that letter, drawing attention to Tolstoy's words: 'A commercial company enslaved a nation comprising 200 million. Tell this to a man free from superstition and he will fail to grasp what these words mean. What does it mean that thirty thousand people, not athletes but rather weak and ill-looking, have enslaved 200 millions of vigorous, clever, strong, freedom-loving people? Do not the figures make it clear that not the English but the Indians have enslaved themselves?' I ended the Preface with: 'He is sincere and in earnest. He commands attention.'[302]

Next, I wrote in Gujarati some chapters on the subject of Indian Home Rule which I ventured to place before the readers of *Indian Opinion*. My work on Tolstoy's letter and this project of mine were connected.

Dr Mehta had been intrigued by what Tolstoy had written and he and I discussed the idea of bombs and independence. At first, although he loved me, he thought I was foolish and sentimental. But I did place my point of view before him. It appealed to his heart. His attitude changed.

After that discussion I had to write what I wrote because I could not restrain myself. The text took the form of a dialogue between the editor (myself) and a reader, whose views and arguments represented those Dr Mehta had used in our discussions. I had read much, pondered much, during the stay, for four months in London, of the Transvaal Indian deputation. I discussed things with as many of my countrymen as I could. I met, too, as many Englishmen as it was possible for me to meet. I considered it my duty to place before the readers of *Indian Opinion* the conclusions, which appear to me to be final. These views were mine, and yet not mine. They were mine because I hoped to act according to them. They were almost a part of my being. But, yet, they were not mine, because I could lay no claim to originality. They had been formed after reading several books.[303]

The following featured, among other exchanges, in it:

READER: At first, we shall assassinate a few Englishmen and strike terror; then, a few men who will have been armed will fight openly. We may have to lose a quarter of a million men, more or less, but we shall regain our land. We shall undertake guerrilla warfare, and defeat the English.

EDITOR: That is to say, you want to make the holy land of India unholy. Do you not tremble to think of freeing India by assassination? What we need to do is to sacrifice ourselves. It is a cowardly thought, that of killing others. Whom do you suppose to free by assassination? The millions of India do not desire it. Those who are intoxicated by the wretched modern civilization think these things. Those who will rise to power by murder will certainly not make the nation happy. Those who believe that India has gained by Dhingra's act and other similar acts in India make a serious mistake. Dhingra was a patriot, but his love was blind. He gave his body in a wrong way; its ultimate result can only be mischievous.

'There is no end to the work I have put in on the steamer this time,' I wrote to Maganlal. 'I have many things to say but that must wait till we meet. Just now, I shall write only what is necessary.' He had written to me about the Phoenix Settlement's name and made some suggestions. I responded to that by saying: 'It seems quite appropriate that the name of Phoenix should be that and nothing else. I wish that my name is forgotten, and only my work endures. The work will endure only if the name is forgotten. And even when a name is given, we shall have to find a common word over which the question of Hindu or Musalman will not arise. The word 'math' or 'ashram' has a particularly Hindu connotation and therefore may not be used. 'Phoenix' is a very good word which has come to us without any effort on our part. Being an English word, it serves to pay homage to the land in which we live. Moreover, it is neutral. Its significance, as the legend goes, is that the bird Phoenix comes back to life again and again from its own ashes, i.e., it never dies. The name Phoenix, for the present, serves the purpose quite well, for we believe that the aims of Phoenix will not vanish even when we are turned to dust. We shall see what we can do later on. At present our whole structure and behaviour is that of the bird Phoenix.'[304]

Nine

BACK TO STRUGGLE AND A NEW EXPERIMENT

I must live there even for the sake of the struggle.

I expected to be arrested on landing in South Africa before reaching Johannesburg. With that in mind I wrote from the ship to Kallenbach in Johannesburg on 25 November: 'Whichever turn the struggle takes, it is the best discipline I can have. Whilst I work strenuously to bring it to close, I continue in it as if it was to last a lifetime.' I also shared with him some concerns about Phoenix, the equations between Desai, the school principal, and Cordes, the teacher and the family: 'Cordes continues to cause trouble. He has been swearing, it appears, at Purushottamdas Desai who, so far as I know, is a very quiet and amiable man. He has felt it terribly, I do not want to write to Cordes for fear I may offend him without doing good. There seems to have been some financial trouble also. I fear that Phoenix has to be supplied with funds. What the condition there is, I do not know. I can only leave the matter in your hands to do the best you can and to ease the situation at Phoenix. Devadas, I notice, was very ill and had not recovered quite at the time they wrote to me.'

I wrote to Maganlal in Phoenix on 27 November: 'Phoenix will be put to test now. Probably we may not get money from Johannesburg. Our pledge is that we shall bring out at least a one-page issue of *Indian Opinion* and distribute it among the people as long as there is even one person in Phoenix. Do not allow any intrigues to flourish there.... I intend to sacrifice Manilal in the struggle if he is willing and if Ba agrees. That will calm his restless mind. In fact, he wanted it himself. But if this does not materialize, it is just as well that he goes to Durban, and you remain in Phoenix.'

And, on the same day to young Ramdas: 'I write this letter to you as I do not know when we shall meet. Do not be angry with me if I have not brought anything for you. There was nothing I liked. What could I do if nothing European appealed to me? I like everything Indian. The people of Europe are good, but their way of life is not good. I shall explain this to you in detail when we meet. Do not be upset if I go to gaol; rather you should rejoice. I should be where Harilal is. I must live there even for the sake of the struggle. Be cheerful. I want to see you stout and strong.'[305]

On the day we reached Cape Town (30 November) a welcome surprise awaited us.[306] We received a cablegram from Professor Gokhale informing us that Mr Ratanji Jamshedji Tata of Bombay had given 25,000 rupees in aid of the Transvaal struggle. This munificent aid showed that the motherland is fully alive. It required passive resisters to show they are prepared to die for a cause that is righteous, godly, and national. I cabled Professor Gokhale:

> Pray thank Mr Tata for munificent timely help. Distress great. Prisoners' lot hard. Religious scruples disregarded. Rations short. Prisoners carry slop-pails; for refusing, put on spare diet. Solitary confinement. Prominent Moslems, Hindus, Parsis in jail. Gandhi.

On 5 December, I paid a visit to Mr Rustomji in Diepkloof Gaol. He was very much broken down; he did not receive the medical food that was prescribed for him at Volksrust. The Parsis—I mean the orthodox Parsis—never take off their caps, but Mr Rustomji had by now been compelled to remove his cap, although he was allowed to keep it on at Volksrust and Houtpoort. He had been put on stone-breaking while suffering from a constitutional disease; his eyesight was affected; he was a most pitiable and piteous sight.[307] I apprised Professor Gokhale of this and other difficulties and also our achievements in a letter that I wrote to him on 6 December: 'Some of the bravest Indians representing all races are at present in Diepkloof Gaol. The foremost among them I count Mr Rustomji, who has now finished over nine months of continuous imprisonment. He is very much shattered in health. I paid him a visit yesterday; he is resolved upon dying in gaol if need be. Another is a cultured Mahomedan priest, Imam Abdul Kadir Bawazeer. The third is a Mahomedan merchant of standing, Mr Ebrahim Aswat from the Surat District. The fourth is an undergraduate and Jain, Mr Nanalal Shah. The fifth is a Brahmin from Ahmedabad, Mr Umiashanker Shelat. He has refused to carry slop-pails, and is now confined in a solitary cell. But perhaps the bravest and the staunchest of all is the indomitable Thambi Naidoo. I do not know any Indian who knows the spirit of the struggle so well as he does. He was born in Mauritius, but is more Indian than most of us. He has sacrificed himself entirely, and has sent me a defiant message, saying that, even though I may yield and accept anything less than Lord Ampthill's amendment, he alone will offer resistance and die in the Transvaal gaols. I may perhaps add to this list another young man, Mr Sorabji. He left a lucrative post in order to lay the foundation of the second stage of the struggle and claim entry as an educated Indian. He came light-heartedly not knowing what was in store for him, but for the last eighteen months he has been practically in gaol. I could continue to multiply the names. In all, there are about thirty Indian passive resisters in the gaols at present; many more would certainly claim the honours if the government would give them.'

On 20 December, I wrote a letter to the Editor of *Indian Opinion*: 'I hope that I shall find myself lodged in gaol before this letter appears in print. My second son (Manilal) lives with me. For some time past I had been thinking of asking him to join the struggle. He was insistent. It appeared to me, on deep reflection, that it would be right to bring him in. I believe that to go to gaol or suffer similar hardships with a pure motive for the sake of the motherland is the truest kind of education. Since I look upon gaol as a kind of palace, how can I deny the privilege of being there to those whom I hold dear? My son has attained the age when he can think for himself. For my part, I should like to tell all Indian parents and all Indian youths that success will attend those who have joined the struggle. It is they that do the fighting who profit most from it. To those who are in gaol now I make this request, that they should make up their minds to return to gaol the moment they are released, without so much as pausing for breath. An exception may be made only in the case of Mr Rustomji. If he is not arrested [on his release], he would do well to go to Durban for a month. But as soon as a month is over, it will be his duty, so at least it appears to me, to return [to the Transvaal], whatever the state of his health. Those who are outside should think of possible ways of getting into gaol. Failing everything else, it will be easy enough for them to fill the gaols in January or February. Whether or not others fill them, it is obviously the duty of those who would do so for the sake of India not to pause even a moment for breath.'

On 22 December, Manilal and I accompanying six others crossed the Natal–Transvaal border and were not challenged by enforcers of the immigration procedures. This was I believe so as to avoid causing a sensation at the session of the Indian National Congress then taking place in Lahore.* Polak who was in India and had met Gokhale had spoken to several audiences about happenings in the Transvaal. On 29 December, the Congress session in Lahore passed a resolution expressing admiration for the struggle in South Africa and urged the ending of indenture.

Polak returned to South Africa at the end of December. Along with Parsi Rustomji and others from the family I went to Port Durban to receive him. As the ship neared the pier, Polak waved from the deck. When, standing on the deck with Prabhudas, Chhaganlal waved back, a port official brusquely asked him to step back. Chhaganlal held his ground. 'Don't you hear me?' the white employee shouted at Chhaganlal. 'Hey you! I am asking you to move and you are not?' Saying that he moved threateningly towards Chhaganlal when I shouted back, twice as loud, 'HE SHAN'T MOVE AN INCH'.

---

*At the Lahore Congress, Gokhale said: 'It is one of the privileges of my life that I know Mr Gandhi personally and I tell you that a purer, a nobler, a braver and a more exalted spirit has never moved on this earth.... He is a man among men, a hero among heroes, a patriot among patriots, and we may well say that in him humanity at the present time has reached its high watermark.'

The man was stunned and was moved away by his colleagues.[308]

Harilal was out of gaol in May and went to Phoenix to be with the family for a while before returning to struggle and to gaol.[309]

The British Constitution keeps the king outside of politics. His personal qualities alone count. When, in the beginning of May, the death was announced of King Edward, *Indian Opinion*, in a boxed item with thick black lines, said: 'Indians will best remember His late Majesty as a sovereign who followed in the footsteps of his mother of revered memory. Like her, the late king had shown a warm corner in his bosom for the people of India. And that will always be a title to our affection for his memory. The Indian people, whatever their views on British policies, will always bear the purest affection for the king.'[310]

On march through Volksrust crossing into the Transvaal.
Courtesy: Sabarmati Ashram Preservation and Memorial Trust, Ahmedabad.

BOOK V
1910 to 1913

Gandhi in South Africa is now being 'made' on that iconic terrain. His body, mind, and soul are being bronzed in the Phoenix Settlement and on Tolstoy Farm. His colleagues and his family, with his wife foremost among them, go through the same fiery test as he does. There is no guarantee of success, only of suffering. There is no telling whether the struggle will avail or when, if at all. And yet they are all in it. Prison gates await and engulf them, men and women, young, and those not young at all.

Gandhi's sons are Gandhi's sons and Kasturba's, but they are also their own selves—with abilities and aspirations, fragilities and failings. They are guided by their resolute father and tended by their mother but they question the man who is now so clearly a mass leader, about his own ideals, his vision for them, his and their future. Harilal sees in Gandhi's drenching of his soul in the cause of Indian South Africans a parching of his care for the family, particularly for his mother. Gandhi contests the charge.

And all this against the backdrop of his galvanizing an upheaval among the Indian population, led as he says, most notably, by its Tamil segment. The Great March of 1913, presaging the ones that are going to shake India, crowns Gandhi's two decades' strivings. Overseen by the Indian statesman Gopal Krishna Gokhale, Gandhi's decisive steps lead to a thawing of South Africa's and Smuts's attitude to Gandhi and to the Indians' cause and a solution begins to come into view.

One

TOLSTOY FARM

*The weak became strong on Tolstoy Farm
and labour became a tonic for all.*

Till now the families of jail-going satyagrahis were maintained by a system of monthly allowances in cash according to their need. There was only one long-term solution for this difficulty, namely, that all the families should be kept at one place and should become members of a sort of cooperative commonwealth. Thus there would be no scope for fraud nor would there be injustice to any.

But where was the place for a settlement of this nature? The place would have to be in the Transvaal and near Johannesburg.[311] What came as a rescue was this letter from Hermann Kallenbach formalizing an idea that had been brewing in his mind:

30 May 1910

Dear Mr Gandhi,

In accordance with our conversation, I offer to you the use of my farm near Lawley for passive resisters and their indigent families; the families and passive resisters to live on the farm free of any rent or charge, as long as the struggle with the Transvaal government lasts.

They may also use, free of charge, all the buildings not at present used by me. Any structural alterations, additions or improvements made by you may be removed at your pleasure on the termination of occupation, or they will be paid for by me at a valuation in the usual manner, the terms of payment to be mutually agreed upon by us.

I propose to pay, at a valuation in the usual manner, [for] all the agricultural improvements that may have been made by the settlers.

The settlers to withdraw from the farm on the termination of the struggle.

Yours sincerely,

H. Kallenbach.

Closing with the offer the same day, I wrote to him:

Dear Mr Kallenbach,

I have shown your kind letter to Mr Cachalia and other fellow passive resisters, and I have to thank you for your generous offer on their and my own behalf. I accept your offer, and I need hardly say to what extent your offer will relieve the financial pressure. As to the improvements and additions referred to in paragraphs 2 and 3 of your letter, I shall keep an accurate account, which shall be open to your inspection, and I shall not undertake improvements or additions without your approval.

I am,

Yours sincerely,

M. K. Gandhi.[312]

Two days after this, on 1 June 1910, the new Union of South Africa was born. On 2 June, I sent a letter to the press saying:

The union has been ushered in among very general rejoicing among the European races of South Africa. Asiatics have also been expected to share in these rejoicings. If they have not been able to respond to these expectations, the cause, so far at least as the Transvaal is concerned, is not far to seek. On the day of the advent of the union, nearly sixty families were deprived of their supporters and were being maintained out of public funds. On the first working day of the union, a cultured Indian and representative Parsi, Mr Sorabji, who has already suffered six terms of imprisonment was re-arrested and is now under orders of deportation. Other passive resisters too continue to be arrested. Mr Joseph Royappen, the barrister and Cambridge graduate, and his companions are again in prison. What can a union under which the above state of things is continued mean to Asiatics except that it is a combination of hostile forces arrayed against them?[313]

Upon the farm of about 1,100 acres were nearly 1,000 fruit-bearing trees and a small house at the foot of the hill with accommodation for half a dozen persons. Water was supplied from two wells as well as a spring. We decided to build houses upon this farm and to invite the families of satyagrahis to settle there.[314]

As regards accommodation for families we resolved from the first that the men and women should be housed separately. The houses were therefore to be built in two separate blocks, each at some distance from the other. For the time it was considered sufficient to provide accommodation for ten women and sixty men. Then again we had to erect a house for Mr Kallenbach and by its side a school house as well as a workshop for carpentry, shoemaking etc.[315]

Kallenbach and I together decided to name the settlement 'Tolstoy Farm'. This was shortly before the great Russian died.

The weak became strong on Tolstoy Farm and labour became a tonic for all.[316]

By June I could write to Dr [Pranjivan] Mehta:

> ...I prepare the bread that is required on the farm. The general opinion about it is that it is well made. Manilal and a few others have learnt how to prepare it. We put in no yeast and no baking powder. We grind our own wheat. We have just prepared some marmalade from the oranges grown on the farm. I have also learnt how to prepare caramel coffee. It can be given as a beverage even to babies. The passive resisters on the farm have given up the use of tea and coffee, and taken to caramel coffee prepared on the farm. It is made from wheat which is first baked in a certain way and then ground. We intend to sell our surplus production of the above articles to the public later on. Just at present, we are working as labourers on the construction work that is going on, on the farm, and have no time to produce more of the articles above mentioned than we need for ourselves.[317]

Two

HARILAL REVOLTS

...one day in early May 1911, when Harilal and I were both in Johannesburg, he just left.

With Manilal and Ramdas, I moved to the Farm on 4 June, asking Maganlal to send to me by goods train a pair of my sandals lying in Phoenix as the one I was using had almost worn out, and Manilal's pair as well, along with his silk suit. Chhaganlal had gone to England to study law and Maganlal had taken over his elder brother's responsibilities on the *Indian Opinion* team. Given the uncertainties of our lives, I asked Chanchal to go back to India. Harilal had a second-class ticket reserved for her.[318]

Harilal could not go to India, escorting Chanchi. We were poor and not in a position to spend money like that. Moreover, having joined the struggle he could not have thus gone away for three months—the time it would have taken for him to go and settle her in and return. So it was decided that Chanchi should go in some good company. 'We do not want our women to remain delicate,' I wrote to Maganlal. Tolstoy Farm had, meanwhile, completely changed my life. I had become a farmer. The whole day was spent in digging the land and other manual labour instead of in writing or explaining things to people. Ramdas dug a pit three feet deep and three feet broad and half of another, working till 1 o'clock. And now I did not see him engrossed in thought as he used to be in Phoenix.[319]

Kastur and Deva joined us on Tolstoy Farm, so except for Harilal who was in and out of gaol, all the boys were with us. Chanchi, with Rami, was back in India. She sent a long and interesting letter which both Kastur and I read with interest. I wrote to Chanchi on 8 November saying that I would show it to Harilal the following day when he is due to come out of gaol. I also told her that she should not wear jewellery for fear of being criticized for not wearing it. There is no beauty in jewellery, I told her. Our custom of wearing ornaments on the nose and ears seems to me to be barbarous. There is no beauty in perforating the nose and ears and inserting something there or in wearing ornaments around the neck or the arms. However, I told Chanchi, I would not say anything about putting bangles on the wrists as their absence would suggest something inauspicious. I told her Harilal, on being released, would be free for some time as they were not making arrests now. He was in excellent health in Johannesburg gaol.[320]

Ramdas and Devadas were very cheerful on the Farm and, with about twenty other boys there, quite at home. Kastur was also happy in the company of other women. She gave up tea and was now habituated to bathe in cold water.[321]

On a January day, all the boys, with Harilal, walked from the Farm to Johannesburg, a distance of 40 miles, and back. I had suggested this to save money, they had agreed and were tested. Devo too had joined. Their health had improved here.[322] I was also busy making sandals on the Farm. I liked the work which was essential too. When I had made about fifteen pairs, I wrote asking Maganlal in Phoenix, when new ones were needed there, to send me the measurements. And to remember to mark the places where the strap is to be fixed—that is, on the outer side of the big toe and the little toe.[323]

Kastur was back in Phoenix later in 1911 when I got a letter from Harilal. It was least expected because any letter from him was a surprise. The general expectation was to have no letter from him. It was meant to speak for her, suggesting that I had stipulated conditions for her returning to Phoenix and that she was scared of going against them. I replied on 5 March to say: 'What you write about Ba is not true.... The fact is that Ba does not know her own mind. However I have nothing to say against your pleading for her.' He had also written about his desire for further studies and about his being weak in Mathematics and general literary education. 'You could have had them had I given you the necessary opportunity,'

I conceded. 'I will not stand in the way of your studies or other ambitions that you may have,' I wrote, 'provided there is nothing positively immoral about them.' I asked him to cast off all fear and pursue studies if he wished to for as long as he liked.'[324]

Harilal was in Phoenix with Kastur and the others for the next few weeks. I visited them when I could or needed to. Once he met me at the Phoenix station and walked with me to our home, carrying my heavy leather bag on his shoulder, Devadas walking behind us. He could not have followed our conversation but he could not have missed the fact that we were both engaged in deep conversation.[325]

I wrote to Maganlal on 19 March: 'The more defects you discover in Harilal, the more love you should have for him. One requires a great deal of water to put out a big fire. To overcome the baser element in Harilal's nature, you have to develop in yourself and pit against it a more powerful force of goodness. Give him the coat too when he asks for a shirt.'[326]

The long-expected immigration bill was received at the beginning of March. It was very complicated and comprehensive. To me it contained the following meaning: (1) The Asiatic Act 2 of 1907 (the 'Black Act') was to be repealed, save in so far as it protects the rights of minors. (2) Act 36 of 1908 was not to be repealed. (3) It seemed, but it was not clear, that those who pass the language test can enter the Transvaal and not be liable to registration. (If that were so, it would stop passive resistance.) (4) The wives and minor children of domiciled Asiatics did not seem to be protected. (5) The granting of certificates of domicile to Asiatics in Natal and the Cape was at the discretion of the authorities. (6) The education test was of so drastic a character that not a single Indian may be allowed to enter the union. (7) No facilities seemed to exist for the protection of those who may be wrongly prohibited by an officer.[327]

I wrote to the private secretary of General Smuts on 2 March saying I was most desirous of helping, to the best of my ability, to end the prolonged Asiatic struggle in the Transvaal and making detailed suggestions. I also consulted a senior lawyer and sent letters embodying his remarks which supplemented mine. Smuts replied positively on 7 March: 'The legal questions raised by your counsel are being gone into by minister with legal advisers.'[328]

Our goals seemed to be within sight and I wrote to Maganlal on 9 March: 'It appears that the struggle will definitely come to an end. No one is likely to stay here at the Tolstoy Farm after the struggle ends. Mr Kallenbach has perhaps spent 600 pounds on buildings alone. I see that the whole burden will fall on him. To prevent this, I propose to stay on at the Farm and make good as much of the loss as possible by means of physical labour. How can I leave Mr Kallenbach immediately after the struggle is over? At the same time, it is necessary for me to go there (Phoenix) but I do not see how it will be possible. My struggle will not be over even when our satyagraha struggle ends. It is as it should be.'

I then gave Maganlal a piece of information which I had thus far withheld: 'Ba became nervous when she had a sudden attack of acute pain. I was busy and could not go to see her a second time. She must have got angry and when I went to her she burst into tears and made it appear as if she would die. I felt somewhat awkward, but immediately recovered myself and said to her with a smile, 'Nothing to worry about if you die. There is plenty of wood. We shall cremate you on this Farm itself.' At this she also laughed. Half the pain disappeared with the laugh. Then I decided that very strong remedies were called for. Earth alone would not do. So I suggested to her that she should give up vegetables and salt altogether. She should live on wheat and fruits only. She might take, if she wanted, saltless rice with ghee. She said, 'Even you cannot do it.' I said, 'From today I give up salt, vegetables, etc.' How could she take these things then? The result is that for the last one month both of us have been taking food without salt, vegetables, and pulses. As for myself, I have no desire for other food. Ba has it sometimes. Once when she could not restrain herself, she took a little gavar*. Otherwise it appears she has lived on this diet. There was a miraculous change for the better. The bleeding stopped immediately. I got the incidental benefit of extra

---

*Cluster beans.

self-control. This is my argument as regards the eschewing of salt: Salt is a powerful chemical. Even a little when added to something changes its quality and taste. Its effect must be to thin the blood. So far as I can think, salt is bound to have an instant effect on the sick—and mostly adverse at that. Even though Ba may continue her [saltless diet] throughout this month, she won't keep it up beyond that. I think of carrying on the experiment as long as possible.'[329]

I have seen acrobat rope-walkers in India. They walk on a rope fixed to poles in mid-air quite twenty feet or more from the ground. They walk with a bamboo stretched along their outstretched arms and their gaze steadily in front of the other end. They may not go away a hair's breadth from their path. Well, that of spiritual rope-walkers is a millionfold more difficult. Happily, they have also correspondingly greater strength.[330]

The community urged on 10 March, that in the Union Immigrants' Restriction Bill an amendment be made exempting educated Asiatics from provincial registration laws and protecting the rights of wives and minor children of registered Asiatics.[331] And we were of course asking the Government of India to suspend the practice of indenture emigration.

I met Smuts on 27 March. The following conversation ensued (Excerpts):

> S: You see, Gandhi, I am giving you everything. I could have done so by regulation but now I am protecting wives and children in the bill. I do not know why, but I know that everybody suspects me. I am also recognizing domicile. But you are very unreasonable.
>
> G: How can you say so, General Smuts? Are you not creating a racial bar?
>
> S: No, I am not. Can you show it to me?
>
> G: Certainly. Will you admit that throughout the four years we have been simply fighting against the racial or colour bar?
>
> S: (Started and said after some hesitation): Yes.

G: You know that in the Transvaal Immigration Law there is no colour bar, but you read sub-section 4 and the Asiatic Act, and you have the bar.

S: There you are unreasonable.

G: I must deny the charge. I am sincerely anxious to help you.

S: You do not know my difficulties.

G: I do. If you send for the Law, I will show you what I mean.

S: (Sends for the Law): But the (Orange) Free Staters will never consent.

G points out the section from which the exemption is to be granted.

S: Yes, I now see what you mean.

G: I for one do not wish to offer passive resistance for material gains, but the racial bar we can never accept.

S: But you have no idea of my difficulties.

G: I know that you are quite able to overcome greater difficulties.

S: All right, I shall now talk to the Free State members. I hope you will keep the Cape and the Natal Indians silent.

G: They will certainly not remain silent. I have just got a wire from Natal. It is absolutely necessary to protect existing rights. The question of domicile is ticklish and section 25 requires amending. Certificates should be issued for the asking.

S: What are you doing in Jo'burg, etc.?

G: Looking after the families of passive resisters, etc.

S: It has hurt me more than you to imprison these people. It has been the unpleasantest episode of my life to imprison men who suffer for their conscience. I should do the same thing for conscience' sake.

On 1 April 1911, the Government of India officially announced that emigration of indentured labour to South Africa was to cease from 1 July. This was a triumph not only for us in South Africa but for those, such as the South African League in Madras which was agitating for this step. Stopping the export before the new unified South African Parliament banned the import was important. Smuts had now become Interior Minister for the whole of South Africa. Indians in all the four territories—the Transvaal, Cape, Natal, and Orange Free State were now his charge. Smuts knew our major demands: repeal of the Black Act, restoration of legal equality by permitting the entry into the Transvaal of educated Indians (six or so), and protection of the rights of all bona fide former residents, including arrested or deported satyagrahis. And we knew that he wanted the Indian community's acceptance of a new countrywide immigration law to replace the immigration laws of the four former colonies—the Union Immigrants' Restriction Bill. I spent practically the whole of April in Cape Town canvassing support for amendments in that bill, keeping the Indian community involved with every stage of the delicate negotiations.[332]

And in the midst of this, the family went through a crisis.

A little later one day in early May 1911, when Harilal and I were both in Johannesburg, he just left. He did so without telling me, only leaving a letter which reproached me for being a deficient father. Harilal said in it that he was breaking all family ties. I noticed, though, that he had not forgotten to take a photograph of mine with him. I searched all over Johannesburg for him and learnt from Joseph Royappen that Harilal had slipped away to Delagoa Bay, on his way to India. I wrote to Maganlal that Harilal was not blame, I was.[333]

Kallenbach then rushed to Delagoa Bay, found Harilal, brought him back to Johannesburg on 15 May. He and I then talked from sundown to sunrise. I was told I never praised my sons, favoured Maganlal and Chhaganlal. Harilal said he would go to India and make his own life.[334]

On 17 May, he left. I was among several who saw him off at the station. Just before the train steamed off, I kissed my son, gave him a gentle slap on his cheek and said: 'If you feel your father has done any wrong to you, forgive him.' I wrote to Maganlal: 'It is just as well that Harilal has left. He was much unsettled in his mind. He bears no ill-will towards any of you. He was angry with me, really. He gave vent to his pent-up feelings on Monday evening. He feels that I have kept all the four boys very much suppressed, that I did not respect their wishes at any time, that I have treated them as of no account, that I have often been hard-hearted. He made this charge against me with the utmost courtesy and seemed very hesitant as he did so. In this he had no thought of money at all in his mind. It was all about my general behaviour. Unlike other fathers, I have not admired my sons or done anything specially for them but always put them and Ba last; such was the charge. He seemed to me to have calmed down after this outburst. I pointed out his error in believing what he did. He saw it partly. What remains he will correct only when he thinks further. He has now left with a calm mind. He is resolved to learn more about those things on account of which I was displeased. He is strongly inclined to study Sanskrit. Thinking that since Gujarati is our language, his education should be for the most part in Gujarat, I have advised Harilal to stay in Ahmedabad. I believe that is what he will do. However, I have left him free. I feel it will turn out well.'[335]

When he stopped in Zanzibar on his way to India, Harilal was recognized and given a welcome by the Zanzibar Indians. He demurred but to no avail. He was taken to Mr Wali Mohammed Nazir Ali's residence where he was entertained lavishly. Replying to a reception given there in his honour, he pointed out what an unfailing remedy satyagraha was. Should there be foul play yet again, he told his audience, satyagrahis, wherever they were, would return to the struggle.[336]

I was glad that Harilal's audience comprising mostly Khojas were not put off by the mention of satyagraha. I found Harilal's comments to be good and we carried a short paragraph on it in *Indian Opinion*. 'Your brothers are all happy,' I told him in a letter that I wrote at 7.30 p.m. from Tolstoy Farm on 3 July. 'They are sitting beside me as I write this.'[337]

Dr Pranjivan Mehta, who had earlier believed I would send Harilal to England to avail his offer of a scholarship, not Chhaganlal, had reconciled to Chhaganlal's having to leave London on account of the severity of its winter and his own poor health and was now dealing with the prospect of Sorabji Shapurji Adajania coming in Chhaganlal's place. And so in his munificence suggested that Harilal should go to Rangoon (where he was based). I dissuaded him from proceeding with this plan. 'Please do not press Harilal to live in Rangoon,' I told the doctor. 'It is best that he should be allowed to live in freedom. It will be a different matter, of course, if he goes to Rangoon or comes over here of his own accord having failed in his plans,' I said.[338] Determined to pass his matriculation examination, Harilal joined a school in Ahmedabad. He said to me that so long as he does not do so he will not be rid of his infatuation nor acquire self-confidence in his own powers. Since he had this intention, I had no desire to stop him.[339]

Three

SMUTS RETREATS

General Smuts as a responsible minister with a parliamentary majority behind him has bound his government to introduce the necessary legislation.

On 27 May, I was able to inform the community through the columns of *Indian Opinion*:

A Provisional Settlement of the Asiatic trouble in the Transvaal has at last been reached. Two things were stated to be essential for satisfying passive resisters, namely: (1) Repeal of Asiatic Act 2 of 1907 and (2) legal equality for immigrants to the Transvaal. It was stated on behalf of the community that those who were actually fighting would, if required, forgo their individual rights and cease passive resistance if only the above demands were granted. General Smuts was at one time reputed to desire to fling the demands of the community contemptuously back in their faces. In that event, the sacrifice above referred to would have been needed. But God willed otherwise. General Smuts reconsidered his position and eventually accepted the co-operation of the passive resisters. He could not carry his legislation during the last Parliament and yet, owing evidently to the Imperial Conference and the approaching coronation, desired cessation of passive resistance. The passive resisters then offered to suspend their operations if General Smuts undertook to grant their cardinal demands and to pass them into law next session of Parliament and further promised not to penalize passive resisters for their passive resistance. But will the promise be redeemed? This question has been asked from many quarters. Ordinarily there can be no doubt about it. General Smuts as a responsible minister with a parliamentary majority behind him has bound his government to introduce the necessary legislation. If the Parliament does not accept it, it will amount to a vote of no-confidence entailing the resignation of the Ministry of which he is perhaps the most important member. But we are free to admit that General Smuts will not take any such heroic steps over an Asiatic question. Nevertheless the remote contingency of the Parliament rejecting his measure could not be allowed to stand in the way of our accepting the olive branch. Our quarrel hitherto was with General Smuts. He was the stumbling block in the way of our reaching the goal. He has now softened his heart and is pledged to concede what only a few months ago he declared he would on no account give. Such being the case, passive resisters properly decided upon a cessation of their activity.[340]

Polak, in a statement, described this as a compromise. L. W. Ritch discussed this with me. I corrected Polak: 'You have called it a compromise. Is not settlement a better term? Ritch points out that compromise may presuppose give and take whereas we have yielded nothing.'[341]

Harilal had written to me immediately after leaving to say he wanted to get some chocolates for little Rami but then decided against it. I wrote to him on 27 May—the same day as I explained the Provisional Settlement in *Indian Opinion*—saying he had done the right thing but cautioned him against taking the line that 'this must be done because Bapu wants it so'. From among the ideas that I suggest, I told him he should put into practice only those that appealed to him. 'I should like you to grow up in freedom,' I wrote.[342]

In June, on the conclusion of the Transvaal satyagraha, as Sorabji was going to India, a farewell function was organized by the Natal Indian Congress for him in Durban. I said in my speech on the occasion: 'As a satyagrahi, Mr Sorabji has displayed many fine qualities. He has rightly been described as the greatest of the satyagrahis. From one point of view I place Mr Thambi Naidoo on par with him. (Applause.) Another person who can match Mr Naidoo in self-sacrifice is unlikely to be found even in India. To be sure,

Mr Sorabji stands out from the rest because he volunteered for suffering. He came from Natal and was the first from that colony to join the campaign. Complaints were frequently made against the satyagrahis in gaol, but never against Mr Sorabji. He is by nature a mild and amiable person. That cannot be said even of Mr Thambi Naidoo. No improper word was ever heard to escape his mouth. He has none of the Parsis' faults but I have found in him all their finer qualities. Though so well endowed, he is without a trace of pride. Though a Parsi, he is an Indian first. Hindus, Muslims, and Christians alike admire him. That he continues firm on his course, having once set it, and that he tries to understand every issue, is his fourth virtue. Mr Sorabji is without compeer. The best way of honouring such a man is to emulate him. India will prosper only when it produces many more Sorabjis.'[343]

The satyagraha had ceased following the Provisional Settlement and Smuts's promise to introduce the amended legislation next year, but the burden on me at Tolstoy Farm was especially heavy. This is how things went on: Physical labour on the Farm up to 10 a.m.; teaching work at the school from 1 to 4.30 p.m.; meal at 5.30 p.m.; office and other correspondence at night. As I did everything single-handedly, I had no time left and I did writing work till late at night.[344]

I can say I was chained to the school from 1 to 4.30 p.m., letting it off only on Mondays when I had to make my weekly visit to Johannesburg. The school kept working on Sundays also. We also had school in the mornings for three hours when only manual labour was done—domestic chores or work on the farm. Because of these things, I saw the bodies and minds of the children improved from day to day. There were a total of twenty-five pupils, eight of them Muslims, two Parsis, and the rest Hindu. Among the last, five were from Madras, one from Calcutta and the rest were Gujaratis. I read *Indian Idylls* (by Edwin Arnold) to the boys. It has excellent translations from the Mahabharata. Among them I found *The Enchanted Lake* to be superb.[345]

A number of Indians wondered if satyagraha has achieved

anything. All that they saw was that people were tortured in gaol and put up with the suffering, and the utmost that was achieved in the end was theoretical equality of rights in the matter of new immigrants, which is unintelligible to most and unavailing in practice. The only outcome of any value, they thought was that (a few) highly educated men would now be able to enter the Transvaal every year. For their benefit I enumerated in *IO*, point by point, the several gains resulting from the campaign.

1. The Indian community's pledge taken at the mammoth meeting of Indians in the Empire Theatre, Johannesburg, on 11 September 1906, to the effect that they would not submit to the Asiatic law Amendment Ordinance, the forerunner of the Asiatic Registration Act, has been redeemed.
2. The Obnoxious Act will be repealed.
3. Public opinion has been roused all over India about our disabilities.
4. The entire world has learnt of our struggle and has admired the Indians' courage.
5. A law has been passed (in India) to prohibit the emigration of indentured labour to Natal.
6. Satyagraha helped bring about whatever improvement there has been in Natal's licensing legislation.

Apart from these, we have also won the sympathy of many. The prestige of the Indian community has risen.[346]

In the last week of September 1911, the Natal Indian Congress received a cablegram from the Indian National Congress in Calcutta asking whether I could preside over the Congress to be held in December that year in Calcutta. The NIC communicated this to me by telegram and telephone strongly urging acceptance. I said it was not possible for me to leave the Transvaal at the present time but at length conveyed acceptance if that would serve the motherland and on the condition that I would be allowed to return to South Africa immediately after the Congress.[347] I sent a private cable saying I should be asked only if my freedom would not be compromised and if my presence was thought necessary.³⁴⁸ I wrote to Harilal on 7 October: 'I have received what looks like an invitation to be President of the Congress. I have accepted it on the condition that I will have the utmost freedom to express my views. I do not covet this position but if I do have to come we shall have occasion to meet.'³⁴⁹

Since no reply came for many days, I inferred that the cable from Calcutta was not an invitation but a mere enquiry, or that my condition was found unacceptable.³⁵⁰ It became clear a little later into October that the cable from Calcutta was only an enquiry. So I cabled before the election of the President* due on 28 October saying my name should not be discussed.³⁵¹

In October occurred the Hindu festival of Diwali and some Hindus burst crackers in Durban. The Durban police went into a huff over this. A leading Hindu gentleman was arrested. This reached the ears of Mr Dawad Mahomed and Mr Parsi Rustomji. They hurried off to the mayor, and argued that, after all, the whites also exploded crackers during Christmas. Why then should the Hindus, they asked, not do so during their festivals? Why should they have to take special permission for this purpose? No one seeks such permission during Christmas. 'If, in spite of this, you wish to harass Hindus for exploding crackers, we shall also join them in this as a mark of sympathy. You may then arrest anyone that you like.' The matter was not serious and the victory not much of a triumph. The significance of the event, however, was great. Because we boldly came forward to suffer the consequences of doing what was right, we had, it transpired, nothing to suffer and our self-respect was preserved. This was satyagraha. Another, more significant, feature of this case was the fact that a Muslim and a Parsi rushed to help in a matter which concerned Hindus alone. The outcome was indeed happy. If the right course is followed in one case, it is bound to happen that it will be adopted on other occasions as well. If one knot in a tangled piece of string can be unravelled, the other too can easily be undone. How can Hindus, Muslims, Parsis,

---

*Pandit Bishan Narayan Dar (1864–1916) became president of the INC for that year, succeeding Sir William Wedderburn (1838–1918) and was succeeded by R. N. Mudholkar (1857–1921).

and Christians all be united? Mr Mahomed and Mr Rustomji had provided the answer. If Muslims come forward to sympathize with Hindus in what concerns the latter alone, if Hindus do the same, and if both these communities act in this manner towards Parsis, will there be anyone so bereft of reason as to seek to come in the way of affection developing among them? Let people's religions be different. You worship a Being—a single Entity—as Allah and another adores Him as Khuda. I worship Him as Ishwar. How does anyone stand to lose by this arrangement?[352]

While Harilal was trying his luck with matric studies in Ahmedabad, Chanchi was bringing up her two children, Rami and Kanti, in her mother's home in Rajkot. Chanchi asked me about Mellin's Food and if she could give that to Kanti. 'Our children grew well enough in the olden days without these foreign foods; hence, my advice is that we should do without them,' I advised. 'Wheat well roasted, ground fine and mixed with a little gur will serve the same purpose as Mellin's Food'. She wanted, naturally, to be where her husband was. How good would that be for his studies? 'I do not at all wish to come in your way in this,' I wrote to her. 'Live, both of you, as you wish.'[353] To him, I wrote: 'I have no objection to your living together; do as you like and live as you deem proper.'[354]

Harilal had taken strong objection to my proposal that Sorabji goes to England to become a barrister, availing the scholarship surrendered by Chhaganlal. He would have liked the chance to be given to him or at east to Medh, one of the satyagrahis in South Africa. I had to tell him: 'You have not understood the step I have taken in regard to Sorabji. The chief thing is that he is a Parsi and it befits a Hindu to encourage him. If Sorabji succeeds in becoming a barrister, his responsibilities will increase. How then could I ever encourage you to become one? If I did, all my ideas would go by the board though at present you will not appreciate them. Just now you should only attend to the strengthening of your character in your own way—that is all I want.'[355]

Another observation that I had to make to Harilal in the same letter was about Chanchal being with child again*: 'You have again succumbed to passion in regard to Chanchal. I can well understand it. The fault does not lie with the Ahmedabad atmosphere. The thing itself is so difficult that you cannot attain it without great effort and careful and sustained thought. If you however continue in your endeavour, you may some day overcome the weakening passion. You will be a different man altogether when you have succeeded in overcoming it. You will have a new strength.'

---

*Their son Rasik was born later that year.

Four

PROFESSOR GOKHALE VISITS SOUTH AFRICA

An address was presented to Gokhale at the station itself, engraved on a solid heart-shaped plate of gold from the Rand mounted on Rhodesian teak.

On 30 October, I wrote to Professor Gokhale: 'Will you never be able to travel outside India and England? British statesmen do; why cannot Indian statesmen? If you could possibly pay a brief visit to South Africa, it would not be now a question of your courting imprisonment, but it would still serve a double purpose. It would bring the people here nearer to India, and it would give me the privilege of so nursing you as to restore you to health. In my opinion, we have at Tolstoy Farm, as also at Phoenix, convenience enough for patients like you. I am quite sure that I can anticipate Mr Kallenbach's warm welcome to you at Tolstoy Farm, and, of course Phoenix you could treat as your own home.'[356]

In December, I urged Professor Gokhale once again to visit South Africa to see things for himself and for the sake of his health. 'Do please decide to come,' I wrote to him on 8 December 1911.[357] It was decided later that month that he would do that in the following summer, to 'study the situation on the spot'. We announced this in *Indian Opinion* in a paragraph titled 'A Joyful News'.[358]

Even as preparations for Professor Gokhale's visit began to take shape,[359] Kastur fell very ill and I had to move her, with Devadas, in September, from the Farm to Phoenix. Devadas was very keen to go there and my understanding with him was that he should continue staying there till my next visit, learn composing and live on a salt-free diet for twenty-eight days in a month.[360]

Preparations for Gokhale's visit meant briefing him on the issues facing us. These included the Provisional Settlement of course but also specific issues as related to the former territories. One of these was the 3-pound tax.

In the year 1905, it had been found that a great many ex-indentured Indians were not paying the 3-pound tax, for the simple reason that they were too poor to do so. Consequently an Act was passed which prohibited any person from employing or letting land to an ex-indentured Indian who could not produce his 3-pound licence for the current year. A contravention of this Act meant a fine of 5 pounds to the employer. It also provided that an employer could pay the 3 pounds and deduct the amount from the wages of the Indian. In this way it was thought to force the Indians to pay the 3-pound tax or leave the country. The tax itself we have always fought against, tooth and nail, and we shall continue to do so until this pernicious and unjust law is wiped off the statute book.[361]

And then came the text of the new bill. The union immigration bill was partly intended to satisfy the Transvaal Indian passive resisters. It was in some respects a better bill than that of the last year. But it did not quite fulfil the promise made by General Smuts. He had undertaken not to disturb the existing legal status throughout South Africa in any general bill designed to meet passive resisters. The existing legal position is among other things that, at any rate, at the Cape and the Transvaal, domicile and the rights of minor children and wives of non-prohibited immigrants are dependent on a decision of the highest tribunal of justice; that British Indians of the Transvaal passing the ordinary simple education test can easily enter the Cape or Natal; and that Indians of Natal have until lately received certificates of domicile as a matter of right upon proving domicile. Under the new bill the Immigration Officer constitutes the highest court of justice to consider the rights of domiciled Asiatics and their wives and children; educated Indians of the Transvaal have to pass the stiffer test under the new bill on entering the Cape or Natal and the Natal Indians will be unable to demand certificates of domicile as a matter of right. Now these are new disabilities which passive resisters could not be expected to accept.[362]

Life on the Farm* went on according to our best intentions. On 8 April 1912, we had a sports event for the children. We got the parents to donate prizes. Fifty other people attended. I wrote to Manilal (who was in Phoenix) about it while advising him not to let anything disturb his studies. Some things in Phoenix were disturbing him. 'Turn your mind,' I wrote, 'to the counsel in the Gita: "What is *apariharya*—that for which one has no remedy—one must resign oneself to".'[363] I had to write to him on 13 April again on a photograph of him that I saw: 'I saw your photograph. Your out-and-out English dress is not of a kind to please me. Even the collar starched? Certainly, you must have clean dress. But it does not go with our way of living to dress like a fastidious Englishman. It would even be better if you made it a rule to wear the Indian-style cap. Do not be dismayed by criticism of you in these matters. You may ignore what I say if it does not appeal to you. I do not want you to change your way of life just to please me. You need change only if my argument convinces you and you feel you are strong enough to act on it.'[364]

With the visit approaching, *Indian Opinion* had to educate its readers about the visitor. We printed the matter on Gokhale, with a picture added, carrying the words 'the Honourable Mr G. K. Gokhale' in full.[365] I did not expect Gokhale's visit to result in a final settlement of all questions; they were too large to be settled in the course of a single visit by one distinguished legislator. But I did hope, however, that the visit would result in a better understanding between Europeans and Indians, and that a better tone would be adopted by the two communities towards each other.[366]

Immediately on arrival, the distinguished guest was given a reception in the City Hall, Cape Town, Mayor Harry Hands presiding. In my comments, I said the name of Mr Gokhale was sacred to me; Mr Gokhale was my political teacher, and whatever I had been able

---

*Gandhi lived on Tolstoy Farm from June 1911 to the middle of January 1913.

to do in the service of my fellow countrymen in South Africa—of which I claimed to be a citizen—was due to Mr Gokhale. (Cheers.) This South African question was not a new one to Mr Gokhale; but we loved him not only for his interest in that question, but because of his life's work. Although Mr Gokhale was a candid critic of the Indian government, I said, he was also a friend to it. (Applause.) I thought it a hopeful sign that they had this representative gathering over which the mayor of the city presided. And the hospitality accorded to Mr Gokhale showed that though there had been hard knocks given between the European and Indian communities, there was not bitterness. In every town where these meetings were to be held, the mayors had signified their intentions to preside over meetings welcoming Mr Gokhale.[367]

A banquet was given by Kimberley Indians, with the Mayor of Beaconsfield, T. Pratley, presiding.

Kimberley is a mining district and Mr Francis Oats, the diamond mines owner, had been good enough to take the guest of the evening over his great mine, and over those huge pieces of machinery. I had also gone with Mr Gokhale and one thing struck me forcibly when watching the machinery, and that was that if we, human beings, worked as well together as this marvellous piece of machinery, what a happy family we would be. Then, indeed, our swords would be beaten into ploughshares, and the lions would certainly lie down with the lambs. I said also that if one nut in that piece of machinery went loose, it was possible for the whole machinery to become disjointed, and to carry that analogy to human beings, we had seen so often that one obstreperous man could break up a whole meeting, and one rogue in a family could damage the reputation of that family. Similarly, to take the reverse position, if the chief part of the machinery did its work regularly, we would find the other pieces working in harmony without being disjointed. It was a matter of pride to me that Mr Gokhale had been instrumental in bringing about such a happening in Kimberley at that meeting of the most representative Europeans and Indians at a common board.[368]

When the special train carrying Gokhale reached Johannesburg punctually to the minute, he was welcomed on the platform which had a dais specially erected for the occasion and covered with rich carpets. Present to receive him was the Mayor of Johannesburg who placed his car at Gokhale's disposal during his stay in the Golden City. An address was presented to Gokhale at the station itself, engraved on a solid heart-shaped plate of gold from the Rand mounted on Rhodesian teak. On the plate was a map of India and Ceylon, and it was flanked on either side by two gold tablets, one bearing an illustration of the Taj Mahal and the other a characteristic Indian scene.[369]

In Johannesburg the British Indian Association hosted a banquet, with Mayor Ellis in the chair. This was the largest of its kind, about 500 persons, including 150 Europeans, attending. A copy of the menu—which was purely vegetarian without any wines—printed on satin was presented to the guest. Indians were admitted by tickets costing a guinea each, an arrangement which enabled us to meet the expenses of the banquet.[370]

To this gathering Gokhale addressed his longest and most important speech in South Africa, in preparing which he subjected us to a very full examination. He asked me to put down on paper what I would like him to say from my point of view, but asked me not to be offended if he did not utilize a single word or idea from my draft. Gokhale did not make any use of my language at all. I cannot even say he adopted any of my ideas.[371]

From Johannesburg, Kallenbach and I took Gokhale to Tolstoy Farm. There was no cot on the Farm, but we borrowed one for Gokhale. There was no room where he could enjoy full privacy. For sitting accommodation we had nothing beyond the benches in our school. I was foolish enough to imagine that he woud be able to put up with a night's discomfort and to walk about a mile and a half from the station to the Farm. I had asked him beforehand and he had agreed to everything without bestowing any thought to it, thanks to his simplicity. It rained that day, as Fate would have it. The hardship was too much for him to bear and he caught a chill. We could not take him to the kitchen and dining hall. He had been put up in Kallenbach's room. His dinner would get cold by the time we brought it from the kitchen to his room. I prepared a special soup and Kotval special bread but these could not be taken to him hot. Gokhale uttered not a syllable but I could understand from his face what a folly I had committed. When Gokhale came to know we all of us slept on the floor he had his own bed also spread on the floor. This whole night was one of repentance for me. The only consolation was that Gokhale wore a smile on his face all the while.

The next morning he allowed no rest either to himself or to us. He corrected all his speeches which we proposed to publish in book form. When he had to write anything he was in the habit of walking to and fro and thinking it out. He had to write a small letter and I thought he would have soon done with it, but no. As I twitted him upon it he read me a little homily. 'I will not do even the least little thing in a hurry. I will think about it and consider the central idea. I will then deliberate as to the language suited to the subject and then set to write.'[372]

On 3 November, from Tolstoy Farm I wrote what was my first letter to V. S. Srinivasa Sastri, Gokhale's valued colleague in the Servants of India Society. 'Dear Mr Shastriar, I have heard so much of you that I almost feel we know each other: hence the familiar style. Mr Gokhale is taking rest for a day or two here—such as he can get after a most strenuous fortnight. I have insisted on Mr Gokhale taking the rest he needs. He has therefore commissioned me to write to you. The receptions throughout the tour have been very flattering. Europeans—many prominent leaders—have taken part in them as you will see from the papers sent to the society. In my opinion Mr Gokhale's mission is bound to be fruitful.'[373]

Durban hosted Gokhale to a grand reception on 8 November 1912 at the Town Hall. Barrister Joseph Royeppen read the address. It was engraved on gold plate and the shield was mounted on ebony. In my remarks, I addressed those present as 'my fellow citizens' and explained myself: 'By an accident, my name has got into some corner of the Voters' Roll and I am therefore able to address this audience— the whites in it—as my fellow citizens.' Introducing the guest, I said:

'Viceroys have called upon him to give them advice, because he has been able to keep his fingers on the pulse of India. He has guided the deliberations of the National Congress of India, and is one of the greatest educationists of the country. Had he been born in England, he would today be occupying the position Mr Asquith occupied. Had he been born in America he probably would be occupying the position to which Dr Woodrow Wilson had been elected, and if he had been born in the Transvaal, he would be occupying General Botha's position.'[374]

From Natal, Gokhale went to Pretoria where he was put up by the union government at the Transvaal Hotel. The purpose was to meet Prime Minister General Botha and Interior Minister General Smuts. We decided that I would not accompany him to this meeting as my presence would raise a sort of barrier between Gokhale and the ministers who would be handicapped in speaking out without reserve. Also, if I was present, they could not with an easy mind make any statement of future policy if they wished to make it. His meeting lasted for about two hours. When he returned, he said, 'You must return to India in a year. Everything has been settled. The Black Act will be repealed. The racial bar will be removed from the emigration law. The 3-pound tax will be abolished.'

'I doubt it very much,' I said. 'You do not know the ministers as I do. But it is enough for me that you have obtained this undertaking from the ministers. But I do not think I can return to India in a year and before many more Indians have gone to jail.'[375]

At his wish, Kallenbach and I accompanied him as far as Zanzibar. On the steamer we had arranged to have suitable food for him. We had ample time on board to talk to our heart's content. Our talks were confined now to India. He analysed for me the characters of all the leaders in India and his analysis was so accurate that I have hardly perceived any difference between Gokhale's estimate and my own personal experience of them.[376]

After we had parted, I wrote to him: 'And now will you forgive me for all my imperfections? I want to be a worthy pupil of yours. This is not mock humility but Indian seriousness. I want to realize in myself the conception I have of an Eastern pupil. We may have many differences of opinion, but you shall still be my pattern in political life.'[377]

But I could not resist giving some advice of my own: 'One word from the quack physician. Ample fasting, strict adherence to two meals, entire absence of condiments of all kinds from your food, omission of pulses, tea, coffee, etc., regular taking of Kuhne baths, regular and brisk walking in the country (not the pacing up and down for stimulating thought), ample allowance of olive oil and acid fruit and gradual elimination of cooked food—and you will get rid of your diabetes and add a few more years than you think to your life of service in your present body.'[378]

Five

THE STRUGGLE NOT AVAILETH

One can only die in the attempt to find the truth. I am passionately in search of it.

Back on the Farm, I directed my health-related advice to my nephew Jamnadas in Phoenix, who had asked me a lot of questions: 'I feel that the kernel in the almonds and other nuts contains more nourishment than fresh fruit. I can think of two reasons why you got boils. Because of unsuitable food the blood became weak and the enervating air at Phoenix had an immediate effect on you. Or else, Phoenix water affects only the skin, in the same way that mere contact with cactus will affect the skin of a person even if his blood is pure. If some air enters the stomach through an enema, no harm will come out of it. At the worst, there might be stomach ache, as the body has no use for air entering this way. When this happens, one should go to the toilet and strain, so that most of the wind is expelled.'[379]

Jamnadas had also asked me a question relating to the Ramayana. I told him: 'It was certainly not right of Sugriva to have had Vali killed. He can be defended up to a point. It is surely not possible to defend all the actions of the virtuous in the Ramayana and the Mahabharata. Even the poet has not visualized them as perfect.'[380]

He had also asked me about a craze of his—cycling. I told him from my knowledge: 'If you are so crazy about a bicycle, use it, and then rid yourself of the craze. While riding to a village on a bicycle, one has to face danger from cattle. The latter are utter strangers to our bicycle and, being frightened, charge at us.'[381]

On 8 January, I went to Phoenix with my students where Kastur was. Tolstoy Farm was closed for some time at this point.

The evening before I left, I had a long and momentous talk with

Kallenbach. He was unsettled in mind, wondering if he too should go to Phoenix or—to India. 'I think that you ought not to think of India or work in Phoenix just now,' I wrote to him on 9 January. 'I feel sure, as I did not up to last night, that your duty is just now to adhere to your practice and your material advancement. In doing so, you have to watch yourself. You must not abandon the simple life, you must not revert to the rake's life....'[382]

I wrote to Kallenbach again on 11 January from Phoenix: 'One can only die in the attempt to find the truth. I am passionately in search of it. May you not for the time being follow my career from a distance? Poor Mrs Gandhi and poor you! Mrs Gandhi must have felt simply shocked to see her neat little home turned into a menagerie. But she took it all quite calmly. Your case is somewhat different. She is bound up in my life. She is not on the fence. You are not bound up in me and you are on the fence. All these things should put you on your guard. I therefore urge again: do not be hasty, nurse your office in terms of my letter, come to Phoenix whenever you like, partly to share my life but not wholly, and you will test yourself. Watch me just now not with a friendly eye but a highly critical and fault-finding eye. Assimilate the joint life as we have lived it hitherto but in my flight now hesitate, watch, and wait. More when you come here. You will observe things for yourself. Please understand me. I do not want to put you off.'[383]

Harilal wrote reporting his failure at the matric examination. I replied saying: 'I have not felt disappointed over your failure. Since you have resolved to pass that examination, go on working for it again. Send me your question papers. You must have preserved them. Let me know in which subject you failed.' He had attended a reception for Gokhale convened by the Sheriff of Bombay on 14 December 1912 on his return to India and I was pleased about that: 'I read in *Mumbai Samachar* that you were present at the Gokhale meeting.' I told him I was planning on returning to India if a law satisfying to our demands was passed. I described to Harilal my Phoenix routine: 'There are in all thirty children to be taught, including those in Phoenix. Jekibehn, Miss West, one Patel named Maganbhai,

Kashi, and I do the teaching. I get up at 4.45 in the morning and wake up the children at 5. The press hands, the schoolchildren, and I do farming from 6 to 8. Between 8 and 8.30, the students and the press hands have breakfast. At 8.30, all the press hands return to the land and work there until 11. I take the children to the school, where they are taught to read and write from 8.30 to 10.30. From 10.30 to 11, again, they learn farm work. Between 11 and 12.30, people bathe and eat. From 12.30 to 4.30, work in the press where the older boys train for two hours; the last two hours [are spent on] reading and writing in the school.'[384]

Harilal's letter gave me occasion to ask myself a question and to answer it: 'Have I failed to take my sons' interests into account? My answer is "No". I did consider their interests, too, according to my own lights. Whether my judgement was right or wrong, time alone will show to us both.'[385]

The waking of children in the morning at Phoenix was to be recorded by Prabhudas in the following description of how his mother, Kashi, would wake him: 'Bapuji would leave his bed, light a lamp, and write till morning with single-minded concentration. My mother would wake me up when the dark of the morning was about to recede. 'See...Bapu is waking up Devadas kaka. You should also wake up, do get up now.' I would remain in bed, half in sleep. My eyes would not open but my ears were alert. I could hear the cocks crowing in the huts across the hills and the voices of the natives hurrying towards the railway station and these sounds would be punctuated by Bapu's robust call: 'Deva! Deva...!' It would take a quarter of an hour or even half an hour of persistent calling for Devadas kaka to wake up from his sleep. Bapu's calls of 'Deva, o Deva!' would reverberate through the hills of Phoenix....'[386]

In March, when I was teaching the children, I came across excerpts from John Bunyan's allegorical work *The Pilgrim's Progress*. I found them soul-stirring and wrote to Kallenbach 'I thought it so fitted your case at many points that I would have it copied. Please read and reread and come out of Doubting Castle after having killed Giant Despair.'[387]

Harilal wrote after many months. He had failed his exam and his mind was not calm. He wanted to continue living in Ahmedabad and with Chanchi. 'You may live as it suits you best,' I wrote to him, 'though even if I give you this freedom you have to depend on me for money.' I asked him to send me his question papers if he had preserved them. And for the names of the books he was reading for his examination. And samples of his composition. Manilal, I told him, was deep into his studies and as he was interested in them, I gave him an hour and a half every day. 'Ramdas and Devadas also study well,' I informed him 'but they have no interest in their studies.'[388]

My nephew Jamnadas had left South Africa in December 1912. He would write to me from India. I read [his letters] with great interest because they asked specific and general questions. I showed them to Manilal. I thought it was in his interest that he should read them, so admirable they appeared to be. In reply to one such I wrote to him two days after I wrote to Harilal, on 14 March, giving him some response to his questions and comments, a few of them being:

1. 'If we must know English we should know it well'—from this we cannot conclude that if we must travel by railway, we should travel first or second.
2. A ship is bound to look after the needs of deck passengers.
3. If you interrupted your studies to offer some little flour to Brahmin beggars who had no business to go begging, you would only be sacrificing your studies. I would not think that in doing so you had done honour to the Brahmins; I would rather count it as your timidity or want of judgement.
4. Give up the afternoon nap, forcing yourself if need be. When you feel the urge coming over you, take a bath.
5. Do not be eccentric in your dress.
6. I agree that you should not give up milk or curds, but do not give them the chief place. They make us more indolent.[389]

Six

THE LAST STRAW

In the eye of the law, Mrs Cachalia, Mrs Naidoo, Mrs Cama and Mrs Gandhi were concubines....

On the same day—14 March 1913—came the judgment of Justice Searle of the Cape Supreme Court on the question of marriage that changed the overall situation dramatically. Hitherto the judgments that had been given affecting the question of marriage had been more or less enigmatic. On the occasion in question, a clear-cut issue had been presented involving a decision of an Immigration Officer. The case was admitted to be a test case and the judgment went against us Indians. The judge was, no doubt, helpless. The Immigration Officer could not be held to blame. He had to administer an Act and he had done so. But the meaning of the judgment was that every Hindu and Mahomedan wife was in South Africa illegally, and, therefore, at the mercy of the government, whose grace alone could enable her to remain in this country. And no one could be blamed but ourselves if in the future, Indian wives—Hindu, Mahomedan or Parsi—were turned out. This was a state of things which our self-respect forbade us from tolerating. Through *Indian Opinion*'s issue of 22 March 1913, I called upon every anjuman, every association, and every dharma sabha 'to send respectful representations to the government urging that the new immigration bill should be altered so as to admit the legality of marriages celebrated according to the recognized Indian religions'. I also said this was a question which demanded that we Indians sacrifice our all—businesses, money, ease—which will have been dearly bought at the price of the nullity of their or their brethren's marriages. No consideration should be allowed to come in the way of their taking prompt and energetic action.[390]

A mass meeting was called by the British Indian Association on 30 March 1913 in Johannesburg. It gave the storm signal. Ahmed Mahomed Cachalia, Chairman, British Indian Association, gave a respectful but firm warning that there were some Indians in South Africa who were prepared to give their all for the sake of their and their country's honour. The meeting passed resolutions which we doubted not would receive the government's earnest attention.[391]

On 1 April 1913, I wrote to General Smuts:

> Dear Sir, Mr Justice Searle's decision regarding the validity of Indian marriages and the statement said to have been made by the Immigration Officer in Natal, to the effect that no boys or girls claiming to be the children of resident Indians would be admitted unless they or their parents produced certificates of birth, have created great consternation among my countrymen. And passive resisters have also felt compelled to examine their own position. According to Justice Searle's decision, no Indian marriage whether celebrated in South Africa or elsewhere can be recognized unless it is in accordance with the marriage laws of the Cape Province, i.e., every Indian marriage is invalid that is not registered before a Marriage Officer or celebrated according to the Christian rites. This, in my humble opinion, is an intolerable position and disturbs rights hitherto exercised by Indians. I need hardly draw the attention of the Hon'ble Minister to the fact that marriages celebrated according to the Hindu, Mahomedan, or Parsi rites are fully recognized in India by Indian law. With reference to children, it is a well-known fact that very few births are registered in India. Registration of birth is not universally compulsory. And it is practically impossible to produce certificates of birth except in rare cases. The practical result of both the cases is almost completely to prevent the entry of wives and minor children of domiciled Indians. In the circumstances, I venture to submit that, apart from other considerations, it is necessary in order to give full effect to the Provisional Settlement to so frame the new immigration bill as to restore the position as to wives as it availed before Justice Searle's decision and to revoke the instructions regarding children.

May I also suggest that it would be better if the leading members of the community were consulted regarding proof required by the government as to marriages or the age or sonship of boys. I am sure that the Indian community has every desire to co-operate with the government in facilitating the examination of relationships of wives and children so as to avoid fraud or deception. I remain:

Yours faithfully,

M. K. Gandhi.

I was ever following news about Gokhale and so came to learn that a point had been raised questioning his election to represent the non-official members of the Bombay Legislative Council in the Viceregal Council, as he was an 'official' drawing remuneration from the public treasury as a member of the Public Services Commission. Gokhale set the matter at rest, in characteristic fashion, by declining to accept the remuneration to which he would have been entitled. Such things are expected from such a man whose whole life has been one of self-abnegation in the service of the public. We do not congratulate him upon what he would himself regard as a perfectly natural act, but we sincerely congratulate the motherland upon the possession of so rare-minded a son.[392]

To my letter to General Smuts of 1 April, I received a reply dated 10 April that argued in favour of status quo and said: '...from the earliest times, following the introduction of European civilization into South Africa, the law of the land has only recognized as a valid union the marriage, by a recognized Marriage Officer, of one man to one woman, to the exclusion, while it lasted, of any other. A very old established section of the Cape population, and a large one in point of numbers, viz., the Cape Malay community, has always followed the Mahomedan faith and conducted its marriages according to the tenets of that religion; but such unions, unless solemnized by a Marriage Officer, are not recognized under the Marriage Order-in-Council or officially recorded in any way.' The operative part of the reply was: '...It is not possible, therefore, to accept your contention that marriages according to Indian custom, but not celebrated before a Marriage Officer, have hitherto been recognized as valid here; nor is it possible to consider the introduction of any law which would have the effect of disturbing the position so far as it affects the Cape Malay or the Indian sections of the population.'[393]

The draft of the new immigration bill which was to activate the Provisional Settlement was open to serious objections. And General Smuts, we were informed, would be in charge of the bill. On 9 April, I sent to General Smuts's secretary an unambiguous letter: 'I certainly never dreamt that Indian marriages that have been hitherto recognized by the Courts of Law in the union were unlawfully recognized. It cannot for a moment be denied that the Searle judgement shakes the existence of Indian society to its foundation. Will you place this letter before General Smuts and, even if he is not to be in charge of this bill, may I look to him for support? I know he will accept my assurance that I am not itching for passive resistance, indeed, I was so sure of the bill carrying out the Provisional Settlement both to the letter and in the spirit that I was preparing for a visit to India in June, but I fear that, if the objections are not met, revival of the awful struggle is a certainty.'[394]

Mr Cachalia received an apparently soothing reply from the government on the resolutions of the Johannesburg mass meeting. The government assured Mr Cachalia and, through him, the community, that they did not intend to disturb the practice that had hitherto existed, in spite of the Searle judgement. 'We accept the assurance,' I wrote in *Indian Opinion*, 'but in vital matters, assurances which are in conflict with an actual legal position can afford little relief.'[395] The question was not that of introducing a few Indian wives into the union per year, but one of determining the theoretical status of Indian women. In plain language, the Searle judgement reduced their status from that of being honoured and honourable wives of their husbands to one of concubinage. In the eye of the law, Mrs Cachalia, Mrs Naidoo, Mrs Cama and Mrs Gandhi were concubines, and their offspring not honoured and beloved sons or daughters of their parents but illegitimate children.

A legal appeal against the judgement was considered but it was clear to me that satyagraha would have to be resorted to even if such an appeal was made and if it was rejected. We decided to offer stubborn satyagraha, with the women coming into line with the men. We first invited the women in the Natal who had lived on Tolstoy Farm. They were only too glad to join. I warned them they might be given hard labour in jail, made to wash clothes, and even subjected to insult by the warders. But these sisters who were all, with one exception, Tamilians feared none of these things. They entered Transvaal at Vereeniging without permits but were not arrested. They then took to hawking without licences but were again not arrested.[396]

I had contemplated sacrificing all the settlers in Phoenix at a critical period. That was to be my final offering to the God of Truth. I went to Phoenix and spoke to the settlers about my plan. The women there I spoke to first. They were all my relatives, Gujarati-speaking. They fell in with my plan which involved the husbands leaving their wives free to take this step.

When Kastur understood the marriage difficulty, she was incensed and said to me: 'Then I am not your wife according to the laws of this country?' I replied that that was so and added that their children were not their heirs. 'Then,' she said, 'let us go to India.' I replied that that would be cowardly and that it would not solve the difficulty. She then said emphatically that she wanted to court arrest. I hesitated.

'What defect is there in me that disqualifies me for jail?'

'I would only be too glad if you went to jail but it should not appear at all as if you went at my instance.'

'You are not asking me to do so.'

'If I asked you, you might be inclined to go just for the sake of complying with my request and then if you began to tremble in the law court or were terrified by hardships in the jail, I could not find fault with you but how would it stand with me?'

'You may have nothing to do with me if by being unable to stand jail I secure my release by an apology. If you can endure hardships and so can my boys why cannot I? I am bound to join the struggle.'

'Then I am bound to admit you to it.'

The step was momentous.[397]

Gokhale I had to take into confidence about Kastur's determination. He himself had been unwell, suffered a nervous breakdown. He was on his way to England when I wrote to him: 'Mrs Gandhi made the offer on her own initiative and I do not want to debar her.' But I did make a request: 'The matter of Mrs Gandhi's intention has not yet been made public. Will you also not mention it anywhere for the time being?'[398]

Around this time came from London reports about the Suffragette movement and the courage of its leaders, especially Emmeline Pankhurst. A little earlier, we gathered, the house of Mr Lloyd George, the finance minister, was burnt down at Mrs Pankhurst's instigation. She willingly took on herself the entire responsibility for this. She was prosecuted and was sentenced to three years' imprisonment. Even in gaol, these ladies were bent on harassing the authorities and so getting themselves released. Accordingly, though Mrs Pankhurst was offered a variety of delicious dishes in gaol, she refused to touch them and fasted for eight days. She was about to collapse, and was, therefore, released. And now this brave lady was in hospital in a critical condition. This kind of fighting was not satyagraha. A satyagrahi's object is to get into a prison and stay there. He will not even dream of harming others. If, however, we were to leave aside her mode of fighting and only think of the suffering she has borne, we would find much to learn from her. I wrote as much in *Indian Opinion*.[399]

Phoenix was my base during this time and I spent much time with the family. On 25 April 1913, I treated Kallenbach to a happy home vignette from Phoenix: 'You will be pleased to know that Devadas and Fakiri ran to the station* and back in thirty-five minutes and Shivpujan in 29....'[400] But not much after that, to another one that was not happy. I wrote to Kallenbach: 'Devadas ate stolen lemons at

---

*Lawley, the station near the Farm, was one mile away. The boys running two miles in thirty-five minutes was an achievement fit for a father to be proud of.

Inanda Falls although he had promised not to do such a thing again. When he was faced with the fact, he was inclined to be naughty and sharp. This grieved me much. And his last defence broke me entirely. He said he did not immediately confess his guilt as he was afraid of being hit by me, as I am in the habit of hitting boys. And so I felt that by way of a lesson to him I would deposit a few slaps on my cheeks which I did and then felt the grief so much that I wept bitterly.'[401]

Along with everything else, we learnt from an authoritative source that, owing to the exigencies of the political situation, the government did not intend to introduce this session a bill to repeal the 3-pound tax required, under Act 17 of 1895, of ex-indentured Indians who remain free in Natal at the expiry of their contracts. This news came as a shock and a bitter disappointment, not only to those immediately affected, but to the entire Indian community, who rightly regarded the impost as a tax upon its honour and social integrity.[402]

In early June it was observed that the government proposed to ask Parliament to remove the tax only on women. From this, I presumed, that they have no intention at present of removing it from men. I apprised Gokhale of the position as follows:

1. The bill has received the royal assent.
2. Passive resistance will be resumed probably [at] the beginning of the next month.
3. In order to court imprisonment we will enter all the provinces in disregard of the new Act and will refuse to show certificates or any other papers. Both educated and uneducated Indians will join the struggle.
4. So far as I can judge at present, 100 men and 13 women will start the struggle. As time goes, we may have more.
5. I do not expect to raise much cash but I do not anticipate any difficulty about getting sufficient food and clothing by begging. If we all go to gaol, Kallenbach has undertaken to do the begging himself. He can be thoroughly relied upon to see that no family is starved so long as he has life in him. If

no funds arrive unasked from India or elsewhere, we shall perform our wanderings on foot, and no money will then be spent on telegrams and cables. Some of my private burdens are being found by Dr Mehta.

6. The struggle is expected to last a year but if we have more men than I anticipate, it may close during the next session of the union Parliament.

And I urged:

'My prayer to you is: Please do not worry about us, do not beg for funds publicly and do not injure your health for the cause. This prayer is selfish. I am anxious to meet you in the flesh in India, work under you and learn, may I say, at your feet, all I want to and must. In some things I want to be disillusioned if I am in the wrong and I want you to be disillusioned if I am in the right and we do not agree. I shall not misunderstand you if I do not receive any letters from you. But whenever you have time and health, I shall value your letters and advice. They would be a source of comfort.'[403]

A letter from Jamnadas required me to tell him on 2 July: 'God exists, and yet does not. He does not, in any literal sense. The atman that has attained moksha is God and therefore omniscient. The true meaning of bhakti is search for the atman. When the atman realizes itself, bhakti is transformed into jnana.'[404]

Seven

A CRISIS AT HOME AND A GREAT LOSS

Never before had I spent such days of agony as I did then.

In those days I had to move between Johannesburg and Phoenix. On 12 July 1913 when I was in Johannesburg, I received tidings of the moral fall of two of the inmates of the Ashram*—Jaykunvar, daughter of Dr Pranjivan Mehta, and Manilal. News of an apparent failure or reverse in the satyagraha struggle would not have shocked me but this news came upon me like a thunderbolt. The same day I took a train for Phoenix. Kallenbach insisted on accompanying me. He had noticed the state I was in. He would not brook the thought of my going alone for he happened to be the bearer of the tidings. During the journey my duty seemed clear to me. I felt that the guardian or teacher was responsible, to some extent at least, for the lapse of the ward or pupil. So my responsibility regarding the incident in question became clear to me as daylight.

My wife had already warned me in the matter but being of a trusting nature I had ignored her caution. I felt the only way the guilty parties could be made to realize my distress and the depth of their own fall would be for me to do some penance. So I imposed upon myself a fast for seven days and a vow to have only one meal a day for a period of four months and a half.[405]

On reaching Phoenix I confronted Manilal and Jeki. She confessed the whole thing.

Millie Polak would recount later that my appearance shocked her. Looking depressed and ill I apparently greeted her without my 'usual warmth'. She said I 'looked as though the light had been quenched'

---

*Phoenix Settlement.

276

within me that I 'sat slack, with all the fight' taken out of me. She was perplexed because she had not heard of what had happened. The conversation with her went as follows:

M: What is the matter? Are you not well or has something happened?

G: The worst has happened!

M: The worst? What do you mean?

G: A dreadful thing has happened among ourselves. __ has been guilty of destroying her chastity. She has had a physical relationship with __ .

M: That is terrible! Are you sure it is true?

G: Only too true. She has confessed it all to me.

M: Still, I don't quite understand. How could it happen? When did it happen? I thought you knew how she spent all her time, and where she went. How then could this have taken place?

G: I thought I knew her movements but it seems I did not. When I thought she was simply taking a walk with her book, she was meeting __, with the results I have told you.

M: Has it been going on for long?

G: Yes, some time. I seem to be almost the only one quite ignorant of what was going on around me. And now what am I to say to her family? I am responsible to them for her!

M: But surely you are not blaming yourself for this, are you? How could you possibly have suspected that such a shocking thing could happen?

G: Whom else should I blame if not myself? I must have neglected something. The responsibility must fall on me.

M: I do not think so. Of course you cannot be held blameworthy. __ was not ignorant. She knew what she was doing. She has behaved disgracefully. It is dreadful for you, I know. But no one can hold you responsible for it. What are you going to do next?

G: I must tell her family at once and accept their rebuke. __ is full of remorse. She realizes how wicked she has been and has done nothing but cry for the last twenty-four hours and is starving herself.

M: Well, a fast will do her good. I have no sympathy at all with her. But I am sorry for __. What could he know of sex-passion before this? He has just been trapped. However, what are going to do about him?

G: I do not know what to do about either of them yet. They must both punish themselves. Of course, I cannot trust them to meet each other again unless someone else is present and I cannot send either way from my care.

M: Is there to be a baby?

G: No, thank God! At least that much is spared me!

M: Well, that is something to be thankful for! It is indeed dreadful enough for you without that to complete it.

G: I have told—that I must share the burden of her guilt and I hope by fasting to expiate it.*

The strain told on Kastur. She became bedridden.[406]

Manilal insisted on observing the same penance vow as mine. His fast too therefore starts from the same day. And yet I knew that in spite of all that, there may be no change of heart. But I decided I must continue to trust and believe.[407]

Never before had I spent such days of agony as I did then. I talked and smiled, walked, ate and worked, all mechanically. But I could do no writing whatever. The heart seemed to have gone dry. Ringing noises in the ears were there before but they were now very persistent. I was not capable of great physical effort. It was an effort now to get up at 4.30 a.m.[408] The agony I was going through was unspeakable. I had during this period often wanted to take the knife

---

*Millie Graham Polak in *Mr Gandhi: The Man*, pp. 142–46. The author withheld the names which have been subsequently mentioned in published records and in Uma Dhupelia-Mesthrie's biography of Manilal Gandhi.

from my pocket and put it through the stomach. Sometimes I felt like striking my head against the wall opposite, and at other times of running away from the world.[409]

On 15 August, the great and altruistic Joseph J. Doke gave up his earthly life. The pen shook in my hand even in writing that sentence for *Indian Opinion*.[410] Together with his son, Clement, he had decided to visit a lonely mission station in northwestern Rhodesia close to the Congo border, and on 2 July they set out on this trip, which was to take about six weeks. Mr Doke was also entrusted by the South African Baptist Mission Society to visit a mission station near Umtali, they taking advantage of his being in Rhodesia to secure particulars which they wanted. Mr Doke enjoyed the trip to the 'Ndla District immensely, and maintained good health throughout. He suffered, however, from footsoreness—the distance to be traversed was some 350 miles—and he travelled most of the way by 'machilla'—a hammock slung on a pole and carried by two natives—but despite this he was in the best of spirits and had the greatest hope for the success of his mission. Through an interpreter he spoke at numerous villages, and he did a great deal of writing and took many photographs with a view to lecturing on his return. On 4 August, Broken Hill was reached, and on 7 August, Mr Doke parted from his son at Bulawayo, the latter being called home by business duties. Mr Doke then proceeded to Umtali, after a few days' waiting at Bulawayo, reaching the end of his train journey on the morning of the 9th instant. Here the Rev. Woodhouse met him and the greater part of the day was spent in the discussion of missionary matters. In the afternoon the party proceeded to the residence of Mr Webber—a friend—just outside the town, where, owing to Mr Doke's feeling too unwell, they remained for the night. The next morning, Mr Doke was up before sunrise, feeling very ill, and all thought of going to the mission station then was abandoned. Mr Doke complained of severe pains in the back and had to take to his bed again. The usual remedies for fever were applied, but, as there seemed to be no temperature, it was concluded that the malady was not fever, and a doctor was sent for, who at once ordered him to the Umtali Hospital, whither he was conveyed by 'machilla'. Here he was under the best doctors and nursing supervision possible. On the 12th a telegram was sent to Mr Doke's family saying that he had a slight attack of pleurisy, but that there was nothing serious and no one was to come. On Friday evening, the 15th, a further telegram was received by Mrs Doke saying that Mr Doke was seriously ill with enteric. Mrs Doke at once made preparations to leave by Saturday night's train, but on the morning of that day a telegram was received that Mr Doke had passed away at 7 o'clock the previous evening. As a human being, Mr Doke was full of nobility; as an Englishman, his conduct was such that, had all Englishmen been like him, there would be no bitterness between them and the Indians. As a priest, he was a man of faith in God and, although he was very zealous in his religion, he never vilified other religions. Not only that, but he did his best to understand the importance of other religions. However, it is for his excellent services to the Indian community of South Africa that it will for ever cherish the name of Mr Doke.

One of his many hopes was to see a satisfactory solution to our problem, and for achieving this he was ever ready for any sacrifice. We had learnt to look upon Mr Doke as our shield. That shield was now gone. Our duty was clear—to live up to Mr Doke's ideas of us. Mr Doke believed that we were true satyagrahis, that we were ready to sacrifice our lives for the sake of our honour and our religion, that we would not wish ill of anyone who might injure us but, leaving justice in the hands of God, would love even those who bore us ill-will and fight them with the sword of love.

Eight

SATYAGRAHA RESUMED

'See now, your parents have gone to jail and so, though you are children, you ought to exercise some self-control.' They, then, felt a little abashed.

A wire came to me on 10 September from the secretary to General Smuts which included the following: 'With regard to marriage question, cannot give any assurance that a marriage law will be introduced next session on lines asked by you which would apparently alter whole basis of existing law in South Africa.'[411]

I had to inform General Smuts, on behalf of the British Indian Association that, after having read his telegram of 9 September, it had been most reluctantly and with the utmost regret decided to revive passive resistance, owing to the inability or unwillingness of the government to concede the points submitted by me in his letters to him.[412]

A party of sixteen satyagrahis, led by Kastur and including Kashi and Santok, left Durban on 15 September 1913 to cross over into the Transvaal and thereby court arrest. I wrote to Kallenbach the same day: 'When she is sentenced and after you have received permission to give her special food you should take charge of the food and give it to the gaoler. After the sentence and after you have made arrangements, you should give it to the gaoler. So far as possible you would arrange for her to receive the food from the government. She is only fruitarian, for health and religious reasons, and she can take olive oil, bananas, plums, dried figs, almonds, tomatoes, grapes, oranges, lemons, banana flour, apples. You will stay there until everything is fixed up and either come here or return to Johannesburg according to the exigencies of the struggle and of your own personal affairs.'[413]

After seeing the satyagrahis off at the Durban railway station, I wrote to Kashi and Santok letters which I hoped they would get when they reached their destination, namely, jail:

> Parents fondly imagine that their children would not be able to live without them. To uphold their conceit, parents believe that their children will be fretting restlessly in their absence. They do not realize that all the people about them get deprived of their parents and still none of them pines away to death. To children, those who love them at the moment are their parents. Rukhi laughed and frisked about as soon as the train moved out. Radha cried a little after the train had left but when I told her of a prize for her, after about five minutes, she also started talking to others. Krishna and Keshu were not even aware that anything had happened. They were shouting and running all the way back. All of them lifted up one another and played among themselves. When they reached home, they asked for the finest dishes to be served. I even had to tell Krishna and Keshu, 'See now, your parents have gone to jail and so, though you are children, you ought to exercise some self-control.' They, then, felt a little abashed. These two do not call to mind anyone even for a moment. Rukhi and Radha are real ladies. All that Rukhi wants is to be served vegetables. Whatever vegetable is served to her, she likes it as if it were her mother and her father. Children are not born with infatuations of any kind. They forget the infatuation of their previous existence, too. Thus, they are unconsciously like saints who are free from all desires. Grown-up people consciously become sannyasis. Even otherwise, children and sannyasis are alike in their state of mind. I do not wish from this to draw the conclusion that parents should abandon their children. But they should give up their fond attachment and stop believing in what does not exist. They should not shower so much affection on the children that the latter would pine away in their absence, nor should they believe that the children would suffer when separated from them. But children are born as a result of our sin and are dependent on us and therefore we ought to have compassion and love for them. When there are

others to look after the children and it becomes necessary for us to leave them for the sake of some other duty, we should not yield to blind love, nor suffer. The children will get along quite well without us. That we may not do without them is another matter. Even so, we have never heard of any mother who has pined away to death at the loss of her only son. Shravan's parents burnt themselves to death. They were helpless and the significance of that story is quite different. I meant to write to you quite a worldly letter, but have written one with a deeper meaning. So, read it attentively. Show it to Chhaganlal, Raojibhai, Maganlal, and Jeki. If Ba wants to read it, I have no objection but I fear she might not be able to draw the right lesson from it and might unnecessarily be distressed. You know how well I love both of you. I had wanted to tell you many things here but could get no free time. Today the bag of thoughts unfolded itself.

I wrote to Harilal on 18 September, who was unwell—physically and mentally. He had written to me saying he has lost his appetite and also his mental powers. About his health I told him: 'I am very unhappy that your health has gone down. I always thought it would. I even warned you.... There is only one remedy for your dyspepsia—a daily walk of 15 miles. By way of diet, you should have solid food, according to your appetite.'[414]

And about the state of his mind and his attempt at examination-based studies: 'It is not surprising that you have lost your mental powers. The education there is useless because it is ill-conceived. Since you have never reflected over the mental vacuity of thousands of educated people, what can I say and to whom am I to say it? What have your studies been that you should acquire strength of mind through them? Where the aim is merely to pass an examination, the result is bound to be unhappy. I feel that the education you are having is of the wrong kind. You have harmed Chanchi's interests and now you are harming those of the children. Still, I regard you as a friend, with due affection, so that I do not wish to order you. I want to bring you round only by appealing to you. I do not wish to exploit your filial piety to make you do anything. There is no anger in this. I do this as a matter of duty. Still I must advise you to shake off this craze for examinations. If you pass, it won't impress me much. If you fail, you will feel very unhappy. However, take the course you think is best. If you give up the thought of examinations and if, when you get this letter, the struggle here is continuing, come over here along with Chanchi, both of you prepared for imprisonment.'

And then about home and the struggle: 'Ba, Ramdas, Kashi, Santok, Chhaganlal, Kuppu, Govindoo, Revashankar, Shivpujan, Raojibhai, Maganbhai, Sam, Rustomji Sheth, Solomon, and others have set out to get imprisoned. They were arrested at Volksrust on Tuesday. Devadas is in Phoenix. He has acquired great efficiency. I get up at 3.30 a.m. and Devadas at 4.30 a.m. At 5, studies and other activities begin. He has filled out a little. Of course, changes do occur in this schedule. For the present, the boys who have remained behind go without salt on all days except Sunday.... Manilal is in Johannesburg. He has now subjected himself to strict vows and is going through a course of penitence. He will court arrest in Johannesburg. Jeki has accompanied Ba to get arrested. She, too, has changed her way of life altogether.'

And I took Harilal into confidence about my own plans: 'I shall get arrested last. I have thought out a way of getting arrested, one which will require a little especial courage. I am constantly praying to God to grant me that.'

I concluded my letter to Harilal with this postscript: '[PS.] My wish is that whatever steps you take should be without reference to me or my views.'

Manilal had written to me to say he was worried on my account. To him also I wrote on the same day as I wrote to Harilal: 'It is ignorance on your part to be concerned on this account. I can be unhappy only if you misbehave. Whether I am happy or otherwise depends on how you behave. By thinking about what I do, you cannot remove my suffering. You can make me happy if you think of your duty.'

The Phoenix satyagrahis, sixteen-strong, comprised beside Kastur, Kashi (Chhaganlal's wife), Santok (Maganlal's wife), Jeki, Parsi Rustomji, Chhaganlal (the only one not from Phoenix) Ravjibhai Patel, Maganbhai Patel, Solomon Royappen, Raju Govindu, Ramdas, Shivpujan Badari, V. Govindarajulu, Kuppuswami Moonlight Mudaliar, Gokaldas Hansraj, Revashankar Ratansi Sodha. They were arrested on the 22nd and on the 23rd, were sentenced to three months' rigorous imprisonment each. Satyagrahi sisters from the Transvaal who had not been arrested earlier were now arrested and brought to the same prison as the Phoenix party—Maritzburg.

The women's bravery was beyond words. They were considerably harassed in jail. Their food was of the worst quality and they were given laundry work as their task.

The 3-pound tax was the sorest question from many points of view. It was a burden imposed upon a most helpless class and it was a tax which was universally condemned during Mr Gokhale's stay last year in South Africa and, as Lord Ampthill most emphatically stated, 'the ministers in South Africa definitely promised Mr Gokhale that this 3-pound poll tax should be removed and ministers told the governor general that they had given him this promise'. A promise given to Mr Gokhale was a promise given to the Indian community. It, therefore, becomes our sacred duty to offer passive resistance until the tax was repealed.[415]

To place the issue in perspective for all in the satyagraha and in the community, I wrote about the tax in *Indian Opinion*'s issue that appeared the day after the arrest of the Phoenix party: 'The proposal for the 3-pound tax first came up in 1894. The Natal government sent a deputation to India. At that time the Indians protested violently against it. The government's original intention was to levy a tax of 25 pounds and, if any Indian could not pay that tax, the government wanted to be empowered to effect his compulsory repatriation. Thanks to our agitation, the Indian government rejected both the proposals and passed a resolution that an Indian who, after completing his indenture, did not re-indenture himself should either return to his country or pay an amount of 3 pounds tax each for himself, his wife and his children. If anyone did not pay the tax, it could be recovered by auctioning his property, if he had any, but that the government would have no power to imprison him. The Indian community made a strong representation against this too. In 1896, meetings were also held in India in this connection. Nevertheless the tax remained. For some time, thereafter, the government collected the tax from those who paid it. Meanwhile, though there was no provision for imprisonment [in case of default], the government found an indirect way of sending defaulters to gaol. According to a section in the law relating to magistrates' courts, anyone failing to comply with a magistrate's judgement is guilty of contempt of court for which the court could sentence him to imprisonment. Under this section, first a decree would be issued on an Indian to pay his tax. Then, if he did not pay the tax, he would be brought before the court for contempt of court. If he is able to prove his poverty, the court must discharge him. Why should the court believe the evidence of such a miserable wretch? The result was violation of the agreement made with the Indian government. This was breach of trust. And hundreds of Indians found themselves in prison. Several women and young men were also imprisoned. Are we not to blame for all this? An opportunity has offered itself today. We are sure that, if many from the community fight against it, the tax will be repealed forthwith. If only a few do so, there is likely to be delay. But the repeal of the tax is certain. The campaign that is now coming is such that it should be easy for all Indians to join it with zest. So far we could ask nothing of the thousands of ex-indentured Indians. Now, they too can join the fight with all their heart. We are convinced that, if every Indian who is not able to court imprisonment or give money for this cause, just spares one hour of his time to acquaint the poor and the illiterate people with the issue of the tax, there will be a real fight indeed. No one, moreover, should remain complacent in the belief that the tax is bound to be repealed. On the contrary, everyone must do his best.'[416]

Likewise, I set out the marriage question: 'In so far as it has drawn our women into the struggle, the marriage question is of even greater importance than that of the annual exaction from ex-indentured men, women, and children. Never did an Indian have cause to suspect that the legality of marriage might be questioned by the Courts of South Africa on the ground of the want of its Christian character or the want of registration in South Africa. But the union government, in pursuance of their policy of greater repression of the Asiatic than before and not being satisfied with their attack on the male members of the community, wanted to extend their hostile operations to our womenfolk. Some zealous law officer discovered that it was possible to prevent the entry of wives of domiciled Indians by declaring their marriage to be illegal in terms of the South African law. They, therefore, challenged the entry of such a woman at the Cape, and Justice Searle was called upon to decide the issue. The learned judge pronounced marriages performed according to the rites of a religion that allows polygamy to be illegal, and, as the person, claiming before him to be the wife of a domiciled Indian, was a Mahomedan, her marriage could not be recognized by the Courts of the Union. This ruling was followed by the Master of the Natal Provincial Division of the Supreme Court. The Master rejected the claim of the only wife of a deceased Indian for exemption from succession duty by reason of her marriage not being in accordance with the laws of the Union. The doctrine was carried to its furthest limit by Justice Gardiner when he declined to recognize the marriage of an Indian wife when she claimed exemption from liability to give evidence against her husband in a trial against him upon a charge of murder. Thus, suddenly, non-Christian Indians found that, in South Africa, their wives occupied merely the position of concubines and their children were considered illegitimate. The reader must remember that, not only does this discovery of their awful position hurt the susceptibilities of a proud race, but it also effectually prevents the entry of almost every Indian wife and every Indian child. If the government had dared to follow out the consequences of the Searle judgement which they deliberately invited, not an Indian wife or her children could have entered the country. To sum up, then, the demands of the community are simple and threefold: (1) Legalization of monogamous marriages already celebrated and to be celebrated in South Africa; (2) The term 'monogamous' to include marriages celebrated according to the rites of religions that may not prohibit polygamy, so long as the woman whose union is to be recognized is the only wife of her husband; (3) the admission of existing plural wives of domiciled Indians without granting such wives a legal status apart from full residential rights.'[417]

On 2 October, Kallenbach set out from Johannesburg with twelve women satyagrahis to court arrest.

Sonja Schlesin reminded me that day that one year more was written off against me. Olive, my late friend J. J. Doke's daughter, was the second to do so. But the family was either in prison or scattered.

I wrote to Maganlal with news of the satyagrahis in Maritzburg jail, important among which was that orders had been issued for the restoration of the sacred thread and shirt to Parsi Rustomji.*

As the satyagraha gathered momentum, I was able to wire Gokhale on 22 October: Nearly hundred [in] gaol. Nearly two thousand labourers families indentured and free in Natal collieries on strike. Strikers will resume work when government promises repeal three-pound tax.

The strike going on in Natal, by now, was promising to become very formidable. By this time six collieries were affected and 2,000 Indians were on strike. The ladies who had tried to get arrested at Vereeniging and failed, now further crossed over into Natal and asked the men serving on the collieries to strike work pending the promise of removal of the annual tax of 3 pounds which ex-indentured Indians and their wives and children have to pay. The presence of these brave women who had never suffered hardship and had never spoken at public meetings acted like electricity, and the men left their work. The strike was conducted on purely passive resistance

---

*Parsi Rustomji had been deprived of his Zoroastrian sacred shirt and thread in Maritzburg Gaol.

lines, and the men had instructions on no account to use physical force, to retaliate or to defend themselves physically. I saw a man who was severely assaulted at Dannhauser on 22 October, and the assault was cruel. He had gone to fetch water and was assaulted by one of the compound managers. The man himself was able-bodied and well able to defend himself, but on account of the above order having been issued, he did not defend himself, and suffered the severe injury without a word.[418]

I wired Prime Minister Botha the next day: The strike has been advised purely regarding the £3 tax and the step has become necessary owing to the nonfulfillment of the promise made to the Hon. Mr Gokhale that it would be repealed, and as a demonstration against the statement made by the government during the last session that the majority of Natal employers are averse to the repeal of the tax. If government will see their way to promise to repeal it next session, the strikers will be advised to return to work.[419]

The strike was having effect but it was necessary to lift it up from the site of the mines. I realized that the strikers must leave the mines. Otherwise the strike was bound to collapse. I therefore invited them to come out and said if they did that, one of us would march with them to the Transvaal border to court arrest. We would be arrested on the way.[420]

On 24 October, I wrote to Maganlal who was looking after the *Indian Opinion*: 'Great things are happening in Newcastle. There is a move to lead a march of 2,000 men into the Transvaal. Let us see what happens.' And by 4 November I was able to cable Gokhale as follows: Five thousand on strike, of whom four thousand have to be fed, including three hundred women and six hundred children. Three hundred are in jail and two hundred more have been arrested. Fifteen hundred strikers are at Charlestown and the rest are gathering at Newcastle prior to crossing the border to court arrest. There is a growing enthusiasm among the strikers.[421]

We were quite determined to march into the Transvaal on the following day, courting arrest, and if we were unmolested, to march right on until we reached Tolstoy Farm. We would then remain quietly there until satisfactory terms had been made with the government. All arrangements had been made along the route, and food depots established at eight different points along the way. Our object was to court arrest, but we wished to do everything quite openly, and we acquainted the government with our intentions.[422]

Nine

THE GREAT MARCH

No trees or plants on the way should be harmed in the least nor should any article belonging to others be touched.

When all the preparations for the march were completed, I made one more effort to achieve a settlement. I had already sent letters and telegrams. I now decided to phone even at the risk of my overtures being answered by an insult. From Charlestown I phoned to General Smuts in Pretoria. I called his secretary and said: 'Tell General Smuts that I am fully prepared for the march. The Europeans in Volksrust are excited and perhaps likely to violate even the safety of our lives. They have certainly held out such a threat. I am sure that even the General would not wish any such untoward event to happen. If he promises to abolish the 3-pound tax, I will stop the march, as I will not break the law merely for the sake of breaking it, but I am driven to it by inexorable necessity. Will not the General accede to such a small request?' I received this reply within half a minute: 'General Smuts will have nothing to do with you. You may do just as you please.' With this the message closed. I had fully expected this result, though I was not prepared for the curtness of the reply. I hoped for a civil answer, as my political relations with the general since the organization of satyagraha had now subsisted for six years. But as I would not be elated by this courtesy, I did not weaken in the face of his incivility. The straight and narrow path I had to tread was clear before me. The next day (6 November 1913) at the appointed stroke of the hour (6.30) we offered prayers and commenced the march in the name of God. The pilgrim band was composed.[423]

I cabled Gokhale: The strike is continuing. The government is not arresting passive resisters. Monthly expenses exceed £7,000. Local contributions are expected to come up to £1,000 every month in provisions and cash. I am marching on Thursday to Transvaal with four thousand men. Endurance and distress are great. Several births have occurred in the concentration camps which have been formed. Two deaths of babies occurred during the march.[424]

I shall never forget the scene when those men, women and children marched out from Phoenix. Each had but one thought—that this was a holy war and that all were setting out on a pilgrimage. They set out singing hymns, one of which was the famous 'Let not thy mind be affected by joy or sorrow'. The strains of music that issued from the throats of those men, women, and children still echo in my ears. The great Parsi Rustomji was among this band. Many had thought that Mr Rustomji had suffered so much in the previous struggle that he would not join this one. Those who said so did not know his true greatness. That women and children should go forth and he stay behind was unthinkable to him. Two other incidents of this period stand out in my memory. There was an argument between Mr Rustomji and his lion-hearted son, Sorabji, who insisted that he would accompany his father. 'Father, let me go in your place,' he said, 'or take me along with you.' The second incident was the meeting between the late Hoosen Mian and Rustomji. When Mr Rustomji went to see him, tears streamed from his eyes and he said, 'Kakaji, if I had been well, I would have accompanied you to gaol.' Bhai Hoosen loved his country dearly; though bedridden, he gave full support to the struggle and spoke constantly of it to all who visited him. Among those who remained behind in Phoenix were boys under sixteen. Although they and the others who managed the affairs of Phoenix stayed out of prison, they did better work than those who went to gaol. Day and night were one to them. They placed themselves under the strictest vows till such time as their companions and elders should be released, lived on saltless diet, and fearlessly took upon themselves even the most onerous tasks. When the strike began in Victoria County, hundreds of indentured labourers took shelter in Phoenix. To have looked after them was in itself a very great achievement. It was equally an achievement to have gone on doing their work in complete fearlessness in spite of the danger of raids by their masters. When the police came and arrested Mr West, they prepared themselves for the possibility that others also might be taken. But not a single person moved out of Phoenix. When the Phoenix batch went to prison, Johannesburg could not remain behind. The women there became restive. They were fired with the desire to be in gaol. The entire family of Mr Thambi Naidoo got ready. His wife, sister-in-law, mother-in-law, Mr Moorgan's relatives, Mrs P. K. Naidoo, Valiamma, who made herself immortal, and other women came forward. They marched forth with children in their arms. Mr Kallenbach took them to Vereeniging. The idea was that, when they crossed the Free State border and returned, they would be arrested. Their expectations were not fulfilled. They somehow managed to spend a few days in Vereeniging, where they tried to get arrested by going round with baskets, hawking, but they were left free. This frustration held within itself a glorious future. If the women had been arrested in Vereeniging itself, the strike might not have taken place; at any rate it would never have reached the proportions it finally did. But the community was in the [protective] hand of God. He is ever the protector of truth. When the women were not arrested, it was decided that they cross the Natal border. If they were not arrested even there, they were to fix, along with Mr Thambi Naidoo, their headquarters at Newcastle. Accordingly, they proceeded to Natal. At the border, the police did not arrest them. They made their home in Newcastle. There Mr D. Lazarus handed over his own house to the women; his wife and sister-in-law, Miss Thomas, took it upon themselves to look to the comforts of the women satyagrahis. The plan was that in Newcastle the women should meet the indentured labourers and their wives, give them a true idea of their conditions and persuade them to go on strike on the issue of the 3-pound tax.

The strike was to commence on my arrival at Newcastle. But the mere presence of these women was like a lighted matchstick to dry fuel. Women who had never before slept except on soft beds and had seldom so much as opened their mouths now delivered public speeches among the indentured labourers. The latter were roused and, even before I arrived, were all for commencing the strike. The project was full of risk. I got a wire from Mr Naidoo. Mr Kallenbach went to Newcastle and the strike began. By the time I reached there, Indians in two coal mines had already stopped work. I was sent for by the Committee of European Sympathizers presided over by Mr Hosken. I met them. They approved of the strike and decided to support it. I stopped for a day at Johannesburg and proceeded to Newcastle and stayed on there. I saw that the people's enthusiasm was tremendous. The government could not tolerate the presence of the women and finally they were sent to gaol as 'vagabonds'. The house of Mr Lazarus now became a dharamsala for satyagrahis. Food had to be cooked there for hundreds of indentured labourers. Mr Lazarus was not to be daunted. The Indians in Newcastle appointed a committee. Mr Sidaat was elected chairman, and the work proceeded apace. Indians in other mines downed tools. Thus, as the strike by the Indian workers in the mines was spreading, a meeting of the Mine Owners' Association was held. I was invited to attend. A great deal of discussion ensued but no solution was found. Their proposal was that, if we called off the strike, they would undertake to write to the government about the 3-pound tax. This, the satyagrahis could not agree to. We had no quarrel with the mine owners. The object of the strike was not to hurt them but rather to invite suffering on ourselves. And so the suggestion of the owners was unacceptable. I returned to Newcastle.

When I reported the result of this meeting, enthusiasm mounted still higher. Work stopped in more mines. Till then the workers had always resided at the mines where they worked. The Council of Action in Newcastle felt that, as long as the labourers continued to live on their masters' estates, the strike would not have its full effect. There was the risk that they might be either tempted or coerced to resume work. Then again, to live in the master's house or eat his bread while refusing to work for him would be immoral. The workers' continued stay at the mines was morally wrong. This last taint, it was felt, would sully the purity of the satyagraha movement. On the other hand, to house and feed thousands of Indians was a stupendous problem. Mr Lazarus' house was now too small. The two poor ladies laboured night and day but found it impossible to cope with the work. It was decided, even in the face of this, to adopt only the right course, whatever the cost. Messages were sent to miners to stop work and proceed to Newcastle. The moment these messages were received, an exodus from the mines began. Indians from the Belangi mine were the first to arrive. It appeared as though bands of pilgrims were daily streaming into Newcastle. Men young and old, women—some by themselves, others with children in their arms—all arrived with bundles on their heads. The men, one saw, were carrying trunks. Some arrived by day, others by night and food had to be provided for them. How can I describe the contentment of these poor people? They were pleased with what they got, no matter how little. Rarely did one come across anyone with a downcast look. A smile played on every face. To me they appeared to have come from among the 33 crores of gods. The women were like goddesses. From where could shelter be provided for all? For bedding, straw was spread on the earth and the sky was their roof. God was their protector. Someone asked for a bidi. I explained that they had come out, not as indentured labourers, but as servants of India. They were taking part in a religious war and at such a time they must abandon addictions such as drinking and smoking. Those who were unable to give them up should not expect their requirements to be paid for from the common coffers. The good men accepted this advice. I was never again asked for money to buy a bidi. The exodus from the mines continued. One pregnant woman had a miscarriage on the way. In spite of numberless hardships of this kind, no one gave up the struggle or turned back. There was a tremendous increase in the Indian population of Newcastle.

The houses of Indians were overfilled. The number made available was enough to accommodate women and old people. I must state here that the white people of Newcastle showed us great courtesy, even sympathy. No Indian was harassed by them. One good lady even gave her house free for our use; other assistance of a minor nature was also received from a number of whites all the time. It was, however, not possible to keep thousands of Indians permanently in Newcastle. The mayor became apprehensive. The normal population of Newcastle is about 3,000. An additional 10,000 could not be accommodated in such a town. Labourers stopped work in other mines too. And so the question arose: what should be done? The intention behind the strike was to court imprisonment. The government could have arrested the workers if it had so wished, but there were not enough prisons to house those thousands. Hence, they had not so far touched the strikers. The one simple way left to us now was to cross the Transvaal border and get arrested. We thought that the congestion in Newcastle would thereby be relieved and the strikers could also be put to the test. In Newcastle, the agents of the mine owners were trying to lure away the workers. Not a single person had yielded; even so, it was the duty of the Council of Action to keep them away from all temptation. It seemed desirable, therefore, that they should march from Newcastle to Charlestown. The distance is about 35 miles. To provide railway fare for thousands was out of the question. It was therefore arranged that all able-bodied men and women should do the journey on foot. The women who could not walk were to be taken by train. There was a possibility of arrests on the way. Moreover, this was the first experience of its kind for them. It was therefore decided that I should myself take the first batch. It consisted of about 500 persons of whom 60 were women, with their children. I shall never forget that scene. The company walked along raising cries of 'Victory to Dwarkanath', 'Victory to Ramachandra', and 'Vande Mataram'.

Each person was given enough cooked rice and dal to last for two days. Everyone carried his or her things in a bundle. The following conditions were read out to them:

1. It was probable that I would be arrested. Even if this happened, they were to march on until arrested themselves. Though every effort would be made to provide them with meals, etc., on the way, they should not mind, if by chance, food was not available on some day.

2. For the duration of the struggle, they should abstain from drinks.
3. They must not retreat even in the face of death.
4. They should expect no shelter for night halts during the march, but should sleep on the grass.
5. No trees or plants on the way should be harmed in the least nor should any article belonging to others be touched.
6. If the government's police came to arrest anyone, the latter should willingly surrender.
7. No resistance should be offered to the police or any others; on the contrary, beating should be patiently borne and no attempt should be made to protect oneself by offering violence in return.
8. They should cheerfully bear the hardships in gaol and live there as if the gaol were a palace.

There were persons of every caste and community in this pilgrim band. There were Hindus, Muslims, Brahmins, Kshatriyas, Vaishyas, and Sudras. There were men from Calcutta and there were Tamils. Several Pathans and Sindhis from the north found it difficult to accept the conditions requiring them to refrain from defending themselves in case they were beaten; not only did they accept it, however, but, when the testing time came, they actually made no move to defend themselves. And so, the first batch started on its march. On the very first night, we had the experience of sleeping out on the grass. On the way, warrants were received for the arrest of about 150 persons and they surrendered themselves readily. A single police officer had come to make the arrests. He had no assistant; how the arrested men were to be taken away became a problem. We were only 6 miles from Charlestown. So I suggested to the officer that these persons could proceed along with me and that he should take them into custody at Charlestown, or do whatever he thought fit after obtaining instructions from his superiors. The officer agreed and left us.

We arrived at Charlestown. This is a very small township, with a population of barely 1,000. There is only one main road and the

Indian population is negligible. The whites were amazed, therefore, at the sight of our party. At no time had so many Indians appeared in Charlestown. There was no train ready to convey the prisoners to Newcastle. Where could the police keep them? There was not enough room for all these arrested persons at the Charlestown police station. And so, the police handed them over to me and agreed to pay for their food. This is no small tribute to satyagraha. In the ordinary course of things, how could people arrested from among us be placed in our charge? If some of them had escaped, the responsibility would not have been ours. But everyone knew that it was the job of the satyagrahis to court arrest and they had, therefore, full confidence in us. The arrested men thus stayed with us for four days more. When the police were ready to take charge of them, they went away willingly. More and more people were being recruited to our party. On some days, 400 would join, on others even more. Many arrived on foot, while women came mostly by train. These were put up wherever there was space in the houses of Indian merchants of Charlestown. The local corporation also offered us houses. The whites did not give us the slightest trouble. On the contrary, they went out of their way to help us. One Dr Briscoe took it upon himself to give us free medical aid and, when we proceeded beyond Charlestown, he gave us gratis some expensive medicines and useful instruments. Our food was cooked in the mosque premises. The fire had to remain lit all the twenty-four hours. The cooks came from among the strikers. During the final days, 4,000 to 5,000 persons were being fed. Yet these workers never lost heart. In the morning, the meal consisted of mealie pap with sugar and some bread. In the evening they had rice, dal, and vegetables. Most people in South Africa eat thrice a day.

The indentured labourers always have three meals, but during the struggle they remained content with only two. They like to have small delicacies with their meals, but these, too, they gave up at this time. What to do with these huge crowds of people became a problem. If they were kept somehow in Charlestown, there was the likelihood of an epidemic breaking out. Moreover, it was not desirable that so many thousands accustomed to hard work should be kept in a state of idleness. It needs to be mentioned here that, although so many poor people had come together in Charlestown, not one of them committed a theft.

The police had never to be called and they had no extra work on our account. However, it seemed best not to keep waiting in Charlestown. It was therefore decided to proceed to the Transvaal and, if not arrested, to go on ultimately to Tolstoy Farm. Before commencing the march, the government was informed that we were proceeding to the Transvaal to court arrest, that we had no desire to stay there or to claim any rights, but that, as long as the government did not arrest us, we would continue our march and finally stay on Tolstoy Farm. If, however, the government promised to withdraw the 3-pound tax, we were willing to return. But the government was in no mood to consider this notice. It was misled by its informants who assured it that the strikers would soon be exhausted. The government had a notice printed in all languages and distributed among the strikers. At last the time came for us to proceed beyond Charlestown. On 6 November, a party of 3,000 left at daybreak. The procession was more than a mile long. Mr Kallenbach and I were at the rear.

The procession reached the border where a police party stood in readiness. When the two of us reached the spot, we had a talk with the police. They refused to arrest us and the procession went on in a disciplined and peaceful manner through Volksrust. On reaching Standerton Road outside the town, we halted and had some refreshments. It had been arranged that women should not join in this march, but later it became impossible to check the tide of enthusiasm and a few women managed to accompany the procession. However, some women and children still remained behind in Charlestown. After crossing the border at Volksrust, Mr Kallenbach was sent back to look after them.

On the following day, the police arrested me near Palmford. I was charged with having brought unauthorized persons into the Transvaal. There was no warrant for the arrest of anyone else. The procession went ahead. I was produced before the magistrate at

Volksrust. I did not, of course, wish to defend myself. But as some arrangements had yet to be made regarding those who had gone beyond Palmford and those left behind at Charlestown, I asked for time. The government pleader objected, but the magistrate pointed out that bail could be refused only in a case of murder. He then asked me to furnish a bail of 50 pounds and gave me time for a week. The amount was immediately paid by a merchant in Volksrust. As soon as I was released, I went straight to the marchers. Their enthusiasm was doubled. Meanwhile, a wire came from Pretoria to say that the government had no intention of arresting the Indians who were with me. Only the leaders were to be arrested. This did not mean that all the rest would be allowed to go free. But the government had no desire to make our work easy by arresting all of us or to provoke agitation in India on this account. Mr Kallenbach followed with another large batch. Our party of over 2,000 was nearing Standerton. There, I was again arrested and the hearing was fixed for the 21st. We, however, proceeded on our way. But now the government could stand this no longer and it took the step of separating me from the rest. At this time, preparations were afoot to send Mr Polak to India with a deputation. He came to see me before leaving. But 'our undertakings remain unfinished, and the will of God prevails'. This is what happened.

On Sunday I was arrested, for the third time, near Greylingstad. The warrant this time was issued from Dundee and the charge was that of instigating the workers to stop work. I was removed from there to Dundee in utmost secrecy. I have mentioned above that Mr Polak was in the march with us. He now took charge. My case came up for hearing in Dundee on Tuesday. All three charges against me were read out and I pleaded guilty to all of them. I made myself quite comfortable in gaol. Afterwards, proceedings were taken against me in Volksrust and I was given another three months of gaol, besides the nine months I got at Dundee. About this time, I learnt that Mr Polak had been arrested and that instead of going to India he found himself in gaol. I, for one, was delighted, because this, to my mind, was a far more weighty deputation than the other one. Soon after this, Mr Kallenbach was arrested and he also, like Mr Polak, found himself lodged in gaol for three months. The government was sadly mistaken when it imagined that, once the leaders were arrested, the people would surrender. All the strikers were put into four special trains and taken to mines in Dundee and Newcastle. They were subjected to much cruelty and they suffered terribly. But they had come forward to suffer. They were their own leaders. They had to demonstrate their strength, left as they were without any leaders, so-called; and they did so. How well they did is known to all the world.[425]

During the satyagraha struggle, 1914
Courtesy: Sabarmati Ashram Preservation and Memorial Trust, Ahmedabad.

BOOK VI
1913 to 1914

Two decades after Gandhi's first arrival in South Africa, he is now a force to reckon with, among his own people and in the echelons of official power. Smuts sees in him a person he cannot but admire and a force he cannot but resist. And the all-powerful Minister for the Interior finds that the force that he is resisting is not the kind that can be locked up or silenced by threats. On the contrary, Gandhi celebrates imprisoning and only grows in influence through each and every method employed to restrain him. And he has become a catalyst for a disciplined mass movement the like of which has not been seen before.

If the 3-pound tax has been an irritant for Indian South Africa, the judgment of Justice Searle derecognizing marriages outside Christian auspices becomes an affront to the community's self-pride in its most intimate domain—the family. Gandhi's wife smarts under the judgment's implications as do all affected by it. High and low, educated and unlettered, all Indian South Africans now move into defiance that is given a spirit of its own by women. Gandhi is to describe this reaction in 1921 thus: 'The whole community rose like a surging wave. Without organization, without propaganda, all—nearly 40,000 courted imprisonment. Nearly 10,000 were actually imprisoned. A bloodless revolution was effected after strenuous discipline in self-suffering.'[426]

India is stirred by reports and C. F. Andrews is deputed by Gokhale to witness and help what seems like the denouement in the struggle. He and his colleague W. W. Pearson do more on coming to South Africa. They tell the authorities in no uncertain terms that South Africa is being judged by what is happening. And in a series of rapid moves, the government advances to a solution—the Smuts–Gandhi agreement of 30 June 1914 under which all the demands of the satyagraha are conceded.

Gandhi, accompanied by Kasturba, leaves South Africa for India via England with a sense of completion, but not of contentment, for he knows India beckons him with stronger pulls, more intense urgings. And he also knows that while the causes of Indian unrest have been addressed in South Africa, that nation is yet to redeem itself from racism. He had told the Reverend Joseph Doke, his first biographer: 'When the moment of collision comes, if, instead of the old ways of massacre, assegai and fire, the natives adopt the policy of passive resistance, it will be a grand change for the colony.'[427]

When, a quarter of a century later, on 1 January 1939, an African leader, the Reverend S. S. Tema of the African National Congress meets Gandhi in India, Gandhi would say to him something that encapsulates Gandhi's vision: 'The Indians (in South Africa) are a microscopic minority.... You, on the other hand, are the sons of the soil who are being robbed of your inheritance. You are bound to resist that. Yours is a far bigger issue....'[428]

~

One
ARREST

20 pounds, or three months' imprisonment, with hard labour.... I said in a clear and calm voice: I elect to go to gaol.

I was arrested near Palmford and charged with having brought unauthorized persons into the Transvaal. I then sent General Smuts this telegram:

> Whilst I appreciate the fact of government having at last arrested prime mover in passive resistance struggle, cannot help remarking that from point view humanity moment chosen most unfortunate. Government probably know that marchers include 122 women, fifty tender children, all voluntarily marching on starvation rations without provision for shelter during stages. Tearing me away under such circumstances from them is violation all considerations justice. If untoward incidents happen during further progress march or if deaths occur, especially among women with babies in arms, responsibility will be government's.[429]

I was produced before the magistrate at Volksrust, released on bail. A representative of Reuter asked me what I thought would be the outcome of the demonstration. I said: The like of this struggle will not come again. We have reached the limit now. The courage that the indentured labourers have shown and the suffering they have gone through have been boundless. How many men will be ready to foot 24 miles a day on one and a half pounds of bread and a little sugar? This is what our poor brethren have done. They have suffered horses' kicks. They have silently endured kicks and blows by whites. Women have walked in the heat of the noon, two-month-old babies in arms and bundles on head. Everyone has braved the rigours of weather, heat and cold and rain.

I was re-arrested the next day at Standerton, released and was arrested for the third time, on 9 November, at Teakworth. I was taken to Heidelberg and produced before the magistrate on the following day. I applied for remand of the case. Before I was to be tried at Dundee, I sent a message on 11 November: Such sacrifice will no doubt result in repeal of the 3-pound tax but what is more, it will enhance India's prestige. I consider the Transvaal March to have been perfectly successful. The object was to get arrested and all have been arrested. It is only now, however, that the struggle will grow really exciting. Hundreds of men, who are not ready for gaol, can play their part. They have only to resolve that they themselves will go without meals but feed the strikers. Whether or not any money arrives from India, we must supply the food from here. We should put courage in the strikers' hearts and advise them not to retaliate even if mercilessly kicked. All Indians can do this. An opportunity like this will not come again. Every Indian may take a pledge. He can cut out a meal every day, and with the money so saved provide food to the hungry. Decency requires that traders in every place should give food and shelter to any striker who might find his way to that place and then send him on to where facilities exist for feeding large numbers. If any Indian fails to play his part in this great venture, I for one will consider him an unfortunate man indeed.

On 11 November, I was charged before the resident magistrate, Mr J. W. Cross of Dundee, with inducing indentured immigrants to leave the province. The court was crowded with Indians and Europeans. Mr W. Dalzell-Turnbull was specially instructed by the attorney general to appear for the prosecution, and Advocate J. W. Godfrey appeared for me. I pleaded guilty to the charges. Mr Turnbull read the section and left the matter in the hands of the magistrate. Mr Godfrey stated that he was under an obligation to the defendant not to plead in mitigation in any way whatsoever. The circumstances, he said, which had brought me before the magistrate were well known to all persons, and he was only expressing the desire of the defendant when he stated that the magistrate had a duty to perform, and that he was expected to perform that duty fearlessly, and should therefore not hesitate to impose the highest sentence upon the prisoner if he felt that the circumstances in the case justified it. I obtained the permission of the court, and made the following statement: As a member of the profession, and being an old resident of Natal, I think that, in justice to myself and the public, I should state that the counts against me were of such a nature that I took the responsibility imposed upon me, for I believed that the demonstration for which these people were taken out of the colony was one for a worthy object. I said I felt that I should say that I had nothing against the employers of indentured labour, and regretted that in this campaign, serious losses were being caused to them. I appealed to the employers also, and said I felt that the tax was one which was heavily weighing down my countrymen, and should be removed. I also felt that I was in honour bound, in view of the position of things between Mr Smuts and Professor Gokhale, to produce a striking demonstration.... On the whole, I felt I had not gone beyond the principles and honour of the profession of which I was a member, had only done my duty in advising my countrymen, and it was my duty to advise them again, that until the tax were removed, to leave work and subsist upon rations obtained by charity. I was certain, I said, that without suffering it was not possible for them to get their grievance remedied. I having pleaded guilty, the magistrate accepted that plea, and passed the following sentences: Count 1: 20 pounds, or three months' imprisonment, with hard labour; Count 2: 20 pounds, or three months' imprisonment, with hard labour, to take effect upon the expiration of the sentence in respect to Count 1; Count 3: 20 pounds, or three months' imprisonment, with hard labour, this to take effect upon the expiration of the sentence imposed in Count 2. I said in a clear and calm voice: I elect to go to gaol. A large crowd of friends waited outside to see me come out, but the police took me away secretly and no one knew how I was taken away.[430]

From my cell in Dundee gaol, I wrote to Maganlal: 'I have got nine months and if I get six months each at the other two places, that will make twenty-one months; I shall be most lucky in that case. That I could get into gaol without having to disguise myself was so much the less bother.'[431]

Polak too had been arrested.

I was produced in court before Mr Jooste, assistant magistrate and charged under Section 20 of the Immigration Regulation Act.[432] I pleaded guilty, but the formal evidence of a resister named Poldat was called. Witness stated he belonged to Ballengeich Mine, and remembered during the current month proceeding with a number of Indians into the Transvaal. Poldat said I was leading them from Charlestown to Johannesburg. Poldat recognized me as the leader. Poldat knew he had no right in this province, because he was a prohibited immigrant. I said he would like to ask witness two questions. Why did Poldat enter the Transvaal? Poldat said he entered the Transvaal as a protest against the 3-pound tax. Would Poldat have gone back to the mines if that 3-pound tax had been repealed? Poldat said yes; if the government had agreed to repeal the 3-pound tax, he would have gone back.

I was asked if I wished to make a statement. I said I admit that I advised not only the last witness but hundreds of other Indians, whom I knew to be prohibited immigrants, to cross the border from Natal into the Transvaal. Of my intention to do so I had given the Minister of the Interior due notice and I specially interviewed the Immigration Officer at Volksrust, and informed him even of the date on which I proposed to cross the border. I told both the government and the Immigration Officer that in doing so my only object was to make a demonstration against the 3-pound tax which was weighing heavily upon those who were affected by it, and to court for myself and the party who crossed with me imprisonment. I assured them that nothing could be further from my wish than to desire that a single one of those men who crossed the border should remain in the Transvaal and settle there. I said also that, with such a large number crossing with me, I might be totally unable to prevent them for all time from roving about the country and that, therefore, I hoped that the government would take charge of the men. Throughout the march into the Transvaal, I endeavoured to keep the men under control and to prevent them from dispersing, and I claim that not a single Indian left the column if it may be so called. I heard something at Heidelberg about the formation of a Vigilants Committee at Volksrust, whose aim I understand was to make the government enforce the Immigration Act. There is, therefore, common cause between the committee and my co-workers and myself. Through the court I begged to make the assurance that the present movement has nothing whatsoever to do with the unlawful entry for purposes of residence in the Transvaal of a single Indian. I think, I said, I may fairly claim that my whole career in the Transvaal has been actuated with the motive of assisting the government in preventing surreptitious entry and unlawful settlement, but I have pleaded guilty as I know that I have committed a technical breach, on a vast scale, of the section under which I am charged. I am aware too that the steps I have taken are fraught with the greatest risks and intense personal suffering by those who have accepted my advice, but after very mature consideration, based upon twenty years' experience of South Africa, I have come to the conclusion that nothing short of such suffering will move the conscience of the government as also of the inhabitants of the union of which, in spite of the so-called breach of the Statutory Laws of the Union, I claim to be a sane and law-abiding citizen. The court then adjourned for a quarter of an hour for the magistrate to consider his decision. On resuming, Mr Jooste passed sentence of three months' imprisonment.

Polak and Kallenbach were arrested at Charlestown on 10 November. Polak was charged before Mr Jooste, assistant magistrate, under Section 20 of the Immigration Act, but declined to plead guilty to the charge. The evidence of five witnesses including Kallenbach and myself was called. I gave evidence that the march to the Transvaal was fixed without consultation with Mr Polak, who intended leaving for India on 14 November, and he knew all arrangements had been made for Mr Polak's departure from Durban. Had it not been for witness's arrest before reaching Greylingstad, Mr Polak would certainly have left at that station. Under the circumstances, I thought Mr Polak should lead the column to its destination, so that the men would not disperse. In my opinion, if Mr Polak was guilty of aiding and abetting, so also were the troopers who guided the column on its way. The men had been handed over to Mr Polak because Mr Cachalia had not then arrived on the scene.

Rifleman Joubert stated that he had seen Polak asking me for instructions at Balfour and thought that Polak was one of the leaders of the movement. Constable Kneen stated that Polak had addressed the Indians and advised them to return to Charlestown. Kallenbach said that Polak's intention had been to return to Durban. His purpose was to discuss certain matters with me regarding his departure for India. Polak was found guilty and was awarded three months' simple imprisonment without hard labour.

I wrote to Millie Polak: 'You are brave. So I know you will consider yourself a proud and happy wife in having a husband who has dared to go to gaol for a cause he believes in. The 3-pound tax cause is the cause of the helpless and the dumb. And I ask you to work away in the shape of begging, advising, and doing all you can. Miss Schlesin knows the struggle almost like Henry. Assist her. I have asked her to move forward and backward and assume full control. Draw upon West and Maganlal for your needs. May you have strength of mind and body to go through the fire.'[433]

Two

GAOL

I had not had time to study for years, particularly since 1893, and the prospect of uninterrupted study filled me with joy.

Kallenbach, Polak, and I now thought the three of us could live together in the Volksrust Gaol for three months. But the government was not going to allow it.

Yet, in the few happy days that we did spend there new prisoners came every day and brought us news of what was happening outside. Among these was Harbutsinh, of about seventy-five years in age. He was not a miner and therefore was not one of the strikers.

'Why are you in gaol?' I asked him, alluding to his age.

'How could I help it?' he replied when you, your wife, and even your boys have gone to gaol for our sakes?'

'But you will not be able to endure the hardships of gaol life. I would advise you to leave gaol. Shall I arrange for your release?'

'No, please, I will never leave gaol. I must die one of these days. And how happy I should be to die in gaol.'

My head bent in reverence before this illiterate sage. Harbutsinh, who was shifted to the Durban Gaol, had his wish, and he died in Durban Gaol on 5 January 1914. His body was cremated according to Hindu rites in the presence of hundreds of Indians.

The government did not want prisoners coming to Volksrust to carry any messages from me or news of Kallenbach, Polak or me on their release or transfer. And so they decided to separate the three of us. Kallenbach was moved to Pretoria and Polak to Germiston. I was taken to a place where no Indian would see me. I was moved to Bloemfontein, the capital of Orangia which had no more than fifty Indians living there—all waiters in hotels. I was not troubled by this isolating of me but hailed it as a blessing. I had not had time to study for years, particularly since 1893, and the prospect of uninterrupted study filled me with joy.

The Bloemfontein gaoler could think only of his own powers but the medical officer of the hall became my friend. At that point I was a fruitarian, taking neither milk nor ghee nor food grains. I lived on a diet of bananas, tomatoes, raw groundnuts, limes, and olive oil. The doctor added almonds, walnuts, and Brazil nuts to my diet. He inspected everything ordered for me in person and for better ventilation in my cell tried his best to have the cell doors kept open for me, but in vain. The gaoler threatened to resign if the doors were kept open. I fully understood the gaoler's standpoint.[434]

But the experience of others was different. In a letter to *The Natal Advertiser* I said: Parsi Rustomji, who took a leading part in the previous campaigns and had experience of the gaols in Volksrust, Heidelberg, Diepkloof, and Johannesburg, on being sentenced at Volksrust, was brought to the Pietermaritzburg Gaol and later removed to the Durban Gaol. He had a taste of the Maritzburg Gaol, but his experience in the Durban Gaol, he told me, was the worst. Mr Rustomji declared, that the native warders used to assault the resisters, with no fear of consequences. One, Mr P. K. Desai, was assaulted so violently that the blow sent him reeling to the ground and from there he was dragged to his cell. The treatment of the injuries kept him in the hospital for eleven days. Mr Rustomji and his fellow prisoners had to resort to a fast to secure him [permission to wear] his shirt and sacred thread. A good Parsi will not move a single step in the absence of these two things. Mr Rustomji was also assaulted twice by native warders. The matter was brought to the notice of the superintendent, but to no purpose. A youngster was beaten for standing out of line. On one occasion, several passive resisters went on a fast to register a strong protest against such treatment. At the end of four days of complete fasting, the boy referred to above was forcibly fed while he kept shrieking in protest all the time. Even the prison doctor in charge is reported to have condemned this display of barbarism and stated that he did not accept responsibility for the forcible feeding. The fact that the prisoner was a vegetarian was ignored: the milk which was fed to him was mixed with eggs. The prisoners were supplied dirty clothes which could be a menace to their health. The food was poor and was served half-cooked in rusted tin bowls, and the prisoners report that in consequence many of them got dysentery. Cockroaches and insects were found in the food, and, when the matter was reported to the officer, his reply was that a prison was no hotel and that even in a hotel one found insects in food.

Most of the passive resisters were men of good education. Though well used to reading, they were not given books to read from the prison libraries nor permitted to read any of their own. Despite protests, all the gaol officers, from the highest to the lowest, used to address the passive resisters as 'coolies'. The more they resented this, the more obstinate the officers became. They [also] report that the present doctor pays no attention to their health. During these three months, the magistrate visited the gaol only once. He did not listen to the complaints of the prisoners. Indian prisoners are generally allowed sandals and socks. In this gaol most of them did not get these; even women were not given any. Quite often the prisoners were supplied only one blanket each, and that a torn one. They were refused permission to see their lawyers and were not even allowed to write to the Director of Prisons. All this is but a brief summary of the tales of suffering I heard from my countrymen.[435]

Cablegrams regarding these outrages were sent to India addressed to Gokhale who, though in sickbed, would inquire if even on a single day he did not receive a full detailed message. It was then Lord Hardinge, the viceroy, made his famous speech which created a stir in South Africa and in England. He spoke of his and of India's 'sympathy, deep and burning', for the sufferings being borne by Indian labourers in South Africa and said that this passive resistance movement had been 'dealt with by measures which would not for one moment be tolerated by any country that calls itself civilized'.

The satyagraha had become international news.[436] The government now took recourse to a time-honoured tradition of appointing a commission of inquiry. 'Indian Inquiry Commission' with Sir William Solomon as chairman was set up by the union government on 11 December, to inquire into the causes of the strike and the disturbances in connection with it.

On 14 December, from my Bloemfontein cell, I wrote to Miss Ada West, who was taking care of the family at Phoenix:

> As I do not know where everybody else is, it is the most appropriate for me to write to you. I am quite happy and well here. It is almost as hot here as in Phoenix this time of the year. Hope that you and others are keeping good health and that Devadas, Prabhudas, and the other boys are observing the discipline that was introduced after the ladies' withdrawal from Phoenix and that the boys are thriving under it. Pray remind Devadas of the promises he has made me at various times. Ask him if he can recall them all. When you or someone else writes to me, I should like [to know] the day's routine for the boys. Is Shanti giving trouble? Is Navin obedient? And are Sivparsad and Chhotam as playful as ever? I hope that Rukhi causes no extra trouble to you or to Maganlal. Krishna, Radha, and Keshu are not out of my mind, but they are used to being with Maganlal and, therefore, do not call for special inquiry.
>
> When the ladies and the boys return, please tell Mrs Gandhi that she will please me immensely by not disturbing the routine established after her withdrawal and I hope that Ramdas and the other boys will fall in with it. Your reply to this should be sent after their return, so that you may give me full information about them. I shall not withdraw any other letter but the reply to this. I hope Mrs Gandhi's old trouble did not revive and that she kept good health. Please let me know too how the other ladies fared. Jekibehn should adhere to the promises made by her to me. Please tell that hardly a day passes when I do not give much thought to her. As for her diet, I do not bind her to any promises or resolutions she may have made. She may take whatever suits her constitution. But she must keep not only good health but be robust....[437]

On the Solomon Commission's recommendation, Polak and Kallenbach and I were brought to Pretoria and released unconditionally on 18 December.[438]

Three

NEGOTIATIONS

Are you prepared to share the fate of those of our countrymen whom the cold stone is resting upon today?... (Cries [from the gathered Indians] of 'Yes.')

We were accorded a reception on reaching Johannesburg in the evening at the old Gaiety Theatre. I said in my response that I was not the least thankful for having been released, for I preferred solitude and the peace of prison because it gave me opportunity and time for meditation; but, having been released, I said I would now resume the work upon which I was engaged when I was convicted. I said I was not satisfied with the Indian Commission appointed by the government as I was uncertain whether it would be effectual, and whether it would be in the interests of the Indian population. However, it had been decided that I and Messrs Polak and Kallenbach should proceed to Durban in the morning, and, when there, decide whether they would accept the commission as it was at present constituted.

I would not positively say at the present time that I would not give evidence before the commission, but my inclinations were that way as the commission was loaded against us. I also added that my prison experience, just over, had been a change from that I had undergone on previous occasions. I had been treated with the utmost courtesy, and I would like publicly to record the excellent manner in which the prison officials had considered my comfort.

I told the Johannesburg audience that we were on the eve of a most momentous decision, and that they would be called upon to decide was whether they could in honour tender evidence to a commission which had been constituted without any reference to Indian wishes or opinion, and also whether the personnel of that commission could be regarded as fair and impartial. After, Polak, Kallenbach, William Hosken, and I had addressed the meeting, it was unanimously resolved not to tender evidence before the commission as then constituted.

We then went to Durban on 21 December 1913. On reaching Durban station, Polak, Kallenbach, and I were garlanded and taken in a procession to the office of the Natal Indian Congress where we addressed a large gathering attended by about 6,000 to 7,000 persons including some prominent Europeans. Abdul Kadir presided. As I rose to speak, I was greeted with cheers and a bunch of flowers was placed in my hand by one of those near the platform. I was looking different as I had changed my dress from that I had been using for the last twenty years. I had decided on the change when I heard of the shooting of our fellow countrymen. No matter whether the shooting was found to be justified or not, the fact was that they were shot, and those bullets shot me through the heart also. I felt how glorious it would have been if one of those bullets had struck me also, because might I not be a murderer myself by having advised Indians to strike? My conscience cleared me from this guilt of murder, but I felt I should adopt mourning for those Indians as a humble example to my fellow countrymen. I was not prepared myself to accept the European mourning dress for this purpose, and, with some modification in deference to the feelings of my European friends, I had adopted the dress similar to that of an indentured Indian. I asked my fellow countrymen to adopt some sign to show to the world that they were mourning, and further to adopt some inward observance also. And perhaps I said I might tell them what my inward mourning was—to restrict myself to one meal a day.

I said that I would have preferred to speak first in one of the Indian tongues, but in the presence of Messrs Polak and Kallenbach, my fellow convicts, feelings of gratitude compelled me to speak first in the tongue they knew. They had been released, I continued, not on any condition, but on the recommendation of a commission appointed by the government, in order that every facility might be given not only to them, but to the Indian community, to bring before the commission any evidence that the community might have in its possession. I thought that it was a right and proper thing that the government had appointed a commission, but I thought the commission was open to the gravest objection from the Indian standpoint; and I was there to tender my humble advice to them that it was impossible to accept the commission in a form in which the Indians had no voice. This was one of the serious fundamental objections. The other objection was that it was a partisan commission; therefore, the Indians wanted their own partisans on it. This they might not get, but they at least wanted impartial men, who had not expressed opinions hostile to their interests, but gentlemen who would be able to bring to the deliberations of the commission an open, just and impartial mind. (Applause.) 'Therefore,' I said, 'I hope you will hold yourselves in readiness to respond to the call the government may make by declining our just and reasonable requests, and then, to force the pace by again undergoing still greater purifying suffering, until at last the government may order the military to riddle us also with their bullets.'

'My friends,' I asked, 'are you prepared for this?' (Voices: 'Yes.') 'Are you prepared to share the fate of those of our countrymen whom the cold stone is resting upon today? Are you prepared to do this?' (Cries of 'Yes.') 'Then, if the government does not grant our request, this is the proposition I wish to place before you this morning: That all of us, on the first day of the New Year, should be ready again to suffer battle, again to suffer imprisonment and march out.' (Applause.)

Immediately after the mass meeting, Polak, Kallenbach, and I wrote to General Smuts:

> Sir, we understand from the papers that our release from imprisonment, before the natural period of the respective terms to which we were sentenced, was due to the recommendation of the members of the commission which has been recently appointed to investigate the causes that led up to the strike of indentured and other Indians in Natal and other Indian matters. We fully appreciate the reasons which moved the commissioners to make the recommendation, and the government's

acceptance thereof, and we are desirous of helping the commission to investigate the causes. We beg to express our gratefulness for the appointment of a commission for the purpose above indicated, but we are reluctantly obliged to inform the government that we shall be unable to render the assistance which it is in our power to do, unless the objections presently to be set forth are met by the government. We have ascertained that the Indian community of South Africa has not been given the opportunity of making any nomination on its behalf to the membership of the commission.

We hold that Colonel Wylie, by reason of his prominent connection with the military, is naturally an interested party. Against Mr Esselen and Colonel Wylie, as South African statesmen, we can have nothing to say, but we cannot help fearing that they share the common human failing of not being able to divest themselves entirely of their bias. Much, however, as we regret the appointment on the commission of these gentlemen, we do not propose to raise any objection to their nomination; but, in order to counterbalance the effect that their bias may have on the finding of the commission, we submit that it is absolutely necessary to appoint gentlemen of South African standing known to possess no anti-Asiatic bias to the commission and, as such, we venture to suggest the names of the Hon. Sir James Rose-Innes and the Hon. W. P. Schreiner. We hope and pray that the government will be pleased to accede to the submission and nominate on the commission the gentlemen whose names have been proposed by the meeting. If the nomination is accepted, we beg to state that, before we can tender our evidence to the commission and advise the community to offer the overwhelming evidence which is in its possession, it will be necessary to release the passive resisters who are presently undergoing imprisonment, whether in the ordinary gaols or in mining compounds which have been turned into gaols. We beg to reiterate the declaration we have often made that, as passive resisters, we countenance no violence, even by way of retaliation, on the part of those who take part in the movement, whether as strikers or otherwise. We have repeatedly given effective advice, which has been acted upon, to the effect that passive resisters must submit to personal violence in the course of their passive resistance, even though such violence may entail death. It becomes necessary for us to redeclare the above view, as after our incarceration, we observe that it has been alleged that, on some estates, strikers used violence.

Four

SUSPENSE

On landing, Andrews...asked: 'Where is Mr Gandhi?'
Polak then turned and pointed to me.

On the release on 22 December of Kastur and the others from Maritzburg Gaol, a procession was taken out which terminated in a reception meeting. Addressing the audience on behalf of the released passive resisters, I said: 'This is a very sad time for us. We can have no joy in gatherings and celebrations. All the same, I give thanks to you, on behalf of my wife and the other ladies, for the welcome you have accorded them. My brethren have lost their lives, killed by bullets, and I feel extremely sad, at a time like this, in taking part in this reception even to the extent that I have done. In gaol, I was free from all anxieties. My Indian brothers and sisters can at this time express their sincere sympathy with the helpless widows and orphans by themselves observing mourning in various ways. Men can leave off tobacco, betel leaves and betel nut; women may lay aside ornaments and fine dresses.'[439]

Gokhale had received Reuter's summary of a report of our position on the Solomon Commission and the following cable to me arrived at 10 p.m. on 21 December: 'Reuter cables substance your interview. After Solomon's speech fear boycotting inquiry will be grave mistake, alienating sympathy Government of India and many friends England. Engage best counsel and yourself Polak assist offering evidence. Inquiry does not concern general grievances passive resisters but it is most important, opportunity offered producing evidence support allegations cruelties should not be refused. I venture suggest draw up protest against Esselen and Wylie, explaining fully objection to both and appear under protest.'

I apprised Gokhale of our position on 22 December: 'Unable assist commission by evidence unless community right to be consulted matters affecting it recognized and partisan character commission counterbalanced by appointment Schreiner appellate judge Rose-Innes or others equally impartial approved by community and unless nearly four thousand passive resistance prisoners in ordinary and mine gaols released. In event unfavourable reply people must hold readiness march foot starvation rations from Durban to Pretoria seeking rearrest. Discovered our release people large numbers had shown unexpected powers endurance sufferings. We were staggered unlooked for ability indentured Indians acting perfect co-operation discipline determination.'

After a meeting in Maritzburg, I apprised Gokhale through a cable of a hard fact: 'Been Maritzburg which at mass meeting endorsed yesterday's Durban resolutions. Impossible accept commission unless suggestion adding to commission, release prisoners accepted. People earnest enthusiastic. They will not listen. Advice acceptance commission except on above conditions. Agitation which is assuming almost uncontrollable proportions. My firm conviction that mass people so indignant that if attempt were made ask them accept present commission, they would kill leaders. Strong protests were lodged with government from most centres before our discharge and many demanded not addition but substitution Esselen Wylie. It required considerable tact calmness induce people accept Esselen Wylie even if our nominees appointed.'[440]

In another cable from Durban sent on 24 December, I reiterated this: 'My firm conviction any one of us especially I advising people now accept commission without addition would be very justifiably killed. We are gaining ground here; but whether or not we retain or lose hold on masses struggle must continue till the few perish in attempt.[441]

On receiving a slight opening I cabled him again on 25 December: Government's reply our letter received. Though rejecting demand addition commission, it leaves openings negotiation. Have asked for private interview. Gandhi.'

And on 26 December: 'March will be postponed almost certainly. Whilst there is hope of peace am not fixing preliminaries necessary providing probably five thousand marchers whose ranks may swell, twenty thousand....'

Gokhale, from the depths of his concern and his ill-health, asked C. F. Andrews if he would be in a position to go to South Africa to help find both justice and bring about an accord. Andrews agreed at once and sailed for Durban with his friend W. W. Pearson, both valued by Rabindranath Tagore. Viceroy Hardinge, in the meantime, decided to send an emissary of his own, Sir Benjamin Robertson, to depose before the Solomon Commission.

I received on 26 December from Gokhale the following: 'Understand if Robertson starts twenty-ninth will reach about eighth. But arrangements departure suspended pending your definite promise that he will have at least one week there before you renew struggle. Viceroy meanwhile undertaking move Lord Crewe secure adjournment commission till end week. Do you promise? Cable explicitly. You certainly entitled if your present negotiations fail announce reason postponement struggle, also to abstain from participation inquiry if commission not adjourned. Public reception Robertson desirable.'

I cabled Gokhale on 27 December: 'I promise suspend march upto one week after Robertson's arrival provided he leaves twenty-ninth. Meanwhile hope pressure will be exercised from India England regarding my proposal submitted yesterday and asking General Smuts grant request without reference Robertson's arrival. Miss Hobhouse, staunch friend government, has just wired asking me suspend march and she is intervening. Similarly sympathy being gained here. This position should not be disturbed either by viceroy or Lord Crewe under pressure from union government as happened during Passage Immigration Bill by either approving union government action or condemning ours.'

Gokhale sent two cables the following day. Gokhale cabled: 'Viceroy wires: "In view promise given by Gandhi and my intense desire secure peaceful settlement, Robertson will leave first January arriving Durban about eleventh. Have asked Lord Crewe endeavour arrange with union government short postponement meeting commission." Viceroy wants you communicate freely with Robertson on arrival. He goes to give fullest assistance community. Viceroy, however, thinks it desirable you should know that if community resort passive resistance or violence, Robertson will immediately dissociate himself.'

I responded: 'Will announce that at viceroy's desire, because Robertson coming, we have suspended march without committing ourselves to commission at present constituted and without taking part at its sittings. This announcement will not be made until I have despaired of negotiations with Smuts. Andrews will be fully honoured. So will Robertson. Gandhi'

In reply to Gokhale's cable of 31 December, inquiring if Andrews and Pearson had arrived safely on board SS *Umtali* which had encountered stormy weather and actually reached Durban harbour five days later than scheduled, I wired saying: 'The Rev. C. F. Andrews and the Rev. W. Pearson have arrived and were accorded a most cordial reception by the Indian community. They had a very rough passage. We are now trying to secure the addition to the commission of at least one European member in whose impartiality we have confidence. The planters, if necessary, are to be allowed to nominate one on their side. I sincerely hope India will support us in this.'

I met them at the wharf with several Indian associates including Polak, West, and a number of European clergymen including the Rev. Archdeacon Gregson. On landing, Andrews greeted Polak and asked: 'Where is Mr Gandhi?' Polak then turned and pointed to me.*

Gokhale cabled on 2 January: 'Robertson started yesterday. Communicated your intention giving reception arrival. He, however, thinks best plan small deputation meet him, demonstration might cause misunderstanding. He has sent message he will do his best for community. Am suffering accumulation fluid cavity heart result extreme exhaustion system. Must lie bed several days. Your statement published yesterday made up of various cables and elaborated to nearly two thousand words. Bringing public opinion strongly round your side. Has Reuter cabled summary.'

Andrews and Pearson were given a reception by the Indian Hawkers' Association at the Surat Hindu Association Dharamsala in

---

*Andrews bent down swiftly and touched Gandhi's feet.

Victoria Street, Durban, at which I was given a purse of 60 pounds as donation to passive resistance funds.*

On 4 January 1914 from Phoenix I wrote to Manilal who was serving a three-month sentence in gaol: 'I was delighted to receive your letter. In the first place, ever since my discharge, I have had not a minute's rest and I hardly get full sleep any day. In the second place, there were so many to whom I should have written, that I thought I would neglect you all and you would understand the reason why; but your letter compels me to write to you. I think that, on your discharge, you will see both mother and me. Ramdas is looking well and has done well. Devadas has proved a hero. He has developed a sense of responsibility which was unexpected. Purbhoodas did almost equally well, but he is not so quick as Devadas. All the womenfolk are well and are looking forward to meeting you all. I am sorry that you were not able to read much. I think that, if you approach the magistrate for more books, he will grant you the permission and you may remind him that you had all the books you desired granted to you at Johannesburg and elsewhere. You will be pleased to hear that I had become a most industrious student at Bloemfontein and I was sincerely sorry to have my studies interrupted. I gave about eight hours a day to solid reading and writing, principally Tamil. The authorities kindly gave me every facility.'[442]

I was continually with Mr Andrews in Cape Town from rising hour to bedtime talking about the question or religious topics. I would often say to myself how nice it would have been if Kallenbach could

---

*By this time, South Africa's Africans seemed to nurse silent support for the Indian satyagrahis. This came across in 1914 when Pearson interviewed John Dube. Recalling to Pearson a scene near Phoenix station that he had personally witnessed during the Indians' campaign the previous November, Dube said he was 'amazed' by the nonviolence and forbearance with which the Indians faced police brutalities, and by their love for Gandhi 'Raja' (king), as they called him. Dube thought Gandhi had tapped a vein in the Indian character that he was not sure existed in the Africans. In a comparable situation, Dube added, the Africans would hit back recklessly. 'If any brother of mine kills a white man after being excited, it would precipitate a great disaster upon us.' Quoted in Ravjibhai Patel, *The Making of the Mahatma*, Ahmedabad: Navajivan, 1989, pp. 216–17.

have been with us. But, as I told him, I was sure that it was the best thing for him not to have come and joined us in Cape Town.[443] He would have been held up like us, waiting for meetings and, what is worse, Mr Andrews would never have talked with the same freedom if he had to talk to two instead of one as now.

Andrews, I saw, entirely lived the Indian life and loved to live among and with Indians. He had a two-hour interview (private) with the Governor General Lord Gladstone and he preached at the cathedral here last Sunday. Kallenbach was, at this time, with Kastur in Phoenix and so I was free from all anxiety.

When the interview with General Smuts did come about (16 January) I asked for definite assurances on four points: (a) The 3-pound tax, (b) the marriage question, (c) the admission of South Africa-born Indians into the Cape Province, (d) the declaration said to be required under the Orange Free State Law. General Smuts sought certain clarifications from me on all these. He ended the interview by promising to consider my proposals and give me an answer as soon as possible.[444]

Governor General Gladstone was to report to the Secretary of State for the Colonies: 'I am glad to be able to report that the prospects of an early settlement of the principal points at issue between my government and the Indian community in this country have distinctly improved during the past week. Obstacles which it would be imprudent to disregard still exist, and others, either unforeseen or only dimly foreseen at present, may yet arise before mutually acceptable legislation can be passed. But on the whole the situation is more hopeful now than at any previous period of my term of office. Numerous personal interviews have taken place between General Smuts and Mr Gandhi, General Smuts and Sir Benjamin Robertson, and Sir Benjamin Robertson and Mr Gandhi. Mr Andrews also has had conversations both with the minister and with Sir Benjamin Robertson. General Smuts has shown a most patient and conciliatory temper. In spite of a series of conflicts extending over many years, he retains a sympathetic interest in Mr Gandhi as an unusual type of humanity, whose peculiarities, however inconvenient they may be to the minister, are not devoid of attraction for the student. Sir Benjamin has proved himself tactful, judicious, and reasonable. He has established excellent relations not only with General Smuts but also with the prime minister, and is on friendly terms with the other members of the Cabinet whose acquaintance he has made, while on Mr Gandhi his firmness and shrewd common sense would seem to have exercised a salutary restraining influence. It is no easy task for a European to conduct negotiations with Mr Gandhi. The workings of his conscience are inscrutable to the occidental mind and produce complications in wholly unexpected places. His ethical and intellectual attitude, based as it appears to be on a curious compound of mysticism and astuteness, baffles the ordinary processes of thought. Nevertheless, a tolerably practical understanding has been reached.'[445]

The Indians had demanded that a member should be co-opted to the commission to represent Indian interests. But on this point General Smuts would not give in. 'That cannot be done,' said he, 'as it would be derogatory to the government's prestige and I would be unable to carry out the desired reforms. You must understand that Mr Esselen is our man, and would fall in with, not oppose, the government's wishes as regards reform. Colonel Wylie is a man of position in Natal and might even be considered anti-Indian. If therefore even he agrees to a repeal of the 3-pound tax, the government will have an easy task before them. Our troubles are manifold; we have not a moment to spare and therefore wish to set the Indian question at rest. We have decided to grant your demands, but for this we must have a recommendation from the commission. I understand your position too. You have solemnly declared that you will not lead evidence before it so long as there is no representative of the Indians sitting on the commission. I do not mind if you do not tender evidence, but you should not organize any active propaganda to prevent anyone who wishes to give evidence from doing so, and should suspend satyagraha in the interval. I believe that by so doing you will be serving your own interests as well as giving me a respite. As you will not tender evidence, you will not be able to prove your allegations as regards ill-treatment accorded to the Indian strikers. But that is for you to think over.'

Five

AGREEMENT

Andrews has done most wonderful and ceaseless work.

During the last days of the negotiations, news reached me that Kasturba was seriously ill in Durban. At a moment, on 21 January, when the talks had reached a deadlock over a phrase which General Smuts had wanted to insert in the proposed agreement, an urgent telegram summoned me to Durban; but I refused to leave till the deadlock had been removed. Andrews recorded what happened during that critical night in these words: 'That night we talked till 1 a.m. Finally, an alternative phrase occurred to me. The difference seemed to be very slight, but Gandhi found it acceptable. "If General Smuts will accept your phrase," he said, as we went to bed, "then everything is finished." In the morning, saying nothing to Gandhi, I went to Smuts and at eight o'clock found him alone. I told him Gandhi's personal anxiety, and showed him the suggested wording.

'I don't mind a bit, it makes no difference as far as I am concerned.'

'Would you make the change and sign on the spot?'

'Certainly.'

The settlement reached, Andrews and I left for Durban, by the 11 o'clock train, on 22 January. General Smuts knew something of my domestic situation. Before leaving for Phoenix I wrote to his secretary to convey my thanks to General Smuts for the patient and kindly interviews that he had been pleased to grant me during a time of overwhelming pressure. 'My countrymen,' I said in my letter, 'will remember with gratitude his great consideration.' But I also stated: 'I understand that the minister is unable to accept (with regard to the Indian Inquiry Commission) either (1) my suggestion that a member representing Indian interests should be co-opted when questions of policy are enquired into; or (2) my suggestion that a second commission, with Indian representation, should be appointed to deal with these questions only; the present commission in that case becoming purely judicial. I submitted a third proposal also, but this, in view of the government's decision, I need not state here. Had any of my suggestions been viewed favourably by the government, it would have been possible for my countrymen to assist the labours of the present commission. But with regard to leading evidence before this commission (which has a political as well as a judicial character), they have conscientious scruples, and these have taken with them a solemn and religious form. I may state briefly that these scruples were based on the strong feeling that the Indian community should have been either consulted or represented where questions of policy were concerned. The minister, I observe, appreciates these scruples, and regards them as honourable, but is unable to alter his decision. As, however, by granting me the recent interviews he has been pleased to accept the principle of consultation, it enables me to advise my countrymen not to hamper the labours of the commission by any active propaganda, and not to render the position of the government difficult by reviving passive resistance, pending the result of the commission and the introduction of legislation during the forthcoming session. If I am right in my interpretation of the government's attitude on the principle of consultation, it would be further possible for us, without violating the spirit of the vow we have taken, to assist Sir Benjamin Robertson, whom the viceroy with gracious forethought has deputed to give evidence before the commission. A word is here necessary on the question of allegations as to ill-treatment during the progress of the Indian strike in Natal. For the reasons above stated the avenue of proving these through the commission is closed to us. I am personally unwilling to challenge libel proceedings by publishing the authentic evidence in our possession. I would far rather refrain altogether from raking up old sores. I beg to assure the minister that as passive resisters we endeavour to avoid as far as possible any resentment of personal wrongs. But in order that our silence may not be mistaken, may I ask the minister to recognize our motive and reciprocate by not leading evidence of a negative character before the commission on the allegations in question. Suspension of passive resistance moreover carries with it a prayer for the release of the bona fide passive resistance prisoners now undergoing imprisonment either in the ordinary gaols or the mine compounds which have been declared as such.'

Finally, I said, it might not be out of place to recapitulate the points on which relief has been sought. They are as follows: (1) Repeal of the 3-pound tax in such a manner as the Indians relieved will virtually occupy the same status as the indentured Indians discharged under the Natal Law 25 of 1891. (2) The marriage question. (3) The Cape entry question. (This requires only administrative relief, subject to the clear safeguards explained to the minister.) (4) The Orange Free State question. (This requires merely a verbal alteration in the assurance already given.) (5) An assurance that existing laws specially affecting Indians will be administered justly and with due regard to vested rights.

I sent a cable to Gokhale on this immediately: 'Letters exchanged government self promising provisional agreement. Government unable accept any of three commission proposals submitted but declare themselves desirous speedy solution. They accept principle consultation and give fullest opportunities. We cannot break vow and give evidence but will assist Robertson where possible. Appreciating government's position, we suspended passive resistance, having assurance proposed legislation during forthcoming session. Regarding allegations as passive resisters we refrain from reviving old sores by publishing our authentic evidence. Government recognize our motive and themselves give no evidence on allegations of negative character. Releasing all prisoners. Am now submitting my action for ratification community. We took consideration every circumstance including yours and viceroy's feelings. Agreement joint work Andrews self. Andrews present last interview.'[446]

And another on 25 January: 'Provisional agreement reached. We not assisting commission owing solemn declaration but helping Robertson. Suspending passive resistance pending legislation which government promises after commission. Principle of Indian consultation acknowledged. Government Robertson both satisfied. Prisoners being released. Opportunity for settlement now more favourable.'

A mass meeting attended by about 3,000 people was held in Durban on 25 January where I explained the terms of the provisional agreement.[447] I had to announce at the meeting that Mr Andrews had received a letter from England preparing him for the death of his beloved mother, whom he had expected to meet on his arrival in England. I also added that Mr Andrews was suffering from fever due to the strain under which he had worked in Pretoria in connection with the agreement. Notwithstanding these facts, Andrews had insisted on attending the meeting.

I addressed the meeting at length, both in English and Hindustani; my remarks being subsequently rendered into Tamil. I said that those to whom I was addressing my remarks in English would, I hoped, have read what had been published in the papers, but I would give them the purport of the agreement with the government. The government should grant the community's request in terms of the five points (1) the repeal of the £3 tax; (2) the restoration of the status of Indian wives as it existed before the Searle judgement; (3) the restoration of the right of South Africa-born Indians to enter the Cape; (4) the removal of the little difficulty that still exists with reference to the racial bar regarding the Orange Free State; and (5) the question of just administration of existing laws with due regard to vested rights. The last three points could be dealt with administratively; the first two only by amending legislation, and I had ventured to submit to General Smuts the easiest and the quickest way in which the matter could be dealt with. General Smuts had said that he would consider the matter, and after I had considered and conferred with the Cabinet, he said, in the presence of Mr Andrews, that the government were willing to grant these things, but wanted the commission to sift them, and that they could not possibly, though they would gladly have met the community, meet them at that stage with reference to its propositions regarding the commission.

After Polak, Andrews, and Kallenbach had spoken, the following resolution was moved by Parsi Rustomji and unanimously passed: 'This mass meeting of British Indians, held under the auspices of the Natal Indian Association, after having heard the terms of the provisional agreement arrived at between the government and Mr Gandhi, hereby endorses Mr Gandhi's action, and earnestly and respectfully hopes that the prayer of the Indian community, as set forth in Mr Gandhi's letter, will be granted.'

I was soon back in Cape Town to see to the formalization of the settlement. Kastur, who continued to be ill, was with me, as were Manilal and Jamnadas. We stayed with Dr Gool and family.

On 28 February, I wrote to Kallenbach from there: 'There is no doubt that Andrews has done most wonderful and ceaseless work. As soon as Andrews is gone I would like to send Manilal to Johannesburg. I am here for a month or more. Whether you come here or not, I think the best thing is for Manilal to stay and work at Mountain View (Johannesburg) by himself. But you will have to be fairly strict with him. He has not gained by his gaol experiences. And you may leave him only after he is in fairly full swing. But please let me know what you feel about this. I would like him to come out to Johannesburg as soon as Andrews is off, subject to your consent. You may, therefore, wire if you think fit.'[448]

Manilal and Jamnadas, I found, had to leave Cape Town. The atmosphere was enervating for both the boys. I had therefore to send Manilal and Jamnadas away, Manilal to Johannesburg and Jamnadas to Durban. There was nothing too wrong with Manilal, but he needed, I could see, a calmer and quieter atmosphere, which Mountain View would provide.

We got news at this time that Valliammah Moonsamy, a passive resister girl, had died in Johannesburg.

Mr Andrews continued to remain a rare man to me. He acquired a marvellous hold on the elite of Cape Town and calmed the atmosphere in a wonderful manner. His affection for Tagore was phenomenal. He called him his Guru at the university lecture, which was a treat.

Six

CAPE TOWN CAPERS

I have grown very tender to Ba, as she has observed.

By 24 February, Kastur had had a relapse.
Kallenbach wrote to me, enclosing Ramdas's and others' letters.[449] I told Kallenbach in my reply he might well want to treasure Ramdas's letter. It was a gem. The boy seemed to be shaping beautifully. If the composition was his own, it was also good. I informed him that Kastur was better but she had ups and downs and continued to cause anxiety.

She and I went over to see Miss Emily Hobhouse. We saw there Mrs Botha, wife of the prime minister and Lady Gladstone, wife of the governor general. Miss Hobhouse has a divine face. Have never seen a diviner face. Gokhale, by his features, had taken me by storm. Miss Hobhouse did likewise, only more so. I felt like gazing at her in awe for hours.

Meanwhile came the report of the Solomon Commission. It was very fair and reasonable. It was a creditable document and a complete vindication of our position.

I wrote for *Indian Opinion* a tribute for the Tamil martyr:

Miss Valliammah Moonsamy, a young lady not yet in her twenties, was one of those devoted Indian women who sought imprisonment in protest against a marriage law that dishonoured her parents' marriage and cast a stigma upon her own birth. Her sudden and unexpected demise, two days after her return home, holds in it all the elements of tragedy. We mourn the loss of a noble daughter of India who did her simple duty without question, and who has set an example of womanly fortitude, pride, and virtue that will, we are sure, not be lost upon the Indian community. We tender to her family our most respectful sympathy. It appears that she was taken to bed immediately after her conviction, and also after her release was suffering greatly. The late Miss Valliammah was born in Johannesburg in 1898 and attended the Government School. She joined the passive resistance struggle on the 29th October last and proceeded to Newcastle with a party of ladies. She afterwards rendered assistance at Charlestown, Dundee, Ladysmith, Dannhauser, Maritzburg, Tongaat, and Durban. She eventually re-crossed the Transvaal border and was convicted, with her mother and others, at Volksrust on the 22nd of December 1913, to three months' imprisonment with hard labour and was discharged on the 11th instant in terms of the Provisional Agreement. Her father is one of the pioneer Indian settlers of the Transvaal. He was once in gaol as a passive resister and during the last campaign was very ill and only came out of the hospital where he underwent an operation recently. We share the sorrows of the parents and express our deepest sympathy at their irreparable loss.[450]

Meanwhile Kastur hovered between life and death. Her appetite seemed to be coming to her. But she again developed the ominous swellings which frightened Dr Gool who asked to examine her urine. His examination led to no results. And the swelling persisted. Also, I was becoming a society man and Miss Molteno was the instrument. She insisted on introducing Kastur and me to all the families she knew. Yesterday, we went to the great estate of the Moltenos and met several people. That was the nature of work.

I again had to advise Kallenbach about Manilal: 'I hope you will try to be with him as much as you can. If he remains morose, I suggest your taking him with you to your office and using him for office work in so far as you may and can. I should like you to take your meal with him for the time being.' And to Jamnadas, who had told me as he was leaving that I was acting like a lawyer, I wrote on 26 February: 'You have found my excess of love scorching on this occasion. That happens. Calm yourself down, though. I have not acted without thinking. You are wrong in charging me with arguing like a lawyer. Once before also you said this. I find from experience that I possess in an especial degree the gift of analysis and of discriminating right from wrong and, in the result, my nice arguments sound like special pleading to others. All the same, you may unhesitatingly say whatever you wish to in self-defence or with a view to putting me right. That is your duty.'

To Manilal who told me I was being cruel, as well: 'You have sinned, without knowing it, in charging me with cruelty. How could I have grown cruel in fifteen days? I have given no such impression to others. Nothing of the sort happened in Phoenix. I have grown very tender to Ba, as she has observed. If I turned cruel to you, what little goodness I claim would be no more than a show and I would think that my life had been wasted. But I shall no doubt appear cruel to you at present for, like a physician, I must make you swallow bitter draughts. I have grown impatient to help you to become perfect. Impatience is my weakness. To the extent that I am impatient, I am but a fond lover. I have fondness enough in me yet to make me attached to you for being my son. When that has gone, even the cruelty that you think you see in me you will see no more. Meanwhile, please bear with me. And now for the contradictions in your letter. For three days you did not [as you say] go out to see Cape Town because of my harsh words. And yet, when leaving, you expressed a desire to do so, though I was in a rage. The harsh words had been there, even on Sunday. Believing that I was cruel, how could you hope to learn anything by living with me? You showed yourself very keen on visiting Table Mountain. When I told you then that you would see much more, what did you find in that to take offence? Well, what has happened has happened. It is your duty not to take notice of my faults. A son should have devotion enough to his father not to notice his shortcomings but to think only of his virtues. I should like to see this trustfulness in you. I don't want to make an ascetic of you. I want to see your character pure, to see in you truthfulness, chastity, straightforwardness, tenderness, self-confidence, humility, and goodness. I want to see you indifferent to the common pleasures of the world. I doubt, however, if you have these at present. I am not asking you to start doing immediately everything I do. But I want you to understand my deepest feelings and so attain true success in your life'

Dealing with misunderstanding among loved ones was my portion at this time. Kallenbach was worrying over what he regarded as lapses from the food regime. And over C. F. Andrews. I wrote to him on 27 February: 'Why very Low, Lower House? I see nothing wrong in your letter regarding food. I have seen nobody who has been able to deny himself so much of the world's good things of life as you have. And what does it matter if you have been taking macaroni about which you have so satisfied yourself? We are food reformers and so we cannot help it. When our reform becomes part of our nature, we shall cease to discuss it. If I discuss it less than you do (which I doubt) it must be because mine has become more natural to me than yours to you. Though I love and almost adore Andrews so, I would not exchange you for him. You still remain the dearest and the nearest to me and so far as my own selfish nature is considered I know that in my lonely journey through the world, you will be the last (if even that) to say goodbye to me. What right had I to expect so much from you!'

I had to tell him about Manilal and Jamnadas. 'Now about Manilal. I have given you some idea. He and Jamnadas appeared to me unbalanced. They did the very things that they used to criticize in others. For instance, they give themselves every indulgence that they denied themselves at Phoenix. If Hanif took something outside Phoenix, both of them used to bring it to my notice. In spite of Manilal's sad experience, both took the greatest freedom with the girls in the Gool household. They were surrounded with much attention and love from all the members of the family. Dr Gool who is such a noble soul but yet youthful, made a deep impression on them by his suave nature. The result was that the boys' faculty for thinking, study or work was paralysed. Manilal and Jamnadas rose after 6 a.m. They never studied. Their talk seemed to me to be unnatural. They found themselves placed in gaudy surroundings which unhinged them for the moment. I felt that to give them a month of this life would be to hurt two very sensitive young promising plants. I spoke very sharply and bitterly to them. They have resented my tone and my speech as also my action. The discovery I made on arrival was so shocking that I certainly became impatient. But I am sorry neither for my action nor for my speech. I had a right to expect them not to misunderstand me. After all, I have sent them away to my personal discomfort and for their advantage. My presence in their midst could not have counterbalanced the unperceived mischief that was working its way into their system. Jamnadas must therefore naturally go to Phoenix and Manilal not to Phoenix whilst Jeki is there and that when I am away. The only alternative for him was to be at Mountain View where he can do the right thing just to the extent that he is able. I wished to place both in circumstances most favourable to their spiritual growth. I have advised Manilal that he ought to religiously avoid baker's bread, tea, and coffee and that he should rarely go to town, never eat the town food and never sleep in town. But I have told him he is a free agent. He need only adopt that part of my advice which appeals to him and no more. I do not want him to do anything for my sake. I want him to become not a creeper but a vigorous tree.'

Apprising him with the political issue, I said: 'I had another glorious interview with Miss Hobhouse yesterday. We discussed you fairly fully and I have told her that it is likely you might be here whilst I am also here. She is General Smuts's guest. Miss Molteno too has been attentive and helpful. Will you select a tablet for the two deceased?* Valliamma's death I felt most keenly. I am unable to stare a Tamil in the face when I recall these deaths. It is weakness I know. But it is there. Consult Naidoo about the stone, please, and both can be put on when I am passing through Johannesburg. I should be delighted.'

I also shared with Kallenbach another deep thought triggered by the deaths of Nagappen and Valliammah: '...the desire in me to die is overpowering.' And I confided: 'My first disappointment was

---

*Nagappen and Valliamma.

that not a single Gujarati had died. I was left alive when those that did not want to die had gone.' And turning to Kastur's health, told him: 'There is no guarantee even now that she will live. But she seems to be rallying and would certainly have succumbed under the orthodox treatment.'

I wrote next to Gokhale about the current political scene and also my future course: 'For the time being I am at Cape Town watching the course of events. I do not want to inflict on you any news about the struggle. I shall be as brief as I possibly can. Mr Andrews and Mr Pearson are truly good men, we all like them very much. Sir Benjamin has disappointed us. He has hardly done any good and he may do a great deal of harm. He is weak and by no means sincere. Even now he has hardly grasped the details. And he undoubtedly, consciously or unconsciously, fosters divisions among us. Mr Andrews will tell you all about him. But I thought that I should give you my impressions of Sir Benjamin. If there is a settlement in March, I propose to leave for India in April. I shall have with me probably about twenty men, women, and children who will live with me. These will include the school children who are likely to come. I do not know whether you still want me to live at the Servants of India quarters in Poona. I shall be prepared to do so immediately after I have paid a visit to the members of my family. It is likely that the number living with me may be augmented by some members of my family who may wish to share my life and work. Please do not consider yourself bound to keep me at the society's quarters. I am entirely in your hands. I want to learn at your feet and gain the necessary experience. No matter whether I am staying somewhere under your guidance or not, I shall scrupulously observe the compact of silence for one year after my arrival in India. The vow of silence as I have understood it does not include the South African question and may be broken at your wish for furthering any project about which both of us hold the same view. My present ambition you know. It is to be by your side as your nurse and attendant. I want to have the real discipline of obeying someone whom I love and look up to. I know I made a bad secretary in South Africa. I hope to do better in the motherland if I am accepted. May you benefit in health by the change and the calmer atmosphere on the continent. This letter will be in your hands about the middle of March. If you deem it necessary to say anything to me about my movements, you will of course cable. I assume too that you will not want me to go to Poona before you return. If you did, I should of course go. If I am enabled to leave for India in April, I propose to use the funds you have sent for our passages which shall be all deck. I have no means of my own and Phoenix can hardly supply funds now. It is drained totally dry. I remain, Yours sincerely, M. K. Gandhi.'[451]

Manilal wrote in return to my letter, saying he was sorry.[452] I responded: 'I know that you are sorry. You haven't the courage to answer when someone asks you why you went away. It shouldn't be difficult for you to say that you were sent away to live by yourself because father did not like your ways. You should realize that in releasing you from attendance on Ba and asking you to go without thinking of my personal convenience, I must have acted with the purest of love. More than your services, I want good behaviour from you. If you become so good that you will never make a slip, I should ask for no more. I would tell Ba too that it was as well you had left.'

And then I gave him a description of the Gool home scene: 'For the last four days I have been seeing that there is meat on the table thrice a day. I manage to finish my meals earlier since I have changed the hours. It hurt me very much yesterday to have to see all that meat in front of me and I simply did not know what to do. I have now decided that, as far as possible, my meal hours shall not be the same as theirs. They are not at fault in this matter. They tell me quite frankly that I can fix my own hours. Formerly, I was not sensitive about this. It is only now that I am growing so. This sensitiveness on my part is a good sign. At the same time, they are not to be blamed for having all these things prepared. But I would certainly not wish you to be placed in such surroundings. At present, all sorts of things are being prepared. They have bun and also jam; and even groundnut is cooked. But for Ba being with me, I would touch none of the preparations. Of course, this is not the reason for my sending you away. But having regard to this as well, I think it is good you have left. So long as Mr Andrews was here, he acted as a shield for you, but they would not have desisted from meat-preparations on your account. Your going away can do you nothing but good. If you are keen on serving Ba or me, you will certainly have the opportunity to do so. That will be only when you are earnest in your desire, or when, wanting your services out of our pure selfishness, I spoil you. This can never be, so that your serving [us] depends entirely on the effort you make. Consider the full meaning of this letter and ponder over it. Do not be angry with father.'

Kastur wanted medicine to be administered.[453] She had it in the mildest form from Dr Gool and was, subsequently, laid up with fever, aches all over, and pain in the stomach. The crisis may have been coming and the medicine may have nothing to do with this serious relapse. Anyhow the relapse was there and there was no escaping it. The thought did come to me that for her, death would be the finest deliverance. But we are in God's hands. Let His will and not ours be done. I was by her side day and night. I commenced reading the Ramayana to her. She could not listen longer than hour. Yet it was something. She was certainly most resigned and was at peace. She needed support even when she wanted to sit up in the bed. She lived for the most part on neem juice, taking grapes or orange juice occasionally.

Harilal sent a letter at this time, apologizing for not writing regularly. I replied saying 'You apologize in every letter of yours and put up a defence as well. It all seems to me sheer hypocrisy now. For years, you have been slack in writing letters, and then coming forward with apologies. Will this go on till death, I forgiving every time? And what is the point of my forgiving? Forgiving has a meaning only to the extent that the person who has apologized does not err again. My forgiving you all the time means that I should go on doing my duty as father though you may not do yours as son.'[454]

He also said he wanted to see us. 'I don't believe,' I said, 'that you are impatient to see us both; equally, this idea that you were to come here sounds insincere to me. Does one who really means to come trumpet it aloud? Now, of course, your coming is pointless, as you say.' He had also alluded to his monetary needs, his desire to study further despite a breakdown in health, start a new business venture, and perhaps move to Bombay. 'I wrote to Revashankerbhai that he should have a talk with you and give you more money as may seem necessary. You were asked never to go in for studies at the cost of your health. You have failed to take care of it. No wonder that Ramdas and Manilal have outdone you. And Ramdas has put in a fine effort, indeed, and grown in size as well. Manilal, too, has plenty of strength and would have been stronger yet if he had not taken to the evil ways of pleasure. Even their studies I take to be sounder than yours. Your mind is now running after Bombay. You say you have Revashankerbhai's consent for that. What weight can that consent carry with me? I would submit in all humility to Revashankerbhai's judgement of a diamond. How could I listen to him in the matter of studies? You are, so it seems to me, in a state of stupefaction. What, then, am I to say.... I would only advise you to do nothing. Wait till my return. Meanwhile, read as you like. Do not, however, start a new venture. I shall supply your needs. Weighing my advice against that of others, do what you think best.'

I told him honestly: 'I am a father who is prejudiced against you. I do not approve of your ways at all. This statement sounds very harsh, but I see extreme insincerity in your letters. Nevertheless, I am so proud a father that I attribute perfection to my children. I become angry when writing to you and also feel like crying. This is my ignorant state, my lack of enlightenment. I ought not to be so much attached to you. I will free myself from this. Be patient with me till I succeed. Now I have given you too long a lesson. I will write no more. I shall be satisfied if you treat me as a friend and show me the regard due to a friend.'

He wanted to know the state of his mother's health. 'Just now I am in Cape Town,' I said to him, 'Ba is with me. She lies hanging between life and death. Till yesterday, she was very bad indeed. There is again a little improvement. She is a mere skeleton. She gives me no trouble, but, not having succeeded yet in disciplining the palate, she suffers and pines. I am by her side the whole day. Between yesterday and today, she must have consumed the juice of two tomatoes and a teaspoonful of oil.'

Devadas had written too. And I replied to the fourteen-year-old: 'Ba's condition has grown very bad of late. She and I both believe that medical treatment has had altogether an adverse effect on her. She herself had asked for such treatment. After she had had two or three doses, her condition became serious. She can eat no food at present. She took a few grapes yesterday, but it seems they did not agree with her.'[455]

I thought I must prepare him for any eventuality and so said: 'Even if the end is death, we have made up our minds to have no fear of it. You need not worry, therefore. The body is sure to fall, and that, on the appointed day. Remedies occur to us accordingly. The atman, besides, is immortal and, though we seem to be concerned only with the body, our real concern should be for the atman. For a truth, we don't preserve the body for any length of time after the soul has left it. So thinking, I take the necessary measures for Ba's health and then stop worrying, and I would ask you all to do the same. Realizing, then, the fate of the body, we should cultivate goodness and disinterestedness. Goodness does not mean outward indifference to objects of desire or a wandering life, but purity of character. Disinterestedness does not mean gloominess but aversion to the pleasures of the senses and absence of interest in the things of this world. If you learn this during Ba's illness, that will be evidence, indeed, of your true devotion to her.'

My brother Lakshmidas passed away, during this troubled time. This loss of one who had been a pillar of strength to me despite our recent differences and even discord, was a blow.

Gokhale, who despite his own ill-health had sent cables enquiring about Kastur and, of course, about the political situation, had to be kept informed. He was on a heath-cure tour of Europe. He had urged that I go to London and meet him there. 'I doubt,' I said to him, 'whether Mrs Gandhi will survive the settlement. I am writing this by her bedside. I have to be her doctor, nurse, and everything. Then my brother's death leaves the sole charge of five widows and their children in my hands. Dr Mehta is just now paying the expenses of the others. To this he will, I do not doubt, add the maintenance of my brother's widow. But she and the others are most naturally anxious to have me with them at the earliest possible moment. I would, therefore, grudge having to go to London unless you consider it absolutely necessary. If you do, I shall certainly come if Mrs Gandhi dies or is better—so well, that is to say, as to permit of my being away from her, I suppose, at least for two months. I do hope that you will materially benefit by the cure at Vichy. Wherever I may be placed in India I shall carry out my compact with you, viz., that I should observe absolute silence except on the S[outh] A[frica] question for one year at least after my landing in India and about everything else I have promised. I am, Yours sincerely, M. K. Gandhi'.[456]

Seven

PHOENIX AND A FAST

...you cannot attach yourself to a particular woman and yet live for humanity.

When Kastur was a little better, we returned to Phoenix.

Envy, resentment are inherent in human nature and misunderstanding is part of it. Owing to my having been absorbed in Kastur's illness, I had asked Sonja Schlesin to keep friends apprised of her condition and she had sent a collective letter. Kallenbach misunderstood that. I had to reassure and reproach him. 'Your letter of the 9th is petty, touchy, and spiteful. It has made me sad and shows that all your so-called reforms there are simply superficial. What you call a circular letter is no circular letter. It was addressed to you and Polak. You, Polak, and Manilal are sufficiently interested in her health to want to know about it daily; hence the letter from Miss Schlesin and the instructions that she herself should write as often as possible. There would have been no such letter had Mrs Gandhi not been sick. Now tell me wherein I was wrong in sending you what you call a circular letter. Do you see my point and your pettiness?'[457]

Kallenbach had also admitted to feeling jealous of our old associate, Sonja Schlesin, and our new friend, Andrews. 'You are entirely right', I said, 'when you say you are jealous (and wrongly so) of Miss Schlesin and Andrews. Because she wrote the letter, it became an offence to you. And as if your letter, warning me not to send you a circular letter was not enough, you must perforce remark underneath Miss Schlesin's letter, "Please do not send me such circular letters henceforth". You should be ashamed of having done this.'

And then I, on my part, had to take Kallenbach into confidence about Kastur: 'Mrs Gandhi is much better but an event happened yesterday which once more proved what I have told you, namely, that she has both the devil and the divine in her in a most concentrated form. She made yesterday a most venomous remark: "Who has opened Devadas's drawer?" suggesting that Jeki had tampered with it. She spits fire on Jeki. I gently remarked that I had opened it. "Why?" was the growling query. I said, "In order to see whether I could find a sheet for you." "That does not contain sheets," was the retort, so much as to convey to me that I had not opened the drawer but I was telling a fib to shield Jeki. This was too much. And I again gently but rebukingly remarked that she was sinful in her thought and that her disease was largely due to her sins. Immediately she began to howl. I had made her leave all the good food in order to kill her, I was tired of her, I wished her to die, I was a hooded snake. The manner of the delivery of these remarks was most vicious. I told her even though she was ill, I could not pity her in her sins. The more I spoke the more vicious she became. I kept completely self-possessed. I apologized to her and told her that henceforth even to that extent I would not remonstrate with her. She has a character and she has none. She is the most venomous woman I have ever met. She never forgets, never forgives. She is quite normal today. But yesterday's was one of the richest lessons of my life. All the charges she brought against me she undoubtedly means. She has contrary emotions. I have nursed her as a son would nurse his mother. But my love has not been sufficiently intense and selfless to make her change her nature. Truly she has so far been my best teacher. She teaches me emptiness of the world, she teaches me patience, forgiveness, greater need for self-sacrifice, for love and charity. The incident leaves me, I hope, a better, wiser, more loving man if it also leaves me sadder. Yes, a man who wishes to work with detachment must not marry. I cannot complain of her being a particularly bad wife or bad woman. On the contrary no other woman would probably have stood the changes in her husband's life as she has. On the whole, she has not thwarted me and has been most exemplary. But how can a leopard change his spots? And yesterday's incident would probably not have happened either in an ordinary household. My point is that you cannot attach yourself to a particular woman and yet live for humanity. The two do not harmonize. That is the real cause of the devil waking in her now and again. Otherwise he might have remained in her asleep and unnoticed.'

In two other letters written from Phoenix after Kastur and I had returned there, I continued: 'I have gone through mental shocks and agonies I have never gone through before. I do not want to write anything. I do not want to talk to anybody. I want to live in solitude and yet I am talking, writing, and living in company. In the daytime I can do little writing. I am unable to get up early in the morning. Can you not enter into my feelings and let your love overlook the omissions and the faults? Love is mute, it does not complain. Love is blind, it sees no fault. Love is deaf, it hears no tales. Love ever gives never demands. Love is constant, never varying whether in adversity or prosperity. Love is never hurt. Love never tires. How has yours fared of late!'[458]

I told him in the same letter about Jeki and the two Manilals, the first my son and the second, Manilal Doctor, now in Fiji, my valued friend Dr Pranjivan Mehta's son-in-law. Manilal Doctor had written complaining bitterly. 'Manilal knows nothing of Manilal of Fiji. He is an infatuated lad. Now that I know Jeki, I know that she is not a patch upon Manilal of Fiji. The latter is an honest man.'

And I went on a self-disciplining fast of fourteen days. 'I have not the energy,' I wrote to Kallenbach, 'to write to you myself, but it is better that I dictate something rather than I should let you remain without any letter at all. This fast has been a very rich but very bitter and painful experience. I have suffered tortures and I am still suffering. It has left me utterly exhausted...' And after the ordeal was over, 'This fast has brought me as near death's door as possible. I can still hardly crawl, can eat very little, restless nights, mouth bad. But it would be all right. The fast was a necessity. I was so grossly deceived. I owed it to Manilal of Fiji, to Dr Mehta, and to myself. It was one of the severest lessons of my life. The discipline was very great. Everyone around me was most charming. Mrs Gandhi was divine. Immediately she realized that there was no turning me back, she set about making my path smooth. She forgot her own sorrows and became my ministering angel. And she still remains the same. The result is that she is better in health. I appealed to all not to go in for fasting but to rejoice that one of themselves was trying to purify himself. All caught the fire and I was helped all along. I felt it my duty not to let you or Polak know because that would have thrown additional care on me and no good purpose could be served by informing you. The step had to be taken by me prayerfully and I took it. I would not miss the experience.'[459]

Eight

THE BEGINNING OF THE END

The struggle of eight years' duration thus, at last, finally closed.

While waiting for the next session of the union Parliament, the Solomon Commission set to work. Only a very few Indian witnesses appeared before it, furnishing striking evidence of the great hold which the satyagrahis had over the community. Sir Benjamin Robertson tried to induce many to tender evidence but failed except in the case of a few who were strongly opposed to the satyagraha. The boycott of the commission did not produce any bad effect. The commission's work was shortened and its report was published at once. The commission:

1. Strongly criticized the Indians for withholding their assistance.
2. Dismissed the charges against the soldiers for their role in the Great March.
3. But recommended compliance without delay with all the demands of the Indian community, such as, for instance, the repeal of the 3-pound tax, and the validation of Indian marriages.

Thus the report of the commission was favourable to the Indians.

With this, Andrews left for England, and Sir Benjamin for India.

We received assurance that the requisite legislation would be undertaken with a view to implement the recommendations.

Within a short time the government published in the official Gazette of the Union, the Indians' Relief Bill. I went at once to Cape Town where the Parliament sits. There was a long and pleasant debate in the union Parliament over the bill. Administrative matters which did not come under the bill were settled by correspondence between General Smuts and me.[460]

The struggle of eight years' duration thus, at last, finally closed.[461] The Indians' Relief Bill and the correspondence between the government and me embodied a complete and mutually satisfactory and honourable settlement of the problems that were affected by the passive resistance movement. For this happy ending we had to thank the Imperial, Indian and union governments, the motherland, guided and moved by Mr Gokhale, and Mr Andrews' mission.

The sufferings of thousands of passive resisters, the martyrdoms of Valliammah, Narayansamy, Nagappen, and Harbutsinh brought these forces into being. Passive resistance, as a lawful weapon, has thus once more been vindicated. The lengthy reference made by Lord Gladstone to the settlement showed its importance. It now remained for the union government to follow up this happy solution of a difficult problem by a sympathetic and just administration of the laws that affect the Indian community and for the latter to show by its action that it was ever worthy of just treatment.

Though there was cause for thankfulness in that the most pressing grievances have been removed, we still laboured under legal disabilities which intense colour prejudice had brought into being. Administration of trade licence laws, largely on racial lines, the deprivation of the right to own land in the Transvaal, the precarious position under the Transvaal Gold Law, inter-provincial restrictions—these and many other such limitations of our liberty showed how true were Lord Gladstone's words when he said that the Indians' Relief Bill did but the barest justice. The struggle, therefore, could give much more than the bill and the administrative measures; it could alter the repressive policy of the government to a progressive one, such that we may look forward to a steady improvement in the future.

Nine

FAREWELL

The creeper of love I have planted and watered with tears.

It was decided that Maganlal would take all the Phoenix children to Bombay from Durban, and Kastur and I, with Kallenbach accompanying us, would sail from Cape Town to London to meet Gokhale and those who had helped us and, after a brief stay there, take a steamer home, to India.

The *Transvaal Leader* sent a correspondent to interview me in Johannesburg on 14 July. I said, replying to questions: 'I am going to India for good. I am going with the intention of never returning, and if ever I have to return to South Africa or leave India, it will be owing to circumstances beyond my control, and at present beyond my conception. The settlement I consider to be entirely honourable to both parties. I believe both General Botha and General Smuts have acted most justly. There has been no mental reservation whatever. The one desire on the part of General Smuts was that there should be no misunderstanding left, and he endeavoured to appreciate the Indian standpoint at every stage of the interviews that he gladly gave me, even when he was pressed with work. And I do feel that nothing could have been finer than the co-operation that the Opposition gave whole-heartedly. And it will be a thousand pities if either my own countrymen, by excessive agitation, or Europeans, spoil that tone and destroy the good effect produced by the settlement.'[462]

> Q: Is the struggle really at an end—will Indians here not fight, constitutionally, no doubt, for political equality?
>
> A: We have never asked for political equality. We do not hope to get that.

Q: You want the vote?

A: No; my view on that would be to leave the question of the political vote severely alone, and my firm conviction is that passive resistance is infinitely superior to the vote. I have never asked for the vote. What I always have insisted on was the removal of racial distinctions, not for equality.

I then recalled some of the more remarkable incidents from the march of the Indian strikers into the Transvaal in November 1913, little acts of kindness that were done by obscure individuals like that of the stationmaster who brought me a glass of milk and a couple of boiled eggs, and many other delicacies to tempt a starving man. It seemed rank ingratitude to refuse them, but I kept to my vow, and I explained to the stationmaster that I seldom ate eggs, and could not taste the milk and the other nice things he had brought, because I had to accept the same treatment as the rank and file. He seemed hurt, and I was sorry, but I hope the kind soul understood. At another place, the proprietor of a hotel said to me: 'You are shivering. Come to my hotel, and I will put you up.' I thanked him, but declined, and, pointing to my companions, I said: 'They too feel the cold, and are shivering.' His kind offer I was obliged to decline. At another place we reached, a woman who ran a small store placed everything she had at our disposal. I remonstrated, but she would have her way. She said: 'Though you are all Indians, you are suffering and I hope I have enough of the old British sense of sympathy left in me to help you.' At Charlestown and Newcastle the whole community helped us, and we helped them. There was no pilfering, no drunkenness. We rose before the sun in the morning and did the best of our day's march before food passed our lips. Then we halted for a small ration of bread and sugar. It was a wonderful thing for 2,000 men to have marched so far without violating the law, without stealing or rioting.

The Gujarati community of Johannesburg organized a farewell event on 16 July 1914. I spoke frankly: 'My Gujarati brethren have done a great deal for me and Mrs Gandhi but they did not, I must say, render as much service in the cause of the struggle as the Tamil community did. I wish the Gujaratis to learn a lesson from the Tamils. Though I do not know their language, they gave me the greatest help in the fight. On the other hand, though I can explain my aims best to Gujaratis because I know Gujarati, they have failed in their duty. They cared more for money. It makes me very unhappy to hear that some members of the community have fallen a prey to drink. They must be pitied. Those who know better have a duty to help such persons break free from the vicious habit. Some are engaged in smuggling gold. They believe that thereby they are helping India economically. Ill-gotten money, however, is never secure. I have not yet attained a state in which I would not seek monetary help. Even so, I would on no account accept help offered from such ill-gotten money. You will perhaps feel that, every time I speak to you, I use fairly harsh language. My bitter words will, however, prove wholesome to you in the end. I am going far away from you, to the motherland, but I can never forget your affection.'

In Cape Town itself, on the day of our departure, 18 July 1914, I drafted a farewell letter. I released this to Reuter's agent at Cape Town. Addressed to Indians and Europeans in South Africa, it was also published in the *Rand Daily Mail*, 20 July 1914, and *The Transvaal Leader*, 24 July 1914.

I said in it: 'I would like, on the eve of my departure for India, to say a few words to my countrymen in South Africa, and also to the European community. The kindness with which both European and Indian friends have overwhelmed me sends me to India a debtor to them. It is a debt I shall endeavour to repay by rendering in India what services I am capable of rendering there; and if, in speaking about the South African Indian question, I am obliged to refer to the injustices which my countrymen have received and may hereafter receive, I promise that I shall never wilfully exaggerate, and shall state the truth and nothing but the truth. A word about the settlement, and what it means. In my humble opinion, it is the Magna Carta of our liberty in this land. I give it the historic name, not because it gives us rights which we have never enjoyed and which are in themselves new or striking, but because it has come to us after eight years' strenuous suffering that has involved the loss of material possessions and of precious lives. I call it our Magna Carta because it marks a change in the policy of the government towards us and establishes our right not only to be consulted in matters affecting us, but to have our reasonable wishes respected. It moreover confirms the theory of the British Constitution that there should be no legal racial inequality between different subjects of the Crown, no matter how much practice may vary according to local circumstance. Above all, the settlement may well be called our Magna Carta, because it has vindicated passive resistance as a lawful, clean weapon, and has given in passive resistance a new strength to the community and I consider it an infinitely superior force to that of the vote, which history shows has often been turned against the voters themselves. The settlement finally disposes of all the points that were the subject matter of passive resistance, and in doing so it breathes the spirit of justice and fair play. If the same spirit guides administration of the existing laws, my countrymen will have comparative peace, and South Africa will hear little of the Indian problem in an acute form. Some of my countrymen have protested against it.'

On 18 July 1914, Kastur, Kallenbach, Mr and Mrs Polak, Miss Schlesin, and I arrived at Monument Station, Cape Town, by the Imperial Mail. The party was received by a large number of European and Indian friends and was taken in procession to the docks. Here I was presented with gifts, an address by the Madras Indian Association, and another telegraphed by Port Elizabeth Indians. At a farewell event in Cape Town I thanked my hosts most heartily and sincerely for the honour they had done my wife and myself on the departure from the land of our adoption. I said I wished I deserved even one-tenth of what they, in their generosity, had been good enough to say about the little service that I might have rendered to my countrymen in South Africa. But if I had done anything for my countrymen in South Africa, that in itself was sufficient reward for me. You have presented me with costly gifts. If you have at all followed my life, you would know how inconsistent these gifts are with the life I have endeavoured to lead, in however small a manner, during the past few years, the life which I have sketched out for myself in India. However I take these rich gifts as an indication of your love, of your sympathy, and your support. May God grant that I should so behave in India as to retain this love of yours. May God grant that this love, although distance may separate us, will extend as the ages go by.'

The sad news had come of the passing away of Lady Hardinge, India's vicereine. Speakers had referred to that and I said that they had done well in referring to the loss sustained by that noble viceroy and faithful friend of ours. It was very hard for me, I said, to part from them, but though I was apart from them in body, I was sure that in spirit we would be knitted together.

'It was twenty-one years ago,' I said, that I landed on the shores of Natal, as a stranger in their midst. I did not know any of my countrymen in South Africa; they did not know me. I knew not a single European. I had only a vague knowledge of the geography of the country. And now, I was leaving a country with great resources, with beautiful scenery, and with a beneficent climate, and certainly, in spite of the hard knocks I had received, a land that had a great future.'

Turning and placing my hand on the shoulder of Mr Kallenbach, I then said: 'Why, I carry away with me not my blood brother, but my European brother. Is not that sufficient earnest of what South Africa has given to me, and is it possible for me to forget South Africa for a single moment? (Cheers.) Our difficulties—your difficulties—are by no means over, but I do hope and trust you will treat this generous settlement that has been given to us in the spirit in which it has been given, backed as it is by those long-drawn-out sufferings extending over a period of eight years, backed as it is by those historic debates in both Houses of Parliament, and backed as it is by the Imperial and Indian governments—a settlement so well meant, so well conceived should be fruitful of a great future. But the future is entirely in your own hands.

'Rightly or wrongly, for good or for evil, Englishmen and Indians have been knit together, and it behoves both races so to mould themselves as to leave a splendid legacy to the generations yet to be born, and to show that though empires have gone and fallen, this Empire perhaps may be an exception and that this is an Empire not founded on material but on spiritual foundations. That has been my source of solace all through. I have always believed there is something subtle, something fine in the ideals of the British Constitution. Tear away those ideals and you tear away my loyalty to that Constitution; keep those ideals and I am ever a bondman. (Cheers.) Both races should see that those ideals of the British Constitution always remained a sacred treasure. I say goodbye, farewell. I shall never forget you. So much love, so much sympathy has overwhelmed me in spite of my trials and tribulations in South Africa, and that love and that sympathy which I have received, not only from my fellow countrymen, but from my European friends, will never be forgotten, but will always remain a sacred memory. (Cheers.)[463]

Just before SS *Kinfauns Castle*, by which we were sailing, weighed anchor, a *Cape Argus* representative approached me for 'any final remarks you would like to make'.

> Let me say that I shall carry away with me the happiest recollections, and that I hope it will be my pleasure while away to find that my countrymen are being treated with justice in South Africa. May I convey, on behalf of Mrs Gandhi, Mr Kallenbach, and self, our deepest thanks to hundreds of senders of telegrams from all parts of South Africa which awaited us upon our arrival on board. These telegrams, containing messages of love and sympathy, will be an additional reminder to us of what South Africa has meant to us. We trust that the goodwill shown to us personally by so many European friends will be transferred to those to whose cause our lives in South Africa were dedicated.

From board the ship I wrote to Chhaganlal who had stayed back at Phoenix to attend to *Indian Opinion*:

> All three of us* are keeping excellent health. Ba behaves wonderfully. She gives no trouble about food. She has reduced the intake of wheat

---

*Kasturba, Kallenbach, and Gandhi.

to a minimum. She lives for the most part on raw banana, boiled groundnut, and milk. After the wheat bati* brought from there has run out, she is inclined to give up even wheat for the present. For one hour I teach Gujarati to Kallenbach and for one hour, at seven in the evening, I explain the Gita to Ba and read the Ramayana to her. She attends to both with great interest. I do not feel any of the inconveniences usual in the third class, but see many advantages. We do not come into contact with other passengers and that saves us plenty of time. We have framed time-tables and the fixed routine is never upset. The company has stocked all fruit so that we get bananas, oranges, etc., in plenty. It also supplies almonds, etc. If any cooking has to be done, it is attended to by Mr Kallenbach.

The party† who were to leave for India must have done so and, therefore, I address nothing to them. The separation this time was a very painful experience.

I received much love in Phoenix.

The creeper of love I have planted and watered with tears. I can utter this from my own experience and rich has been the harvest[464] I have reaped.

---

*A kind of wheat cake traditionally baked in the fire of cow-dung cakes.
†A batch of some twenty-five Phoenix students including Manilal, Ramdas, Devadas and Prabhudas, a few teachers, and Maganlal Gandhi left for India in the first week of August 1914, to join Tagore's Visva-Bharati at Santiniketan.

ACKNOWLEDGEMENTS

Vidvan T. M. Krishna, out of the blue, asked me one day in 2015: 'Gopal, why don't you do a new autobiography of Gandhi?' I was sure I had misheard him. 'You mean a new biography, right?' 'No, no,' he said. 'I mean a new autobiography, putting together what Gandhi has said, in his own words, about his life, his family, outside the public sphere, outside *The Story of My Experiments With Truth* which is so...so...brief....'

The idea was novel and after mulling it over I sounded out David Davidar, the 'ultimate' in terms of book concepts. 'Occasionally,' David wrote back at once 'book ideas give you goosebumps. A new Gandhi autobiography is one such.' Encouraged by him, I started work on the project but had to abandon it unavoidably for as long as five years. A combination of propitious circumstances enabled me to resume it in 2020 and bring it to partial completion in the form of this volume covering Gandhi's home-cum-public life from his birth to his departure from South Africa for India in 1914. And, so, my thanks must start with the Vidvan and my publisher, David Davidar, for conceptualizing this work.

My sister, Tara Gandhi Bhattacharjee, blessed this project with all her heart and I place my gratitude in her hands with love and respect.

My brother Rajmohan Gandhi, a Gandhi biographer with matchless veracity was also enthused by the idea of giving Gandhi's less-known words the light of a new imprint. To him go my profound gratitude for green-flagging this slow coach on its bullock, rail, road, sea, and war-torn tracks.

The Center for Contemporary South Asia, located at Brown University's Watson Institute for Public and International Affairs, Providence, RI, USA, administers the Meera and Vikram Gandhi Fellowship to enable scholars and public figures working on India to undertake substantial projects while in residence at Brown. I was awarded this Fellowship for the Spring of 2020, enabling me to work for about six weeks on campus and another six weeks in India on this and another, related, Gandhi-based study based on Gandhi's letters to his son (and my father), Devadas Gandhi. I am deeply grateful to the Center and its Director, Professor Ashutosh Varshney, for this.

The major part of the material in this compilation has come from *The Collected Works of Mahatma Gandhi*. I have used both sets of that monumental volume, namely, the 'original' collection available on the Gandhi Heritage Portal and the one put out by the Publications Division of the Government of India in 1999. In essence, this work is nothing but a recasting of the *CWMG*'s autobiographical content in chronological order. The sourcing in the end notes ascribes the excerpts appropriately. And so great thanks, amounting to an expression of debt, no less, is owed to Professor K. Swaminathan, long-serving editor of the series and his distinguished colleague, C. N. Patel, both of whom have set an example in collection, editing, and presentation the like of which the world of scholarship has rarely seen.

I gratefully acknowledge inestimable help received by me from the highly knowledgeable Kinnari Bhatt at the Sabarmati Ashram Archives; the single most authentic go-to-person for Gandhi scholarship, Dina Patel; the Gandhi scholar and translator Tridip Suhrud and the incisive historian Ramachandra Guha.

Invaluable assistance for details of individuals and episodes, especially useful for footnotes came to me from Uma Dhupelia-Mesthrie, Shanti K. Gandhi, Tushar A. Gandhi, Venu Madhav Govindu, Arun Mehta, Rudrangshu Mukherjee, Rajendra Prasad Narla of the Tata Central Archives, Anil Nauriya, Pesi Padshah, Madhavan Palat, Dinyar Patel, Jairam Ramesh, Murali Ranganathan, Enuga S. Reddy, Rupert Snell, A. R. Venkatachalapathy, and Thomas Weber. My grateful thanks to all of them.

To Pujitha Krishnan I offer admiration and gratitude for her astonishingly perceptive editing of this work in which the text was that of a master of English expression but across different stages of his way with that language.

And most fundamentally, in this work centred on Gandhi's home life, I need to thank Tara, my wife, for her monumental patience with her husband's preoccupation with the 'past', invariably at the expense of the wayward present and an enigmatic future.

REFERENCES

1. Joseph J. Doke, *An Indian Patriot in South Africa*, Publications Division, Government of India, 1909, p. 38.
2. Pyarelal, *Mahatma Gandhi: The Early Phase*, Ahmedabad: Navajivan, 1965, p. 212; CWMG, Vol. 1, p. 1.
3. *Harijan*, 11 March 1939, CWMG, Vol. 69, p. 9.
4. A note written after June 1940 (CWMG, Vol. 72, p. 127)
5. J. M. Upadhyaya, *Mahatma Gandhi as a Student*, Publications Division, Government of India, 1965.
6. CWMG, Vol. 1, p. 9.
7. Navajivan, 7 September 1924.
8. Dadabhai Naoroji, *Poverty and un-British Rule in India*, Publications Division, Government of India, first published 1901.
9. Letter to the family in November 1888, cited in C. B. Dalal (ed.), *Gandhiji Ni Dinavari*, Ahmedabad: Navajivan, 1976.
10. *Guide to London*, a 20,000-word manuscript (CWMG, Vol. 1, p. 68 onwards) written by Gandhi to be of assistance to young Indian students aspiring to studying in England and 'as a postscript to his own struggle for a career in the law', Pyarelal in *Mahatma Gandhi: Early Phase*, p. 285.
11. Louis Fischer papers deposited in the New York Public Library.
12. *Autobiography*, pp. 75–80 (hereafter, A).
13. CWMG, Vol. 68, p. 171.
14. Interview with Christian missionaries, before 12 December 1893.
15. *The Natal Advertiser*, 5 June 1896 (CWMG, Vol. 1, p. 340).
16. CWMG, Vol. 2, pp. 51 and 53.
17. Letter to F. S. Taleyarkhan dated 10 October 1896 (CWMG, Vol. 2, p. 61).
18. *The Hindu*, 28 October 1896; CWMG, Vol. 2, p. 92.
19. *The Natal Advertiser*, 14 January 1897 (CWMG, Vol. 2, p. 126).
20. *Satyagraha in South Africa*, p. 54 (hereafter SiSA)
21. CWMG, Vol. 51, pp. 24–25.
22. CWMG, Vol. 2, pp. 229–230.
23. CWMG, Vol. 2, pp. 126–127.
24. May 1897 (CWMG, Vol. 2, p. 255)
25. *The Diary of Mahadev Desai*, Vol. 1 (1932), pp. 53–54.
26. CWMG, Vol. 10, p. 296.
27. CWMG, Vol. 3, pp. 152–53.
28. At public meeting in Calcutta, on 27 January 1902 (CWMG, Vol. 3, p. 263).

29 *Indian Opinion*, 20 October 1903 (*CWMG*, Vol. 4, p. 24).
30 As related by Gandhi to Pyarelal, in Pyarelal, *Mahatma Gandhi*, Vol. 2, Bombay: Sevak, 1980, pp. 282–283 and cited by Rajmohan Gandhi in *Mohandas*, pp. 95–96; *CWMG*, Vol. 63 p. 379.
31 *CWMG*, Vol. 3, p. 159.
32 *CWMG*, Vol. 3, pp. 160–61.
33 *CWMG*, Vol. 3, pp. 176–77.
34 *CWMG*, Vol. 3, p. 177.
35 *CWMG*, Vol. 3, p. 204.
36 *CWMG*, Vol. 3, p. 206.
37 *CWMG*, Vol. 3, p. 212.
38 *CWMG*, Vol. 3, pp. 215–16.
39 *CWMG*, Vol. 3, p. 230.
40 *CWMG*, Vol. 3, pp. 230–31.
41 *CWMG*, Vol. 3, p. 235.
42 *CWMG*, Vol. 3, p. 241.
43 A, 183–185
44 *CWMG*, Vol. 3, pp. 246–47
45 Ibid., p. 249.
46 *The Times of India*, 20 December 1901 (*CWMG*, Vol. 3, p. 250).
47 *CWMG*, Vol. 3, p. 257.
48 See fn. 65.
49 *CWMG*, Vol. 3, p. 258.
50 *Young India*, 30 June 1927.
51 Mahadev Desai in his *Diary* of 1 June 1932.
52 A, pp. 200–01.
53 *CWMG*, Vol. 3, p. 271.
54 *CWMG* Vol. 3, pp. 272–73.
55 *CWMG*, Vol. 3, p. 313.
56 *CWMG*, Vol. 7, p. 113.
57 *CWMG*, Vol. 3, p. 315.
58 *CWMG*, Vol. 3, p. 315.
59 A, Chapter 23.
60 *CWMG*, Vol. 3, p. 332.
61 Rajmohan Gandhi, *Mohandas*, New Delhi: Penguin/Viking, 2006, p. 103.
62 *CWMG*, Vol. 3 p. 332.
63 Ibid., p. 335.
64 Ibid., pp. 424–26.
65 5 February 1903; *CWMG*, Vol. 3, p. 336.
66 *SiSA*, p. 4.
67 Letter to *The Vegetarian*, 25 April 1903 (*CWMG*, Vol. 3, p. 345).
68 *CWMG*, Vol. 3, pp. 424–26.
69 Ibid.

70 Ibid., p. 426.
71 23 February 1903, *CWMG*, Vol. 3, p. 341.
72 10 May 1903, *CWMG*, Vol. 3, p. 362.
73 *Indian Opinion*, 6 August 1903 (*CWMG*, Vol. 3, p. 478).
74 *Indian Opinion*, 4 June 1903 (*CWMG*, Vol. 3, p. 380).
75 Ibid.
76 *CWMG*, Vol. 4, pp. 129–31.
77 A, pp. 177–179
78 In a letter dated 31 October 1904 to Dadabhai Naoroji (*CWMG*, Vol. 4, pp. 286–87).
79 *Indian Opinion*, 24 March 1904 (*CWMG*, Vol. 4, p. 153)
80 *Indian Opinion*, 30 April 1904 (*CWMG*, Vol. 4, p. 176)
81 Indian Opinion, 9 April 1904 (*CWMG*, Vol. 4, p. 160)
82 *Indian Opinion*, 31 December 1904 (*CWMG*, Vol. 4, p. 326)
83 *Indian Opinion*, 12 November 1904 (*CWMG*, Vol. 4, p. 296)
84 *CWMG*, Vol. 4, p. 290
85 A, pp. 181–182
86 Prabhudas Gandhi, *Jivan nu Parodh*, translated into English by D N Kalhan, The Hindustan Times Press, 1957, p. 37 (hereafter JnP, E.tr.)
87 *CWMG*, Vol. 4, p. 320.
88 JnP, E.tr., pp. 38–39.
89 Ibid.
90 *CWMG*, Vol. 4, p. 332.
91 *Indian Opinion*, 25 March 1905 (*CWMG*, Vol. 4, p. 387)
92 *CWMG*, Vol. 4, p. 428.
93 *CWMG*, Vol. 5, p. 5.
94 *Indian Opinion*, 26 August 1905 (*CWMG*, Vol. 5, p. 50).
95 *Indian Opinion*, 2 September 1905 (*CWMG*, Vol. 5, p. 57).
96 *Indian Opinion*, 26 August 1905 (*CWMG*, Vol. 5, p. 50).
97 *CWMG*, Vol. 5, p. 9.
98 *CWMG*, Vol. 5, p. 28.
99 *CWMG*, Vol. 5, p. 21.
100 *CWMG*, Vol. 5, p. 44.
101 *Indian Opinion*, 2 September 1905.
102 *Indian Opinion*, 17 March 1906.
103 *SiSA*, p. 165–66.
104 A, pp. 171–72.
105 *CWMG*, Vol. 84, p. 295.
106 In Milie Graham Polak, *Mr Gandhi: The Man*, London: G. Allen & Unwin, 1931.
107 *Indian Opinion*, 27 January 1906 (*CWMG*, Vol. 5, p. 181).
108 *CWMG*, Vol. 5, p. 197.
109 JnP, E.tr. pp. 42–43.

110 *Indian Opinion*, 7 April 1906 (CWMG, Vol. 5, p. 266).
111 Adapted from letter in CWMG, Vol. 5, pp. 334–35.
112 See fn 182.
113 *Indian Opinion*, 14 April 1906 (CWMG, Vol. 5, p. 282).
114 *Indian Opinion*, 28 July 1906 (CWMG, Vol. 5, p. 368).
115 *Indian Opinion*, 28 July 1906 (CWMG, Vol. 5, pp. 369–73).
116 *SiSA*, pp. 89–91.
117 CWMG, Vol. 68, p. 269.
118 A, pp. 193–194.
119 JnP, E.tr., p. 42.
120 Pyarelal, *Mahatma Gandhi*, Vol. 3, p. 483.
121 Rajmohan Gandhi, *Mohandas*, p. 121.
122 *Indian Opinion*, 8 April 1906 (CWMG Vol. 5, p. 412).
123 Ibid.
124 Ibid.
125 CWMG, Vol. 5, p. 416.
126 Transvaal Leader, 22 September 1906 (CWMG VOL. 5, p. 435).
127 CWMG, Vol. 5, p. 438.
128 *SiSA*, pp. 109–10.
129 Plate facing p. 472 of CWMG, Vol. 5.
130 CWMG, Vol. 6, pp. 18–20.
131 Ibid.
132 CWMG, Vol. 6, p. 84.
133 CWMG, Vol. 6, p. 4.
134 CWMG, Vol. 6, p. 13–14.
135 CWMG, Vol. 6, pp. 19.
136 CWMG, Vol. 6, pp. 13–14.
137 CWMG, Vol. 6, pp. 26.
138 CWMG, Vol. 6, p. 23.
139 CWMG, Vol.6, pp. 29–30.
140 CWMG, Vol. 6, pp. 33–34.
141 CWMG, Vol. 6, p. 66.
142 CWMG, Vol. 6, pp. 81–82.
143 CWMG, Vol. 6, p. 99.
144 *SiSA*, p. 110.
145 CWMG, Vol. 6, p. 137.
146 CWMG, Vol. 6, p. 138.
147 Ibid.
148 CWMG Vol. 6, p. 258.
149 CWMG, Vol. 6, p. 235.
150 CWMG, Vol. 6, p. 245.
151 CWMG, Vol. 6, p. 260.
152 CWMG, Vol. 6, p. 264.

153 *CWMG*, Vol.6, p. 273.
154 *CWMG*, Vol. 6, p. 305.
155 *CWMG*, Vol. 6, p. 309.
156 *CWMG*, Vol. 6, p. 344.
157 *CWMG*, Vol. 6, pp. 386–87.
158 *CWMG*, Vol. 6, p. 407.
159 *CWMG*, Vol. 6, pp. 415–16.
160 *CWMG*, Vol. 6, p. 424.
161 *CWMG*, Vol. 6, p. 425.
162 Undated letter from this period in Nilam Parekh, *Gandhiji's Lost Jewel*, p. 130.
163 *CWMG*, Vol. 6, p. 429.
164 *CWMG*, Vol. 6, pp. 430–32.
165 *CWMG*, Vol. 6, p. 435.
166 JnP, E.tr., p. 40.
167 *CWMG*, Vol. 6, p. 439.
168 *CWMG*, Vol. 6, p. 468.
169 *Indian Opinion*, 1 June 1907 (*CWMG*, Vol. 7, p. 5).
170 *CWMG*, Vol. 7, pp. 80–82.
171 *CWMG*, Vol. 7, p. 89.
172 *CWMG*, Vol. 7, p. 32.
173 *CWMG*, Vol. 7, p. 53.
174 *CWMG*, Vol. 7, p. 258.
175 Ibid.
176 *CWMG*, Vol. 7, p. 164.
177 *CWMG*, Vol. 7, p. 173.
178 *CWMG*, Vol. 7, p. 187.
179 *CWMG*, Vol. 8, p. 24.
180 *Indian Opinion*, 11 January 1908 (*CWMG*, Vol. 8, pp. 22–23) and A, p. 194.
181 *CWMG*, Vol. 8, pp. 31–33.
182 *CWMG*, Vol. 8, pp. 36–37; *SiSA*, p. 138.
183 *SiSA*, pp. 142–43.
184 *CWMG*, Vol. 8, p. 136.
185 *CWMG*, Vol. 8, pp. 121.
186 *CWMG*, Vol. 8, p. 139.
187 *CWMG*, Vol. 8, pp. 39–40.
188 *CWMG*, Vol. 8, p. 159 (GS).
189 *CWMG*, Vol. 8, p. 140–41.
190 Ibid.
191 *CWMG*, Vol. 8, p. vi.
192 Ibid and *CWMG*, Vol. 8, pp. 65–66.
193 *CWMG*, Vol. 8, pp. 66–67.

194 *CWMG*, Vol 8. p. 66.
195 *SiSA*, p. 144.
196 *SiSA*, p. 145.
197 *CWMG*, Vol. 8, p. 69.
198 *SiSA*, Vol. 8, pp. 148–51.
199 *CWMG*, Vol. 8, p. 45.
200 *CWMG*, Vol. 8, p. 61.
201 *CWMG*, Vol. 8, pp. 56–57.
202 *CWMG*, Vol. 8, p. 57.
203 Polak, *Mr Gandhi*.
204 Raojibhai Patel, *Gandhijini Sadhana*.
205 *CWMG*, Vol. 8, pp. 93–94.
206 *CWMG*, Vol. 8, p. 95.
207 *SiSA*, pp. 153–57.
208 *CWMG*, Vol. 8, p. 94.
209 *CWMG*, Vol. 8, pp. 75–76.
210 *SiSA*, p. 169.
211 *SiSA*, pp. 170–71.
212 Prabhudas Gandhi, JnP, E.tr., p. 44.
213 JnP, E.tr., pp. 44–46.
214 Ibid.
215 JnP, E.tr., p. 44–46.
216 Ibid.
217 *The Hindustan Times*, 3 July 1948, p. 5, columns 3–5.
218 Parekh, *Gandhiji's Lost Jewel*, p. 18.
219 JnP, E.tr., p. 45.
220 Ibid.
221 *CWMG* (PD1999), Vol. 8, pp. 233–34.
222 *CWMG* (PD1999), Vol. 8, p. 212.
223 *CWMG* (PD1999) Vol. 8, p. 231.
224 Ibid.
225 *CWMG* (PD1999) Vol. 8, p. 325.
226 Cited in *Harijan*, 29 May 1937 from Mahadev Desai's weekly letter.
227 *CWMG* (PD1999) Vol. 8, p. 326.
228 *CWMG* (PD1999) Vol. 9, p. 1.
229 *CWMG* (PD1999) Vol. 9, p. 8.
230 *CWMG* (PD1999) Vol. 9, p. 15.
231 *CWMG* (PD1999) Vol. 8, pp. 432–33.
232 *CWMG* (PD1999) Vol. 8, p. 455.
233 *CWMG* (PD1999) Vol. 9, p. 33.
234 *CWMG* (PD1999) Vol. 9, pp. 10–11.
235 *CWMG* (PD1999) Vol. 8, p. 458.
236 *CWMG* (PD1999) Vol. 9. p. 67.

237 *CWMG* (PD1999) Vol. 9, p. 92.
238 *CWMG* (PD1999) Vol. 9, p. 133.
239 *CWMG* (PD1999) Vol. 9, p. 155.
240 JnP, E.tr., pp. 49–59.
241 Ibid.
242 *CWMG* (PD1999) Vol. 9, p. 189.
243 JnP, E.tr., p. 55–56
244 *CWMG* (PD1999) Vol. 9, pp. 160–61 and p. 165.
245 *CWMG* (PD1999) Vol. 9, pp. 193–94.
246 Gillian Berning (ed.), *Gandhi Letters: From Upper House To Lower House (1906–1914)*, Durban: Local History Museum, 1994, p. 11.
247 *CWMG* (PD1999) Vol. 9, p. 208.
248 Ibid
249 *CWMG* (PD1999) Vol. 9, p. 197.
250 *CWMG* (PD1999) Vol. 9, p. 253.
251 *CWMG* (PD1999) Vol. 9, p. 254.
252 *CWMG* (PD1999) Vol. 9, pp. 245–47
253 *CWMG* (PD1999) Vol. 9, p. 255.
254 *CWMG* (PD1999) Vol. 9, p. 256.
255 *CWMG* (PD1999) Vol. 9, p. 269–70.
256 *CWMG* (PD1999) Vol. 9, p. 270.
257 *CWMG* (PD1999) Vol. 9, pp. 271–72.
258 *SiSA*, p. 201.
259 *CWMG*, Vol. 9, p. 603.
260 *CWMG* (PD1999) Vol. 9, p. 211.
261 *CWMG* (PD1999) Vol. 9, p. 220.
262 *CWMG* (PD1999) Vol. 9, p. 212.
263 *CWMG* (PD1999) Vol. 9, p. 214.
264 A, pp. 272–74.
265 From letter to Kallenbach, Berning (ed.), *Gandhi Letters*, p. 12–13.
266 *CWMG* (PD1999) Vol. 9, pp. 257–58.
267 *CWMG* (PD1999) Vol. 9, p. 268.
268 *CWMG* (PD1999) Vol. 9, p. 200.
269 *CWMG* (PD1999) Vol. 9, pp. 343–46.
270 *CWMG* (PD1999) Vol. 9, p. 315.
271 *CWMG* (PD1999) Vol. 9, p. 356.
272 *CWMG* (PD1999) Vol. 9, p. 337.
273 *CWMG* (PD1999) Vol. 9, p. 355.
274 *CWMG* (PD1999) Vol. 9, pp. 318–23.
275 *CWMG* (PD1999) Vol. 11, p. 26.
276 *CWMG* (PD1999) Vol. 9, p. 335.
277 *CWMG* (PD1999) Vol. 9, pp. 372–73.
278 *CWMG* (PD1999) Vol. 9, pp. 377–78.

279 *CWMG* (PD1999) Vol. 9, p. 389.
280 *CWMG* (PD1999) Vol. 9, p. 390.
281 *CWMG* (PD1999) Vol. 9, p. 395.
282 *CWMG* (PD1999) Vol. 9, p. 396.
283 *CWMG* (PD1999) Vol. 9, p. 397.
284 *CWMG* (PD1999) Vol. 9, p. 397.
285 *CWMG* (PD1999) Vol. 9, p. 399
286 *CWMG* (PD1999) Vol. 9, pp. 400–01.
287 *CWMG* (PD1999) Vol. 9, p. 403.
288 *CWMG* (PD1999) Vol. 9, p. 403.
289 *Indian Opinion*, 14 August 1909.
290 *CWMG* (PD1999) Vol. 9, pp. 410 and 424.
291 *CWMG* (PD1999) Vol. 9, p. 436 and 427–28.
292 *CWMG* (PD1999) Vol. 10, p. 11.
293 *CWMG* (PD1999) Vol. 9, p. 457.
294 *CWMG* (PD1999) Vol. 10, p. 25.
295 *CWMG* (PD1999) Vol. 9, p. 435.
296 *CWMG* (PD1999) Vol. 9, p. 448.
297 Nilam Parekh, *Gandhijinu Khovayelu Dhan*, Ahmedabad: Navajivan, 1998.
298 Berning (ed.), *Gandhi's Letters*, p. 14.
299 Ibid.
300 *CWMG* (PD1999) Vol. 9, p. 513.
301 *CWMG* (PD1999) Vol. 10, p. 239 and 323–24.
302 *CWMG* (PD1999) Vol. 10, pp. 240–44.
303 *CWMG* (PD1999) Vol. 10, pp. 245–46, *CWMG*, Vol. 77, p. 357 and Rajmohan Gandhi, *Mohandas*, p. 151.
304 *CWMG* (PD1999) Vol. 10, p. 315–16.
305 *CWMG* (PD1999) Vol. 10, p. 333.
306 *CWMG* (PD1999) Vol. 10, p. 334.
307 *CWMG* (PD1999) Vol. 10, p. 334.
308 JnP, E.tr.
309 *CWMG*, Vol. 10, p. 250.
310 *CWMG*, Vol. 10, pp. 251 and 253.
311 *SiSA*, p. 213–14.
312 *CWMG* (PD1999) Vol. 11, p 56.
313 *CWMG*, Vol. 10, p. 263.
314 *SiSA*, p. 214–17.
315 Ibid.
316 Ibid.
317 *CWMG* (PD1999) Vol. 11, p. 60.
318 *CWMG*, Vol. 10, p. 273.
319 *CWMG*, Vol. 10, p. 308.
320 *CWMG*, Vol. 10, p. 398.

321 Ibid.
322 *CWMG*, Vol. 10, p. 402.
323 *CWMG* (PD1999) Vol. 11, p. 19.
324 *CWMG*, Vol. 10, pp. 428–29.
325 Devadas Gandhi, obituary tribute to Harilal Gandhi, *The Hindustan Times*, 1948.
326 *CWMG*, Vol. 10, p. 476.
327 *CWMG* (PD1999) Vol. 11, p. 221.
328 *CWMG* (PD1999) Vol. 11, p. 254.
329 *CWMG* (PD1999) Vol. 11, pp. 261–62.
330 *CWMG* (PD1999) Vol. 12, p. 93.
331 *CWMG*, Vol. 11, p. 6.
332 *CWMG*, Vol. 11, p. v and Rajmohan Gandhi, *Mohandas*, p. 166.
333 *CWMG*, Vol. 11, p. 68.
334 Rajmohan Gandhi, *Mohandas*, p. 163.
335 *CWMG*, Vol. 11, pp. 77–78.
336 *CWMG*, Vol. 11, pp. 114–15.
337 *CWMG*, Vol. 11, pp. 117–19.
338 *CWMG*, Vol. 11, p. 138.
339 *CWMG*, Vol. 11, p. 147.
340 *CWMG* (PD1999) Vol. 11, pp. 423–24.
341 *CWMG* (PD1999) Vol. 11, p. 427.
342 *CWMG* (PD1999) Vol. 11, pp. 425–27.
343 *CWMG* (PD1999) Vol. 11, p. 445.
344 *CWMG*, Vol. 11, pp. 117–19.
345 *CWMG* Vol. 11, pp. 133–34.
346 *CWMG* (PD1999) Vol. 11, pp. 431–36.
347 *CWMG*, Vol. 11, pp. 162–63.
348 *CWMG*, Vol. 11, p. 166.
349 *CWMG*, Vol. 11, p. 165.
350 *CWMG*, Vol. 11, p. 166.
351 *CWMG*, Vol. 11, p. 168.
352 *CWMG* (PD1999) Vol. 12, p. 82.
353 *CWMG*, Vol. 11, pp. 237–38.
354 Ibid.
355 *CWMG*, Vol. 11, p. 333.
356 *CWMG* (PD1999) Vol. 12, p. 84.
357 *CWMG* Vol. 11, p. 195.
358 *CWMG* Vol. 11, p. 207.
359 *CWMG* Vol. 11, p. 312.
360 *CWMG* Vol. 11, p. 315.
361 *CWMG* (PD1999) Vol. 12, pp. 90–91.
362 *CWMG* (PD1999) Vol. 12, p. 142.

363 *CWMG* (PD1999) Vol. 12, p. 183.
364 *CWMG* (PD1999) Vol. 12, p. 185.
365 *CWMG* (PD1999) Vol. 12, p. 186.
366 *CWMG* (PD1999) Vol. 12, p. 264.
367 *CWMG* (PD1999) Vol. 12, p. 267.
368 *CWMG* (PD1999) Vol. 12, pp. 269–70.
369 *SiSA*, pp. 240–41.
370 *CWMG* (PD 1999) Vol. 12, p. 275.
371 *SiSA* pp. 241–42.
372 *SiSA*, pp. 227–28.
373 *CWMG* (PD1999) Vol. 12, p. 276.
374 *CWMG* (PD1999) Vol. 12, p. 278.
375 *SiSA*, p. 244.
376 *SiSA*, p. 245.
377 *CWMG* (PD1999) Vol. 12, p. 282.
378 Ibid.
379 *CWMG* (PD1999) Vol. 12, p. 285.
380 Ibid.
381 Ibid.
382 *CWMG* (PD1999) Vol. 12, pp. 368–69.
383 *CWMG* (PD1999) Vol. 12, p. 376.
384 *CWMG* (PD1999) Vol. 12, p. 391.
385 Ibid.
386 JnP, p. 233.
387 *CWMG* (PD 1999) Vol. 13, p. 264.
388 *CWMG*, Vol. 11, item 356, 14 March 1913.
389 *CWMG* (PD1999) Vol. 13, pp. 3–5.
390 *CWMG* (PD1999) Vol. 13, p. 10.
391 *CWMG* (PD1999) Vol. 13, p. 40.
392 *CWMG* (PD1999) Vol. 13, p. 6.
393 *CWMG* (PD1999) Vol. 13, pp. 37–38.
394 *CWMG* (PD1999) Vol. 13, pp. 49–50.
395 *CWMG* (PD1999) Vol. 13, p. 56.
396 *SiSA*, pp. 254–55.
397 *CWMG* (PD1999) Vol. 13, p. 52 and *SiSA*, pp. 254–55.
398 *CWMG* (PD1999) Vol. 13, item 60, 19 April 1913.
399 *CWMG* (PD1999) Vol. 13, pp. 81–82.
400 Ibid.
401 Isa Sarid and Christian Bartolf, *Hermann Kallenbach: Mahatma Gandhi's friend in South Africa*, Selbstverlag: Gandhi Information Zentrum, 1997, p. 96.
402 *CWMG* (PD1999) Vol. 13, p. 89.
403 *CWMG* (PD1999) Vol. 13, p. 178.

404 *CWMG* (PD1999) Vol. 13, p. 193.
405 A, pp. 208–209 and Uma Dhupelia-Mesthrie, *Gandhi's Prisoner*, New Delhi: Permanent Black, 2004.
406 *CWMG* (PD1999) Vol. 13, p. 224.
407 *CWMG* (PD 1999) Vol. 13, p. 208.
408 *CWMG* (PD1999) Vol. 13, p. 230.
409 Fragment of letter, 22 April 1914, *Gandhi ni Sadhana* (*CWMG*, Vol. 12, p. 410).
410 *CWMG* (PD1999) Vol. 13, p. 263.
411 *CWMG* (PD1999) Vol. 13, p. 266.
412 *CWMG* (PD1999) Vol. 13, p. 283.
413 *CWMG* (PD1999) Vol. 13, p. 291.
414 *CWMG* (PD1999) Vol. 13, p. 297–98.
415 *CWMG* (PD1999) Vol. 13, p. 305.
416 *CWMG* (PD1999) Vol. 13, p. 325.
417 *Indian Opinion*, 1 October 1913.
418 Interview to Rand Daily Mail 23-10-1913, *CWMG* (PD1999) Vol. 13, p. 374.
419 *CWMG* (PD1999) Vol. 13, p. 377.
420 *CWMG* (PD1999) Vol. 13, p. 381.
421 *CWMG* (PD1999) Vol. 13, p. 381.
422 *CWMG* (PD1999) Vol. 13, p. 397.
423 Ibid.
424 *CWMG* (PD1999) Vol. 13, item 260.
425 *CWMG* Vol. 13 item 381.
426 *Young India*, 21 April 1921.
427 J. J. Doke, *An Indian Patriot in South Africa*, p. 86 (*The London Indian Chronicle*, 1909).
428 *CWMG*, Vol. 68, pp. 272–73.
429 *CWMG* (PD1999) Vol. 13, item 262.
430 *Indian Opinion*, 19 November 1913.
431 *CWMG* (PD1999) Vol. 13, item 268. Letter to Maganlal Gandhi, 11 November 1913.
432 *CWMG* (PD1999) Vol. 13, item 270.
433 *CWMG* (PD1999) Vol. 13, item 269.
434 *SiSA*, pp. 282–84.
435 *CWMG* (PD1999) Vol. 13, item 282.
436 See Robert Payne, *The Life and Death of Mahatma* Gandhi, Brand: Smithmark, USA, 1969, pp. 265–66.
437 *CWMG* (PD1999) Vol. 13, item 271.
438 *CWMG* (PD1999) Vol. 13, item 273.
439 *CWMG* (PD1999) Vol. 13, item 279.
440 *CWMG* (PD1999) Vol. 13, item 283.

441 *CWMG* (PD1999) Vol. 13, item 288.
442 *CWMG* (PD1999) Vol. 14, item 23.
443 *CWMG* (PD1999) Vol. 15, item 30.
444 *CWMG* (PD1999) Vol. 14, item 31.
445. Ibid.
446 *CWMG* (PD1999) Vol. 14, item 39.
447 *CWMG* (PD1999) Vol. 14, item 43.
448 *CWMG* (PD1999) Vol. 14, item 64.
449 *CWMG* (PD1999) Vol. 14, item 71.
450 *CWMG* (PD1999) Vol. 14, item 73.
451 *CWMG* (PD1999) Vol. 14, item 79.
452 *CWMG* (PD1999) Vol. 14, item 83.
453 *CWMG* (PD1999) Vol. 14, item 90.
454 *CWMG* Vol. 14, item 89.
455 *CWMG* (PD1999) Vol. 14, item 93.
456 *CWMG* (PD1999) Vol. 14, item 119.
457 *CWMG* (PD1999) Vol. 14, item 127.
458 *CWMG* (PD1999) Vol. 14, items 143 and 144.
459 *CWMG* (PD1999) Vol. 14, items 145 and 146.
460 *SiSA*, pp. 302–04.
461 *CWMG* (PD1999) Vol. 14, item 185.
462 *The Transvaal Leader*, 15 July 1914, *CWMG* (PD1999) Vol. 14, item 203.
463 *Cape Times*, 20 July 1914. These words are reported in the introductory paragraph of the speech.
464 *CWMG*, Vol. 12, p. 520.

INDEX

3-pound tax, 257, 262, 274, 285, 291, 293, 294, 299, 303, 306, 308, 310, 326, 327, 330, 348

Adajania, Sorabji Shapurji, 183, 248
Aden, 42, 61
ahimsa, 18, 24
Ahnika-Prakasha, 212
Alam, Mir, 168, 171, 172, 173, 178
Alexander, R. C., 87
Alfred High School (also Kathiawar High School), 106
Ali, Justice Ameer, 137
Ally, Hajee Ojer, 134, 135, 136–45
Ambulance Corps, 91, 92, 94
Ampthill, Lord, 219–23, 285
Andrews, C. F., 303, 323, 324, 336
Anglo–Boer War, 83
Asiatic Law Amendment Ordinance (ordinance), 83, 133, 134, 138, 140, 142, 143, 144, 145, 148, 150, 252
Assam, 61, 62

Ballengeich Mine, 308
Bamasaheb, 11
Bambatha Rebellion, 83
Banerjee, Surendranath, 80
Bangabasi, 76, 80
Bania (Modh Vania), 3, 36
Barda Hills, 4
Bawazeer, Imam Abdul Kadir, 230
Benares, 34, 103, 104
Bhagavad Gita (Gita), 10, 159, 195, 212, 258, 356
Bhajekar, B. N., 89

Bhavnagar, 31, 32, 35
Bhownaggree, Sir Mancherji M., 96, 99, 142, 144, 145, 146, 198, 219
Bloemfontein, 311, 312, 314, 325
Boksburg, 190
Botha, General, 148, 167, 262, 350
Brindisi, 43, 62
Bruce, Charles (Lord), 99, 223
Buch, Jayshankar, 31
Buller, General Redvers, 94

Cachalia, Ahmed Mahomed, 269
Cama, N. A., 187, 215
Campbell, Marshall, 123
Cartwright, Albert, 142, 165
Chamberlain, Joseph (Secretary of State for the Colonies), 87, 107, 108, 116
Chamney, Mr, 172, 173
Chanchal (Gulab) (Chanchi), 110, 130, 149, 152, 203, 204, 207, 210, 213, 240, 241, 254, 255, 267, 283, 284
Charlestown, 67, 289, 291, 296, 297, 298, 299, 300, 308, 309, 310, 334, 351
Chieveley camp, 92
Churchill, Winston, 84, 144
Cordes, Mr, 177, 190
Crewe, Lord, 215, 220, 323
Cronje, General, 94
Curzon, Lady, 93
Curzon, Viceroy Lord, 108, 122, 223

Dalmahoy, P. C., 184
Dave, Mavji (Joshiji), 32, 34

Desai, Jhinabhai, 194
Desai, Mahadev, 102
Diepkloof Gaol, 229
Doke, Olive, 216
Doke, Reverend Joseph J., v, xiii, xiv, 172–74, 279, 280,304
Dube, John Langalibalele, xv, 83, 123, 130, 224, 325
Durban Gaol, 311, 312

Elgin, Lord, 134, 142, 143, 144, 146, 148
Escombe, Harry, 86, 87, 92, 94, 108
Essakji, Moosa, 201
Essop Ismail Mia, 187

Gaiety Theatre, 148, 316
Gallwey, Colonel, 92
Gandhi, Chhaganlal Khushalchand, v, xiii, 100, 106, 109, 110, 118, 128, 129, 132, 147, 150, 151, 176–78, 186, 189, 231, 240, 246, 248, 254, 283–85, 355
Gandhi, Daman, 4
Gandhi, Devadas, xiii, 89, 95, 100, 110, 129, 150, 177, 178, 204, 213, 214, 228, 240, 241, 242, 256, 266, 267, 273, 284, 314, 325, 342, 345
Gandhi, Harilal, viii, 36, 64, 82, 85, 100, 106, 109, 110, 122, 128, 130, 149–52, 163, 178, 184–88, 197, 199, 203, 204, 206, 207, 210, 213, 214, 223, 229, 232, 235, 240–42, 246–48, 250, 253, 254, 265–67, 283, 284, 340, 369, 374
Gandhi, Karamchand (Kaba), xi, 7, 19, 21, 47, 150
Gandhi, Karsandas, 9, 23, 27, 28
Gandhi, Kasturba (Kastur, Kasturbai) 19fn, 21, 22, 25, 26, 30, 82, 84, 95, 104, 106, 109, 110, 125, 127, 128, 132, 142, 151, 178, 198, 199, 201, 202–10, 235, 240, 241, 242, 256, 264, 272, 273, 278, 281, 285, 304, 321, 326, 328, 332, 333, 340, 342, 344, 346, 350, 353, 355,
Gandhi, Lakshmidas Karamchand, 9, 19, 21, 27, 34, 36, 122, 129, 130, 342
Gandhi, Manilal, 82, 85, 100, 105, 109, 110, 111, 125fn, 129, 147, 150, 159, 199, 204, 210, 213, 221, 228, 230, 231, 239, 240, 258, 267, 276, 278, 284, 325, 332, 334, 335, 336, 337, 339, 341, 344, 346, 356fn
Gandhi, Prabhudas Chhaganlal, v, xiii, xiv, 1, 129, 152, 176-178, 231, 266, 314, 356
Gandhi, Rajmohan, xii, 37, 357
Gandhi, Ramdas, 14, 24, 82, 89, 95, 100, 110, 125, 129, 136, 137, 150, 172, 176, 177, 204, 213, 214, 216, 229, 240, 241, 267, 284, 285, 314, 325, 333, 341, 356
Gandhi, Tulsidas, 7, 19, 23, 25
Gandhi, Uttamchand Harjivan (Ota Bapa), 4
Germiston, 188, 200, 311
Gibraltar, 43, 61
Girgaum, 105
Gladstone, Governor General Lord, 326
Gokhale, Gopal Krishna, 78, 79, 102, 103, 106, 110, 118, 222, 229, 231, 235, 256–63, 265, 270, 273, 274, 285, 288, 289, 291, 303, 307, 313, 321–24, 330, 333, 338, 342, 349, 350
Gokuldas, 82, 85, 100, 106, 128, 150, 152
Gool, Dr A. H., 139
Gool, Hamid, 139

Gorky, Maxim, 121
Great March, 1913, The, 235
Greylingstad, 300, 309
Griffin, Sir Lepel, 142
Guha, Ramachandra, xii, 358

Habib, Hajee, 133, 134, 215, 216, 217, 219, 223, 224
Hajurasingh, 206, 207
Haloo, S., 187
Hamidiya Islamic Society, 201
Harbutsinh, 311, 349
Hardinge, Lady, 354
Hardinge, Viceroy Lord, 313, 323
Haridas Vakhatchand Vora, 110, 130
Hayashi, Viscount, 116
Het Volk, 180
Hind Swaraj, 163
Hobhouse, Emily, 333
Houghton, K. A. Hobart, 124
Hunt, James D., 34fn

India House, 138, 139
Indian Idylls, 251
Indian Opinion, 84, 111, 112, 115–122, 126, 128, 134, 137, 146, 147, 149, 152, 155, 169, 175, 178, 179, 180, 182, 185, 192, 224, 225, 226, 228, 230, 232, 240, 247, 249, 250, 256, 258, 268, 271, 273, 279, 285, 289, 333, 355
Institute of Booker T. Washington, 124
Irving, Washington, 137

Jabavu, Tengo, 83, 124
Jagjivan, Revashanker, 63
James, L. M., 140
Jaykunvar (Jeki) (Jekibehn), 265, 276, 283, 284, 285, 314, 337, 345, 346
Jhaveri, Abdulla Hajee Adam

(Abdulla Sheth), 66, 67, 69, 70, 72, 88, 110
Johannesburg, 67, 93, 108–117, 119, 125–127, 132, 133, 135, 138, 139, 142, 146, 149, 154, 155, 157, 166, 167, 169, 175, 184, 187, 191, 195–97, 200–204, 214, 216, 223, 228, 237, 240, 241, 246, 251, 252, 260, 269, 271, 276, 281, 284, 288, 293, 294, 308, 312, 316, 325, 332, 334, 337, 350, 351
Junagadh, 3, 5, 6, 8, 31, 32, 37
Junior, Gibson, 172
Justice Ameer Ali, 219

Kallenbach, Hermann, 126, 237
Kalyandas, 112
Kathiawar, 3, 7, 19, 27, 35, 37, 64, 106, 110
Keshavram, Bhatt, 212
Khanmahomed, Sheth Tyeb Haji, 107
Khimoji, Rana, 4, 5
Khushalbhai, 179, 186
Kimberley, 94, 259
Kipling, Rudyard, 116
Koran, 159, 160
Kutiyana, 3, 4, 6

Ladysmith, 93, 94, 95, 97, 334
Lalbahadursingh, 206
Lane, E. F. C., 181
Laughton, Mr, 86
Lely, Frederick S. P., 224
Lew, Yuk Lin, 140
London Vegetarian Society, 59, 72

Madras Mahajana Sabha, 80
Mafeking, 93, 146
Mahomed, Dawad, 198, 206, 253
Majid, Abdul, 41
Ma Ne Shikhaman, 89
Mariji, Hera, 184

INDEX 375

Mazmudar, Tryambakrai, 37
Meghjibhai, 33, 34, 179
Mehtab, Sheikh, 27, 30, 33, 34, 36, 73
Mehta, Dr Pranjivan, 45, 63, 164, 224, 247, 276, 346
Mirza, Hassan, 193
Miss Molteno, 334, 337
Miss Winterbottom, 219, 224
Moodaley, Jack, 176
Moonsamy, Valliammah, 332, 333
Mr Morley, 144, 148
Mrs Cachalia, 268, 271
Mrs Pillay, 210
Mr Vernon, 166

Nagappen, Sammy, 220
Naidoo, P. K., 160, 293
Naidoo, Thambi, 158, 172, 184, 186, 230, 250, 251, 293
Nanji, Dr R. M., 202
Naoroji, Dadabhai, 45, 46, 71, 108, 113, 139, 142, 143, 144, 145, 162
Natal Legislative Assembly, 70, 87
Navajivan, xvi, xvii, 1, 102, 325
Nawab of Junagadh (Muhammad Hamid Khanji II), 6
Nazar, Mansukhlal Harilal, 128

Oceana, 61, 62
Oldfield, Dr Josiah, 59, 139, 141
Osman, Omar, 194

Padshah, Pestonji, 102
Palmford, 299, 300, 305
Pankhurst, Emmeline, 273
Patanjal-Yoga-Darshan, 212
Patwari, Ranchhodlal, 64
Pearson, W. W., 304, 323
Phoenix Settlement, 226, 235, 276
Pietermaritzburg (Maritzburg), 67, 87, 91, 92, 107, 137, 285, 288, 312, 321, 322, 334

Pillay, Sinnappa Rangasamy, 185
plague, 86, 104, 106, 112, 113, 114, 115, 119
Polak, Henry Solomon Leon, 115, 138, 170
Polak, J. H., 138, 139
Polak, Millie (nee Downs), xiii, xiv, 140, 276, 310
Poldat, 308
Porbandar, 3, 4, 5, 6, 7, 9, 14, 15, 16, 17, 19, 20, 32, 33, 34, 47, 65, 100, 104
Porter, Dr C., 111
Port Said, 42, 62
Prince Ranjitsinhji, 17, 45
Putlibai, 8, 9
Pyarelal, xiii, xiv, xvii, xviii, 1, 73

Quinn, Leung, 158, 187

Raja Rammohun Roy, 66
Rajasthanik Court, 8
Rajkot, 7, 8, 9, 11, 16, 17, 20, 26, 27, 31, 32, 34, 35, 36, 37, 39, 52, 64, 65, 73, 76, 77, 100, 101, 104, 106, 110, 130, 179, 254
Raliyat, xvii, 9, 77, 82, 85
Rambhabai (Rambha), 15, 16
Ranade, Justice Mahadev Govind, 77
Raychandbhai, 65, 69, 96
Rhodes, Cecil, 104
Ritch, L. W., 108, 250
RMS *Kenilworth Castle*, 216
Roberts, Field Marshal Lord, 94
Robertson, Sir Benjamin, 323, 348
Robinson, Sir John, 110
Rose-Innes, Hon. Sir James, 319
Royappen, Joseph, 238, 246
Royappen, Solomon, 285
Ruskin, 84, 116, 117, 118, 125, 159, 171
Rustomji, Parsi, 99, 175, 176, 231, 253, 285, 288, 292, 312, 332

Sabarmati Ashram, xiii, 82, 234, 302, 358
Sandhya-ni Gutika, 212
Sastri, V. S. Srinivasa, 261
satyagraha, xi, 155, 169, 180, 182, 191, 196, 199, 200, 211, 216, 243, 247, 250, 251, 253, 272, 273, 276, 285, 288, 291, 294, 298, 302, 304, 313, 327, 348
Schlesin, Sonja, 126, 155, 288, 344
Schreiner, Hon. W. P., 319
Schreiner, Olive, 216
Sepoy War (1857), 10
Sheth, Tyeb, 67, 69
Shivananda, Swami (Taraknath Ghosal), 90
Shukla, Dalpatram, 45, 48, 100, 106
Siege of Mafeking, 93
Singh, Lord Prince Duleep, 223
Singh, Parbhu, 93
Sister Nivedita, 101, 102
Solomon Commission, 315, 321, 323, 333, 348
SS *Armadale Castle*, 135
SS *Clyde*, 31, 37
Standerton, 299, 300, 306
Surti Mosque, 155

Tema, Reverend S. S., 304
The Daily Telegraph, 80
The Enchanted Lake, 251
The Kingdom of God is Within You, 200, 210
The Light of Asia, 116
The London Indian Chronicle, xiii
The Natal Advertiser (also *The Advertiser*), 66, 67, 75, 86, 94, 312
The Natal Mercury (also *The Mercury*), 71, 72, 88, 97

The Story of My Experiments with Truth (also *Experiments* and *Experiments with Truth*), xi, xii, xiv, 357
The Times of Natal, 72
Tilak, Lokamanya, 78
Tolstoy Farm, viii, 126, 235, 237, 239, 240, 243, 247, 251, 256, 258, 260, 261, 264, 272, 289, 299
Transvaal March, 306
Tyabji, Justice Badruddin, 77

Unto This Last, 116, 117
'untouchable', 12, 89

Varma, Pandit Shyamji Krishna, 139
Veda-Shabda-Sangna, 211
Vereeniging, 272, 288, 293
Victoria, empress of India, 95, 96
Vikmatji, Rana, 7
Vivekananda, Swami, 89, 90, 101, 102
Volksrust, 115, 134, 184, 191, 195, 198, 200, 201, 206, 207, 208, 214, 229, 234, 284, 291, 299, 300, 305, 308, 309, 311, 312, 334
Volksrust Gaol, 201, 206, 207, 311
Vora, Haridas Vakhatchand, 110
Vyavaharik, Madanjit, 111, 112

Watson, Colonel, 35, 47
West, Ada, 314
West, Albert, 115, 138, 199
White, Sir George, 93, 94, 95
Wylie, Colonel, 319, 327
Wyllie, Sir Curzon, 219, 220

Zaveri (Jhaveri), Revashanker, 96, 110, 122, 341